THINKING CINEMA WITH PROUST

LEGENDA

LEGENDA is the Modern Humanities Research Association's book imprint for new research in the Humanities. Founded in 1995 by Malcolm Bowie and others within the University of Oxford, Legenda has always been a collaborative publishing enterprise, directly governed by scholars. The Modern Humanities Research Association (MHRA) joined this collaboration in 1998, became half-owner in 2004, in partnership with Maney Publishing and then Routledge, and has since 2016 been sole owner. Titles range from medieval texts to contemporary cinema and form a widely comparative view of the modern humanities, including works on Arabic, Catalan, English, French, German, Greek, Italian, Portuguese, Russian, Spanish, and Yiddish literature. Editorial boards and committees of more than 60 leading academic specialists work in collaboration with bodies such as the Society for French Studies, the British Comparative Literature Association and the Association of Hispanists of Great Britain & Ireland.

The MHRA encourages and promotes advanced study and research in the field of the modern humanities, especially modern European languages and literature, including English, and also cinema. It aims to break down the barriers between scholars working in different disciplines and to maintain the unity of humanistic scholarship. The Association fulfils this purpose through the publication of journals, bibliographies, monographs, critical editions, and the MHRA Style Guide, and by making grants in support of research. Membership is open to all who work in the Humanities, whether independent or in a University post, and the participation of younger colleagues entering the field is especially welcomed.

ALSO PUBLISHED BY THE ASSOCIATION

Critical Texts
Tudor and Stuart Translations • *New Translations* • *European Translations*
MHRA Library of Medieval Welsh Literature

MHRA Bibliographies
Publications of the Modern Humanities Research Association

The Annual Bibliography of English Language & Literature
Austrian Studies
Modern Language Review
Portuguese Studies
The Slavonic and East European Review
Working Papers in the Humanities
The Yearbook of English Studies

www.mhra.org.uk
www.legendabooks.com

MOVING IMAGE

Legenda/Moving Image publishes cutting-edge work on any aspect of film or screen media from Europe and Latin America. Studies of European-language cinemas from other continents, and diasporic and intercultural cinemas (with some relation to Europe or its languages), are also encompassed. The series seeks to reflect a diversity of theoretical, historical, and interdisciplinary approaches to the moving image, and includes projects comparing screen media with other art forms. Research monographs and collected volumes will be considered, but not studies of a single film. As innovation is a priority for the series, volumes should predominantly consist of previously unpublished material.

Proposals should be sent with one or two sample chapters to the Editor, Professor Emma Wilson, Corpus Christi College, Cambridge CB2 1RH, UK.

APPEARING IN THIS SERIES

1. *Spanish Practices: Literature, Cinema, Television*, by Paul Julian Smith
2. *Cinema and Contact: The Withdrawal of Touch in Nancy, Bresson, Duras and Denis*, by Laura McMahon
3. *Cinema's Inter-Sensory Encounters: Krzysztof Kieślowski and Claire Denis*, by Georgina Evans
4. *Holocaust Intersections: Genocide and Visual Culture at the New Millennium*, edited by Axel Bangert, Robert S. C. Gordon and Libby Saxton
5. *Africa's Lost Classics: New Histories of African Cinema*, edited by Lizelle Bisschoff and David Murphy
6. *Agnès Varda Unlimited: Image, Music, Media*, edited by Marie-Claire Barnet
7. *Thinking Cinema with Proust*, by Patrick ffrench
8. *Blanchot and the Moving Image: Fascination and Spectatorship*, by Calum Watt
9. *Chantal Akerman: Afterlives*, edited by Marion Schmid and Emma Wilson
10. *Screening Work: The Films of Christian Petzold*, by Stephan Hilpert and Andrew J. Webber

Thinking Cinema with Proust

PATRICK FFRENCH

LEGENDA
Moving Image 7
Modern Humanities Research Association
2018

Published by Legenda
an imprint of the Modern Humanities Research Association
Salisbury House, Station Road, Cambridge CB1 2LA

ISBN 978-1-78188-635-9 (HB)
ISBN 978-1-78188-636-6 (PB)

First published 2018

Copy-Editor: Charlotte Brown

CONTENTS

	Acknowledgements	ix
	Abbreviations	x
	Introduction	I
I	Reverie in a Dark Room	8
2	Camera Obscura	50
3	Proust's Projections	66
4	The Cinema of Montjouvain	102
5	Theory of Gesture	119
6	Screen Memories/Screen Histories	157
	Conclusion	189
	Bibliography	193
	Index	202

For Sarah

ACKNOWLEDGEMENTS

This book has been woven out of many conversations with colleagues and friends. The list of all those whose words may find traces here would be long, and too long, but I want to thank, in particular, the following: Alan Read, Alexandra Tzirkoti, Anne Mulhall, Barnaby Dicker, Ben Dalton, Bruno Sibona, Calum Watt, Catherine Wheatley, Corinna Guthrie, Emma Wilson, Erica Carter, Hector Kollias, Ian James, Ian Maclachlan, Igor Reyner, Jacob Bittner, Jerôme Cornette, Jo Malt, Joel White, Josh Cohen, Kate Brook, Katrin Yacavone, Martin Brady, Martin Crowley, Max Silverman, Michael Sheringham, Nick Harrison, Nigel Saint, Nikolaj Lubecker, Richard Mason, Roger Lippin, Roland-François Lack, Ros Murray, Russell Goulbourne, Sarah Cooper, Sarah Date, Simon Gaunt, Simone Ventura, Sophie Eager, Suzanne Guerlac, Tim Mathews, Tom Baldwin, Tom Gould, and Ziad Elmasarfy. I am also very grateful to the staff and students of the Department of French and the Faculty of Arts and Humanities of King's College London for their intellectual adventurousness and friendship, and for their socially and culturally exceptional support of the opportunity for intellectual and creative freedom.

The front cover images are taken from the 'Geneviève de Brabant' series of magic lantern slides by Auguste Lapierre, held in the collection of the Cinémathèque française in Paris, photographed by Stéphane Dabrowski. Thank you to Laurent Mannoni for permission to reproduce these slides.

P.FF., London, June 2018

ABBREVIATIONS

References to *A la recherche du temps perdu*, in parenthesis in the text, will be to the current Pléaide edition in four volumes (Paris: Gallimard, 1987), with volumes indicated by Roman numerals. References to the translation into English will be to *In Search of Lost Time* under the general editorship of Christopher Prendergast published in six volumes by Penguin (London: Penguin, 2002): Volume 1: *The Way by Swann's*, trans. by Lydia Davis; Volume 2: *In the Shadow of Young Girls in Flower*, trans. by James Grieve; Volume 3: *The Guermantes Way*, trans. by Mark Treharne; Volume 4: *Sodom and Gomorrah*, trans. by John Sturrock; Volume 5: *The Prisoner* and *The Fugitive*, trans. by Carol Clark and Peter Collier; Volume 6: *Finding Time Again*, trans. by Ian Patterson. The volumes of the translation will be indicated by Arabic numerals. References to other texts will be given in footnotes. Where published translations of French works exist, reference will be to them. All other translations are my own.

INTRODUCTION

Thinking Cinema with Proust, or *Thinking Proust with Cinema*? I would like the conjunction in this title to point in both directions, evoking a sustained oscillation between interpretative engagements with the text of Proust's novel and theories and philosophies of film, in some cases those expressed by films themselves. It must be said at the outset however that readers seeking 'Proustian' analyses of films or an exclusive or exhaustive focus on the cinematographic elements of *A la recherche du temps perdu* [In Search of Lost Time] will be frustrated. Neither will I be especially concerned with the film/television adaptations of the novel, either those undertaken by Volker Schlondorff (*Swann in Love*, 1984) Chantal Akerman (*La Captive*, 2000), Raoul Ruiz (*Le Temps retrouvé* [Time Regained], 1999), and Nina Companeez (*A la recherche du temps perdu*, 2011), or those planned by Joseph Losey with Harold Pinter, and by Luchino Visconti.[1] My starting point is the structural absence of cinema from Proust's novel; written predominantly in the second decade of the twentieth century, and covering, in its fictional diegesis, a period roughly from the turn of the century until the end of World War I, the *Recherche* coincides with the birth of cinema and its rapid expansion as an industry and as a cultural form. Yet no-one goes to the cinema in the *Recherche*, or barely, and among the many cultural references that punctuate the narrator's meditations, on music, painting, architecture, literature, fashion, philosophy, science, biology, zoology, and much more, the cinema is conspicuous by its absence. The novel does feature, however, recurrent reference to devices and motifs from the pre-history of cinema — photography, the magic lantern, the kinetoscope, the stereoscope, the modalities of projection and of the screen. This prompts the hypothesis that the *Recherche* enters into a 'functional competition' with the cinema, which it pursues through a dismantling of the constitutive elements of the cinematographic *dispositif* [apparatus], a regression to earlier forms, and a re-imagining of cinematic experience; the *Recherche* offers an account of a virtual cinema, different from the actualized cinema as we know it.[2] My aim is to bring this account to bear on the critical theories of cinema which, themselves, have sought to deconstruct the institution of film and to think it differently.

In keeping with the absence of cinema from the diegetic and mimetic space of the novel, critical writing on Proust and cinema has tended, in the main, to focus on the adaptations mentioned above. The place of photography in the *Recherche* and in the novelist's imaginary has in contrast generated a number of studies, and this is just one aspect of the substantial body of criticism devoted to Proust and the visual arts.[3] It is telling, however, that in their approach to the role of photography in the novel critics have been led to extend the scope of their object to comprise the late nineteenth-century experiments with the chronophotographic methods employed by Eadweard Muybridge and Etienne-Jules Marey in their attempts to capture and study human and animal locomotion. Mieke Bal, in *The Mottled Screen: Reading Proust Visually*, uses photographic motifs in her reading of the different modes of the visual in the *Recherche*, and extends this to chronophotography in relation to Robert de Saint-Loup (see Chapter Five).[4] She stops short of cinematography, however.[5] The focus of discussion of Proust and cinematography has thus tended to be directed toward the edges, the liminal spaces around the cinema, at least as it was 'invented' by Auguste and Louis Lumière in 1895. Some have seen this as symptomatic of a 'regressive' approach on Proust's part to the culture of the moving image; André Benhaïm has proposed imaginatively that Proust backed away from the cinema because he feared the 'perfection' of its illusion and preferred 'de voir mal' [to see badly].[6] Jean-François Chévrier, in *Proust et la photographie*, has proposed a somewhat schematic mapping of the *Recherche* as moving 'backwards' from a clearly cinematic opening to work through the different stages of the photographic process.[7] This liminal focus foregrounds the historical shape of the cinema, and brings it to light as a 'technique of the observer', or as a *dispositif* specific to the twentieth century, with which Proust's novel enters, as I have suggested, into 'functional competition'.[8] It is significantly at the other end, at the outer limit, so to speak, of cinema, that the presence of Proust comes back into play. As the digital technologies developed in the later decades of the twentieth century begin to compete with the cinematographic apparatus, as new ways of seeing, rival *dispositifs*, start to foreground the historical and technological limits of the cinema, and as experimental practices within film history and around its edges develop, Proust's novel emerges as a theoretical point of reference and a point of comparison. Proust is a recurrent reference, for example, in the work of Raymond Bellour, on what he calls 'l'entre-images' [the between-the-images], on experimental practices within film, between film and video, between film and literature, and in installation art.[9] This is in part because of the emergence, within film, of cinema itself as an object of memory, as a historical object, and due to the complex relations between memory and the photographic and cinematographic image. The cinema as an object of memory and of history is no doubt a concern that is present, at least virtually, across the whole history of the medium, but it emerges with particular clarity at the end of the twentieth century, and in tandem with the possibility of the perspectives in cinema as an object offered by other media. Jacques Rancière has pointed to Gilles Deleuze's two-volume study of the cinema — *Cinéma 1: L'Image-mouvement* [The Movement-Image] and *Cinéma 2: L'Image-temps* [The Time-Image] — and to Jean-Luc Godard's six-part video project *Histoire(s) du cinéma*, as two instances where the cinema comes into play as a historical object, the edges of which are now partially visible.[10] Proust is an important presence in both — Deleuze suggests a fundamental affinity between Proustian involuntary memory, which mobilizes 'un peu de temps à l'état pur' [a bit of time in the pure state], and the experience of the passing of time as such in the cinema of the time-image (in the films of Ozu, for example).[11] Beyond the specific citations of Proust in *Histoire(s) du cinéma* the

Proustian operation of involuntary memory is also at work in Godard's project, mediated, as we will see, through Walter Benjamin's philosophy of history. Miriam Heywood and Alessia Ricciardi have brought out the parallels and the dynamics that play out between Proust's *Recherche* and Godard's *Histoire(s)*, both of them pointing to the critical perspectives this interplay can provoke upon the cinema.[12] Chris Marker's film *La Jetée* [The Jetty] (1962) also emerges as a liminal example in a different way, through its formal experimentation with the tensions between the still and the moving image, and through its related enquiry into the relations between memory and the image.

It is in this space between, in this interplay, that I would like the *thinking with* proposed by the title of this book to take place, or to be received. Several figures emerge as privileged interlocutors in this endeavour. Some of them come into view in relation to the specific motifs or problematics I address across the six chapters of the book. Chapters 1 and 2 engage with the subjective or affective state of reverie, with the figure or space of the room, *la chambre*, and with the related apparatus of the camera obscura, as they emerge across the *Recherche*; and this provokes a series of conversations with Roland Barthes, Jean-Louis Baudry, and Christian Metz around a specific moment in French film theory of the 1970s exemplified in a special issue of the semiotics journal *Communications* on psychoanalysis and cinema.[13] The work of Jonathan Crary on the transformations undergone by the philosophical paradigm of the camera obscura, and on the vicissitudes of attention, also bear upon my consideration of the treatment of these motifs in Proust's novel. In Chapters 3 and 4, in which I move on to the motif of projection, the apparatus and metaphor of the magic lantern, and the incidence of the screen, I engage with Leo Bersani's psychoanalytically-inflected readings of Proust and with Stanley Cavell's conception of the cinema as a projected world. Chapters 5 and 6 see Giorgio Agamben and, increasingly, Walter Benjamin, take centre stage as offering the most significant interpretative frameworks for the understanding of the parallel conceptions of gesture and of memory at work in Proust's novel and in the cinema. I pay close attention to Agamben's postulation, in the programmatic essay 'Notes on Gesture', that the twentieth century was an era that has 'lost its gestures', for which the possibility of a consensual bodily symbolism had receded into the past, and his proposition that the *Recherche* and silent cinema, among other forms, represent attempts 'in extremis' to mark this loss, but also to recover and redeem what was being lost.[14] I follow this argument through a reading of gestures across the novel. But I also show the extent to which Agamben's argument connects with and is influenced by his substantial engagement with Benjamin. In Chapter 5 and in the final chapter, which deploys the Freudian figure of the 'screen memory', Benjamin's philosophy of history is shown to be conditioned by his fraught relation with Proust. Through Serge Daney's melancholic reflection on the critical possibilities of a cinema which is aware of its constitutive relation to historical trauma in the landmark essay 'Le Travelling de *Kapo*' [The Tracking Shot in *Kapo*], I move, still with Benjamin, towards a consideration of the use-value of Proust and of cinema in relation to history.[15]

Thinking Cinema with Proust is also an exercise in reading. The *Recherche* promotes itself as a device by means of which experience, memory, and the figure of the other may become *readable*, albeit as mediated through the consciousness of its narrator. Reading, both literal and metaphorical, functions as a figure through which the novel legitimates itself, and through which the narrator's account of his world and his experience communicates with the activity and agency of the reader.[16] Perceptual experience, memory, the discourse of the other, the complexities of social interaction, the landscape, the visual and the acoustic fields — all are subject to the promotion of readability as the means through which consciousness makes sense of its world. Readability, or intelligibility, is also a defining factor in the philosophy of history of Benjamin, which I address in the final chapter. In Benjamin's account, informed as we will see by the logic of involuntary memory, an awakening from the dream of the past is possible through the temporal spasm of the 'dialectical image', through which an unlived element of past experience interrupts the present in the 'now of intelligibility'.[17] Reading, here, is positioned as a mode of awakening, and the threshold between sleep and awakening thus appears as the liminal state from which such a reading can begin.

A different perspective on reading, awakening, and the cinema is offered in the work of Roland Barthes, also a recurrent reference across this book. Barthes's 'resistance to cinema' is well-known, and one of the predominant features of this resistance lies in his complaint that the unstoppable procession of cinematic images demands a 'voracious' spectator, obliged to devour the image rather than to think it.[18] In a similar vein, Barthes also complains that in the cinema he is forced, through the imaginary pull of the screen-mirror, to 'glue himself' to the screen, so much so that his nose is crushed against it.[19] More often than not, he adds, sound in the cinema is there to reinforce the verisimilitude of the image.[20] Barthes's complaint is that the cinema offers no purchase for reading, that it annuls the temporal and spatial displacement necessary for the activity of reading, and that through the orthodox fusion of image and sound in the *vraisemblable* it disables the *jouissance* of reading, on the one hand, and listening, *écoute*, on the other.[21]

Thinking Cinema with Proust is directed towards a confrontation of the mode and mood of readerly attentiveness which is promoted in the *Recherche* with the experience of cinematic spectatorship. It thus attends to the implicit or explicit appeals to Proust's novel in film theory and film-philosophy which has, in keeping with Barthes's perspectives, sought to disaggregate the hypnotic reality-effects of cinema, to dismantle the apparatus. This encounter, between Proust's novel and a critical film theory (thus also with a critical cinema, or with other audio-visual practices which operate a critique of cinema), has a powerful precedent in Gilles Deleuze's philosophy of cinema, in which, as mentioned above, Proust's *Recherche* works as a sub-text for the 'direct perception of time' in the cinema of the time-image. Deleuze also offers a coherent account of the way in which a properly modern cinema displaces the hierarchy of image and sound and thus subverts the lure of verisimilitude which provoked Barthes's frustration. In the silent era, Deleuze proposes, image and language were split into two separate regimes, the latter, in the form of inter-titles, assumed the function of the law or the symbol, while the image was assimilated to a natural or organic emanation of the real.[22] The era of sound cinema, in its first period, reintegrated image and sound, image and speech, with the effect of affirming visual presence. But the modernity of the cinema does not coincide with the advent of sound cinema; the classical/modern distinction does not map on to the technological division between silent and sound cinema. Rather, cinematic modernity intervenes when the image and sound tracks take on an autonomy in relation to each other, when sound ceases to become a property of the image. This instance of separation, Deleuze proposes, confers a new readability on to the image; the image becomes readable to the same extent that sound — voice, noise, music — becomes audible, subject to what Barthes calls an 'écoute'.[23]

I want to open the proceedings, as it were, with an invitation to see Proust's *Recherche* as operating a similar kind of disjunction, and as offering a paradigmatic model for the re-thinking of cinema at work across the theorists and writers invoked in this book. Deleuze observes that Proust anticipated, in the novel, the 'sociological' perspectives of sound cinema in the emergence of conversation as an object, but is the *Recherche* not also a paradigm for the 'free indirect discourse' in which Deleuze finds one of the modes of the autonomy of sound in relation to the image, and the consequent readability of both?[24] Proust's narrator is enormously sensitive, moreover, to the atmospherics and tonalities of background noise, often in isolation from its location in the visual field; he is often predominantly a listener in addition to and as opposed to a voyeur.[25] Where the voice is present in the diegetic field of the *Recherche* it is often thoroughly mediated, often through technological devices which render it acousmatic; it is always in some sense a voice-off.[26] In other words, Proust practices a disjunction of the acoustic and visual fields which transforms both into spaces of readability, and anticipates the readability of modern cinema in Deleuze's sense. Finally, might we not consider the *Recherche* and the experience of reading it as always and inevitably at a critical remove from the immersive lure of the screen, as an omnipresent voice-off which intervenes to establish the distance necessary for reading and for criticism?

Notes to the Introduction

1. For works which deal, among other things, with the existing screen adaptations of Proust's novel, see Marion Schmid and Martine Beugnet, *Proust at the Movies* (London & New York: Routledge, 2004), Jean Cléder and Jean-Pierre Montier (eds.), *Proust et les images: peinture, photographie, cinéma, vidéo* (Rennes: Presses universitaires de Rennes, 2003), and Thomas Carrier-Lafleur, *L'Œil cinématographique de Proust* (Paris: Classiques Garnier, 2016). For studies of Losey and Visconti's abortive projects, and the affinities between Proust's novel and Visconti's aesthetic, see: Florence Colombani, *Proust-Visconti: histoire d'une affinité élective* (Paris: Philippe Rey, 2006), Peter Kravanja, *Visconti — lecteur de Proust* (Paris: Portaparole, 2005), and *Proust à l'écran* (Paris: Editions internationales, 2003). Edward Said also discusses the Proustian dimensions of Visconti's *The Leopard* (1963) in *On Late Style: Music and Literature Against the Grain* (London: Bloomsbury, 2006), pp. 91–114.
2. I have borrowed the expression 'functional competition' from Christian Metz, who uses it to refer to the relation between cinema and reverie; see Chapter 1. The term *dispositif* indicates the cinema not as an apparatus in the strict sense (a machine) but a whole set of relations, including spectator, screen, space, and the social and historical context in which they inhere.

3. See, among many other titles, Jean-François Chévrier, *Proust et la photographie: la resurrection de Venise* (Paris: L'Arachnéen, 2009); Brassai, *Marcel Proust sous l'emprise de la photographie* (Paris: Gallimard, 1997); *Proust in the Power of Photography*, trans. by Richard Howard (Chicago, IL: Chicago University Press, 2001); Katja Haustein, *Regarding Lost Time: Photography, Identity and Affect in Proust, Benjamin and Barthes* (Oxford: Legenda, 2012).
4. Mieke Bal, *The Mottled Screen: Reading Proust Visually*, trans. by Anna-Louise Milne (Stanford, CA: Stanford University Press, 1997).
5. Ibid., p. 213.
6. André Benhaïm, *Panim: visages de Proust* (Villeneuve d'Ascq: Presses universitaires du Septentrion, 2006), pp. 149–50.
7. Chévrier, *Proust et la photographie*, pp. 14–15.
8. I borrow the expression 'techniques of the observer' from Jonathan Crary, whose book of this title addresses the imbrications of visual technologies and modes of perception and knowledge in the nineteenth century (*Techniques of the Observer: On Vision and Modernity in the Nineteenth Century* (Cambridge, MA: MIT Press, 1990), Chapters 1 and 2).
9. Raymond Bellour, *L'Entre-images: photo, cinéma, vidéo* (Paris: La Différence, 1990); *Between-the-Images*, trans. by Allan Hardyck (Zurich & Dijon: JRP/Ringier & Les Presses du réel, 2012; and *L'Entre-images 2: mots-images* (Paris: POL, 1999).
10. Jacques Rancière, *La Fable cinématographique* (Paris: Seuil, 2001), p. 12; *Film Fables*, trans. by Emiliano Battista (Oxford & New York: Berg, 2006), p. 5.
11. Gilles Deleuze, *Cinéma 2: l'image-temps* (Paris: Minuit, 1985), p. 27; *Cinema 2: The Time-Image*, trans. by Hugh Tomlinson and Robert Galeta (London: Athlone, 1989), p. 17.
12. Miriam Heywood, *Modernist Visions: Marcel Proust's A la recherche du temps perdu and Jean-Luc Godard's Histoire(s) du cinéma* (Bern: Peter Lang, 2012); Alessia Ricciardi, 'Cinema Regained: Godard Between Proust and Benjamin', *Modernism/modernity*, 8:4 (November 2001), 643–61, and *The Ends of Mourning: Psychoanalysis, Literature, Film* (Stanford, CA: Stanford University Press, 2003).
13. *Psychanalyse et cinéma*, ed. by Raymond Bellour, Thierry Kuntzel and Christian Metz, special issue of *Communications*, 23 (1975). See Chapter 1 for references to the individual essays and their translations.
14. Giorgio Agamben, 'Notes on Gesture', in *Means Without End: Notes on Politics*, trans. by Vincenzo Binetti and Cesare Casarino (Minneapolis: University of Minnesota Press, 2000), pp. 49–62.
15. Serge Daney, 'Le Travelling de *Kapo*', in *Persévérance: entretien avec Serge Toubiana* (Paris: POL, 1994), pp. 13–39; 'The Tracking Shot in *Kapo*', in *Postcards from the Cinema*, trans. by Paul Grant (London: Bloomsbury, 2007), pp. 17–38.
16. On Proust and reading, see Adam Watt, *Reading in Proust's A la recherche: 'le délire de la lecture'* (Oxford: Oxford University Press, 2009).
17. See Walter Benjamin, *The Arcades Project*, trans. by Howard Eiland and Kevin McLaughlin (Cambridge, MA, & London: Harvard University Press, 1999), p. 456.
18. Roland Barthes, *La Chambre claire* (Paris: Gallimard, Seuil, Cahiers du cinéma, 1980), pp. 89–90; *Camera Lucida*, trans. by Richard Howard (London: Vintage, 1982), p. 55.
19. Roland Barthes, 'En sortant du cinéma', in *Le Bruissement de la langue* (Paris: Seuil, 1984) pp. 383–87 (p. 387); 'Leaving the Movie Theatre', in *The Rustle of Language*, trans. by Richard Howard (New York: Hill & Wang, 1986), pp. 345–49 (p. 348).
20. Ibid.
21. Roland Barthes, 'Le Troisième sens', in *L'Obvie et l'obtus* (Paris: Seuil, 1982), pp. 43–61, (p. 44); 'The Third Meaning', in *Image, Music, Text*, trans. by Stephen Heath (London: Fontana, 1977), pp. 52–68 (p. 53).
22. Deleuze, *Cinéma 2*, p. 292; *Cinema 2*, p. 225. See also Heywood, *Modernist Visions*, pp. 119–67, for an incisive chapter comparing Proust's and Godard's uses of sound, voice, and music.
23. Deleuze, *Cinéma 2*, p. 320; *Cinema 2*, p. 245.
24. Ibid., p. 314; p. 242.
25. For a profound and exhaustive account of the *Recherche* as both a narrative and a theory of

listening, see Igor Reyner, *Listening in Proust* (unpublished PhD thesis, King's College London, 2017).

26. In his landmark essay on the voice in cinema, *La Voix au cinéma*, Michel Chion uses the episode of the grandmother's telephone call as a paradigm for the elaboration of what he calls, after Pierre Schaeffer, the 'acousmêtre' (*La Voix au cinema* (Paris: Cahiers du cinéma/Éditions de l'étoile, 1982); *The Voice in Cinema*, trans. by Claudia Gorbman (New York: Columbia University Press, 1999)). For further discussion of the 'acousmatic' dimensions of the episode, see Patrick ffrench, 'Barthes and the Voice: The Acousmatic and Beyond', *L'Esprit créateur*, 55:4 (2015), 56–69.

CHAPTER 1

Reverie in a Dark Room

It begins in a dark room. Before coming to the point at which the linear narrative of *A la recherche du temps perdu* can properly commence, Proust must first establish a narrative agent. In parallel to the return to childhood, to Combray and all that belongs to it, but before this memory comes into play, consciousness emerges from a threshold between sleep and wakefulness. In this primordial state, before any certainty in relation to time and place, consciousness is consciousness of a room, but also, strangely, consciousness *as* a room, a chamber.

Before being situated in historical time and geographic space the subject (if we can thus name the consciousness which is barely able to distinguish itself from the objects of its attention) occupies an indistinct and non-specific space and time which nevertheless has the quality of enclosure. The experiencing subject is *in* time, but not yet in a particular present that can be positioned in respect to a past and a future; it is *in* space, but not yet in a particular point of space that can be positioned at a particular distance from locatable objects around it. The indistinct dimensions of this temporality and spatiality, before time as present-ness and space as phenomenologically-centred, intervene throughout the novel to disrupt the narrative agent's occupation of space and time. They give the novel its intermittent coherence. These dimensions, however, remain those of the room, the chamber. Before consciousness situates the subject, there is an experience of enclosure, and a threshold consciousness of a division between interior and exterior which is in some sense the font and the primary condition for thought.

The room is the division, anterior to subjectivity and knowledge, between inside and outside. In the very first sentences of the novel the narrator immediately poses this relation through his attempt, on waking in the middle of the night, to gauge the disposition of the surrounding countryside, the outside, through the sound of passing trains:

> Je me demandais quelle heure il pouvait être; j'entendais le sifflement des trains qui, plus ou moins éloigné, comme le chant d'un oiseau dans une forêt, relevant les distances, me décrivait l'étendue de la campagne déserte où le voyageur se hâte vers la station prochaine; et le petit chemin qu'il suit va être gravé dans son souvenir par l'excitation qu'il doit à des lieux nouveaux, à des actes inaccoutumés, à la causerie récente et aux adieux sous la lampe étrangère qui le suivent encore dans la silence de la nuit, à la douceur prochaine du retour.
> (I, 3–4)

[I would ask myself what time it might be; I could hear the whistling of the trains which, remote or near by, like the singing of a bird in a forest, plotting the distances, described to me the extent of the deserted countryside where the traveller hastens towards the nearest station; and the little road he is following will be engraved on his memory by the excitement he owes to new places, to unaccustomed activities, to the recent conversation and the farewells under the unfamiliar lamp that follow him still through the silence of the night, to the imminent sweetness of his return.] (I, 7)

Exterior space here is conceived as an unknown domain, a blank canvas or screen on which the narrator can project this sketch of a hypothetical traveller, drawing on an emotive register of familiarity, strangeness, voyage out, and return. The passage also functions to introduce, for the first time, the theme of memory as an inscription provoked by the intensity of non-habitual experience. But this brief foray outside the space of the room only serves to emphasize the affective security of the narrator's enclosure in his room and in his bed, a sense of protection which is immediately, in the next paragraph, associated with childhood: 'J'appuyais tendrement mes joues contre les belles joues de l'oreiller, qui, pleines et fraîches, sont comme les joues de notre enfance' ('I would rest my cheeks tenderly against the lovely cheeks of the pillow, which, full and fresh, are like the cheeks of our childhood'). This simile does not, however, suffice to draw the narrator back to what Roland Barthes refers to as 'le bon sommeil' [good sleep], in proximity to the mother, to the maternal space of his childhood room.[1] He remains in 'le mauvais sommeil' [bad sleep], 'loin de la mère' [far from the mother], provoking a new comparison to the room of the convalescent who hopefully perceives 'sous la porte une raie de jour' ('a ray of light under the door') (I, 4; I, 8). Security and anxiety here are being played out around the threshold of the room, a refuge from the strangeness and exposure of the outside, but also a cloistered space of suffering from which a sign of exterior life can promise escape. Consciousness, and the affective being of the subject, fill the space of the room and establish themselves within its limits, to the extent that the subject is identified with this chamber, with an enclosed, interior space.

The *Recherche* begins at a threshold between sleep and wakefulness, but the experience takes place, nevertheless, within the space of a room. Barthes underlines how the incipit of the novel installs a logic of disorganization, announced by the logical and grammatical 'scandal' of such a threshold consciousness:

Un paradoxe le définit bien: il est un sommeil qui peut être écrit, parce qu'il est une conscience de sommeil; tout l'épisode (et, partant, je le crois, toute l'œuvre qui en sort) se tient ainsi suspendu dans une sorte de scandale grammatical: dire 'je dors' est en effet, à la lettre, aussi impossible que de dire 'je suis mort'.

[A paradox defines it nicely: it is a sleep which can be written, because it is a consciousness of sleep; the whole episode (and consequently the whole work which emerges from it) is thus held suspended in a sort of grammatical scandal; to say 'I'm asleep' is in effect as impossible as to say 'I'm dead'.][2]

This scandal suspends the laws of logic and of narrative, and introduces an alternative logic, of 'vacillation', or 'decompartmentalization' (*décloisonnement*).[3] The opening up of partitions — *cloisons* — works here between different states of consciousness, but also as the introduction of continuity and flux into the previously compartmentalized rooms which the narrator has occupied over time, rooms which change their shape and arrangement, but which nevertheless appear to merge into the same room, their rapid succession giving the image of permanence, like a projected strip of photogrammatic frames.

Initially the narrator's intermittence between sleep and the waking state is accounted for through a relation to the room and its furniture:

> Je me rendormais, et parfois je n'avais plus que de courts réveils d'un instant, le temps d'entendre les craquements organiques des boiseries, d'ouvrir les yeux pour fixer le kaléïdoscope de l'obscurité, de goûter grâce à une lueur momentanée de conscience le sommeil où étaient plongés les meubles, la chambre, le tout dont je n'étais qu'une petite partie et à l'insensibilité duquel je retournais vite m'unir. (I, 4)

> [I would go back to sleep, and sometimes afterwards woke only briefly for a moment, long enough to hear the organic creak of the woodwork, open my eyes and stare at the kaleidoscope of the darkness, savour in a momentary glimmer of consciousness the sleep into which were plunged the furniture, the room, that whole of which I was only a small part and whose insensibility I would soon return to share.] (I, 8)[4]

This remarkable sentence looks like the acute point of the scandal Barthes identifies, which explodes the certainty of the Cartesian subject, and more, the modalities of the Kantian subject — the a priori modalities which form a capacity to establish a position in time and space.[5] What vacillates, or oscillates here, around the threshold, is consciousness *of* the room, and consciousness *as* the room. The room exists on either side of this intermittence. Before becoming a consciousness *of* this room, consciousness is *in* the room, or is the room itself. This suggests a different elaboration from the phenomenological *conscience de*, an elaboration according to which consciousness is not primarily *of*, but exists on the same plane as that of which it becomes conscious through a kind of fold, a pocket within the room from which point it becomes an object of consciousness.[6] The room is primordial in that it exists before and is the first condition for the awakening of consciousness. This is 'scandalous' in Barthes's sense, in that it operates a suspension of consciousness at its limit, but more so, and in a specifically grammatical sense, in that writing transgresses the grammar which positions a subject in relation to a predicate.[7] What it suspends is the association of the pronoun *je* with a subject, or rather it dislocates the grammatical function of the subject from its psychological foundation, and institutes something like a *je-chambre*, recalling the earlier, oneiric equivalence of the *je* with the object of attention: 'j'étais moi-même ce dont parlait l'ouvrage' ('I was myself what the book was talking about') (I, 3; I, 7). Proust's *Esquisses* offer further examples of this 'scandalous' dislocation, in which consciousness opens as a kind of parenthesis within an ontological and epistemological continuity:

> Autrefois j'avais connu comme tout le monde la douceur de m'éveiller au milieu de la nuit, de goûter un instant l'obscurité, le silence, quelque sourd craquement, comme pourrait le faire au fond d'une armoire une pomme appelée pour un instant à une faible conscience de sa situation. (I, 639)

[Formerly, I had known like everyone else the sweetness of waking up in the middle of the night, of savouring the darkness and the silence, perhaps some muffled creaking, for just a moment, just as an apple in a wardrobe might have done, called for an instant to a frail consciousness of its situation.]

Après avoir surpris sur le fait les remous de l'obscurité et le craquement des boiseries, je me rendormais au plus vite, à peu près comme une pomme ou un pot de confitures qui auraient été appelées un instant à la conscience et après avoir constaté qu'il faisait nuit noire dans l'armoire et entendu le bois travailler, n'auraient rien eu de plus pressé que de retourner à la délicieuse insensibilité de la planche où ils sont posés, des autres pôts de confiture et de l'obscurité. (i, 640)

[Having instantaneously surprised the shifts in the darkness and the creaking of the wooden furniture, I fell back to sleep very quickly, a little like an apple or pot of jam summoned to an instant of consciousness, which once having ascertained that it was pitch dark in the cupboard, and having heard the creaking of the wood, would have nothing more pressing to do than to return to the delicious insensibility of the shelf on which they were placed, the other pots of jam, and the darkness.]

Writing installs a subject which is not that of the psychological person, nor of phenomenology, bearing out Barthes's well-known observation that: 'Le langage connaît un "sujet", non une "personne"' ('Language knows a "subject" not a "person"'), and this places the *Recherche* under the sign of a non-subject, which troubles, albeit partially, any attempts to enlist it to the services of a hermeneutics of the self.[8] What is particularly interesting here is that the continuity from which subjective consciousness emerges is enclosed; as if behind and outside the parentheses of perceptual consciousness there was the sense of being housed, separated from the outside.

The state of sleep is a 'participation' in the room: 'Une sorte de participation à l'obscurité de la chambre, à la vie inconsciente de ses cloisons et de ses meubles, tel ètait mon sommeil' (i, 640) [A sort of participation in the darkness of the room, in the unconscious life of its partitions and its furniture, such was my sleep]. But the room in which sleep participates, a sleep endowed with a kind of agency, is not only or necessarily the room which encloses the narrator in the present. As the narrator says of the linear thread of time and of the hierarchy of years that have led up that point in time, 'leurs rangs peuvent se mêler, se rompre' ('their ranks can be mixed up, broken') (i, 5; i, 9). The *décloisonnement* Barthes names takes place across the temporal partitions that separate different rooms, and therefore different worlds, since the past is a multiplicity of worlds, separated by *cloisons*, which this sleep-writing moves through and across. The transversal movement which opens up one room, one world, to the next, in a non-linear procession, serves to dislocate consciousness from the direct object of perception in the present, qualified by the definite article, *the* room in which I am asleep, and to accentuate the generic quality of being in *a* room, as such.

Proust's textual transgressions, as Barthes construes them, also operate as a pheno-menological investigation which strains at the leash which ties phenomenology itself to the Cartesian subject of knowledge and experience, the notion of 'participation' looking to Merleau-Ponty's chiasmus and to the enmeshing of consciousness in *la chair du monde* [the flesh of the world].[9] But another dimension comes quickly into play, entering into tension with this account of things; if we restrict ourselves to the experiential registering of phenomena we miss entirely the affective intensity with which the experience of the room is endowed. This other dimension is that of childhood and of 'early life' (*la vie primitive*); the threshold at stake is not only that of perception but also that of infancy, and thus of sexuality. It is not completely the case, as Barthes suggests, that 'ce sommeil n'a rien de freudien' ('this sleep has nothing Freudian about it'); it is non-Freudian to the extent that the other logic at stake is not pinned down to that of the dream-work — there are few dreams in Proust, as Barthes observes — but it does appeal to a psychoanalytically-inflected account of childhood through the introduction of the 'terreurs enfantines' [childish terrors] which return in sleep.[10] The moment of the re-unification of the *je* with the room's insensibility is worth a further look:

> Ou bien en dormant j'avais rejoint sans effort un âge à jamais révolu de ma vie primitive, retrouvé telle de mes terreurs enfantines comme celle que mon grand-oncle me tirât par mes boucles et qu'avait dissipée le jour — date pour moi d'un ère nouvelle — où on les avait coupées. J'avais oublié cet événement pendant mon sommeil, j'en retrouvais le souvenir aussitôt que j'avais réussi à m'éveiller pour échapper aux mains de mon grand-oncle, mais par mesure de précaution j'entourais complètement ma tête de l'oreiller avant de retourner dans le monde des rêves. (I, 4)

> [Or else while sleeping I had effortlessly returned to a for ever vanished period of my early life, rediscovered one of my childish terrors such as that my great-uncle would pull me by my curls, a terror dispelled on the day — the dawn for me of a new era — when they were cut off. I had forgotten that event during my sleep, I recovered its memory as soon as I managed to wake myself up to escape the hands of my great-uncle, but as a precautionary measure I would completely surround my head with my pillow before returning to the world of dreams.] (I, 8)

The immersion of the subject in the insensibility of the room is proposed here as alternating with a dreamed return to 'primitive life'. This alternative is not one of mutual exclusion but of series, in keeping with the imperfect tense of the opening of the novel, but it may also have an affective, moral quality; unification with the room and the absorption or savouring (*goûter*) of the sleep into which the room is plunged connoting a security which is disrupted by childhood terror. As we will see later, immersion in the room, the dissipating expansion of the subject into its space, alternates with a near-traumatic experience of its unfamiliarity when attention shrinks back to a more central point of perception. It is not an exaggeration to say that experience is presented as traumatic in itself, when it imposes itself on a subject unable to avoid its demand for attention. Here, however, wakeful consciousness (almost) saves the subject from terror; 'ou bien' [or else] denotes not a logical alternative but a moral one: sleep can be a welcome relief from the demands of the present, but it can also resuscitate the tormentors of the past. A childhood memory can provoke both *terreur* and *jouissance*. Sleeping consciousness does not take account of the events which put an end to infantile terror — the narrator's first haircut, for example — or which have changed its objects, neither does it pay heed to the linear succession of different 'eras' which sub-divide childhood into a litany of different transitional objects of terror and anxiety. So this vulnerability and terror are dreamed as real as they were at the time. Consciousness intervenes to re-establish the dividing lines; waking is an escape from the torment, but it also provokes 'mesures de précaution' [precautionary measures] against the intensity of the affective charge; 'le monde de rêves' [the world of dreams] is experienced not as fantasy or as a radical alterity, but just as real as the objects of perception and the knowledge of the past; a threshold state of consciousness is adumbrated here, akin to a form of hallucination, a form of private cinema. In Proust's local theorization, the phenomenology of threshold consciousness, sleep vis-à-vis wakefulness, is plotted against the different axis of childhood vis-à-vis adulthood. The sensations and affects of 'primitive life' thus return in the present, as if they were actual. Proust's sleep *is* Freudian to this extent, but with significant qualifications which we will encounter further on.

A further resonance with the premises of Freudian psychoanalysis is suggested in the shift of focus from childhood terror to sexual pleasure from this paragraph ('Je me rendormais'; 'I would go back to sleep') to the next ('Quelquefois, comme Ève naquit d'une côte d'Adam'; 'Sometimes, as Eve was born from one of Adam's ribs'). Just as the narrator dreams his great uncle's torment as real and imminent, he dreams the imminent pleasure of the woman his dream has invented, or remembered, as physical and corporeal. In both cases, the imminence of the peak of the affective charge in physical contact — the great uncle's sadistic hands and the body of the woman — makes the narrator wake up. Fear and pleasure are equivalent here in terms of the common limit they encounter, the 'central zone' of *jouissance* where the affect is too intense.[11] The room is also the space of this congruence, where sexual pleasure is associated with guilt and torment. Further on in the *Recherche* the room as a site of cruelty and *jouissance* returns, when the narrator, now a voyeur outside the room, witnesses Mlle Vinteuil spit on the photograph of her father to inflame her lover, and when he spies on Charlus's flagellation in Jupien's brothel.[12]

In his account of the infinitesimal process of awakening Proust conceives of different degrees of contraction of the concentric circle of time around 'un homme qui dort' [a man asleep].[13] The elasticity and variability of time is such that morning can be mistaken for evening, day for night. It is the body's posture which measures the distortion. A greater or lesser divergence of the body from its habitual sleeping position determines the degree of divergence between 'le point de la terre qu'il occupe' [the point on the earth he occupies] and the spatial and temporal location of the place in which he thinks he has awakened. But Proust also proposes that at an extreme point, at the full stretch of time's elasticity, so to speak, temporality is unleashed from what connects it to the 'point of the present'. What he will later call 'un peu de temps à l'état pur' [a bit of time in the pure state] is no longer characterized by concentric organization around the subject's present location.[14]

The dilation of time occasioned by deep sleep reaches beyond memory, however disordered, to provoke, on awakening, a pure feeling (*sentiment*) of existence:

> Mais il suffisait que, dans mon lit même, mon sommeil fût profond et détendit entièrement mon esprit; alors celle-ci lâchait le plan du lieu où je m'étais endormi, et quand je m'éveillais au milieu de la nuit, comme j'ignorais où je me trouvais, je ne savais même pas au premier instant qui j'étais; j'avais seulement, dans sa simplicité première, le sentiment d'existence comme il peut frémir au fond d'un animal; j'étais plus dénuée que l'homme des cavernes. (I, 5)

> [But it was enough if, in my own bed, my sleep was deep and allowed my mind to relax entirely; then it would let go of the map of the place where I had fallen asleep and, when I woke in the middle of the night, since I did not know where I was, I did not even understand in the first moment who I was; all I had, in its original simplicity, was the sense of existence as it may quiver in the depths of an animal; I was more bereft than a caveman.] (I, 9)

At this extreme point there is a fundamental intimation of exteriority; the bare feeling of existence is that of an animal with fewer means, or more impoverished, than the man of the caves; the implication is that what the being in this state lacks is shelter and enclosure. The deeper the sleep, the less contracted the mind, the more, paradoxically, one finds oneself 'outside' upon awakening. Proust does, then, conceive of a radical exteriority, a distant outside to this chamber *of* and *as* consciousness. It is one that rarely intervenes, and its indication here serves to reinforce the extent to which the borders of human subjectivity are those of an enclosed space, made of layers or sheets of time, and experienced as memories.

Memories of different places, of rooms, draw the narrator back inside, away from 'the void' (*le néant*):

> Mais alors le souvenir — non encore du lieu où j'étais, mais de quelques-uns de ceux que j'avais habités et où j'aurais pu être — venait à moi comme un secours d'en haut pour me tirer du néant d'où je n'aurais pu sortir tout seul; je passais en une seconde par-dessus des siècles de civilisation, et l'image confusément entrevue de lampes à pétrole, puis de chemises à col rabattu, recomposaient peu à peu les traits originaux de mon moi. (I, 5–6)

> [But then the memory — not yet of the place where I was, but of several of those where I had lived and where I might have been — would come to me like help from on high to pull me out of the void from which I could not have got out on my own; I passed over centuries of civilisation in one second, and the image confusedly glimpsed of oil lamps, then of wing-collar shirts, gradually recomposed my self's original features.] (I, 9)

It is significant that the redemptive agency of memory is described here as separate from the *je*, which cannot do the work alone, as if memory were not tied to the individual consciousness but did indeed operate over and above the self, as an exterior agency, 'venant d'en haut' [from on high], supplementary to it. It is also significant that memory is described as operating by means of images, but that the recomposition of the self is written in graphic terms. The self, 'le moi' which is thus rescued from oblivion (from forgetfulness) is an entity composed (thus written) of or with images. The original characteristics of the self, or, if we read 'traits' at the most literal level, strokes, graphic marks, or lines, appear as historically contingent and somewhat banal in relation to the metaphysical register which the text has engaged. Why petrol lamps and shirts with turnover collars? These images, 'confusément entrevue' [confusedly glimpsed], are the nearest detectable markers of the past over centuries (fifty, Proust calculates in one of the drafts); the speed at which the *je* is moving through time, from the prehistoric time of caves to the present moment, slows down as it nears the present enough to enable such details to be drawn. The 'original' self is *re*composed, but the originality of this composition is suspended and undermined by the graphic nature of the marks that make it; that the *moi* is made of graphic strokes undermines its status as origin; it is a form of writing. The original strokes or marks of the self as a graphic composition are repeated — a contradictory conflation of creative composition and the re-assembling of something pre-existent.

The capacity to draw or to visually register a mark depends upon the right speed. Things have to slow down enough to allow us to fix ourselves in relation to them, to immobilize them and thus to immobilize ourselves. We project immobility and fixity onto things, whereas, before our own certainty immobilizes them, they are in constant motion, and at varying degrees of speed: 'Peut-être l'immobilité des choses autour de nous leur est-elle imposée par notre certitude que ce sont elles et non pas d'autres, par l'immobilité de notre pensée en face d'elles' ('Perhaps the immobility of things around us is imposed on them by our certainty that they are themselves and not others, by the immobility of our mind confronting them') (I, 6; I, 9–10). Proust portrays waking consciousness in terms of deceleration; located identity in the present is a fixing of the infinite speed of things around us, and this is put in specifically visual terms, already introduced in the expression 'fixer le kaléidoscope de l'obscurité', the first of many references to visual technologies in the *Recherche*.

The kaleidoscope, however, is not strictly speaking a mechanism whereby moving images are immobilized, but one in which a finite visual arrangement of objects is momentarily fixed from an indefinite number of possibilities. The conceptual point Proust makes here is that the image of things we believe we have in front of us, which also locates us in a reassuring certainty of our own stability, is but one of an infinite number of possible arrangements of things. To *fix* the kaleidoscope of the darkness is to choose one of these possible arrangements, possible universes. In this instance, however, finite fixity in relation to an infinity of possibilities is put in terms of mobile circulation: 'tout *tournait* autour de moi dans l'obscurité, les choses, les pays, les années' ('everything *revolved* around me in the darkness, things, countries, years'); '*tourbillonnaient* dans les ténèbres' ('*spun* through the shadows') (I, 6; I, 9); and later, 'ces évocations *tournoyantes*' ('these *revolving*, confused evocations') (I, 7; I, 10). Proust's figures conflate kaleidoscopic multiplicity with speed and rotation, finitude with immobility, suggesting that the stable image of things in front of us is due to the *arrest* of a flux of moving images.

The images at stake are those of rooms, and they circulate in the darkness of a generic room, an infinity of possible rooms which we might grasp, paraphrasing Proust, with the expression 'the room in its pure state'. Memory is proposed here to be an operation of discernment in relation to infinite speed, which selects, within the genre of the room, the rooms which the subject has inhabited. It is not a cerebral but a corporeal operation, selecting different rooms in relation to the postures of the body, and thus proposing a haptic participation *in* the room:

> Mon corps, trop engourdi pour remuer, cherchait, d'après la forme de sa fatigue, à repérer la position de ses membres pour en induire la direction du mur, la place des meubles, pour reconstruire et pour nommer la demeure où il se trouvait. Sa mémoire, la mémoire de ses côtes, de ses genoux, de ses épaules, lui présentait successivement plusieurs des chambres où il avait dormi, tandis qu'autour de lui les murs invisibles, changeant de place selon la forme de la pièce imaginée, tourbillonnaient dans les ténèbres. Et avant même que ma pensée, qui hésitait au seuil des temps et des formes, eût identifié le logis en rapprochant les circonstances, lui, — mon corps, — se rappelait pour chacun le genre du lit, la place des portes, la prise de jour des fenêtres, l'existence d'un couloir, avec la pensée que j'avais en m'y endormant et que je retrouvais au réveil. Mon côté ankylosé, cherchant à deviner son orientation, s'imaginait, par exemple, allongé face au mur dans un grand lit à baldaquin, et aussitôt je me disais: 'Tiens, j'ai fini par m'endormir quoique maman ne soit pas venue me dire bonsoir', j'étais à la campagne chez mon grand-père, mort depuis bien des années; et mon corps, le côté sur lequel je reposais, gardiens fidèles d'un passé que mon esprit n'aurait jamais dû oublier, me rappelaient la flamme de la veilleuse de verre de Bohême, en forme d'urne, suspendue au plafond par des chaînettes, la cheminée en marbre de Sienne, dans ma chambre à coucher de Combray, chez mes grands-parents, en des jours lointains qu'en ce moment je me figurais actuels sans me les représenter exactement, et que je reverrais mieux tout à l'heure quand je serais tout à fait éveillé. (I, 6)

[My body, too benumbed to move, would try to locate, according to the form of its fatigue, the position of its limbs in order to deduce from this the direction of the wall, the location of the furniture, in order to reconstruct and name the dwelling in which it found itself. Its memory, the memory of its ribs, its knees, its shoulders, offered in succession several of the rooms where it had slept, while around it the invisible walls, changing place according to the shape of the imagined room, spun through the shadows. And even before my mind, which hesitated on the thresholds of times and shapes, had identified the house by reassembling the circumstances, it — my body — would recall the kind of bed in each one, the location of the doors, the angle at which the light came in through the windows, the existence of a hallway, along with the thought I had had as I fell asleep and that I had recovered upon waking. My stiffened side, trying to guess its orientation, would imagine, for instance, that it lay facing the wall in a big canopied bed and immediately I would say to myself: 'Why, I went to sleep in the end even though Mama didn't come to say goodnight to me,' I was in the country at the house of my grandfather, dead for many years; and my body, the side on which I was resting, faithful guardians of a past my mind ought never to have forgotten, recalled to me the flame of the nightlight of Bohemian glass, in the shape of an urn, hanging from the ceiling by little chains, the mantelpiece of Siena marble, in my bedroom at Combray, at my grandparents' house, in remote days which at this moment I imagined were present without picturing them to myself exactly and which I would see more clearly in a little while when I was fully awake.] (I, 10)

Bodily memory is well in advance of 'my mind' (*esprit* or *pensée*), which remains on the other side of the threshold of time and distinguishable forms. Different body parts are given a form of agency in their quasi-tactile exploration ('cherchait [...] à se repérer [...] pour en induire') of the body's position in relation to surrounding objects. It is as if the body has its own way of sensing, knowing, and remembering the spatiality of its surroundings.[15] The different dispositions of body parts remember specific rooms ('se rappelait pour chacun'), which are presented successively, while thought judges between them ('rapprochant les circonstances'), as if for each bodily position and state of intensity there corresponded a room which remained actual and present, of which the body or its part was the faithful guardian. The body is given a moral agency here in the preservation of the past and as a guarantee against the judgments and syntheses, thus the need to forget, of the mind. Proust proposes, in short, a powerful affirmation of the process of memory through haptic participation or proprioceptive perception rather than synthetic conceptualization.[16]

The successive rooms, momentarily and provisionally frozen, yet sensed as no less actual for all this, in the swirling motion of possible rooms, are now figured as the successive images of a proto-cinematographic device, the *kinétoscope*:

> Ces évocations tournoyantes et confuses ne duraient jamais que quelques secondes; souvent, ma brève incertitude du lieu où je me trouvais ne distinguait pas mieux les unes des autres les diverses suppositions dont elle était faite, que nous n'isolons, en voyant un cheval courir, les positions successives que nous montre le kinétoscope. (I, 7)

> [These revolving, confused evocations never lasted for more than a few seconds; often, in my brief uncertainty about where I was, I did not distinguish the various suppositions of which it was composed, any better than we isolate, when we see a horse run, the successive positions shown to us by a kinetoscope.] (I, 11)

What is significant here is the way in which Proust keys in his concerns with the physiological processes of awakening with a question about visual perception very much linked to a near-contemporary context in which science merges with cultures of entertainment and curiosity: the pre-history of the cinema in those 'techniques of the observer' that had been popular since the mid-nineteenth century.[17] The issue concerns the narrator's capacity to distinguish between the different rooms his body had imagined, and the capacity to visually fix an image in motion. Again, it is a question of speed. The shift from the context of the subject's consciousness to that of contemporary science and culture is marked by the change in pronoun, from 'ma brève incertitude' [my brief uncertainty] to 'nous'; the kinetoscope is part of 'our' culture, part of the cultural context of the late nineteenth century. In fact the word *kinétoscope* first entered the French language, according to the *Petit Robert*, in the 1890s, following the invention and naming of the device by Thomas Edison and William Dickson in the late 1880s, in the United States, and its presentation at the Exposition Universelle of 1889. The machine created a moving image by means of the movement of a perforated strip of consecutive images in front of a light source, which would be seen through an aperture in the machine itself; it was a version of the 'phenakistoscope' invented and patented by Joseph Plateau in 1834 and an object of curiosity for Baudelaire in the essay 'La Morale du joujou' [The Moral of the Toy].[18]

Proust's metaphor, however, somewhat confuses the issue through allusion to the quasi-scientific experiments with the recording of motion carried out in the 1880s by the amateur photographer Eadweard Muybridge in California, commissioned by the entrepreneur Leland Stanford. Muybridge's celebrated experiments featured the horse 'Occident' and were intended specifically to record whether a horse's hooves were or were not in contact with the ground at full gallop. The published results fed into Edison's more industrial endeavours in the United States, which were also informed by, and in turn influenced the work of Étienne-Jules Marey, who had been exploring similar inventions in France in a context more allied to science and medicine.[19] The use of photographic film in Edison's kinetoscope was influenced by an earlier device of Marey's, the *chronophotographe*.[20] Proust's reference to the image of the horse shown by a kinetoscope is thus an allusion to a contemporary object of curiosity and exhibition, which conflates (or condenses) different cultural contexts, with which one might assume he was familiar. The condensation is extended if one takes into account an earlier version of the text, which has 'cinématographe' rather than 'kinétoscope' (I, 1090). This places the mechanism within a French context, the *cinématographe* having been patented in 1895 by the Lumière brothers Louis and Auguste.

While the substitution of *kinétoscope* for *cinématographe* is suggestive, as we will discuss further on, the underlying analogy between the narrator's capacity to isolate one room from the many possible rooms that are revolving around him in an indistinct blur and the improbability of the isolation of successive positions in 'our' perception of animal locomotion remains the same. Proust is contrasting the physiological perception of motion with its analytic reduction to a succession of sequential instants. Movement is irreducible to a series of 'points' of the present. In this Proust and his narrator follow Henri Bergson's critique of the 'cinematographic illusion' in *L'Évolution créatrice* (1907). As Deleuze paraphrases Bergson: 'vous ne pouvez pas reconstituer le mouvement avec des positions dans l'espace ou des instants dans le temps, c'est-à-dire avec des "coupes" immobiles' ('you cannot reconstitute movement with positions in space and instants in time: that is, with immobile sections').[21] This operation construes movement on the basis of fixed positions or instants, and adds the 'abstract idea' of succession, whereas for Bergson movement as such has a qualitative duration of its own ('sa propre durée qualitative'; 'its own qualitative duration').[22] Proust thus joins Bergson in condemning the cinematographic for giving a false perception of movement, positioning himself on the side of the duration and intuition of time as opposed to its decomposition in the work of Marey and Muybridge.[23]

As Sara Danius notes, in the context of her work on modernist literature and technology, Proust distances the operation of memory, here, from any equivalence with photography.[24] The operation of the threshold consciousness does not work with a succession of photogrammatic snapshots of the rooms which the narrator has inhabited; all is in continual motion and flux. The virtual rooms from which the narrator will eventually come to distinguish the actual room he is in are not, like the actual room, a succession of static images, but an image in motion, a 'movement–image', to adopt Deleuze's expression. The key distinction here is between a theorization of the moving image which thinks it as an animated series of static instants, and one which grasps movement as a distinct concept and object, irreducible to the abstraction of the instant. As we have seen, Bergson in particular would be critical of the cinematographic abstraction of movement in this vein. The distinction recurs in the fairly stark difference between photogrammatic theories of film, such as those grounded in the ontology of the photographic image (André Bazin and Roland Barthes) and the radical departure of Gilles Deleuze in the mid-1980s with the two volumes of *Cinéma*, *L'Image-mouvement* and *L'Image-temps*, which returned to Bergson, correcting his criticism of cinema and proposing that in cinema a perception of time 'in its pure state' were possible. We will return to this critical nexus further on.

Writing, nevertheless, does distinguish and isolate one room from another. There is a dislocation between the logics of perception and of consciousness that Proust is attempting to convey here, and the logic of writing by means of which he conveys it. Writing, following Barthes's naming of its propensity to 'scandal', does not follow the rules of normative human perception. Moreover, the perpetual motion with which Proust qualifies the 'évocations tournoyantes' pertains to the hypnagogic state of threshold consciousness, in contrast to the sequential and distinct memories — 'tantôt l'une, tantôt l'autre' [sometimes one, sometimes another] — he recalls when now fully awake. Conscious and voluntary memory is, we might infer, qualitatively and radically different in nature to the memory which inhabits the body. Threshold consciousness, the consciousness of *rêverie*, which Proust expresses here as 'ma brève incertitude', does not analyze, does not differentiate the 'suppositions dont elle [est] faite' [the suppositions of which it [is] composed]; it is nevertheless made of such suppositions, just as the film strip in the kinetoscope or the camera/projector *is* made of sequential photogrammatic images, and the moving image of *a* room provokes a subsequent, analytic, and sequential review of the different rooms that make up the mobile room which threshold consciousness had experienced: 'Mais j'avais revu, tantôt une, tantôt l'autre, des chambres que j'avais habitées dans ma vie, et je finissais par me les rappeler toutes pendant les longues rêveries qui suivaient mon réveil' ('But I had seen sometimes one, sometimes another, of the bedrooms I had inhabited in my life, and in the end I would recall them all in the long reveries that followed my waking') (I, 7; I, 11). Conscious, reflective memory is analytic, and does isolate each of the rooms, now one, now the other, classifying them within the clauses and syntax of a single sentence, introduced here, which thus operates a montage of rooms; the flow and elongation of the sentence nevertheless loosens the distinction of each image, each room, and thus constitutes the movement-image of the room, in the famous elongated sentence of the rooms which the narrator has inhabited. It is now worth citing the whole sentence:

> Mais j'avais revu, tantôt une, tantôt l'autre, des chambres que j'avais habitées
> dans ma vie, et je finissais par me les rappeler toutes pendant les longues rêveries

qui suivaient mon réveil; chambres d'hiver où quand on est couché, on se blottit
la tête dans un nid qu'on se tresse avec les choses les plus disparates: un coin de
l'oreiller, le haut des couvertures, un bout de châle, le bord du lit, et un numéro
des *Débats roses*, qu'on finit par cimenter ensemble selon la technique des
oiseaux en s'y appuyant indéfiniment; où, par un temps glacial le plaisir qu'on
goûte est de se sentir séparé du dehors (comme l'hirondelle de mer qui a son nid
au fond d'un souterrain dans la chaleur de la terre), et où, le feu étant entretenu
toute la nuit dans la cheminée, on dort dans un grand manteau d'air chaud
et fumeux, traversé des lueurs des tisons qui se rallument, sorte d'impalpable
alcôve, de chaude caverne creusée au sein de la chambre même, zone ardente et
mobile en ses contours thermiques, aérée de souffles qui nous rafraîchissent la
figure et viennent des angles, des parties voisines de la fenêtre ou éloignées du
foyer, et qui se sont refroidies; — chambres d'été où l'on aime être uni à la nuit
tiède, où le clair de lune appuyé aux volets entrouverts, jette jusqu'au pied du
lit son échelle enchantée, où on dort presque en plein air, comme la mésange
balancée par la brise au pointe d'un rayon; — parfois la chambre Louis XVI,
si gaie que même le premier soir je n'y avais pas été trop malheureux et où
les colonnettes qui soutenaient légèrement le plafond s'écartaient avec tant de
grâce pour montrer et réserver la place du lit; parfois au contraire celle, petite
et si élevée de plafond, creusée en forme de pyramide dans la hauteur de deux
étages et partiellement revêtue d'acajou, où dès la première seconde j'avais été
intoxiqué moralement par l'odeur inconnue du vétiver, convaincu de l'hostilité
des rideaux violets et de l'insolente indifférence de la pendule qui jacassait
toute haute comme si je n'avais pas été là; — où une étrange et impitoyable
glace à pieds quadrangulaire, barrant obliquement un des angles de la pièce,
se creusait à vif dans la douce plénitude de mon champ visuel accoutumé un
emplacement qui n'était pas prévu; — où ma pensée, s'efforçant pendant des
heures de se disloquer, de s'étirer en hauteur pour prendre exactement la forme
de la chambre et arriver à remplir jusqu'en haut son gigantesque entonnoir,
avait souffert bien de dures nuits, tandis que j'étais étendu dans mon lit, les
yeux levés, l'oreille anxieuse, la narine rétive, le cœur battant: jusqu'à ce que
l'habitude eût changé la couleur des rideaux, fait taire la pendule, enseigné la
pitié à la glace oblique et cruelle, dissimulé, sinon chassé complètement, l'odeur
du vétiver et notablement diminué la hauteur apparente du plafond. (I, 7–8)

[But I had seen sometimes one, sometimes another, of the bedrooms I had
inhabited in my life, and in the end I would recall them all in the long reveries
that followed my waking: winter bedrooms in which, as soon as you are in
bed, you bury your head in a nest braided of the most disparate things: a corner
of the pillow, the top of the covers, a bit of shawl, the side of the bed and an
issue of the *Débats roses*, which you end by cementing together using the birds'
technique of pressing down on it indefinitely; where in icy weather the pleasure
you enjoy is the feeling that you are separated from the outdoors (like the sea
swallow which makes its nest deep in an underground passage in the warmth
of the earth) and where, since the fire is kept burning all night in the fireplace,
you sleep in a great cloak of warm, smoky air, shot with the glimmers from
the logs breaking into flame again, a sort of immaterial alcove, a warm cave
dug out of the heart of the room itself, a zone of heat with shifting thermal
contours, aerated by drafts which cool your face and come from the corners,
from the parts close to the window or far from the hearth, and which have
grown cold again: summer bedrooms where you delight in becoming one with

the soft night, where the moonlight leaning against the half-open shutters casts its enchanted ladder to the foot of the bed, where you sleep almost in the open air, like a titmouse rocked by the breeze on the tip of a ray of light; sometimes the Louis XVI bedroom, so cheerful that even on the first night I had not been too unhappy there and where the slender columns that lightly supported the ceiling stood aside with such grace to show and reserve the place where the bed was; at other times, the small bedroom with the very high ceiling, hollowed out in the form of a pyramid two stories high and partly panelled in mahogany, where from the first second I had been mentally poisoned by the unfamiliar odour of the vetiver, convinced of the hostility of the violet curtains and the insolent indifference of the clock chattering loudly as though I were not there; where a strange and pitiless quadrangular cheval glass, barring obliquely one of the corners of the room, carved from deep inside the soft fullness of my usual field of vision a site for itself which I had not expected; where my mind, struggling for hours to dislodge itself, to stretch upward so as to assume the exact shape of the room and succeed in filling its gigantic funnel to the very top, had suffered many hard nights, while I lay stretched out in my bed, my eyes lifted, my ear anxious, my nostril restive, my heart pounding, until habit had changed the colour of the curtains, silenced the clock, taught pity to the cruel oblique mirror, concealed, if not driven out completely, the smell of the vetiver and appreciably diminished the apparent height of the ceiling.] (1, 11)

Proust's sentence elaborates a logic of the room and its relation to the affective, embodied subject, which then provokes a meditation on habit. The underlying motif of the contrasting pair of the first two types of rooms — 'chambres d'hiver' and 'chambres d'été' — is a kind of contraction and dilation of the embodied consciousness of the subject, a relation to the space it inhabits which one might render in terms of intimacy: there are rooms whose function is to establish an enclosed space and thus a division between interior and exterior, which is also a division between social space and the space of the subject, but within these rooms the subject contracts into a smaller space, a nest constructed, through *bricolage*, with what is closest to hand, or rather closest to the body. A relation to the room is established such that the body-subject draws its spatiality, its proprioception, *in* towards itself, to the closest possible proximity to itself, but nevertheless installs a heterogeneous and sensory envelope, an alcove or cavern within the room which concentrates intimacy and controls the degree of exposure to the outside. The summer room, on the other hand, encloses a dilated subject, which has expanded to almost exceed the limits of the enclosure itself, so that 'on dort presque en plein air' [you sleep almost in the open air]. What is experimented here is a dynamic relation between embodied consciousness and the space of enclosure, with the flexible possibility of a concentrated alcove within the room, on the one hand, and a thinning out of the room's *cloisonnement* [compartmentalization] from the outside, on the other. With the second pair of rooms, which this time are specific, located rooms rather than being types of rooms defined by the season, Proust stages this dynamic in terms of the degree to which the subject can inhabit the room, which is to say the degree to which s/he can 'fill it with himself'. The possibilities for the room-subject here are, however, dependent not on seasonal, sensory conditions so much as temporal ones; the Louis XVI room is well-proportioned enough, its scenography sufficiently dramatic so as to diminish the trauma of entering a new space, one which the body-subject has not furnished with himself over time. The high-ceilinged room with violet curtains presents more of a challenge, but for both rooms the issue is one of habitation, which is made equivalent to filling the room with oneself, diminishing its sensory intrusions and altering the space through a form of proprioceptive transformation. Inhabiting is both a spatial and a temporal work; thought ('ma pensée') suffers if it cannot, through a distortion of its dimensions and its contours, occupy the space it inhabits; habit intervenes to change and reduce both the dimensions and the foreign sensory intrusions, but there is a fundamental drive at work here to inhabit and occupy the room, to take its form: 'pour prendre exactement la forme de la chambre' [to assume the exact shape of the room].

From within the dark room, then, there is a consciousness, enclosed within the room yet somehow aware of an outside, thus aware of its enclosure and of the limits of its space. This consciousness is at the threshold, neither subject nor object, neither wakeful reason nor dream, but reverie, a threshold state between the two. The consciousness inhabits a dark and mobile room, a room that is spinning in space and time, as its attention slows down enough to be able to fix an unstable, evanescent present.

In 'Infancy and History: An Essay on the Destruction of Experience' Giorgio Agamben counters the ostensibly dominant image of Proust's *Recherche* as the redemptive triumph of the hermeneutic subject over temporality through the recapturing of lost time and the aestheticization of experience. He argues that Proust's work constitutes the 'most peremptory objection' to the modern concept of experience, since its object, involuntary memory, is 'something which has been neither lived nor experienced', and that the established conceptions of the subject of knowledge and of the subject of experience, of the subject as such, are thrown into question. Agamben suggests that 'what Proust has in mind' is rather 'certain crepuscular states like drowsiness or a loss of consciousness'. Nor, Agamben argues, it is a question of the Bergsonian subject of intuition, since precisely what lacks in Proust is a subject; what emerges is an experience 'with neither subject nor object, absolute'. For Agamben, following Walter Benjamin, the *Recherche* is the index of a consciousness so blown apart by the shock experience of modernity that its dominant mode is that of distraction, fragmentation, and a loss of the capacity to synthesize, to bind. Far from proposing the triumph of the hermeneutic, contemplative, or intuitive subject over an exploded and aleatory temporality, the *Recherche*, for Agamben, gives us an image of Proust closer to the contemporary reality of 'an infinite drifting and a casual colliding of objects and sensations'.[25] This account of Proust's *Recherche* harks back to the opening of the essay, where, following a quotation from Benjamin's 'The Storyteller', Agamben writes:

> Today, however, we know that the destruction of experience no longer necessitates a catastrophe, and that humdrum daily life in any city will suffice. For modern man's average day contains virtually nothing that can still be translated into experience. Neither reading the newspaper, with its abundance of news

that is irretrievably remote from his life, nor sitting for minutes on end at the wheel of his car in a traffic jam. Neither the journey through the nether world of the subway, nor the demonstration that suddenly blocks the street. Neither the cloud of tear gas slowly dispersing between the buildings of the city centre, nor the rapid blasts of gunfire from who knows where, nor queuing up at a business counter, nor visiting the Land of Cockayne at the supermarket, nor those eternal moments of dumb promiscuity among strangers in lifts and buses. Modern man makes his way home in the evening wearied by a jumble of events, but however entertaining or tedious, unusual or commonplace, harrowing or pleasurable they are, none of them will have become experience.[26]

Agamben thus transforms Proust's novel into a prescient diagnosis of the anomie of contemporary life akin to those of the Situationists of the 1950s and after. The enlisting of Proust for a critique of everyday life may be extreme, but the consistent factor here is the absence or loss of the capacity for a centering and synthetic capacity in a subject, and the reference to 'certain crepuscular states'. For Agamben, then, Proust's novel displaces and dissolves the Kantian subject, whose synthesizing capacities were assured through the a priori structures of cognition, the spatial and temporal situatedness of consciousness.

Barthes's observation in 'Longtemps je me suis couché de bonne heure', cited earlier, that the incipit of the novel is the logically inadmissible proposition 'je dors' [I am asleep], and that Proust's narrative world is thus generated from a disordered or 'disorganized' state of consciousness and temporality, draws Agamben's argument down to the detail of the novel's beginning and into the dark room we have been exploring. Agamben interrogates the other (non-Kantian) subject that operates in this state of sleep, or, to be more exact the zone of non-distinction between sleep and wakefulness which conditions this space and this experience. How can we name this subject and the writing which is woven around it? A cluster of terms forms around it, rather than a system of oppositions (sleep/wakefulness; consciousness/unconscious). The terms in question sit in between and trouble the epistemology these oppositions support: *conscience de sommeil* [consciousness of sleep], *démi-réveil* [semi-wakeful state], *veille paradoxale* [paradoxical wakefulness], *reverie*, and *hypnosis*.

With these last two terms we engage with a series of questions which, as Jonathan Crary has persuasively shown, were a particular focus of discursive activity in the last quarter of the nineteenth century. Crary identifies in this period a discursive pressure towards the disciplining of processes of attention in the service of capitalist modes of production, alongside a wide interest in 'pathologies' of attention which he describes as 'state[s] of being suspended, a looking or listening so rapt that it is an exemption from ordinary conditions, that it becomes a suspended temporality, a hovering out of time'.[27] It is also a period which, among many other 'technologies of the observer', sees the invention of the cinema in the form in which it would become technologically fixed. These factors, the invention of the cinema and of cinematographic experience, and the concurrent invention (as a discursive problematic) of pathologies of attention, intersect in the dark room in which the *Recherche* begins.

Crary shows through a wide-ranging survey of discourses and practices around attention in the late nineteenth century that what he calls the 'classical' model of the centered, rational subject, exemplified by the *dispositif* of the camera obscura, no longer held authority or certainty. Instead of the Kantian subject for whom the perceived world could be rendered coherent through transcendental synthesis, perceptual experience was characterized as a 'relation of forces', both internal and external, 'an economy of forces rather than an optics of representation'.[28] A key factor in this shift is the work of Schopenhauer, whose work *The World as Will and Representation* (1844) opens 'a window onto the cognitive chaos of modernity against which attention will be summoned to do battle'.[29] The shift is from the a priori capacities of the subject, situated firmly in relation to an exterior world of perceptions, to a notion of the '*physiological* conditions of knowledge'.[30] What holds successive perceptions together, for Schopenhauer, what binds time, is the will, or as Crary puts it, 'the instinctual desiring economy of one's physical existence'.[31] When temporality became an object of anxiety, since consciousness could no longer bind or synthesize it, attention and attentiveness became a disputed terrain where what was at stake was the 'disciplining' of the attentive and productive body:

> We see the disintegration of the epistemological tradition running from Descartes to Kant for which consciousness or the cogito is the ground of all knowledge and certitude. For it is only when consciousness ceases to have an unquestioned foundational priority that attention emerges as a problem — when a subject ceases to be synonymous with a consciousness that is essentially self-present to itself, when there is no longer an inevitable congruence between subjectivity and a thinking 'I'.[32]

Crary adopts a Foucaultian approach to the numerous discourses around attention, which he shows to be particularly active in the last quarter of the nineteenth century, in arguing that these discourses both supported and were driven by a disciplinary regime whose aim was to stabilize, but also to police, the field of attentiveness through technologies of attention. However, just as in Foucault (as commented by Judith Butler), subjectivizing power produces an excess, these technologies of attention also produced the conditions of their own undermining:

> But scientific psychology never was to assemble knowledge that would compel the efficient functioning of an attentive subject, or that would guarantee a full co-presence of the world and an attentive observer. Instead, the more one investigated, the more attention was shown to contain within itself the conditions for its own undoing — attentiveness was in fact continuous with states of distraction, reverie, dissociation and trance. Attention finally could not coincide with a modern dream of autonomy.[33]

The normative process of technologies of attention inevitably produced pathologies of attention, but the boundaries between the normal and pathological were uncertain and fluid. Not only did it emerge that attentiveness implied a necessary quotient of forgetting or automatism (attentiveness implied a concentration on something at the expense of something else), but attention also began to be seen as blending or bleeding into modes of distraction; the border between attentiveness and states of reverie was porous:

In one sense, attentiveness was a critical feature of a productive and socially adaptive subject, but the border that separated a socially useful attentiveness and a dangerously absorbed or diverted attention was profoundly nebulous and could be described only in terms of performative norms. Attention and distraction were not two essentially different states but existed on a single continuum.[34]

States such as reverie and hypnosis bordered the terrain of normative attention in this period; they were objects both of intense critical attention and troubling anxiety. The cinema, as Crary points out, is chronologically coincident with and is one of the modes of the technology of attention described above, in which hypnosis and reverie emerge as problematic states of consciousness. Proto-cinematic and cinematic apparatuses alike were deployed in this discursive context and should be seen as informed by it. Following the logic articulated above, we might see that if the cinema, as it emerged and became stabilized as an apparatus and as an experience, was one of 'various techniques for imposing specific kinds of perceptual synthesis', it was also a site and a space in which the pathologies of attention — hypnosis and reverie — came into play.[35] As a discursive form and as a technology of attention, the cinema is a space in which a discursive excess arises which retrospectively unsettles the perceptual norms it is intended to uphold. And if hypnosis and reverie emerge as specific modes of this excess, they also play this role, both chronologically and methodologically, in relation to psychoanalysis. These are the conflicts, tensions, and resonances I see at play in the dark room of the *Recherche*.

Crary argues that 'perhaps nowhere else in the late nineteenth century is the ambivalent status of attention as visible as in the social phenomenon of hypnosis'.[36] For him, while hypnosis 'seemed to offer new possibilities of clinical power and medical benefits, it disclosed the unsettling outlines of a subject whose uncertain makeup could evade both intellectual and institutional mastery'.[37] What emerges in hypnosis, and in the discourse on hypnosis, is the threat of a powerful, but unmasterable alternative to consciousness, and thus a threat to both the classical notion of the rational consciousness, and the disciplinary technologies of attention. It is perhaps the anxiety around this question which determines the rapid turn away from hypnosis at the outset of the twentieth century, and its difficult status in the work of Freud and in psychoanalysis more generally. Put crudely, hypnosis, as a state and as a practice, is foreclosed from a picture structured by a fundamental opposition between consciousness and the unconscious, or between wakefulness and dream. The continuum of attention is replaced by a structured topology which, while introducing the radical otherness of the unconscious, repositions and re-stabilizes consciousness and excludes the hybrid, troubling, in-between states which were so prevalent as objects of concern in the late nineteenth century.

Reverie is a similarly unsettling critical object (Crary suggests that the history of the daydream 'will never be written').[38] While it occupies some of the same scientifically disputed terrain as hypnosis, and shares the same difficult status as hypnosis in psychoanalysis, reverie is also a fundamentally literary preoccupation and topos which extends from Montaigne through Rousseau and Nerval to Proust. In his critical survey of reverie in Romanticism and post-Romanticism Marcel Raymond finds the definitive elements of reverie in a sense of 'immersion' in an imaginary substance ('Ainsi vivons-nous comme immergés dans une "substance" imaginaire' [We thus live as if immersed in an imaginary 'substance']), which draws on memory and particularly on childhood.[39] He compares it to 'une seconde existence [qui] nous habite obscurément' [a second-level existence which inhabits us obscurely].[40] Echoing Agamben's 'crepuscular state', it also provokes a suspension of space and time: 'Sorte d'état second, proche de l'hypnose, où les coordonnées de l'espace et du temps sont comme suspendues' [A sort of secondary state, close to hypnosis, in which the coordinates of space and time are as if suspended].[41] Reverie, Raymond suggests, blurs or dissolves the division between subject and object (and here we find an echo of the decompartmentalization or *décloisonnement* we encountered earlier): 'Toute cloison brisée entre le sujet et l'objet, les puissances de l'homme s'unifient comme pour réaliser sa totale identification à "ce qui est"' [With all of the partitions between subject and object broken, the powers of man unite as if to realize a total identification with 'what exists'].[42] The etymology of reverie relates it to a 'wandering' state and to a detachment from reality (close to the French word *divaguer*). However the earlier associations of the term with madness were to wane progressively, and from the time of Montaigne onwards reverie would qualify not only a psychic state of absorption in the inner self and a concomitant detachment from exterior reality, but also a formal quality of writing, signifying an errant, wandering form, lacking narrative or conceptual rigour. From Rousseau's *Rêveries du promeneur solitaire* to Nerval's *Filles du feu*, writings which explore reverie involve, on the part of their narrators, and demand on the part of their readers, a relaxation of the attention which diffuses the urgency of narrative events and didactic intervention. In the state of reverie the time of the present and the need for action and movement can relinquish their hold on the attention and allow it to be suffused with memory and imagination. The referential real recedes, to become one layer among others of the palimpsestic text of thought. Rousseau, whose *Rêveries* make him the nodal reference point for the form, drew on the work of Mme de Scudéry and Fontanelle, for whom the form and mood of reverie allowed a lessening of the demands of reason, and a 'heightened sensibility'; reverie was a pleasurable disorder which also appealed to the less ordered state of nature and the principles of sensualist philosophy.[43] Both in its formal qualities, and in its etymological lineage, reverie occupies a space between — between rational order and the chaos of madness, between fixed forms and formless disorder.[44] But as Russell Goulbourne points out, for Rousseau, 'reverie is also an epistemological project'; the 'errant' form is also a means of access to the truth of the self, and Rousseau draws here on Montaigne, for whom reverie was both a self-mocking ironization of his 'ravings', and a form which allied self-reflection with an improvisatory movement.[45]

For Baudelaire, writing on Victor Hugo in 1861, reverie appears similarly as a faculty which involves the contemplation of mysteries or enigmas not solvable by reason, 'metaphysical' mysteries such as 'la contemplation suggestive du ciel' [the suggestive contemplation of the heavens].[46] The advances of science are not, Baudelaire adds, 'si grande que la rêverie ne puisse se loger dans les vastes lacunes non encore explorés par la science moderne' [so significant that reverie cannot occupy the vast spaces as yet unexplored by modern science].[47] The notion of reverie as an epistemological project, or indeed, looking forward to Proust, as a 'recherche', is active here, but so is the sense of experimental movement and form: 'Très légitimement, le poète laisse errer sa pensée dans un dédale enivrant de conjectures' [Legitimately, the poet lets his thought wander in an intoxicating labyrinth of hypotheses].[48] Baudelaire defends in Hugo's late poetry the tendency to metaphysical speculation, which he calls 'hypothesis' ('la conjecture'), versus less interesting forms of didacticism; poetry as a form of theory, supplementary to science, takes the form of reverie. To abandon oneself to 'toutes les rêveries' is a legitimate epistemological and formal enterprise.[49]

Reverie as form is articulated further in the preface to Baudelaire's *Spleen de Paris* of 1869, the dedication to Arsène Houssaye, where Baudelaire famously wonders:

> Qui est celui de nous qui n'a pas, dans ses jours d'ambition, rêvé le miracle d'une prose poétique, musicale sans rythme et sans rime, assez souple et assez heurtée pour s'adapter aux mouvements lyriques de l'âme, aux ondulations de la rêverie, aux soubresauts de la conscience?

> [Which of us has not, in his ambitious days, dreamt the miracle of a poetic prose, musical without rhythm or rhyme, supple enough and striking enough to suit lyrical movements of the soul, undulations of reverie, the flip-flips of consciousness?][50]

The final three clauses of this statement, which qualify the form of which Baudelaire dreams, and which, one assumes, he has given to the prose poems of the *Spleen de Paris*, can be seen to move from the classical topos of the soul's innate lyricism, through the wave-like motion (elsewhere 'ondulations' is replaced by 'langueurs')[51] of reverie, to the jibes or 'shocks' of consciousness; this is a movement towards modernity, and thus towards the everyday life of the modern city which will be one of the principal emphases of the collection. Reverie stands at a threshold — between the more or less grounded certainties of the sacred and the alienation of modern consciousness. The solitary walker (*promeneur solitaire*, in fact one of the rejected titles for the volume, along with 'Rêvasseries en prose')[52] proposed by Baudelaire moves around in the crowded streets of Paris, rather than the pastoral spaces of Rousseau's solitary walks.

For Jean-François Delasalle, as for Claude Pichois, Baudelaire's project is prefigured by Edgar Allan Poe's earlier speculation in 1846 (in his *Marginalia*), about what would come to be called 'hypnagogic hallucination'. Poe writes:

> There is, however, a class of fancies, of exquisite delicacy, which are not thoughts, and to which, as yet, I have found it absolutely impossible to adapt language. [...] They arise in the soul (alas, how rarely!) only at its epochs of most intense tranquility — when the bodily and mental health are in perfection — and at those mere points of time where the confines of the waking world blend with those of the world of dreams. I am aware of these 'fancies' only when I am upon the very brink of sleep, with the consciousness that I am so. I have satisfied myself that this condition exists but for an inappreciable point of time — yet it is crowded with these 'shadows of shadows'; and for absolute thought there is demanded time's endurance.[53]

Poe remarks on the other-worldliness of these impressions, but nevertheless has faith in the power of language to convey them. He describes how once being aware of the particular quality of these 'psychal impressions' or 'fancies' he is able to arrest the condition at will, by 'startling himself into wakefulness' when on the point of 'lapsing' 'from this border-ground into the dominion of sleep'.[54] For a brief period he is then able to 'transfer the point itself into the realm of Memory' and subject the impressions to 'the eye of analysis'.[55]

Reverie is subtly different from the hypnagogic state although it may share some of its characteristics and draw on the same crepuscular zones of the mind. Poe is defending the capacities of language to comprise and to represent threshold states of consciousness, while Baudelaire, in his dedication to Arsène Houssaye, intends a prose form that would 'adapt to' or take the shape and form of the undulating, errant form of reverie and its looser hold on consciousness. Baudelaire wants poetic form to have a plasticity that can respond to affective currents which the rhymes and fixed rhythms of verse form constrain and foreclose. This project informs at least some of the prose poems of the *Spleen de Paris*, and in particular 'La Chambre double' ('Double Bedroom'), where the poet conjures the vision of reverie as a space: 'une chambre qui ressemble à une rêverie' ('a room resembling a reverie'), where the 'ressemblance' is not that of representation, but of a kind of contagion; in this room distinct objects and qualities tend to blend into one another.[56] The space is 'quelque chose de crépusculaire, de bleuâtre et de roseâtre; un rêve de volupté pendant une éclipse' ('something crepuscular, bluish and rose pink, voluptuous dream during an eclipse').[57] Even the furniture is 'douée d'une vie somnambulique' ('endowed with a somnambulistic life').[58] Proust's depiction of the room in which his narrator awakens in *Du côté de chez Swann* has a close relationship to the room Baudelaire paints here; both are spaces of reverie, inhabited by their subjects to the point where they become indistinguishable from the space itself, where the subject merges into the space and the affect of the space.[59]

Proust's interest in Gérard de Nerval's *Sylvie*, manifest in the essay included in *Contre Sainte-Beuve*, speaks to his interest in reverie, and to the extent to which the literary genre which Nerval had perhaps brought to its epitome had informed the mood and form of the opening of the *Recherche*. Proust points to the moment in *Sylvie* when its narrator hovers on the threshold of sleep:

> Plongé dans une demi-somnolence, toute ma jeunesse repassait en mes souvenirs. Cet état, où l'esprit résiste encore aux bizarres combinaisons du songe, permet souvent de voir se presser en quelques minutes les tableaux les plus saillants d'une longue période de la vie.
>
> [As I lay between sleeping and waking, my whole youth passed through my memory. That state of mind where intellect still holds out against the fantastic contrivances of dreaming often lets one see the most striking scenes of a long period in one's life huddled into the space of a few minutes.][60]

Proust comments on the evanescent quality of such visions:

> Donc ce que nous avons ici, c'est un de ces tableaux d'une couleur irréelle, que nous ne voyons pas dans la réalité, que les mots même n'évoquent pas, mais que

parfois nous voyons dans le rêve, ou que la musique évoque. Parfois, au moment de s'endormir, on les aperçoit, on veut fixer et définir leur charme, alors on s'éveille et on ne les voit plus, on s'y laisse aller et avant qu'on ait su les fixer on est endormi, comme si l'intelligence n'avait pas la permission de les voir. Les êtres eux-mêmes qui sont dans de tels tableaux sont des êtres rêvés.

[So what we have here is one of those rainbow-painted pictures, never to be seen in real life, or even called up by words, but sometimes brought before us in a dream or called up by music. Sometimes in the moment of falling asleep we see them, and try to seize and define them. Then we wake up and they are gone, we give up the pursuit, and before we can be sure of their nature we are asleep again as though the sight of them were forbidden to the waking mind. The inhabitants of these pictures are themselves of the stuff of dreams.][61]

The interest in threshold or crepuscular states of consciousness is allied here with the epistemological project of fixing an implicitly mobile procession of sensations, of finding the form which will retain the impression and the unreal colours of these moving pictures ('tableaux'). It is an inherently cinematographic project, which expresses a desire for cinema.[62]

The notion of reverie as an 'epistemological project' also implicitly poses the question of its relation to knowledge and the status of the consciousness it pertains to. In light of our discussion of Crary above we might see this as a degree of attentiveness to an object, a question of the degree to which the object of knowledge is focused, is in focus, and the linearity and directness of the mode of access to it. In reverie access is somewhat aleatory, and attention is diffuse. In psychoanalytic terms this positions reverie somewhere between the primary processes (of the unconscious) and the secondary processes (of the conscious mind), and this has led to a somewhat problematic status in psychoanalytic thought. The psychoanalyst André Green has usefully summarized the hybrid status of reverie:

S'il existe une division tranchée entre processus secondaires et processus prim-aires, cette division peut engendrer des formations de compromis — ce sang-mêlé, comme dit Freud — autrement appelé 'rêverie'. Dans tous les cas, c'est l'adjectif *libre* qui est important. En musique (*Rêverie* de Schumann), comme en literature (*Rêveries du promeneur solitaire* de Rousseau) le mot 'rêverie' désigne une activité de l'esprit qui va sans but précis, sans rigueur méthodique, comme un bouchon qui se laisse emporter au grè des vagues sous l'influence des courants qui animent la mer.[63]

[If there is a strict division between primary processes and secondary processes, this division may still engender compromise formations — the half-blood, as Freud says — otherwise called 'reverie'. In each case it's the adjective *free* which is important. In music (Schumann's *Rêverie*), as in literature (Rousseau's *Reveries of the Solitary Walker*) the word 'reverie' designates an activity of the mind that moves without a precise aim, without methodical rigour, like a cork which lets itself be carried away by the waves under the influence of the sea's currents.]

Aimless thought and passive movement are closely associated to the errant and free-associative form of reverie here. Reverie is a compromise, neither one thing nor another, but as a form it remains a privileged mode of access, and thus of epistemological value.

Somewhat in the same vein, reverie is a key concept in the work of French phenomenologist Gaston Bachelard, whose global enterprise is to constitute an ontology through an exploration of poetic images, thus to gain insight into what he calls 'la conscience rêveuse' [dreaming consciousness].[64] His account of reverie is valuable insofar as he dissociates it from dream and from sleep, and considers it the font of a language 'au seuil de l'être' [on the threshold of being]:

> À elle seule, la rêverie est une instance psychique qu'on confond trop souvent avec le rêve. Mais quand il s'agit d'une rêverie poétique, d'une rêverie qui jouit non seulement d'elle-même, mais qui prépare pour d'autres âmes des jouissances poétiques, on sait bien qu'on n'est plus sur la pente des somnolences.

> [In itself, reverie constitutes a psychic condition that is too frequently confused with dream. But when it is a question of poetic reverie, of reverie that derives pleasure not only from itself, but also prepares poetic pleasures for other souls, one realizes that one is no longer moving in the direction of somnolence.][65]

For Bachelard, in *La Poétique de l'espace*, our relation to space is determined at a fundamental level by the image or motif of the house, or rather of being housed: 'tout espace vraiment habité porte l'essence de la notion de maison' ('all really inhabited space bears the essence of the notion of the house').[66] Any enclosed or sheltered space thus has a resonance with the earliest and most fundamental dimensions of the psyche (and thus with what Proust calls 'le sentiment d'existence' [the feeling of existence]): 'la rêverie s'approfondit au point qu'un domaine immémorial s'ouvre pour le rêveur du foyer au delà de la plus ancienne mémoire' ('the reverie deepens to the point where an immemorial domain opens up for the dreamer of a home beyond man's earliest memory').[67] The habitation thus has an intimate connection to the capacity for reverie: 'la maison abrite la rêverie' ('the house shelters reverie').[68] Childhood, moreover, is a privileged focus for literature and especially for poetry, and it is through reverie that it persists: 'C'est sur le plan de la rêverie et non sur le plan des faits que l'enfance reste en nous vivante et poétiquement utile' ('It is on the plane of reverie and not on that of facts that childhood remains alive and poetically useful within us').[69] From this point of view, the childhood room has an acute importance as concerns memory, and it is intimately associated with reverie.

From a more psychoanalytically-oriented perspective, which Bachelard's explorations suggest but do not perhaps sufficiently theorize, the room of childhood has an acute importance because it is the space and time in which intimate space, the spatial envelope of the body, is explored and negotiated as a substitute for the mother and in the process of separation from her, a process that corresponds to the concept of the transitional object or space in the work of British psychoanalyst Donald Winnicott. In Winnicott's work, particularly in *Playing and Reality* (1971), the transitional object or space is theorized as a 'transitional environment' or 'potential space' in which the infant can explore and play with her separation from the mother.[70] Both Winnicott and his colleague Wilfred Bion offered conceptualizations of the mother's role as one of 'holding' or 'containment' that resonate with the motif of the room of childhood.[71] For Bion, significantly, this capacity for containment is linked to the mother's capacity for reverie: through her reverie the mother provides thoughts ('alpha' elements) vicariously for the child, who is capable only of instinctual drives and impulses ('beta' elements).[72]

The rooms which Proust's narrator inhabits, and which he reflects upon in the reveries that follow his awakening, are variations, to this extent, of the childhood room, the first transitional space; in this space he negotiates the limits of his body and of his consciousness and the extent to which he can dilate it, stretch it out, and fill the room. The capacity for reverie is a significant factor in this transition. While Bachelard focuses on the house as a space which should permit reverie, for Winnicott and Bion as well it is the mother's capacity for reverie which can permit a successful negotiation of transitional space, and transitional space itself must allow for reverie, for a relaxed quality of attention. It is the absence of this quality in the psychotic patient which suggests to Bion its pertinence both in the analytic session (the reverie of the analyst) and in the mother–infant relation. In the *Recherche*, insofar as the sequence of rooms, one of the first operations of retrospective memory which drive the novel (in dynamic tension with the interruptive punctuations of involuntary memory), is introduced as a reverie, one can infer that one of the preconditions for the *Recherche* as such is something like the room of reverie, a room which the narrator proprioceptively inhabits to such an extent that the room and its furnishings cease to be an object for consciousness, and consciousness can take the form of a room.

Is the cinema such a room? Some of the early theorists of cinema certainly thought so. Maxim Gorky's celebrated and oft-cited report 'From the Realm of Shadows', giving his first impressions of the Lumière cinematograph, emphasized the spectral quality of the images rather than their realism. The early twentieth-century film writer Ycham wrote in 1912 of the proximity between cinema and dream state, and of film as 'L'Art de suggérer des rêves' [The Art of Suggesting Dreams].[73] He would also exploit a recurrent motif in suggesting a parallel between the experience of the spectator and that of the hypnotized subject:

> L'obscurité de la salle constitue un facteur important qui, par le receuillement qu'elle produit, contribue, bien plus qu'on ne pourrait le croire à l'impression produite; l'attention du spectateur se trouve appellée et concentrée sur la projection lumineuse sans qu'aucune distraction puisse se produire du fait de la salle.[74]

> [The darkness of the space constitutes an important factor, which through the state of reverence it creates, contributes much more than one might believe to the impression that is produced; the spectator's attention is claimed and concentrated on the luminous projection without any distraction from the space itself.]

In 1911 Jules Romains would write about the cinema in a prose poem with the title 'Le Rêve de la foule commence' [The Dream of the Crowd Begins].[75] The early film theorists of the 1920s postulated an analogical relation between the film and the unconscious mind. The contemporary film-philosopher Daniel Frampton has pointed to the ways in which in this period film was understood as 'a visualization of thoughts and memories (Henri Bergson, Germaine Dulac, Pierre Quesnoy) or similar in form to our subconscious (Emile Vuillermoz, Ricciotto Canudo)'.[76] For writers like Dulac or Quesnoy the justification of the analogy lay in the mobility common to the mind and the film.[77] For Vuillermoz and Canudo film could capture thoughts and affects that the conscious mind could not; Canudo in particular proposed that film captures 'another kind of thought', expressed in the notion of the soul, a thesis recently explored both historically and theoretically by Sarah Cooper.[78] The more explicit analogy between film and dream, or the proposition of film as dream, by writers such as Paul Ramain and Jean Goudal would, however, prove limiting, since as Frampton notes, it was generally 'proposed', rather than argued, and turns out to be of limited value when comparing the logic of dreams and the order of filmic syntax and narrative.[79] Dream-films by Surrealists like Buñuel and Dalí, or proto-Surrealists like Cocteau, were exceptions, and explicitly closer to what Freud would call the dream-work. The Surrealists would for their part be critical of the tendency to assimilate films to dreams or to the 'dream-like', perhaps justifiably seeing it as a watered-down version of the true logic of the unconscious.

These reservations do not however prevent the return of the analogy between film and dream, or between film and the unconscious, in film theory of the 1960s and 1970s, where it is informed by the textual materialism of the *Tel Quel* group. While the earlier film theories of Vuillermoz, Canudo, Epstein, and others were historically distant for writers such as Christian Metz, Jean-Louis Baudry, and Roland Barthes, contributors to the landmark 1975 issue of the journal *Communications*, *Psychanalyse et cinéma*, it is also the case that from the strictly Freudian point of view adopted in *Tel Quel* such a compromise formation as reverie was deeply suspicious, the symptom of an *après-coup* through which the radicality of the Freudian unconscious would be obscured.[80] The same held for hypnosis which, as Barthes (somewhat more sympathetically) remarks, was generally treated as an embarrassing moment of pre-history.[81] As we will see, however, in our exploration of the essays of Metz, Baudry, and Barthes, despite this critical stance the motif of reverie cannot be so easily rejected.

Before coming to this point, however, I want to take a step back and come at things from a slightly different angle. In keeping with Crary's account of the crisis of the Kantian subject in the late nineteenth century, theorists and historians of proto-cinema and of early cinema have pointed to the ways in which spectatorship is a mobile terrain of affective suggestion, bodily innervation and imitative performance, rather than one determined by a grounded, located Subject, positioned vis-à-vis a discernable representation of the world. Rae Beth Gordon has pointed to the multiple levels of continuity between the corporeal movements of epileptics and hysterics, studied and captured photographically and chronophotographically under Charcot and his assistants at the Salpetrière hospital, and the performances of the café-concerts and Grand Guignols which prefigured and initially accompanied the first cinematic spectacles.[82] For Gordon, early cinema drew on an already well-established repertoire of the 'epileptic genre' or style, which itself was well-embedded in a medical discourse culturally disseminated beyond the limits of the medical institution. But it was not only in terms of the imitation of a bodily style or the cultural currency of a performative style that such pathologies as hysteria, epilepsy, and somnambulism bore upon early cinema — it was also on the terrain of suggestion, and in reference to the specificities of cinematographic technology. Gordon points to the co-incidence, around the *fin de siècle*, of pathologies and theories of suggestion or suggestibility. The quarrel between Charcot at the Salpetrière and Hippolyte Bernheim at the Nancy School is well known; for Charcot hypnotic suggestibility, or hypnosis as such, was applicable and pertinent only to those of an inherently hysterical etiology, while for Bernheim a propensity to hypnotic suggestion was inherent in everyone. This account of suggestion would be drawn on by Gabriel Tarde, in whose work (against the structures of belief and identificatory sacrifice proposed by Durkheim), suggestion was the essence of sociality. Gordon draws on the contemporaneity of Tarde's work to support the thesis that the enervated and spasmodic bodies of early cinema (in the work of Mèliès, for example) themselves induced mimetic effects in the spectators. The 'impression of reality' of early cinema has less to do, from this perspective, with the ontology of the photographic image (as it does for Bazin, later) than it does with the transmission, so to speak, of a motor effect from screen to spectator. The innervated, spasmodic or somnambulist body on screen produces or provokes a nervous reaction — the beginning of a motor reaction — and acts directly on or in the body. This continuity of affect and thought between the film on screen and the body and mind of the spectator will be theorized by early film theorists such as Artaud and Epstein. It is taken up again by Deleuze and Jean-Louis Schefer, and discussed by Daniel Frampton with the idea that in the cinema we find an autonomous form of thought (a 'filmind' in Frampton's case) that acts directly on the brain, a 'spiritual automaton' (Deleuze), or 'experimental chamber' (Schefer) that can think beyond our normative modes of thought and 'shock' us into thinking, at last.[83]

This notion of an affective continuity between screen and spectator, and the concomitant loosening of the structural matrix of Subject and Representation exists in interesting tension with structuralist or apparatus theory accounts. The apparent embarrassment of Christian Metz's attempt, in his essay for the *Communications* issue, to deal with the 'impression of reality' might be seen as a symptom of a split in accounts of spectatorship and of modes of considering this impression: from the point of view of the theories of affective continuity the image is not real because it looks *like* the real, but because it has an effect on the spectator which *is* real.

But there is also a historicity to account for here; if Metz and Baudry only concerned themselves with film spectatorship as classically established, even while (in Baudry's case) aiming to subvert it, it is also in part because they had, as mentioned earlier, limited access to earlier impressionist modes of film theorization, even those of Artaud, surprisingly. These earlier theories themselves did not draw on the Freudian model of primary and secondary processes or the Freudian paradigm of the individual psyche and unconscious. The earlier film theorists such as Epstein, Delluc, Dulac, Canudo, or Vuillermoz referred not to the Freudian model of consciousness/dream/fantasy but to pre-Freudian psychologies in which the boundary between conscious and unconscious thinking were far more porous and fluid. In fact, consciousness as such was thought to be far more volatile and subject to automatisms and affective mutability. In effect, the Freudian paradigm, while it gave a more radical alterity to the unconscious, (re)positions the conscious subject with more security and certainty, as ego. It is in some regard a rearguard action, warding off the spectre of suggestion and automatism, inoculating this threat by eroticizing it around the dynamics of libido and repression. To take account of earlier theories, while not dismissing the later (Freudian and Lacanian) paradigms, is to acknowledge that there are other accounts of the psyche and of the ways thinking and feeling work, which might operate outside the subject, on different terrain. It is also to think differently about the relation between spectator and screen, subject and image.

This brings us to the work of Crary and to the post-Kantian parenthesis, if I can put it that way, during which thought and emotion are in motion outside the secure province of the centred Subject. In an echo of the proposition by Agamben cited earlier, that Proust's *Recherche* gives us the image of 'an infinite drifting and a casual colliding of objects and sensations', we also encounter the continuity of thought and image, affect and screen, in the reverie room in which we began.

The *Psychanalyse et cinéma* volume of the semiotics journal *Communications*, which we will now turn to in more detail, was convened by Thierry Kuntzel, Raymond Bellour, and Christian Metz, and is a significant event in the history of film theory. Many of the essays included in the volume would prove influential in their own right, particularly in the translation and exportation of French materialist film theory into the United Kingdom: this pertains to Kristeva's 'Ellipse sur la frayeur et la séduction spéculaire' [Ellipsis on Dread and Specular Seduction], Baudry's 'Le Dispositif' [The Apparatus], Barthes's 'En sortant du cinéma' [On Leaving the Movie Theater], and the dual contributions by Christian Metz. The essays by Baudry, Metz, and Barthes, however, are particularly interesting for their attempt to elaborate an account of cinematic experience (what Barthes, echoing Sartre, calls the 'la situation du cinéma', and Baudry the 'dispositif') which seeks to locate itself in relation to a Freudian theory of consciousness, but which in interesting ways is obliged to refer to the hybrid objects of reverie and hypnosis, and to the enclosed space in which the experience takes place, the cinema as a room.

In a key section of his first essay 'Le Film de fiction et son spectateur' [The Fiction Film and its Spectator], Christian Metz works through the structural relations between a number of terms — dream, daydream, fantasy, and the 'filmic state'. Both the filmic state and the daydream share the characterization of a 'reduced' state of wakefulness: 'L'état filmique et le fantasme conscient supposent également un degré assez semblable de vigilance' ('The filmic state and the conscious fantasy suppose a rather similar degree of wakefulness'); but also a maintenance of the belief in the 'imaginary' status of the images:

> Dans l'état filmique comme dans la rêverie, le transfert perceptif s'arrête avant
> son terme, l'illusion vraie fait défaut, l'imaginaire reste senti comme tel: de

même que le spectateur sait qu'il voit un film, la rêverie sait qu'elle est une reverie.

[In the filmic state as in the daydream, perceptual transference stops before its conclusion, true illusion is wanting, the imaginary remains felt as such; just as the spectator knows he is watching a film, the daydream knows that it is a daydream.][84]

In the Freudian terms which Metz deploys, while primary processes are entertained to some degree in both states, they do not impinge to the extent of affecting the perceptual apparatus; regression stops short of 'perceptual transference' ('transfert perceptif').[85] The filmic state is akin to that of the daydream in several important ways, through the fact that both are undertaken in solitude, and therefore involve a kind of narcissistic withdrawal ('se replie pour un temps sur une base plus narcissique'; 'withdraw for a time to a more narcissistic base'), and that both are modes of contemplation rather than of action: 'La vision du film, comme la rêverie, procède de la contemplation et non de l'action' ('Film viewing, like daydreaming, is rooted in contemplation and not in action').[86] Thus, for Metz, drawing back to a more social perspective, film (the fiction film specifically) enters into 'functional competition' with reverie: 'Dans la vie sociale de notre époque, le film de fiction entre en concurrence fonctionnelle avec la rêverie' ('In the social life of our age, the fiction film enters into functional competition with the daydream').[87]

Around these terms there is a degree of translational difficulty and slippage, indicative of the troubling status of the hybrid, in-between states which are at stake. Metz writes:

En essayant de préciser les relations entre l'état filmique et l'état onirique, parentés partielles et divergences incomplètes, on rencontre à chaque pas le problème du sommeil, ou de son absence, ou de ses degrés intermédiaires. Aussi est-on inévitablement amené à introduire dans l'analyse un terme nouveau, la rêverie, qui, comme l'état filmique et contrairement au rêve, est une activité de la veille. Le français, lorsqu'il veut distinguer plus nettement le rêve de la rêverie, appelle cette dernière, d'un syntagme figé et en fait redondant, 'rêverie éveillée'. C'est le 'Tagtraum' de Freud, le rêve de jour, bref le fantasme conscient.

[In trying to specify the relations between the filmic state and the dream state, the partial kinships and incomplete differences, we encounter at every step the problem of sleep, its absence, or its intermediate degrees. Thus we are inevitably led to introduce a new term into the analysis, the daydream, which, like the filmic state and unlike the dream, is a waking activity. When in French we wish more clearly to distinguish the dream and the daydream, we call the latter, in a fixed syntagm which is fact redundant, the 'waking daydream'. This is Freud's 'Tagtraum', the daytime dream, in short the conscious fantasy.][88]

In keeping with the Freudian paradigm which determines his approach, Metz is led to define reverie in relation to dream, supplementing reverie, albeit hesitantly, with the qualifier 'éveillée' [waking] in order to ward off the threat introduced by the homophony in French of 'rêve' and 'reverie'. Reverie, then, is defined within the parameters of the Freudian paradigm and its topological structure, which opposes conscious to unconscious, dream to wakefulness. The same definition of reverie as a lesser form of the dream (lesser in the sense that as Metz argued regression is only partial) is imposed in Freud's German term *Tagtraum* and a further terminological slippage or transference is manifest in the way that Metz, following Freud, draws reverie towards fantasy through the coincidence in both of elements of narrative (Freud's references to the 'petit roman' or 'story' aspect). This is manifest in Metz's note on terminology: 'Freud en emploie également d'autres: day-dream, "rêve eveillée" dans le sens français de rêve diurne, c'est-à-dire justement de "reverie"' ('Freud also employs others: the English word "daydream", "waking dream" in the French sense of a daytime dream, that is to say, precisely, a "reverie"').[89] The distinction of reverie is in each of these cases drawn away through comparison and contrast to other states — dream, fantasy. However, the global impact of Metz's essay, alongside those of Baudry and Barthes as we shall see, is to qualify the psychic state of the spectator in the cinema as akin to reverie, to the 'crepuscular state' noted by Agamben as the paradigm of Proustian consciousness.

In his contribution to the special issue of *Communications* the critic and novelist Jean-Louis Baudry, a former member of the *Tel Quel* group, explores the same terrain as Christian Metz, that is to say the analogical relations between the dream and the film, and the issue of the 'impression of reality'. His aim in this the second of two essays which would be hugely influential in film theory, is to discern what he calls the 'désir de cinéma' [desire for the cinema], and the 'effet-cinéma' [the cinema-effect], which is to say that he is not concerned with specific films or, as such, with the cinematic apparatus as it is actualized, but with the desire that produces, that has given rise to what he calls the 'dispositif', to this particular *arrangement* of the subject and the machine.[90] What is it that is desired, in cinema? Following a discussion of the scene of Plato's cave, and of Freud's references to photographic technologies, Baudry pursues his response to this question via reference to the American psychoanalyst Bertram D. Lewin's elaboration of the hypothesis of the 'dream-screen'. Lewin had described, in essays of the late 1940s and early 1950s, the manifestation in a dream of a screen, often as a blank surface.[91] Following Lewin, Baudry theorizes this as 'le support indispensable à la projection des images' ('the indispensible support for the projection of images'), as the 'arrière-fond blanc' ('blank background'), on which the dream appears to be 'projected'.[92] The term was suggested to Lewin, as Baudry notes, by the cinema because, just as the dreamer does not usually mark the 'background' of the dream, the cinema spectator does not notice the screen as such. Seeking to understand of what the screen, in the dream, is the representation, Lewin sees it as the hallucinatory representation of the mother's breast on which the infant has fallen asleep, which has been somehow 'flattened out'.[93] The screen which appears in the dream is, Lewin hypothesizes, the representation or memory of a state of satisfaction which harks back to the oral phase and to the infant's experience of the limitlessness of her body, and a lack of distinction between herself and the body of the mother. The dream screen, Baudry and Lewin propose, is the remnant of archaic mnesic traces; it refers back to a phase of indistinction between representation and perception, body and breast, and to what Baudry calls 'une mode d'identification antérieur au stade du miroir ('a mode of identification prior to the mirror stage').[94] This indistinction is also present as a contradictory merging of a desire for perception and a desire for hallucination, giving rise to the dream as a 'réel-plus-que-réel' ('real-more than real').[95] This hypothesis, Baudry says, enters into play in the 'cinema-effect', which describes the particular quality and structure of the arrangement of a projected image which gives the impression of reality, in an enclosed, interior space.

The cinema, Baudry says, is an apparatus of simulation, not just of reality, but also of 'subject effects' ('effets-sujet').[96] Film theory has looked for the impression of reality in the image and in technique, rather than in the psyche of the subject. Psychoanalysis inaugurates an approach to film which includes the subject in the 'framework' (or *dispositif*), while the 'apparatus' (*appareil*) considers the subject as abstracted from the situation. Baudry's *dispositif* of the cinema is proposed as an artificially regressive state, the response to a desire to find this situation again, an enveloping or absorbing relation to reality in which the limits of the self are blurred, in which 'l'absorption d'images est en même temps absorption du sujet dans l'image, préparé, prédigéré par son entrée dans la salle obscure' ('the absorption of images is at the same time the absorption of the subject in the image, prepared, predigested by his very entering in the dark theatre').[97]

The distinction between *dispositif* and *appareil* is a well-established critical landmark in film studies. Although the title of Baudry's 1975 essay in *Communications* is often translated as 'apparatus', it is nevertheless distinct from this term, which Baudry had developed in the earlier essay 'Cinéma: effets idéologiques produits par l'appareil de base' [Ideological Effects of the Basic Cinematographic Apparatus]. With *dispositif*, which might, rather, be translated as 'arrangement', or even 'technique', in the sense that Crary uses the term, Baudry intends to comprise the subject, and the psychic state of the subject, in the structure that is being analyzed; the subject is not simply the transcendental subject proposed or assumed by apparatus theory, or by the pre-modern paradigm of the camera obscura, as we will see further on. The subject is, as Baudry suggests above, psychically enveloped by the image, and absorbed by it. What Baudry calls the 'salle obscure' [dark room] is a space of absorption rather than of observation, and this begins to offer an account of the way the subject occupies the space. The key element is the screen, which Baudry theorizes, via Lewin, as a motif of absorption and of indistinction, representative of a desire for regression. We will have occasion to return, further on, to the motif of the screen. For the moment, however, I want to turn to another key essay in the special issue of *Communications*, and to an essential, yet fascinatingly oblique text of film theory, Barthes's 'En sortant du cinéma'.

Barthes opens his seminal yet idiosyncratic essay with a critical device which resonates deeply with my approach in this book: to leave the cinema, the better to see it, to think it, to rethink it. Later in the essay the device will be reconfigured as a move to 'unstick' oneself from the film, from the image on screen, the better to grasp the physicality and the arrangement of the space of the cinema, of the cinema as room; 'Comment se décoller du miroir?' ('How to come unglued from the mirror') as Barthes puts it.[98] But as he points out, the word *décoller* has other meanings — to 'take off', or to 'get off' (on) — 'Risquons une réponse qui sera un jeu de mots, en "décollant", au sens aéronatique et drogué du terme' ('I'll risk a pun to answer: by *taking off* (in the aeronautical and narcotic sense of the term').[99] Through this departure Barthes seeks to bring to light the 'situation' of the cinema in all the senses of that term, that is, not only the optical, physical, and phenomenological qualities of spectatorship (which Metz and Baudry, in their essays, variously call the 'apparatus' or the 'dispositif'), but also the affective, social, and moral characteristics of the space and of the practice of going to the cinema. To leave the film, to unstick one's gaze from the screen, the better to ask where and how we are situated, in the cinema. Barthes's first answer to this question introduces the theme and topos of reverie, and thus conjures the 'impossible' subject of the 'Longtemps je me suis couché de bonne heure' essay, while adding a theoretical reference to hypnosis, thus implicitly determining a reference to psychoanalysis.

The essay begins: 'Le sujet qui parle ici doit reconnaître une chose: il aime à *sortir* d'une salle de cinéma' ('The subject speaking here has something to confess: he likes to leave a cinema').[100] 'Ici' ('here') refers, at least in part, to the special issue on cinema and psychoanalysis of the semiotics journal (*Communications*) which Barthes had helped to found in 1960. What the subject must recognize, here, is that he *likes* to *leave* the cinema. Barthes's strategy is one of deflation and displacement; he turns from signs to affects, from what he might decipher to what he likes and loves. And this turn is also a turn away, from the screen and from the film, a movement in which the contours and dimensions of the cinema as a space, as a room, and as what Barthes will call a 'situation', come into view and come into play. The account Barthes gives is thus focused on the affective and physiological qualities of his body on leaving the cinema:

> Se retrouvant dans la rue éclairée et un peu vide (c'est toujours le soir et en semaine qu'il y va) et se dirigeant machinalement vers quelque café, il marche silencieusement (il n'aime guère parler tout de suite du film qu'il vient de voir), un peu engourdi, engoncé, frileux, bref, ensommeillé: il a sommeil, voilà ce qu'il pense; son corps est devenu quelque chose de sopitif, de doux, de paisible; mou comme un chat endormi, il se sent quelque peu désarticulé, ou encore, (car pour une organisation morale le repos ne peut être que là) irresponsable.

> [Back on the more or less empty, more or less brightly lit street (it is invariably at night, and during the week, that he goes), and heading uncertainly for some café or other, he walks in silence (he doesn't like discussing the film he's just seen), a little dazed, wrapped up in himself, feeling the cold — he's sleepy, that's what he's thinking, his body has become something *sopitive*, soft, limp, like a sleeping cat, and he feels a little disjointed, even (for a moral organization, relief comes only from this quarter), irresponsible.][101]

His body is in a state of rest, and this extends to a state of moral irresponsibility; he is also relieved from social demand. These qualities of affective and moral regression lead Barthes to the conclusion that what he is leaving is a hypnotic state: 'Bref, c'est evident, il sort d'une hypnose' ('In other words, obviously, he's coming out of hypnosis').[102] Strategically, although he will come back, later in the essay, to the Lacanian concepts of Imaginary, Real, and Symbolic, to an implicit echo of the mirror stage, and to the issue of narcissism, while also hinting at the Kleinian/Winnicottian pair of mother and infant, at this point he seems to want to displace psychoanalysis, to position himself outside or at its threshold. The context is significant once more; in order to address the relation between cinema and psychoanalysis Barthes is obliged to take his departure from both. This gesture returns us to the pre-psychoanalytic (and eminently literary) scene of reverie, but also more specifically to the threshold of hypnosis. It was, we can recall, through hypnosis that Freud would come to the recognition of the unconscious, the influence of sexuality, the agency of repression, and the practice of the talking cure. Freud's visit to the Salpetrière hospital in the mid-1880s, his meeting and subsequent work with Jean-Marie Charcot (as well as his encounter with the work of Hippolyte Bernheim and the Nancy School) led him to collaborative work with Breuer in *Studies in Hysteria*. Barthes refers to the enlightening and explorative function of hypnosis for psychoanalysis in the metaphor of the lantern: 'vieille lanterne psychoanalytique' [an old psychoanalytic device], but he also notes the condescension or even contempt for hypnosis evinced in current Lacanian theory with the addition of a parenthetical note which refers us to the Lacanian journal *Ornicar*, and to the announcement in its first issue (January 1975) of a seminar series by Khalid Najab on hypnotism from Mesmer to Freud.[103] Barthes's strategy is two-fold — to conjure psychoanalysis, but also to establish a critical distance from it. And this displacement, via a return to a kind of repressed primal scene of psychoanalysis, entails a parallel disjunctive turn to the prehistory of cinema, with the lantern, in which we might also hear the echo of Proust's magic lantern.[104] Barthes's turn away from cinema is a turn towards its pre-history, to its infancy, and towards infancy as such. The cinema, then, is a space of hypnosis, a threshold. As such Barthes sees in it a curative space and a curative experience. Barthes's sleep, and thus Barthes's cinema, is not oneiric, but hypnotic; it is a sleep and a cinema of moral and social relaxation, or regression, rather than of dream. In this it is akin to Proustian sleep, which, as Yves-Jean Tadié has pointed out, is only minimally oneiric.[105] Barthes's sleep resembles that of Proust's narrator in offering: 'le plus vieux des pouvoirs, le guérissement' ('the most venerable of powers: healing').[106]

The affects with which Barthes endows the situation of the cinema thus involve a relaxation, a vacation of and from social demand, and from the conflicts of gregariousness: 'on va au cinéma à partir d'une oisiveté, d'une disponibilité, d'une vacance' ('he goes to cinemas as a response to idleness, leisure, free time').[107] Availability, here, is the mobility and freedom of the body, which is not caught in the demands of the desire of the other, nor by work. The hypnotized body is also available, but also unemployed:

> Tout se passe comme si, avant même d'entrer dans la salle, les conditions classiques de l'hypnose étaient réunies: vide, désœuvrement, inemploi; ce n'est pas devant le film et par le film que l'on rêve; c'est, sans le savoir, avant même d'en devenir le spectateur.
>
> [It's as if, even before he went into the cinema, the classic conditions of hypnosis

were in force: vacancy, want of occupation, lethargy; it's not in front of the film and because of the film that he *dreams* off — it's, without knowing it, even before he becomes a spectator.][108]

A double displacement is effected, here, outside both desire, dream, and work. In this light, the situation of the cinema calls upon theories other than those of Freud and Marx; its space is that of hypnotic reverie and is unemployable, unemployed. It is not far-fetched to postulate, then, that the 'curative' situation of the cinema as Barthes describes it is Proustian, in its luxury and unemployment (outside the social demand of work), its supplementarity, and its status between sleep and waking.

In the term 'situation' Barthes wants us to hear, I think, an echo of Sartre's *Situations* and thus wants to point us towards an existentialist understanding of the cinema, that is an understanding that comprises both its phenomenological characteristics and its social and moral aspects. Or its social and moral aspects as embedded in the concrete and spatial and embodied experience of the subject. In these terms the morality of Barthes's situation involves a regressive relaxation of social censorship, a freeing up of desire, an availability that comes with unemployment, and with a relaxed or collapsed posture of the body. In concrete terms, the dark of the cinema is metonymically contiguous with the 'crepuscular reverie' that precedes hypnosis.[109]

But Barthes extends the crepuscular, threshold state to the whole social and moral situation of the cinema:

> Suivant une métonymie vraie, le noir de la salle est préfiguré par la 'rêverie crépusculaire' (préalable à l'hypnose, au dire de Breuer-Freud) qui précède ce noir et conduit le sujet, de rue en rue, d'affiche en affiche, à s'abîmer finalement dans un cube obscur, anonyme, indifférent, où doit se produire ce festival d'affects qu'on appelle un film.

> [According to a true metonymy, the darkness of the cinema is preceded by the 'twilight reverie' (a prerequisite for hypnosis, according to Breuer-Freud), which precedes it and leads him from street to street, from poster to poster, finally burying himself in a dim, anonymous, indifferent cube where that festival of affects known as a film will be presented.][110]

Socially and morally, the cinema is a place of regression to the threshold of sleep and to the infancy of the subject. The end term of this trajectory is a kind of eclipse of consciousness, an entry into a negative consciousness, without identity, a space we might call one of an affectivity without a subject, which thus resembles the 'crepuscular state' Agamben described as an 'infinite drifting and [...] casual colliding of objects and sensations'.

In the cinema, Barthes has two bodies:

> Il est une autre manière d'aller au cinéma (autrement qu'armé par le discours de la contre-idéologie): en s'y laissant fasciner deux fois: par l'image et par ses entours, comme si j'avais deux corps en même temps: un corps narcissique qui regarde, perdu dans le miroir proche, et un corps pervers, prêt à fétichiser, non l'image, mais précisément ce qui l'excède: le grain du son, la salle, le noir, la masse obscure des autres corps, les rais de la lumière, l'entrée, la sortie: bref, pour distancer, 'décoller', je complique une 'relation' par une 'situation'. Ce

dont je me sers pour prendre mes distances à l'égard de l'image, voilà, en fin de compte, ce qui me fascine: je suis hypnotisé par une distance; et cette distance n'est pas critique (intellectuelle); c'est, si l'on peut dire, une distance amoureuse: y aurait-il, au cinéma même (et en prenant le mot dans son profil étymologique), une jouissance possible de la discrétion?

[But there is another way of going to the movies (besides being armed by the discourse of counter-ideology); by letting oneself be fascinated *twice over*, by the image and by its surroundings — as if I had two bodies at the same time, a narcissistic body which gazes, lost, into the engulfing mirror, and a perverse body, ready to fetishize not the image but precisely what exceeds it: the texture of the sound, the hall, the darkness, the obscure mass of the other bodies, the rays of light, entering the cinema, leaving the hall; in short, in order to distance, in order to 'take off,' I complicate a 'relation' by a 'situation.' What I use to distance myself from the image, that, ultimately, is what fascinates me: I am hypnotized by a distance; and this distance is not critical (intellectual); it is, one might say, an amorous distance: would there be, in the cinema itself, (and taking the word at its etymological suggestion) a possible bliss of *discretion*.][111]

Barthes's spectator is doubly fascinated. In the first instance he is 'glued' to the 'lure' (*leurre*) of the screen. Here Barthes draws on explicitly Lacanian terms — the Image is a lure which captures or captivates the Subject in the adhesive and cohesive *glue* of the Imaginary, which holds everything together, just as the Mirror draws the primitive ego together, orthopedically. The glue of the Image, moreover, is a pseudo-Nature; the Real requires distance, and the Symbolic is the realm of masks, of symbols. The Lacanian and Althusserian tenor of ideological capture by the Image is very evident in Barthes's account of this first level of fascination. It is also implicitly informed, however, by Blanchot's differently inflected account of the Image as that which fascinates.[112]

However, as distinct from Baudry, Marcelin Pleynet, and other advocates of the structuralist materialist theorists of cinema, who promote both an ideological and practical attack on the Imaginary (by means of theory, on the one hand, and through an avant-garde practice of film-making, on the other) Barthes promotes a second level of fascination, a parallel, perverse, and fetishistic investment in an alternative Imaginary of the cinema, that of the *space* rather than of the *screen*. In this Barthes deviates radically from the whole direction of structuralist materialist film theory. Moving away from the Brechtian distanciation techniques which he had broadly championed in the 1950s, Barthes's other cinema foregrounds its material, spatial qualities as a room, and as a projection:[113]

Dans ce cube opaque, une lumière: le film, l'écran? Oui, bien sûr. Mais aussi (mais surtout?), visible et inaperçu, ce cône dansant qui troue le noir, à la façon d'un rayon de laser. Ce rayon se monnaye, selon la rotation de ses particules, en figures changeantes; nous tournons notre visage vers la monnaie d'une vibration brillante, dont le jet impérieux rase notre crâne, effleure, de dos, de biais, une chevelure, un visage. Comme dans les vieilles experiences d'hypnotisme, nous sommes fascinés, sans le voir en face, par ce lieu brilliant, immobile et dansant.

[In that opaque cube, one light: the film, the screen? Yes of course. But also, (especially?) visible and unperceived, that dancing cone which pierces the darkness like a laser beam. This beam is minted, according to the rotation of its particles, into changing figures; we turn our face towards the currency of a gleaming vibration whose imperious jet brushes our skull, glancing off someone's hair, someone's face. As in the old hypnotic experiments, we are fascinated — without seeing it head on, by this shining point, motionless and dancing.][114]

Barthes unsticks his look from the onscreen image to focus on the 'dancing cone' of the projection itself, imagining it to be made of constantly changing particles, implying a quasi-Lucretian image of light as particles entering the eye, or as an optical vibration. The verb on which this extended analogy is based, *se monnayer*, also draws on the quasi-chemical or alchemical register, implying the transformation of base metal into coinage; what we see is the result of a process which produces ('mints', in Richard Howard's translation) the 'coinage' of the image through a process of luminous vibration. Barthes's strategy here — the description of the experience in terms of its physical and spatial properties, but with metaphors which imply the materiality of light (and hark back to earlier scientific accounts of luminosity) and a process of chemical transformation — returns cinema to the conditions of its birth, to the magic, and to the demonic. It is reminiscent of one of the first literary accounts of cinematic projection by Maxim Gorky, mentioned earlier, in whose text 'In the Kingdom of Shadows' we encounter a similar 'turn away' from the screen to the one described by Barthes: 'You are forgetting where you are. Strange imaginings invade your mind and your consciousness begins to wane and grow dim... But suddenly alongside of you a gay chatter and a provoking laughter of a woman is heard, and you remember that you are at Aumont's, Charles Aumont's'.[115]

In a commentary on Barthes's 'En sortant du cinéma' Victor Burgin highlights the condition of 'lassitude' described by Barthes and asks 'whether somnolence itself may not be the spectator's best defence before the spectacle of the Law'.[116] The 'torpidly receptive state' in which Barthes's subject finds himself operates 'not by resisting the perversion, but by doubling it', by an inattentive 'distracted' or 'peripatetic' mode of being, which is 'intermittent', 'flickering'.[117] Burgin relates this to the 'sin' of *acedia*, described as 'a body become soporific, soft, limp; a loss of reality, a porosity to the strangeness of the world, a hallucinatory vivacity of sensations'.[118] This state, reminiscent of the aesthetic receptivity of Proust's narrator, also recalls Baudry's 'absorbed' subject. This is not, then, the transcendental subject of the camera obscura posited by classical apparatus theory, but a subject who is physiologically and affectively enmeshed with the image, even to the point of indiscernibility from it. It is to the body which inhabits the camera obscura that I will turn in the next chapter.

Notes to Chapter 1

1. Roland Barthes, 'Longtemps je me suis couché de bonne heure', in *Le Bruissement de la langue*, pp. 313–25 (p. 316); 'Longtemps je me suis couché de bonne heure', in *The Rustle of Language*, pp. 277–90 (p. 280).
2. Ibid.
3. Ibid., p. 317; p. 281.
4. Lydia Davis translates 'fixer le kaléïdoscope de l'obscurité' as 'stare at the kaleidoscope'. I think that the other definitions of 'fixer' are also at work here, as in: to set, to focus, to establish.
5. The Italian philosopher Giorgio Agamben offers a very clear and condensed version of this point: 'But the most peremptory objection against the modern concept of experience has been raised in the work of Proust. For the object of the *Recherche* is not a lived experience but, quite the contrary, something that has been neither lived nor experienced. And not even its sudden emergence in the *intermittences du cœur* constitutes an experience, from the point when the condition of this emergence is precisely a vacillation of the Kantian conditions of time and space. And it is not only the conditions of experience that are called into question, but also its subject, for the latter is undoubtedly not the modern subject of knowledge (Proust seems rather to have in mind *certain crepuscular states*, like drowsiness or a loss of consciousness: "Je ne savais pas au premier instant qui j'étais" — I did not know who I was at first — is his typical formula' ('Infancy and History: An Essay on the Destruction of Experience', in *Infancy and History* (London: Verso, 1993), pp. 11–64 (p. 42, my emphasis)).
6. This nuances Deleuze's celebrated opposition between Bergsonian and phenomenological accounts of consciousness, according to which: 'Chacun lançait son cri de guerre: toute conscience est conscience *de* quelque chose (Husserl) ou plus encore, toute conscience *est* quelque chose (Bergson)' ('Each had his own war cry: all consciousness is consciousness *of* something (Husserl), or more strongly, all consciousness *is* something (Bergson)') (*Cinéma 1: l'image-mouvement* (Paris: Minuit, 1983), pp. 83–84; *Cinema 1: The Movement-Image*, trans. by Hugh Tomlinson and Barbara Habberjam (London: Athlone, 1986), p. 56).
7. Cf. Barthes, 'Longtemps je me suis couché', p. 316: '[L]'écriture est précisément cette activité qui travaille la langue — les impossibilités de la langue — au profit du discours' ('writing is precisely that activity which tampers with language — the impossibilities of language — to the advantage of discourse', p. 280).
8. Roland Barthes, 'La Mort de l'auteur', in *Le Bruissement de la langue*, pp. 63–69 (p. 63); 'The Death of the Author', in *The Rustle of Language,* pp. 49–55 (p. 51).
9. See, in particular, Maurice Merleau-Ponty, *Le Visible et l'invisible* (Paris: Gallimard, 1964), Chapter 4: 'L'Entrelacs — le chiasme'; *The Visible and the Invisible*, trans. by Alphonso Lingis (Evanston, IL: Northwestern University Press, 1968), Chapter 4: 'The Intertwining — The Chiasm'. Significantly, when Merleau-Ponty wants to give an account of how the experience of something is not reducible to the idea of the thing, but can be accessed only through the embodied experience of the thing ('par une experience charnelle', p. 194; 'in a carnal experience', p. 150) he refers to Proust's *Recherche* and to Swann's attempts to grasp the essence of Vinteuil's 'petite phrase'.
10. Barthes, 'Longtemps je me suis couché', p. 316; p. 280.
11. See Jacques Lacan, *Le Séminaire Livre XVI: d'un autre à l'autre* (Paris: Seuil, 2006), p. 224: 'la dialectique meme du plaisir, à savoir ce qu'elle comporte d'un niveau de stimulation à la fois recherché et évité, d'une juste limite, d'un seuil, implique la centralité d'une zone, disons, interdite, parce que le plaisir y serait trop intense' [the very dialectic of pleasure, specifically the fact of a level of stimulation which is sought and avoided at the same time, the idea of a limit, a threshold, implies the centrality of a zone which we might call forbidden, because the pleasure there would be to intense].
12. See Chapter Four for a more extensive discussion of what I call the 'cinema of Montjouvain'.
13. The expression 'un homme qui dort' was adopted by Georges Perec for the title of his novel of 1967, *Un homme qui dort* (Paris: Denoël, 1967), and the 1974 film of the same title written and directed by Perec and Bernard Queysanne. Both the novel and the film feature multiple

points of connection with the opening of the *Recherche* and the psychic state that it depicts. Carla Ambrósio Garcia has proposed a fascinating analysis of the film in a chapter of her book *Bion in Film Theory and Analysis* (London: Routledge, 2017) which reads it according to the thought of the British psychoanalyst Wilfred Bion (1897–1979) in ways which resonate with my own approach to Proust here. She writes of the protagonist's room, in the film, for example: 'The changes that occur in the experience of this space, as well as of other spaces of the film, both interior and exterior, point to the containment and the problems of containment in the relationship between the protagonist and the spaces that surround him', pp. 115–36 (p. 116).

14. The notion of the 'point of the present' is crucial to Gilles Deleuze's discussion of 'sheets of time' (*nappes de temps*) in *Cinéma 2*: 'Le passé se manifeste [...] comme la coexistence de cercles plus ou moins dilatés, plus ou moins contractés, dont chacun contient tout en même temps, et dont le présent est la limite extrême (le plus petit circuit qui contient tout le passé). Entre le passé comme pré-existence en général et le présent comme passé infiniment contracté, il y a donc tous les cercles du passé qui constituent autant de *régions, de gisements, de nappes* étirées ou rétréciés' (p. 130); 'The past appears [...] as the coexistence of circles which are more or less dilated or contracted, each one of which contains everything at the same time and the present of which is the extreme limit (the smallest circuit that contains all the past). Between the past as pre-existence in general and the present as infinitely contracted there are, therefore, all the circles of the past constituting so many stretched or shrunk *regions, strata* and *sheets*' (*Cinema 2*, pp. 98–99). For a discussion of the 'Proustian' elements of this aspect of Deleuze's writing on cinema, see Patrick ffrench, '"Time in the pure state": Deleuze, Proust and the Image of Time', in *Time and the Image*, ed. by Carolyn Bailey Gill (Manchester: Manchester University Press, 2000), pp. 161–71, and 'Proust, Deleuze and the Spiritual Automaton', in *Beckett's Proust/Deleuze's Proust*, ed. by Mary Bryden and Margaret Topping (London: Palgrave, 2009), pp. 104–16.

15. While this is resonant with Merleau-Ponty's account of the embodied, intentional, and participatory relation of perception to objects in *Phénoménologie de la perception* (Paris: Gallimard, 1945) it also relates to the notion of proprioceptivity discussed below.

16. See Kaja Silverman, *The Threshold of the Visible World* (New York & London: Routledge, 1996): 'Proprioceptivity, which is as central to the formation of the corporeal ego as is the visual imago, derives etymologically from *proprius*, which includes among its central meanings "personal", "individual", "characteristic" and "belonging to"; and *capere*, which means "to grasp", "to conceive" and "to catch". It thus signifies something like "the apprehension on the part of the subject of his or her 'ownness'"'; 'Proprioceptivity would seem to be bound up with the body's sensation of occupying a point in space [...]. It thus involves a non-visual mapping of the body's form' (p.16). Silverman's critical reading of Lacan's mirror stage draws on the work of Viennese neurologist Paul Schilder and French psychoanalyst Henri Wallon to elaborate the sensorial, postural, and spatial dynamics of the ego.

17. See Crary, *Techniques of the Observer*, for a crucial account of the relation between different optical devices and the discourses that supported them. For an extensive historical account of pre-cinematographic technologies see Laurent Mannoni, *Le Grand Art de la lumière et de l'ombre: archéologie du cinéma* (Paris: Nathan, 1999); *The Great Art of Light and Shadow: Archaeology of the Cinema*, trans. by Richard Crangle (Exeter: University of Exeter Press, 2000). See pp. 359–83 (pp. 387–415) for the history of the kinetoscope, which was named by Edison in 1888 and marketed from 1894. It was for an individual viewer and showed a moving image (a 'chronophotographic record') of a short scene on a 35mm film strip. With the kinetoscope, Mannoni remarks, 'la chronophotographie de Marey, entre les mains d'Edison, cesse d'être purement scientifique pour devenir un vrai spectacle populaire' (p. 359) ('Marey's chronophotography, in the hands of Edison, ceased to be a purely scientific instrument and became a truly popular spectacle', p. 387). By the mid-1890s it had been 'demonstrated' in Paris and had become the object of a burgeoning trade. Mannoni adds that 'Marcel Proust s'est peut-être lui aussi dérangé' (p. 379) ('Marcel Proust may also have been entertained by it', p. 410), basing this observation on the reference to it in the novel.

18. See Mannoni, *Le Grand Art de la lumière et de l'ombre*, pp. 203–10; *The Great Art of Light and Shadow*, pp. 215–24. The phenakistoscope was a device consisting of a rotating disc with multiple slots around its circumference through which the viewer looked to see a moving figure on a

further disc. Baudelaire's essay 'La Morale du joujou' appeared in 1853 and is included in *Œuvres complètes*, 2 vols (Paris: Gallimard, Pléiade, 1975–76), I, 581–87.

19. Marey was a (senior) colleague of Proust's father Adrien at the Institut de Médecine, with whom he co-authored a number of articles.

20. See Mannoni, *Le Grand Art de la lumière et de l'ombre*, pp. 299–337 (*The Great Art of Light and Shadow*, pp. 320–63), for details of the history of chronophotography, invented by Marey in the 1870s and 1880s (following his correspondence and encounter with Muybridge) in the context of his scientific study of human and animal locomotion.

21. Deleuze, *Cinéma 1*, p. 9; *Cinema 1*, p. 1.

22. Ibid.

23. Deleuze will argue that Bergson's earlier *Matière et mémoire* (1896) had theorized movement as a 'coupe mobile' [mobile section], which is precisely what, for Deleuze, cinema gives us; movement is perceived not through the perception of a series of instants plus the abstract idea of movement as succession, but by the 'average' image ('l'image moyenne', p. 11; 'intermediate image', p. 2) created through the projection of photograms at a certain speed: 'Le cinema nous donne immédiatement une image-mouvement' (p. 11) ('Cinema immediately gives us a movement-image', p. 2). See also Sara Danius, *The Senses of Modernism: Technology, Perception and Aesthetics* (New York: Cornell University Press, 2002), pp. 102–07, for an insightful account of Bergson's more or less explicit critique of Marey's chronophotography.

24. See Danius, *The Senses of Modernism*, p. 106. See also Donald R. Maxwell, *The Abacus and the Rainbow: Bergson, Proust and the Digital-Analogic Opposition* (New York: Peter Lang, 1999).

25. Agamben, 'Infancy and History', p. 42.

26. Ibid., pp. 13–14.

27. Jonathan Crary, *Suspensions of Perception: Attention, Spectacle and Modern Culture* (Cambridge, MA: MIT Press, 1999), p. 10.

28. Ibid., pp. 15 & 39.

29. Ibid., p. 56.

30. Ibid.

31. Ibid., p. 57.

32. Ibid., pp. 57–58.

33. Ibid., pp. 45–46. See Judith Butler, *The Psychic Life of Power: Essays in Subjection* (Stanford, CA: Stanford University Press, 1997), p. 84: 'The Foucaultian subject is never fully constituted in subjection, then; it is repeatedly constituted in subjection, and it is in the possibility of a repetition that repeats against its origin that subjection might be understood to draw its inadvertently enabling power'.

34. Crary, *Suspensions of Perception*, p. 47.

35. Ibid., p. 14.

36. Ibid., p. 67.

37. Ibid., p. 65.

38. Ibid., p. 77.

39. Marcel Raymond, *Romantisme et rêverie* (Alençon: José Corti, 1978), p. 13.

40. Ibid.

41. Ibid., p. 14.

42. Ibid.

43. Russell Goulbourne, 'Introduction', in Jean-Jacques Rousseau, *Reveries of the Solitary Walker* (Oxford: Oxford University Press, 2011), pp. ix–xxviii (p. xviii).

44. See Robert J. Morrissey, *La Rêverie jusqu'à Rousseau: recherches sur un topos littéraire* (Lexington, KY: French Forum, 1984), for an informative genealogy of reverie from the medieval period to the late eighteenth century.

45. Goulbourne, 'Introduction', p. xix.

46. Charles Baudelaire, 'Réflexions sur quelques-uns de mes contemporains: Victor Hugo', in *Œuvres complètes*, II, 129–41 (p. 137).

47. Ibid., p. 138.

48. Ibid.

49. Ibid., p. 139.
50. Charles Baudelaire, *Le Spleen de Paris: petits poèmes en prose*, in *Œuvres complètes*, I, 273–374 (p. 275); *Paris Spleen: Little Poems in Prose*, trans. by Keith Waldrop (Middletown, CT: Wesleyan University Press, 2009), p. 3.
51. Baudelaire, *Œuvres complètes*, I, 1298.
52. Ibid., p. 1299.
53. Edgar Allan Poe, 'Marginalia', in *The Collected Writings of Edgar Allan Poe*, 5 vols (New York: Gordian Press, 1981–97), II, 258. The reference to Poe is in Pichois's notes to Baudelaire, *Le Spleen de Paris*, p. 1308.
54. Poe, 'Marginalia', p. 259.
55. Ibid. Poe's account is a significant reference in the neurologist Oliver Sacks's essay 'On the Threshold of Sleep', which considers the phenomena of hypnagogic and hypnopompic hallucinations (the latter being those that occur upon waking), and points to their early consideration in the work of French psychologist Alfred Maury in 1848 (in *Le Sommeil et les rêves*, to which Freud refers in *The Interpretation of Dreams*) and Francis Galton in 1883. Interestingly, while noting the 'kaleidoscopic' nature of the hallucinations, Sacks distinguishes them from dreams: 'Dreams come in episodes, not flashes; they have a continuity, a coherence, a narrative, a theme. One is a participant or a participant-observer in one's dreams, whereas with hypnagogia, one is merely a spectator'. See Oliver Sacks, *Hallucinations* (New York: Random House, 2012), pp. 198–217 (p. 209). Anne Henry has analyzed in great detail the extent to which Proust draws on the philosophical, psychological, and scientific discourses of his time, with particular emphasis on Schopenhauer, Bergson, and the German Romantics, but also on the sociology of Gabriel Tarde and the materialist psychology of Maury and Hervey de Saint Denis. She suggests that the opening of the novel owes much to Proust's familiarity with Maury's *Le Sommeil et les rêves* in particular. See Anne Henry, *Marcel Proust: théories pour une esthétique* (Paris: Klinksieck, 1983), pp. 336–44. For more on Proust and Maury, see also Anne Henry, *La Tentation de Marcel Proust* (Paris: PUF, 2000), pp. 97–98, and *Alfred Maury: érudit et rêveur*, ed. by Jacqueline Carroy and Nathalie Richard (Rennes: Presses universitaires de Rennes, 2007), p. 20.
56. Baudelaire, *Le Spleen de Paris*, p. 280; *Paris Spleen*, p. 9.
57. Ibid.
58. Ibid.
59. Baudelaire will go on to ironize his own portrait of the reverie room, revealing its 'double'; a court officer knocks at the door, the vision crumbles and the poet recognizes the 'fetid swamp' of his room, and the vial of laudanum which may have induced the vision in the first place.
60. See Marcel Proust, *Contre Saint-Beuve, précédé de Pastiches et mélanges, suivi de Essais et articles* (Paris: Gallimard, Pléiade, 1971), p. 235; *By Way of Sainte-Beuve*, trans. by Sylvia Townsend Warner (London: Chatto & Windus, 1958), p. 110. The passage from Nerval can be found in Chapter 2 of *Sylvie*, in Gérard de Nerval, *Œuvres complètes*, 3 vols (Paris: Gallimard, Pléiade, 1984–93), III, 540–41. Christopher Prendergast describes the 'between' states favoured by Nerval's *Sylvie* as provoking a 'vacillation in the order of mimesis'. As we saw above, the operation of 'vacillation' is highly resonant with the opening of the *Recherche* and with my concerns here; the crisis of the separated orders of Subject and Representation and the 'crepuscular' merging of one thing or state into another moves towards the identification of a space in which image and affect are coincident. See Christopher Prendergast, *The Order of Mimesis: Balzac, Stendhal, Nerval and Flaubert* (Cambridge: Cambridge University Press, 1986), p. 177.
61. Proust, *Contre Sainte-Beuve*, p. 235; *By Way of Sainte-Beuve*, pp. 110–11.
62. The notion of the 'desire for cinema' comes from Jean-Louis Baudry's essay 'Le Dispositif' [The Apparatus] which we will come to further on in this chapter.
63. André Green, *La Folie privée* (Paris: Gallimard, 1990), p. 402.
64. Gaston Bachelard, *La Poétique de l'espace* (Paris: PUF, 1964), p. 4; *The Poetics of Space*, trans. by Maris Jolas (Boston: Beacon Press, 1969), p. xvi.
65. Ibid., p. 2, 5–6; p. xii, xvii–xviii (translation modified).
66. Ibid., p. 24; p. 5 (translation modified).
67. Ibid., p. 25; p. 5 (translation modified).

68. Ibid., p. 27; p. 6 (translation modified).

69. Ibid., p. 33; p.16 (translation modified).

70. Donald Woods Winnicott, *Playing and Reality* [1971] (London: Routledge, 2005), pp. 135–39.

71. See Donald Woods Winnicott, *Human Nature* (London: Free Association Books, 1988), pp. 119, 62. Cited by Adam Phillips in *On Kissing, Tickling and Being Bored* (London: Faber & Faber, 1993), p. 115. Bion develops the dynamic of container and contained in *Attention and Interpretation* (London: Tavistock, 1970). See André Green, 'La Capacité de rêverie et le mythe étiologique', in *La Folie privée*, for a useful account of the proximity of Winnicott and Bion on this issue.

72. See Wilfred Bion, *Learning from Experience* (Oxford: Aronson, 1962).

73. Yhcam, 'Un réalisme invraisemblable', in *Le Cinéma: naissance d'un art 1895–1920*, ed. by Daniel Banda and José Moure (Paris: Flammarion, 2008), pp. 237–39 (p. 238).

74. Ibid.

75. Jules Romains, 'L'Art de la foule commence', in *Le Cinéma*, ed. by Banda and Moure, pp. 287–88 (p. 287).

76. Daniel Frampton, *Filmosophy* (New York & Chichester: Wallflower, 2006), p. 16.

77. Frampton suggests that Pierre Quesnoy offers a theorization of film as able to 'feel time and memory in ways similar to the novels of Marcel Proust — superimpositions and shifts to markedly different scenes painting the psychological evolution of characters (subjective experience and triggered memories, for instance)' (*Filmosophy*, p. 18). The likely source of Frampton's proposition is Richard Abel, who says roughly the same thing, see *French Film Theory and Criticism: A History/Anthology, 1907–1939*, 2 vols (Princeton, NJ: Princeton University Press, 1988), I, 333. In fact, Quesnoy's essay, *Littérature et cinéma* (Paris: Le Rouge et le noir, 1928), is not so much a contribution to the theorization of cinema as a literary-critical enterprise which finds cinematic qualities in contemporary literary works (so cinematic qualities in Proust, rather than Proustian elements in cinema, as Frampton implies). Quesnoy's essay is nevertheless significant in proposing a fairly substantial account, informed by contemporary film-theorists such as Faure and Epstein, of the cinematographic qualities of the *Recherche*, alongside other novelists and poets such as Ramuz and Cendrars. Quesnoy's argument is that film can inspire a renewal of an otherwise moribund and obsolete literary art, through an injection of speed and movement: 'Peut-être n'est-il que le premier de ces arts dynamiques qui remplaceront les arts statiques et caractériseront notre temps de vitesse et de mouvement' [Perhaps it is but the first of those dynamic arts that will replace the static arts the better to describe our era of speed and movement] (p. 7). Accordingly, Quesnoy sees in the work of Hugo, Aloysius Bertrand, Rimbaud, Nerval and Lautréamont pre-cinematic qualities such as the capacity to create 'une impression générale' [a general impression] (p. 8), the rapid play of superimpositions, a surrealistic play of associations. But it is in the novel, Quesnoy proposes, that the renewal of literary form through its proximity to cinema is most salient, and in this regard, 'Proust est un des plus caractéristiques' [Proust is one of the most exemplary of writers] (p. 15). While it is not a question of 'influence' as such, the parallels are striking, writes Quesnoy. Firstly, around the question of time and duration: ' "le cinéma", déclarait récemment Epstein, est un art à quatre dimensions dont le quatrième est le temps". [...] Cette notion de temps et de durée, c'est Proust qui l'introduisit dans notre littérature' ['cinema', Epstein declared recently, 'is an art of four dimension in which the fourth is time'. [...] This notion of time and duration, has been introduced into literature by Proust] (p. 15). Secondly, the multiple and non-linear presentation and analysis of character corresponds to the multiple angles of film, and to its montage. More specifically, Quesnoy writes, within the form of Proust's writing cinematic techniques are at work: 'à l'intérieur même de ces scènes [the soirées] on peut constater les procédés exacts, les éléments de l'ABC du cinema' [within the scenes themselves [the soirées] one can discern specific procedures, the elements of the ABC of the cinema] (p. 16). Among these is the flashback, which Quesnoy finds in the incidence of involuntary memory; 'un choc sensoriel quelconque' [some sensorial shock] provokes 'le défilé de toute une série d'images passées' [the procession of a whole series of images of the past] (p. 16). Indeed Quesnoy finds in Proust's writing a range of cinematic techniques: 'Flous, accélères, ralentis, gros plans, tout cela se retrouvé également' [Blurred focus, fast motion, slow motion, close-ups, all of this can be found] (p. 18).

78. Quesnoy, *Littérature et cinéma*, p. 19. See Sarah Cooper, *The Soul of Film Theory* (London: Palgrave, 2013).
79. Frampton, *Filmosophy*, p. 19.
80. See, for example, the critical essays on Surrealism in *Tel Quel*, 46 (Summer 1971) by Jean-Louis Houdebine and Guy Scarpetta.
81. Barthes, 'En sortant du cinéma', p. 383; 'Leaving the Movie Theater', p. 345.
82. Rae Beth Gordon, *Why the French love Jerry Lewis: From Cabaret to Early Cinema* (Stanford, CA: Stanford University Press, 2001).
83. Frampton, *Filmosophy*, pp. 49–70. See also Patrick ffrench, 'Memories of the Unlived Body: Jean-Louis Schefer, Georges Bataille, Gilles Deleuze', *Film-Philosophy*, 21:2 (2017), 161–87.
84. Christian Metz, 'Le Film de fiction et son spectateur', *Psychanalyse et cinema*, special issue of *Communications*, 23 (1975), 108–35 (pp. 129, 130); 'The Fiction Film and the Spectator', in *The Imaginary Signifier*, trans. by Alfred Guzzetti (modified by Ben Brewster and Celia Britton) (Bloomington: Indiana University Press, 1982), pp. 99–147 (p. 133).
85. Ibid., p. 109; p. 133.
86. Ibid., p. 109; p. 134.
87. Ibid., p. 132; p. 136.
88. Ibid., p. 127; p. 129.
89. Ibid., p. 129; p. 146 (translation modified).
90. Jean-Louis Baudry, 'Le Dispositif: approches métapsychologiques de l'impression de réalité', *Psychanalyse et cinéma*, special issue of *Communications*, 23 (1975), 65–72 (pp. 62, 68); 'The Apparatus', trans. by Jean Andrews and Bertrand Augst, *Camera Obscura*, 1:11 (1976), 104–26 (pp. 113, 118). See further on for a discussion of Baudry's title.
91. Baudry refers to the English versions of Lewin's 'Sleep, the Mouth and the Dream Screen' and 'Inferences from the Dream Screen', which appeared in *The Psychoanalytic Quarterly*, 15 (1946), 419–34, and *The International Journal of Psycho-Analysis*, 29 (1 January 1948), 224–31, respectively. A translation into French by J.-B. Pontalis of the first essay appeared as 'Le Sommeil, la bouche et le rêve', *L'Espace du rêve*, special issue of *Nouvelle revue de psychanalyse*, 5 (1972), 211–24.
92. Baudry, 'Le Dispositif', p. 66; 'The Apparatus', p. 116.
93. Lewin, 'Le Sommeil, la bouche et l'écran du rêve', p. 213.
94. Baudry, 'Le Dispositif', p. 67; 'The Apparatus', p. 117 (translation modified).
95. Ibid., p. 67; p. 118 (translation modified).
96. Ibid., p. 68; p. 118.
97. Ibid., p. 70; p. 125.
98. Barthes, 'En sortant du cinéma', p. 387; 'Leaving the Movie Theater', p. 348.
99. Ibid.
100. Ibid., p. 383; p. 345 (translation modified).
101. Ibid.
102. Ibid.
103. This issue of *Ornicar* also announced a series of lectures by Gérard Miller on hypnotism and the pre-history of psychoanalysis.
104. See Raymond Bellour, *Le Corps au cinéma: hypnoses, emotions, animalités* (Paris: POL, 2009), pp. 21–123, for an extensive discussion of the historical and conceptual connecting points of hypnosis and cinema.
105. See Yves-Jean Tadié, *Le Lac inconnu: entre Proust et Freud* (Paris: Gallimard, 2012), pp. 15–48; 'Proust est d'abord le romancier du sommeil', p. 20.
106. Barthes, 'En sortant du cinéma', p. 383; 'Leaving the Movie Theater', p. 345. Thinking of the curative effect of the cinema space, Barthes meditates on the possibility of a 'hypnotic music'. 'N'y-a-t-il pas des musiques hypnotiques?' ('isn't there such a thing as hypnotic music?') (p. 383; p. 345). Answering his own question, he refers to the castrato Farinelli, whose voice soothed (or put to sleep) the morbid melancholy of King Phillip V of Spain by singing the same romance every night for fourteen years. This story will return in the chapter on the 'La Retraite' in Barthes's lecture course on the Neutral, a few years later, in the context of the possibility of a specifically 'Proustian' retreat. Proust's retreat, Barthes says, lies in the biographical 'myth'

(which he drew from the 'Castex and Surer' literature 'textbook' devoted to the twentieth century) of the writer's cork-lined room, his withdrawal from society, and so on. Deflecting this myth, however, Barthes points to the morning ritual and specific culinary demands of the writer (fried potatoes in a small silver serving bowl!) as reported by his servants, and thus identifies, as a determining factor of this retreat, 'l'alliance du luxe et de la répétition' ('the alliance between luxury and repetition'). Roland Barthes, *Le Neutre: cours au Collège de France 1977–78* (Paris: Seuil/IMEC, 2002), p. 186; *The Neutral: Lecture Course at the Collège de France (1977–1978)*, trans. by Rosalind E. Krauss and Denis Hollier (New York: Columbia University Press, 2005), p. 144.

107. Barthes, 'En sortant du cinéma', p. 383; 'Leaving the Movie Theater', p. 345.

108. Ibid.

109. Laplanche and Pontalis's entry under 'Etat hypnoïde' in *Vocabulaire de la psychanalyse* (Paris: PUF, 1967), proposes that 'Les états hypnoïdes ont, selon Breuer, deux conditions: un état de rêverie (rêverie diurne, état crépusculaire) et la survenue d'un affect, l'auto-hypnose spontanée étant déclenchée lorsque "l'émotion pénètre dans la rêverie habituelle"'. The quotation here comes from Freud and Breuer's *Studies in Hysteria*, in the 'Preliminary Sketch', in which the authors refer to the hypnoid state as a 'conscience seconde' which blocks associative exchange: 'These hypnoid states, however varied they may be, have one thing in common with each other and with hypnosis, notably that the ideas emerging within them are very intense, but are blocked from associative exchange with the remaining content of consciousness' (Sigmund Freud and Josef Breuer, *Studies in Hysteria*, trans. by Nicola Luckhurst (London: Penguin, 2004), p. 15). Read alongside Barthes's 'En sortant du cinéma' these comments might suggest that the body of Barthes's spectatorship is a quasi-hysterical body, in which control has passed over to this other, 'second' consciousness.

110. Barthes, 'En sortant du cinéma', p. 384; 'Leaving the Movie Theater', p. 346.

111. Ibid., p. 387; p. 349.

112. See Calum Watt, *Blanchot and the Moving Image* (Oxford: Legenda, 2017), pp. 23–35.

113. See Philip Watts, *Roland Barthes's Cinema* (Oxford: Oxford University Press, 2016), pp. 9–34, and Patrick ffrench, *Roland Barthes and Film: Myth, Photography and Leaving the Cinema* (London: I. B. Tauris, forthcoming).

114. Barthes, 'En sortant du cinéma', p. 385; 'Leaving the Movie Theater', p. 347.

115. Maxim Gorky, 'In the Kingdom of Shadows', in Jay Leyda, *Kino: A History of Russian and Soviet Film* (London: Allen, 1960), pp. 407–09 (p. 408).

116. Victor Burgin, 'Barthes' Discretion', in *The Remembered Film* (London: Reaktion, 2004), p. 31.

117. Ibid., pp. 32–34.

118. Ibid., p. 40.

CHAPTER 2

Camera Obscura

In her book *Death 24x a Second* Laura Mulvey points to the importance of the camera obscura as one of the long-term strands of the history of optics which would converge in the late nineteenth century to determine the birth of the cinema. She discusses it in the context of a consideration of different attempts to 'preserve the fleeting instability of reality and the passing of time in a fixed image'.[1] Yet as Mulvey points out, the image projected in the camera obscura was transient and impermanent; cinema, or the desire for cinema, would need the chemical process of fixing the image — the detour into photography — in order for the indexical image of the moving image to be preserved and to persist beyond its evanescence. The camera obscura, literally a dark box or room with an aperture through which light may pass and be concentrated so as to reproduce an inverted image on a wall or screen of the chamber, enabled the exact re-presentation of a mobile and living reality. The camera obscura's reproduction of the real was indexical, yet spectral, ontologically related to the reality it reproduced, but presenting an uncanny, evanescent, and insubstantial double of the real.

These spectral and uncanny properties would, however, be suppressed in the promotion of the device to the status of a philosophical paradigm. It is not so much the indexical and uncanny properties of the camera obscura, its power to offer a spectral and concurrent image of an external reality, so much as its structure as a framing and enclosing device, a *dispositif* which structures the relation of a subject to the perceptual world, which supports the pervasive ideological power of the apparatus. In *Techniques of the Observer* Crary considers the camera obscura as the paradigmatic model of knowledge and certainty, and argues that this model undergoes substantive displacements over a longer timeframe than orthodox histories of art and technology suggest. Crary challenges the prevailing accounts in art history which postulate a key rupture around the end of the nineteenth century, a rupture with broadly realist modes of representation ushering in the modernist epoch. According to the modernist thesis the rupture takes place in the margins. It is 'an event whose effects occur *outside* the most dominant and pervasive modes of seeing'.[2] Crary describes this as producing 'a confusing bifurcated model', whereby Renaissance structures of seeing persist alongside the modernist experiments which disturb them.[3] Both the hegemonic and avant-gardist modes of seeing are sustained without affecting the observer, 'who remains perceptually the same, or whose historical status is never interrogated'. This account obscures what Crary describes as a 'crucial systemic shift', which occurred much earlier in the nineteenth century and indeed was well underway by 1820.[4] This is 'a problem of the observer', where the latter is defined as 'the one who sees within a prescribed set of possibilities'. Crary draws on Foucault to schematize visuality in terms of an 'arrangement of forces' or as a 'hegemonic set of discourses and practices' which situate optical devices (such as the camera obscura or the stereoscope) as 'sites of both knowledge and power that operate directly on the body of the individual'.[5] In this light Crary turns towards earlier periods to describe the camera obscura as 'paradigmatic of the dominant status of the observer in the 17th and 18th centuries'. The 'pervasive suppression' of subjectivity in the seventeenth and eighteenth centuries is contrasted with the priority, from the nineteenth century on, of models of subjective vision.[6] Summarizing the epistemological, discursive, but also technological mutation at stake here, Crary writes that:

> What takes place from 1810 to 1840 is an uprooting of vision from the stable and fixed relations incarnated in the camera obscura. If the camera obscura, as a concept, subsisted as an objective ground of visual truth, a variety of discourses and practices — in philosophy, science, and in procedures of social normalization — tend to abolish the foundations of that ground in the early nineteenth century. In a sense, what occurs is a new valuation of visual experience: it is given an unprecedented mobility and exchangeability, abstracted from any founding site or referent.[7]

Crary thus notes and charts the decline of the 'apodictic claims of the camera obscura to establish it as truth'.[8] The 'subjective vision' which Crary sees as the consequence of the displacement of the camera obscura as conceptual framework and grounding of truth is 'a vision that had been taken out of the incorporeal relations of the camera obscura and relocated in the human body'. This is reflected in 'a passage from geometrical optics to physiological optics', and it establishes the 'constitutive role of the body in the apprehension of the visible world'.[9]

Crary thus shows how, far from being an 'incipient form' on an 'evolutionary ladder' that leads to photography and to cinema, a claim made or implied by conservative and radical histories alike (i.e. those that saw this evolution as a form of progress, and those that saw it as an increasing ideological subjection) the camera obscura device is a site of overlapping knowledge and power.[10] As a 'historically constructed artefact' it 'coalesced' into a 'dominant paradigm' which fixed and regulated the status and position of the observer in the seventeenth and eighteenth centuries. The camera obscura became the usual or normative model for explaining vision and the 'position of a knowing subject [in relation to] an external world'.[11] One of the prominent effects of the camera obscura model was to rigorously demarcate the interior and the exterior worlds, separating the one from the other, to establish the empirical outside as formally exterior, and to fix the 'inside' as the domain of certainty and knowledge, but without any kind of phenomenal thickness. This it did through a delimitation and a demarcation of the visual field, by means of the aperture, which individuated the observer 'as isolated, enclosed and autonomous within its dark confines', by means of withdrawal (or askesis) of the observer from the empirically observable world, and through a concomitant decorporealization of vision. The observer in or of the camera obscura is a 'free, sovereign individual', a 'privatized subject', or a 'monadic viewpoint'.[12] Crucially, the observer is also a 'disembodied witness', since the apparatus of perception is as if given over to the purely mechanical procedure of the device. Crary writes: 'Thus the spectator is a more free-floating inhabitant of the darkness, a marginal supplementary presence independent of the machinery of representation'.[13]

In keeping with another etymology of the word 'chamber', moreover, the disembodied observer of the camera obscura also plays a 'juridical' role.[14] Crary notes that the camera obscura 'allows the subject to guarantee and police the correspondence between exterior world and interior representation and to exclude anything disorderly or unruly'.[15] The camera obscura model is essential, in effect, to the constitution of the Cartesian subject and the concomitant knowable objectivity of the exterior world. It rules over the strict territorial division between Subject and Object and polices the translation from one zone to the other.[16]

Having established the camera obscura as the paradigm for the transcendental subject of knowledge throughout the seventeenth and eighteenth centuries, Crary traces the shift from these conditions of abstracted, disembodied subjectivity to those of the physiological subject, or 'subjective vision'. In this new paradigm, the subject is physiologically involved in what they see; the objects of vision, no longer anchored to the real and true by a firmly positioned and framed subject, circulate in an economy of signs, subject to desire, and as we saw above, subject to the vicissitudes of attention.

Proust's *Recherche* proposes a major dramatization of the tension between the camera obscura model and the 'subjective vision' which displaces it as a philosophical paradigm. On the one hand, the novel is punctuated by recurrent scenes in which the narrator's perception and knowledge of the outside world takes place in the interior space of his room. On the other hand, the security and certainty of this knowledge is compromised by the fact that, in the room, he is not a disembodied and abstracted subject, but a physiological presence, and one whose very presence is mined internally by the intermittences of time and of consciousness. This is a room, we might recall, that he has 'filled with himself'. Moreover, while adopting the skeletal structure of the camera obscura, so to speak, Proust troubles it through the mutual complication of different senses, and through a pervasive attention to the surfaces or limits separating inside from outside.

In the opening of the first volume, for example, the optical operation of the camera obscura motif — the perception of the outside from within the interior space of the room — is definitively annulled. No light enters the room save that from under the door, and the knowledge that it allows the narrator is faulty; it is not morning, and no-one is coming to his aid. Knowledge of the exterior world is afforded through listening — it is through a technique of proprioceptive listening that the narrator is able to judge the distances of the surrounding countryside. This judgment and this knowledge do not have the same certainty, the same philosophical and juridical status, as that afforded by vision, given that they depend on the contingent fact of the sound of a passing train. It is often through the sense of sound and the faculty of listening that the narrator's knowledge of the exterior world, from within his room, is gained; Proust thus implicitly problematizes the conceptual prioritization of vision in the philosophical *dispositif.* The room becomes not so much a camera obscura as an echo chamber.[17]

The emergence in Proust of an ambivalently embodied subjectivity, in the room, is not only due to the visual impairment proposed by darkness and the subsequent intensification of aural sensibility, but by the radical extension of the subject's interior space. Perceptual knowledge of exterior space as the ground and basis of knowledge is troubled by the fact that, crudely, the subject 'does not know who he is'. This is not only because of the shifting movements around the threshold of consciousness, the terrain of hypnagogic consciousness and of reverie, but also because the subject has a vast and multiple extension in time. The kind of vertigo which the narrator confesses to at the end of *Le Temps retrouvé*, as if he is peering down, on stilts, into the far depths of his own temporal existence, may be connected back to the opening of *Combray*: certain knowledge of the exterior world is also ruined by the proposition that the narrator does not know *when* he is. A vast interior space *inside* the subject doubles and multiplies exterior space.

A further, and decisive, subversion of the *dispositif* of the camera obscura is manifest in the challenge posed to its paradigmatic status by its competitor in the stakes of the pre-history of cinema: the magic lantern. If the philosophical paradigm of the camera obscura situates a disembodied subject of knowledge at a fixed point for the reception of perceptual information about the exterior world, the magic lantern colonizes the interior space with an already projected world, a screened world, which is both a substitute for and a rival of the real outside, which, to some extent remains permanently out of reach, permanently set at distance by virtue of the recurrent operations of projection.

If the apparatus of the camera obscura posits an actual, indexical image of the exterior upon its inverted screen, the magic lantern intervenes in that process, interrupts it, thrusting its intrusive illusion onto the walls of the *chambre obscure.* The magic lantern, with the stress upon the first term, magic, disturbs, with its 'revolving evocations', the ontological and epistemological security of the camera obscura. It substitutes for the evanescent and spectral index of the outside an illusory and subjectively tinged, vibrantly coloured image. The magic lantern figures the intrusion of subjective vision into the fixed world of Cartesian certainty; its projection onto the walls, furniture, and objects of the child narrator's room is the radical intervention of the physiological and libidinal subject into the affectively blank *dispositif* of the camera obscura.

We might say in this light that the film is projected as if from the inside, emanating from the point of the subject, rather than playing out on the back wall of the camera obscura from the point of the aperture, a defining feature of the apparatus, the juridical point of articulation between interior and exterior. If the film is already projected, from the inside, then the knowledge of the exterior world guaranteed by this juridical site, and all of the epistemological and moral certainties which come with that, begin to crumble.[18]

In this light we can look again at the opening sentences of the *Recherche*, which position the narrator inside a room, which functions as a generative matrix for the novel as a whole and for the narrator's experience. The narrator, detaching himself from a semi-somnolent state in an as yet unlocated room, finds himself capable of a sensory attention to the world outside the room:

> Je me demandais quelle heure il pouvait être; j'entendais le sifflement des trains qui, plus ou moins éloigné, comme le chant d'un oiseau dans une forêt, relevant les distances, me décrivait l'étendue de la campagne déserte où le voyageur se hâte vers la station prochaine; et le petit chemin qu'il suit va être gravé dans son souvenir par l'excitation qu'il doit à des lieux nouveaux, des actes inaccoutumés, à la causerie récente et aux adieux sous la lampe étrangère qui le suivent encore dans le silence de la nuit, à la douceur prochaine du retour. (I, 3–4, see Chapter 1 for a translation of this passage)

The darkness of the room is the condition for the imaginary reconstruction of the landscape outside premised on the auditory perception of the train's whistle. But this indexical link to the exterior immediately passes into the oneiric picturing of a scene which sits uneasily between metaphor and description, as if the narrating subject had passed back into that semi-conscious state from which he had first emerged. This is one of many instances in which the narrator, usually in his bedroom and usually upon awakening, gauges the quality of the exterior world via a fragile umbilical thread linking his perception to the exterior. An often auditory indexical sign provides the basis for a reconstruction of this exterior world which, while often distorted, comes to fill the interior both of the room itself and of the subject's consciousness. The narrator's consciousness, in these instances, is situated in an uncanny border-zone between imagination and sensation, between indexical description and imaginative representation; attention to the rhetorical structure of the sentence cited above suggests that the fragment 'la campagne déserte où le voyageur se hâte' hides a slippage into metaphor, the elision of which gives the impression that the following sequence about the traveller is part of the real landscape. This uncanny status also characterizes the ghostly image in the camera obscura, which is indexically tied to the reality exterior to the chamber, yet disembodied, the spectral double of the outside.

In another room in which he awakes, at the opening of *La Prisonnière*, the narrator relates that he can sense the quality of the day before turning to see the rays of light entering the room above the curtains. He remarks, as a means of preparing the reader for Albertine's presence in his mother's house, that: 'Ce fut, du reste, surtout de ma chambre que je perçus la vie extérieure pendant cette période' ('It was, in fact, mainly from my bedroom that I perceived the world around me at this period') (III, 520; 5, 3). Of course this does not mean that the narrator does not move and perceive in the exterior world, but this matrix of perception, the exterior sensed in the interior, is the mode of his perceptual interaction, the structure according to which a spectral and distorted, evanescent double of the exterior world will be created in the interiority of the narrator's consciousness, which thus has the status of a room, or a chamber.

That this matrix of perception is fundamental to the way the novel constructs reality is suggested by the association between the outside/inside inversion specific to it and the activity of reading, in *Du côté de chez Swann*. The room in which the narrator has retired to read:

> Protegeait en tremblant sa fraîcheur transparente et fragile contre le soleil de l'après-midi derrière ses volets presque clos où un reflet de jour avait pourtant trouvé moyen de faire passer ses ailes jaunes, et restait immobile entre le bois et le vitrage, dans un coin, comme un papillon posé. (I, 82)

> [Tremulously protected its frail transparent coolness from the afternoon sun behind its nearly closed shutters, through which a gleam of daylight had nevertheless contrived to pass its yellow wings and remained motionless between the wood and window-pane, in a corner, like a poised butterfly.] (I, 85)

Despite the thin ray of light that has passed through an aperture in the shutters there is only just enough light to read, and the full effect of the light outside is only given to the narrator by the sound of the blacksmith's blows, by the buzzing of flies:

> Il faisait peine assez claire pour lire, et la sensation de la splendeur de la lumière ne m'était donnée que par les coups frappés dans la rue par Camus [...] contre les caisses poussiéreuses mais qui, retentissant dans l'atmosphère sonore, spéciale aux temps chauds, semblaient faire voler au loin des astres écarlates; et aussi par les mouches qui exécutait devant moi, dans leur petit concert, comme la musique de chambre de l'été; elle ne l'évoque pas à la façon d'un air de musique humaine, qui, entendu par hasard à la belle saison, vous la rappelle ensuite; elle est unie à l'été par un lien plus nécessaire; née des beaux jours, ne renaissant qu'avec eux, contenant un peu de leur essence, elle n'en réveille pas seulement l'image dans notre mémoire, elle en certifie le retour, la présence effective, ambiante, immédiatement accessible. (I, 82)

> [It was barely light enough to read, and the sensation of the splendid brightness of the day came to me only from the blows struck in the rue de la Cure by Camus [...] against some dusty crates, which, however, reverberating in the sonorous atmosphere peculiar to hot weather, seemed to send scarlet stars flying into the distance; and also by the houseflies that performed for me, in a little concert, a sort of chamber music of summer; this music does not evoke summer in the same way as a melody of human music, which, when you happen to hear it during the warm season, afterwards reminds you of it; it is connected to the summer by a more necessary bond: born of the fine days, born again only with them, containing a little of their essence, it not only awakens their image in our memory, it guarantees their return, their presence, actual, ambient, immediately accessible.] (I, 85)

The narrator proposes that through the buzzing of the flies, ontologically linked to the summer, he has the full sensation of the outside; it is effectively present. As often in the *Recherche*, this is followed by a theorization of perception which corresponds to the model of the camera obscura, while extending it to include senses other than the visual, according to the pretext of Baudelaire's *correspondances*. He proposes that through the inverted image of the exterior world in his room he is able to grasp the totality of the spectacle which if he were outside would only be accessible in fragments:

> Cette obscure fraîcheur de ma chambre était au plein soleil de la rue, ce que l'ombre est au rayon, c'est-à-dire aussi lumineuse que lui, et offrait à mon imagination le spectacle total de l'été dont mes sens si j'avais été en promenade, n'auraient pu jouir que par morceaux. (I, 82)

> [The dim coolness of my room was to the full sun of the street what a shadow is to a ray of light, that is to say, it was just as luminous and offered my imagination the full spectacle of summer, which my senses, had I been out walking, could have enjoyed only piecemeal.] (I, 85)

The shadow is *as* 'luminous' as the ray of light precisely because of the indexical, ontological connection between the two; the full light of the street finds its inverted sensory image in the darkness of the room.[19]

But the narrator goes further than this commentary on the quality and mode of his perceptions, in extending the camera obscura function to that of his consciousness itself:

> Et ma pensée n'était-elle pas aussi comme une autre crèche au fond de laquelle je sentais que je restais enfoncé, même pour regarder ce qui se passait au-dehors? Quand je voyais un objet extérieur, la conscience que je le voyais restait entre moi et lui, le bordait d'un mince liséré spirituel, qui m'empêchait de jamais toucher directement sa matière, elle se volatilisait en quelque sorte avant que je prisse contact avec elle, comme un corps incandescent qu'on approche d'un objet mouillé ne touche pas son humidité parce qu'il se fait toujours précéder d'une zone d'évaporation. (I, 83)

> [And wasn't my mind also like another crib in the depths of which I felt I remained ensconced, even in order to watch what was happening outside? When I saw an exterior object, my awareness that I was seeing it would remain between me and it, edging it with a thin spiritual border that prevented me from ever directly touching its substance; it would dissipate somehow before I could make contact with it, just as an incandescent body brought near a damp object never touches its wetness because it is always preceded by a zone of evaporation.] (I, 86)

Thought itself is like a crèche in which the narrator is semi-buried. Material contact with the exterior world is prevented by this bordering or fringing of conscience; it is always perceived from within the room. And just as the spectral image in the camera obscura vanishes if approached, the material, exterior world has a volatile, evanescent presence. The narrator goes on to compare the state in which he is plunged through reading to the process by which the world is experienced as more true and more essential when perceived in the interior chamber of consciousness.

The *Recherche* and cinema thus share a common situation in the room, the chamber, as an interior space separated from the outside, in which perception of the outside is mediated, as if on a form of screen. The apparatus and the concept of the camera obscura reinforces this connection, even as Proust's deployment of the motif problematizes its philosophical function. The motif of the room may need to be taken further, however; if the opening of the *Recherche*, as I have tried to show, foregrounds an experience which functions as a spectral double of the situation of the spectator, in the cinema, the notion of the cinema as a room as such remains implicit, understated. Barthes's gesture of departure — leaving the cinema — and his exploration of the space and volume of the place, incorporating a consciousness of the other bodies that inhabit it, begin to raise a consciousness of the cinema as an inhabited space, as a room. Indeed it may be precisely only by leaving the cinema, in investigating the liminary spaces around it, that the 'vocation of the room', of the cinema, to adopt an expression from Raymond Bellour which I intend to exploit in concluding this chapter, begins to become visible.[20]

In 1989 Bellour curated an exhibition at the Centre Georges Pompidou Musée national d'art moderne called *Passages de l'image* devoted to the movements between different visual media of photography, cinema, and video. The exhibition featured artists whose work played on and between these media, on the fault-lines and translations between them, including Bill Viola, Gary Hill, Chantal Akerman, Chris Marker, and Michael Snow among others. It was informed by the work Bellour had been doing on different media — cinema, photography, video — since the early 1980s, collected in the book *L'Entre-images*. A second volume, *L'Entre-images 2*, collected essays written between 1988 and 1999, and was largely oriented around the *Passages* exhibition and the artists who participated, but the exhibition itself also explored further the thinking articulated in the first volume, whose title itself, 'l'entre-images', conceptualizes a space and a movement between images, whether it be the interval or cut or splice of the film strip, or the tensions and intensities between the still and the moving image.

Proust's *Recherche* is a recurrent reference across the two volumes of *L'Entre-images*, as if Bellour's exploration of the spaces between cinema and its others necessitated reference back to the liminary role Proust's novel and his writing has in relation to cinema, not so much historically, but symptomatologically — the consciousness of Proust's narrator is coincident with a projection, inside a darkened room, as I have tried to show.[21] Bellour's explorations of the edges and experimental limits of cinema, both internally in its relation to the photograph or the still, and externally, in its relation to video, but also to writing, thus necessarily have recourse to Proust's *Recherche* almost as a kind of primal scene, an alternative to the Lacanian mirror stage in which one can discern the 'threshold of the visible world'. It is significant also that some of the seminal works which Bellour discusses as key to his conception of the 'between-the-images' also deploy references and allusions to Proust, or incorporate Proust's novel in different ways, as if to reinforce the way in which an experimental re-thinking of the cinema is destined at some point to encounter it as its photographic negative.

At the conceptual centre of Bellour's *L'Entre-Images 2: mots, images*, a book which as its subtitle suggests supplements the first volume through a more focused attention to the movements between words and images, and to the place of the word in or as the image, is the essay 'La Chambre', in which Bellour argues for the intrinsic importance of the room in both cinema and literature.[22] Bellour exploits, in this essay, the multiple associations between the cinema and the room. The essay opens with the proposition that the cinema functions as a kind of double of the private, reserved space of the bedroom:

Depuis qu'au XVIIIe siècle la chambre à coucher est devenue l'espace réservé de nos enfances, une relation s'est formée entre les lieux publics où l'homme s'enferme pour capter des visions et ceux où il se retire pour dormir et rêver, pour écrire et jouer, pour jouir ou pour mourir.[23]

[Since in the eighteenth century the bedroom became the reserved space of our childhoods, a relation has been established between the public spaces in which people shut themselves away to capture their visions and those to which they withdraw to sleep and to dream, to write and to play, to make love and to die.]

As a room, the cinema, Bellour proposes, occupies an intermediate space between the social spectacle of theatre and the private space of real bedrooms, into which television often now intervenes as a kind of fourth wall. The cinema's doubling of the intimate room is such that when rooms appear on screen the cinema comes closest to itself: 'c'est parce que sa vocation de chambre est si vive, comme en deça de ce qu'il montre, qu'il arrive au cinéma de se tenir aussi près de lui-même sitôt que de vraies chambres apparaissent' [it is because its orientation toward the room is so vital, as if always behind what it shows, that the cinema is never closest to itself as when real rooms appear].[24] This programmes a number of references on Bellour's part to rooms in films, including those of Fritz Lang, to François Truffaut's *La Chambre verte*, but especially to Samuel Beckett's *Film*. His point, in engaging with *Film*, and with Deleuze's reading of it, is to establish the room as a space, as a volume which embodies a gaze. In the room of *Film*, in which the protagonist takes refuge from any possibility of appearing in the visual field of the other, 'Tout regarde et tout voit' [Everything looks and sees].[25] The final, ostensibly terrifying image of the figure of a face on the headrest of the chair accompanies the extinction of the protagonist's look, which is coincident, in Bellour's reading, with the merging of the look with the space of the room itself. The eyes of the headrest, Bellour suggests:

Accompagnent le processus d'extinction de la vision par une mise en volume du regard comme point de lumière. Lumière physique et mentale ici liée à la chambre, son espace, son temps. Il y a regard tant qu'il y a chambre, chambre dès qu'il y a regard, réfraction de lumière.[26]

[Accompany the process of extinction of vision through a volumizing of the look as point of light. A physical and mental light bound to the room, its space, its time. There is a look as soon as there is a room, a room as soon as there is a look, a refraction of light.]

Bellour's thesis is that the room is intimately tied to the physical and psychical fact of the look, or the gaze. The room is 'la frontière et le point de friction' [the frontier and point of friction] between the eye of the subject, and the immanent plane of vision. In other words, the room is the space of refraction, the space of mediation between the light that is given and the light that is perceived.

This vision of the room ('cette vision de chambre') was brought home to him, Bellour suggests, in his encounters over a short time with a series of experimental video installations, by Gary Hill, Bill Viola, and Thierry Kuntzel.[27] In these works, he pursues, the room as such is addressed, and it becomes a sort of theoretical fiction or symptomatic motif whereby the cinema engages with its own history and pre-history, the history of all of those apparatuses, real or imagined, which it refers back to or which, in film theory as such, it has been understood, the camera obscura included. However, cinema, Bellour argues, can only approach its status as a room, its 'vocation de chambre', with difficulty, since its structure has been reified and fixed as a kind of 'sovereign' installation.[28] It is thus in experimental video art, in the practices and spaces 'between-the-images' that defamiliarize the cinema as a room, that Bellour sees the pursuit of this exploration of the room. Viola, for example, seeks to draw the spectator-subject closer to themselves through an increasing enclosure in the space of the image: 'une tentation d'épuiser les modalités de la chambre tapissée d'images' [an attempt to exhaust the modes of the room-space decorated with images].[29] Hill, on the other hand, disperses the attention of the spectator subject through the dislocation of the screen-form: 'une dislocation de la forme-écran'.[30] Kuntzel draws on film history, evoking the green room of Hitchcock's *Vertigo*, and the room in Chris Marker's *La Jetée* in which the fault-line between the photogrammatic and the moving image becomes suddenly, acutely visible, and *La Jetée* as the 'chamber' through which Kuntzel moved to transform his practice of film-analysis and theory into video art.[31] These installations and practices, and many others, bring the cinema into relief in its status as a 'cube obscur' (dark cube), thus detaching it from the lure, or fascination, of the screen, and from its institutionally immobile structure. It is in the light of this defamiliarizing operation that I now want to address a series of film and installation works which seem to me resonant with Proust's *Recherche*.[32]

In 1972 Chantal Akerman, who would later direct *La Captive* (2000), an adaptation of *La Prisonnière*, directed an eleven-minute experimental silent film called *La Chambre*, her first film made in New York. The film is shot entirely in what appears to be a studio apartment, thus a domestic space which is both bedroom and kitchen. The camera remains at a fixed position and with an unchanging angle and frame in the centre of the room and pans slowly around the room, completing two 360-degree panoramic turns in an anti-clockwise direction before reversing direction about halfway through a third 360-degree turn for four slow panning movements back and forth around the bed.

The camera moves over an old upholstered chair, an antique wooden dresser, a round table littered with food and crockery, a sink, a stove-top with a kettle, an antique desk, and other less identifiable objects. Light comes into the room from three windows with translucent blinds. The central focus, and the apparent fulcrum of the panning movements is a bed occupied by a young woman, Akerman herself. At first we see her sitting up and seeming to look directly at the camera while moving her head from side to side slowly, as if to mimic the movement of the camera. The second panoramic movement is faster, although not so we notice; this time Akerman is lying down in the bed, still facing us, and rocking back and forth under the covers. At the start of the third revolution we see her turning an apple around in her hands; on the reverse pan she is brushing it against her lips, then, in the next two panning movements she is eating the apple, first slowly, and then more voraciously. In the final pan she rubs her face in her hands before settling back into the bed.

Commentary on the film has emphasized the thematics of the everyday and of domestic space, of female captivity and of the female gaze, and the ways in which the film is redolent of Akerman's characteristic visual exploration of space as the predominant narrative movement. This structuralist tendency, which eschews conventional storytelling through shot-counter-shot, point of view, and montage, pares the cinematographic situation down by means of a fixed camera, whose 'structural' revolutions and pans draw attention to its presence in the room, while simultaneously confronting the viewer with the woman's gaze turned back on us. But *La Chambre* also foregrounds its own space, the space of the room, and, in a way that parallels the effects of the video installations of Viola, Hill, and Kuntzel, draws out the volume of the cinema-space we inhabit, while also drawing us back to the bedroom as the space of sleep, pleasure, and interiority. The room of *La Chambre* is definitively an interior space, a space of refuge, retreat, or imprisonment, its enclosure ratified by the circular movements of the camera. It is a room that has been inhabited, filled with objects and furnishings which speak of everyday usage, but also of the past and of memory — an ornate lamp, an upholstered chair, the antique dresser, of personal traces, of the director herself, perhaps of others. The exterior world is present through these objects, it is true, but its intrusion into the room is felt principally in the light that filters through the windows, which seems to be the only light source — the room appears darker in its corners.

In the way that it draws attention to the space of the room and to the cinema's vocation as a room, through its formal and structural qualities, *La Chambre* draws on and cites the experimental work of Canadian director and artist Michael Snow, whose *Back and Forth* (1969) Akerman cites as an explicit influence. But while *Back and Forth* features the same formal camera movements as *La Chambre* — panning at different speeds from right to left and left to right, and up and down, in a room that resembles a classroom — its space is far more open to the outside, through the open doors and several windows of the room, and the indistinct human figures who pass through the room throughout its fifty-two minutes. *Back and Forth* also begins with a short sequence outside the room, and incorporates superimpositions, and intermittent ambient sound, dominated by the noise of the camera. More akin to Snow's *Wavelength*, which is shot entirely within one room from a static camera position with an imperceptibly slow unilateral zoom and which features four events including the apparent death of one of the several human figures who pass through the room, *La Chambre* nevertheless exploits its formal structure in a way that is more attuned to subjective experience, that of its director and protagonist, the semi-autobiographical subject of the film, and that of the viewer.

This proposition might be drawn out further through reading *La Chambre* against the opening of Proust's *Recherche*, and here again the space and time of reading mediate around and between the images in Bellour's sense. Akerman's room is, like the bedroom of Proust's narrator, a space which she has 'filled with herself', and which dilates and contracts around her. It is akin to a camera obscura, like the bedroom at Combray, or the room of *La Prisonnière,* insofar as it establishes a division between interior and exterior and establishes itself as an enclosed space of experience and knowledge, yet it is a camera obscura that has been inhabited by the physiological and experiential body, the body of desire and pleasure. *La Chambre,* however, introduces a major structural displacement; while Proust's subject is the proprioceptive centre of the space, and the room is sensed both spatially and temporally from the central point that he inhabits, around which the room is arranged concentrically ('un homme qui dort tient en cercle les années autour de lui' ('A sleeping man holds in a circle the sequence of the ours, the order of the years and worlds') (I, 5; I, 9), this central point is occupied in *La Chambre* by the camera, from whose viewpoint we can see the subject, whose gaze comes back at us. While we are never given a reflection or an image of Proust's narrator, as if he were never anything other than a viewpoint on the world, an empty apparatus (see Chapter 3), *La Chambre* seems to offer us both the disembodied look of the camera and the embodied image of the subject. Between text and film, then, as readers and spectators we move across different positions, back and forth between subject and body-image, interior monologue and seeing subject.

Between the *Ouverture* of the *Recherche* and *La Chambre* there is also a gender dynamics at stake. If, in my re-imagining of the interplay of novel and film, the text gives voice to the subject, offering its words to the woman in the bed in the silent film, the film returns a female gaze back upon the apparatus of the narrative viewpoint, challenging its ostensibly male vision with another body and another look, as if Albertine were to look back at the narrator and challenge him. *La Chambre* invites us to re-imagine the *Recherche*, just as this reading — between text and film — has invited us to think the film with and through Proust.

Véronique Aubouy's extraordinary video project *Proust lu* proposes a further displacement of the *Recherche*, and a further dialogue with it, in this instance moving against and outside the enclosed space of the room and against the 'vocation de chambre' Bellour finds in the cinema.[33] Aubouy's as yet unfinished project uses digital video to capture over a thousand readers, each of whom read aloud a two-page extract from the novel, to the camera, in a setting of their choice. The only constraints are that the readings should be from the original French and should follow the progression of the text. The readers are drawn from contingent encounters on the part of Aubouy from all manner of social contexts, and from her friends and family, and in this way the project has an autobiographical character bound to the passages and accidents of Aubouy's own life and experience, and incorporated as a span of time and gesturality into her life. The settings vary: there are bedrooms, but also *epiceries*, cowsheds, Metro stations, forests, graveyards, bars, workshops, the water of Lake Como, interior and exterior spaces of all kinds.[34] *Proust lu* democratizes and exteriorizes the *Recherche*, drawing it out of the enclosed space of the room and of reading, and making of reading both a mode of performance and of autobiographical self-expression — through the choice of location and the voice and gesture of reading aloud. Exploiting the greater mobility of digital video, *Proust lu* works and plays upon an inter-medial space, between text and image; the readers' eyes move between the page and the camera, performing Proust through voice and address. While this might seem to emphasize the personal appropriation of the literary epitome that the *Recherche* is, and thus to draw Proust out of the room and the salon, and thus establish a series of individualistic claims upon the text, the very plurality and multiplicity of readers and readings move against this. With its estimated final length of 200 hours of video footage, *Proust lu* is recurrently screened in its entirety in galleries and at festivals; its viewing as a whole is impossible, and the viewing space becomes a site of passage, definitively different from the orthodox situation of the cinema, while resembling the projections *en permanence* of early cinema. In its viewing conditions and in its powerful exteriorization both of Proust's novel, and of the cinematographic *dispositif*, *Proust lu* is definitively outside the room.

The Canadian artist Stan Douglas's installation *Overture*, first created in 1986, features a projector encased in a black box projecting a six-minute 16mm film loop. The film is in fact found footage from the Edison company from around the end of the nineteenth century showing the movement of a train through a series of tunnels in a mountain pass in British Columbia. Douglas has extended the sections when the train passes through the tunnels through black leader. The soundtrack features the Canadian writer Gerald Creede reading sentences from the opening of Proust's *Recherche* which Douglas has selected, re-ordered, and recombined.

At the beginning of her book *Exhibiting Cinema in Contemporary Art* Erica Balsom proposes that Douglas's *Overture* plays with the association of the train with the birth of cinema, referring back to the Lumière brothers' 1895 film *L'Arrivée d'un train à La Ciotat* and exploiting the movement of the train at a time when it was not possible to move the camera. The use of Proust for the installation's voiceover suggests further connections, as Balsom notes:

> Seemingly opposed to the fast-moving views of faraway lands seen on the image track, the voiceover speaks of private, internal experience. And yet, as memories rush in and surround the narrator, he describes the experience in distinctly cinematic terms: 'Everything revolved around me through the darkness: things, places, years'. He then goes on to discuss the inability to separate one sensation from another with reference to the illusion of movement achieved by the proto-cinematic device of the Bio-scope.[35]

Peter Culley has also pointed to the historical concerns carried by Douglas's piece, suggesting that the installation pertains to:

> The historical moment that the beginnings of film share with the end of the novel, when Proust's faith in the tantalizing structures of his great predecessors, Balzac and Wagner, was being undermined by the perceptive discontinuities that film helped to bring about.[36]

Culley suggests, furthermore, that the opening sentences of the novel articulate these discontinuities.

The intermittent consciousness of the opening of the *Recherche* is thus proposed as a symptomatic index of a crisis of representation brought about by the new technologies of cinema, and Balsom's consideration of the later reference to the pre-cinematographic technology of the kinetoscope emphasizes this much. But she also points to the way in which Douglas's work plays on and between interior and exterior, public and private. *Overture* shows us the wide-open space of the American landscape, from the assuredly public site of a moving train, while conjuring the interior space of a scene of awakening through the use of the voiceover from Proust. This also implies a constructive tension between different temporalities. Balsom writes that:

> *Overture* thus brings together two conceptions of time that are central to late nineteenth-century modernity: the public, standardized time that is closely linked to the development of the railway and the subjective time of involuntary memory as elaborated by Proust. Somewhere between them, between regularity and contingency, public and private, lies the time of the cinema.[37]

But Balsom also points to the way in which, as an installation rather than an experimental film, Douglas's work is able to foreground the historical conditions of the *dispositif* of the cinema. Through its historical reference back to the end of the nineteenth century — through the Edison footage, and then through the formal presentation of the projecting apparatus in the gallery space — Douglas brackets the cinema as a historical artefact, incorporating the excerpts from Proust's novel as a similar, if chronologically inexact measure of the same moment. Balsom writes:

> From one fin-de-siècle to another, [*Overture*] is a return to the subjective transformations brought about by the invention of cinema at the end of the nineteenth century amidst those initiated by new electronic media at the end of the twentieth. As an indexical trace of pastness, the grainy footage of the Edison films contains within it the very force of time that Proust's narrator sought to recover, testifying to the way in which the past can be summoned in all its anachronism to challenge the present.[38]

This layering of time and mobilization of obsolescence to provoke both the uncanny return of the historical past and a consciousness of the present is redolent of Bellour's proposition of the passage 'between-the-images' which can extract the spectator from the lure of the screen, in a manner also resonant with Barthes's 'discretion', discussed earlier.[39] Douglas's use of Proust proposes an intermedial and trans-historical play, between text and image, reading and seeing, which introduces fissures into the sovereign technology of film, and invites us to think the cinema differently, again, with Proust.

Notes to Chapter 2

1. Laura Mulvey, *Death 24x a Second* (London: Reaktion, 2006), p. 18.
2. Crary, *Techniques of the Observer*, p. 4.
3. Ibid.
4. Ibid., p. 5.
5. Ibid., p. 6. Crary argues against 'latent or explicit technological determinism' (p. 8), which sees technology and technical apparatuses as subordinate to other forces.
6. Ibid., p. 8.
7. Ibid., p. 14.
8. Ibid.

9. Ibid., p. 16.

10. Ibid., p. 26. In the late 1960s and early 1970s writers such as Baudry and Marcelin Pleynet, associated with the French literary journal *Tel Quel*, and with a satellite film review *Cinéthique*, but also with *Cahiers du cinéma* for a brief moment in the early 1970s, developed a critique of the cinematic apparatus which underlined the way it functioned to affirm the subject-centered character of Western bourgeois ideology. They referred specifically to the legacy of the camera obscura in the development of perspective in the quattrocento, structuring and framing vision around the point of view of the subject. Pleynet writes, for example, that: 'L'appareil cinématographique est un appareil purement idéologique. Il produit un code perspective directement hérité, construit sur le modèle scientifique du quattrocento' [The film camera is an ideological instrument in its own right; it produces and reproduces a directly inherited code of perspective, built on the scientific model of the Quattrocento], Marcelin Pleynet and Jean Thibaudeau, 'Economique-formelle-idéologique', *Cinéthique*, 3 (1969), 7–14 (p. 10). From Crary's perspective, the accounts which locate the ideological basis of the cinematographic apparatus in the rationalist procedures of the Renaissance ignore and occlude the historical shifts in the 'techniques of the observer' which profoundly alter the modes of spectatorship and vision.

11. Ibid., p. 27.

12. Ibid., p. 39.

13. Ibid., p. 41.

14. Ibid., p. 42.

15. Ibid., pp. 42–43.

16. Crary comments on the aperture as the 'single, mathematically definable point', a viewpoint which provides 'a vantage point onto the world analogous to the eye of God' (p. 48), and explores how Descartes had postulated the potential substitution of the eye of a human or an animal (such as an ox) in place of the lens in order to 'found human knowledge on a purely objective basis' (p. 48). Sarah Kofman, to whom Crary refers here, explores the same motif in the chapter 'L'Œil de bœuf: Descartes et l'après-coup idéologique' of her book *Camera obscura: de l'idéologie* (Paris: Galilée, 1973). An uncanny echo can be heard here: in the architectural feature called the 'œil de bœuf', the spyhole window through which Proust's narrator witnesses Charlus's flagellation in *Le Temps retrouvé*, in the scene of Jupien's hotel (IV, 394; 7, 123). The co-incidence of the architectural motif and Descartes's hypothetical experiment points to the way in which the occurrence of the aperture in the *Recherche* undermines the classical structure of the camera obscura model by implicating the subject in the field of vision, predominantly through motifs associated with desire and cruelty. See Chapter Four for an account of this in relation to the 'Montjouvain' episode.

17. I am indebted here to Igor Reyner, 'Listening in Proust'.

18. This possibility is conjured in Gilles Deleuze's re-imagining, in *Le Pli: Leibniz et le baroque* (Paris: Minuit, 1988); *The Fold: Leibniz and the Baroque*, trans. by Tom Conley (London: Athlone, 1993), of the architecture of the baroque period and of the modalities of the Leibnizian monad. Deleuze is concerned in this work with the same kind of terrain as Crary in *Techniques of the Observer*, and Crary will also discuss the connections between Leibniz's monad and the disembodied subject of the camera obscura. For Leibniz, Crary suggests, the problem is 'the reconciling of the validity of universal truths with the inescapable fact of a world consisting of multiple points of view'. The (partial) solution to this conundrum offered by Leibniz is the notion of the monad, which implies 'a fragmented and decentred world'. The monad, nevertheless, 'had the capacity to reflect in itself the whole universe from its own finite viewpoint' (*Techniques of the Observer*, p. 50). Crary suggests the alignment of Leibniz's monad with the camera obscura, which allows 'a parallel reconstruction of a limited (or monadic) viewpoint, and, at the same time, necessary truth'. In *Le Pli* Deleuze also compares the Leibnizian monad with the camera obscura: 'Ce serait la chambre obscure des *Nouveaux Essais,* garnie d'une toile tendue diversifiée par des plis mouvants, vivants. L'essentiel de la monade, c'est qu'elle a un sombre fond: elle en tire tout, et rien du vient du dehors ni ne va au-dehors' (*Le Pli*, pp. 38–39) ('This would be the camera obscura of the *New Essays*, furnished by a stretched canvas, diversified by moving, living folds. Essential to the monad is its *dark background*; everything is drawn out of it, and nothing goes out

or comes in from the outside', *The Fold*, p. 27).

19. See Paul de Man, *Allegories of Reading: Figural Language in Rousseau, Nietzsche, Rilke and Proust* (Newhaven, CT: Yale University Press, 1979), pp. 57–78, for an extended discussion of the passage on reading.

20. Raymond Bellour, 'La Chambre', in *L'Entre-images 2*, pp. 281–317 (p. 281).

21. See, in particular, 'Quand s'écrit la photo du cinéma', Bellour's review of Jean-François Chévrier's *Proust et la photographie* (Paris: L'Arachnéen, 2009), in *L'Entre-Images*, pp. 67–72; 'When the Photograph of Cinema is Written', in *Between-the-Images*, pp. 78–85; and in the essay 'La Double Hélice' (*L'Entre-images 2*, pp. 9–41), Bellour's analysis of the role of Proust in David Larcher's experimental video *Granny's I's* (1989).

22. The essay 'La Chambre' appeared originally in *Trafic*, 9 (1994).

23. Bellour, 'La Chambre', in *L'Entre-Images 2*, p. 281.

24. Ibid., pp. 281–82.

25. Ibid., p. 283.

26. Ibid., p. 285.

27. Ibid., p. 288.

28. Ibid., p. 289.

29. Ibid., p. 294.

30. Ibid., p. 298.

31. Ibid., p. 301. Bellour evokes Kuntzel's lost 'critical-imaginary montage' of Marker's *La Jetée*, titled *La Rejetée* (1974).

32. Bellour cites Barthes's 'cube obscur' from 'En sortant du cinéma', p. 289. Cf. Barthes, 'En sortant du cinéma', p. 384; 'Leaving the Movie Theater', p. 346.

33. See <http://www.aubouy.fr/proust-lu/le-film.html> [accessed 24 March 2017] for Aubouy's own website and presentation of the project.

34. See <http://www.aubouy.fr/proust-lu/images-lecteur.html> [accessed 24 March 2017] for a selection of images of readers in different locations.

35. Erica Balsom, *Exhibiting Cinema in Contemporary Art* (Amsterdam: Amsterdam University Press, 2013), p. 9.

36. Peter Culley, 'Two Works by Stan Douglas', *Vanguard*, 16:4 (October 1987), <http://ccca.concordia.ca/c/writing/c/culley/culo02t.html> [accessed 24 March 2017].

37. Balsom, *Exhibiting Cinema in Contemporary Art*, pp. 10–11.

38. Ibid.

39. It would also be pertinent in this vein to consider Chris Marker's CD-Rom project *Immemory*, and the use of the then new, but now obsolete, technology of the CD-Rom to explore the history and memory of cinema, intertwined with the experience of reading Proust. See Patrick ffrench, 'The Immanent Ethnography of Chris Marker, Reader of Proust', *Film Studies*, 6 (Summer 2005), 87–96.

CHAPTER 3

Proust's Projections

'An illuminated section cut directly out of the unknown'

Introducing what he calls 'this long-distance migrant among themes' in Proust's *A la recherche du temps perdu* — 'the imperious drive to *know*' — Malcolm Bowie cites an expression from *Un Amour de Swann*; the narrator's privilege is:

> To be summoned to the limits of what is thinkable, and to risk everything for a glimpse of what lies beyond. Overshadowing the promise of sexual satisfaction another, improbable, order of pleasure is seen: that of a mind suddenly confronted by, and able to grasp, 'une étroite section lumineuse pratiquée à même l'inconnu'.[1]

Bowie does not discuss in detail the specific context or image of the expression, but goes on to consider another episode in the volume which positions Swann outside his lover Odette's window, meditating on the knowledge of her infidelity he believes he is about to obtain. Bowie thus allows us to infer a threefold association between the screen, a 'luminous cut-out', the acquisition of knowledge, and the surreptitious voyeurism of Swann. I want to begin this chapter with a consideration of these associations, which seem to me to cluster around the figure of the screen. I will attend further on to the two episodes that Bowie conjurs here, but before doing so, following his lead, I will consider more precisely the implications of the expression 'une étroite section pratiquée à meme l'inconnu'.

To read it cold, without context, is to imagine a luminescent aperture, framed by surrounding darkness. The 'cut-out' or frame is given a spatial and an episte-mological status; it is executed or operated, 'pratiquée' 'right up against the surface of the unknown', cut into, but also layered, like a thin film, upon a truth that is there to know, but which is as yet unknown, which it has the potential to illuminate. The fact that, as it turns out, what there is to know here concerns the desire of the other, of Odette in this instance, and Swann's desire for knowledge of Odette's desire, renders the episode and the expression pregnant with questions around the relations between desire, knowledge, and visuality. What interests me are the resonances between Proust's epistemologically voracious subject and the spectator in the cinema. Both are confronted by a screen — a (framed) section, a 'cut out', a thin, film-like surface (which I read into Proust's 'à même', abutting, touching without distance) — and luminosity. The drama and intensity of this part of Proust's novel hinges in part around the conflation of desire and knowledge; in jealousy desire has taken on the form of an 'imperious will to know'. But Bowie also adds to this anxious conflation a specifically optical and spatial disposition. It is significantly narrow: 'une *étroite* section'. Swann has confined and limited himself to 'an unpromisingly narrow [...] observational world'.[2] It is not only that, in this particular instance, the field of knowledge, of what there is to know, is framed or constrained, it is also that Swann's look has narrowed and accommodated itself to the dimensions of the illuminated screen in front of him, in which he believes he will find the knowledge he both craves and fears. Jealousy is a narrowing and a framing of the look.

A major resource in thinking through the rich terrain of associations provoked by Proust's expression is to be found, I suggest, in Jean-Luc Godard's film *Le Mépris* [Contempt] (1963), especially as read by Leo Bersani and Ulysse Dutoit in *Forms of Being*.[3] One of the major thematic strands of the film, adapted by Godard from Alberto Moravia's novel, is the parallel between Paul Javal (played by Michel Piccoli) and the spectator; Paul's look has been narrowed to a unilateral and unique focus on the physiognomy of his wife Camille (Brigitte Bardot). Paul both seeks for and finds in her expressions the signs of her contempt for him. Bersani and Dutoit refer to psychoanalyst Jean Laplanche's notion of the enigmatic signifier to explain this effect.[4] Paul experiences Camille as (with)holding knowledge, a knowledge that pertains specifically to her desire, and he thus constitutes her and her image as a signifier whose meaning is withdrawn or withheld. The spectator of the film is also drawn into this desire. It is Paul's task, and ours, to find or interpret the meaning of the enigmatic signifier of Camille's look; he is constrained to a hermeneutic quest, just as we are as spectators. Paul's look is thus reduced in its range and focus to the unknown or not yet known. Godard's film plays with this narrowing effect in and around the dimensions of the narrative, setting the story of Paul and Camille against the wider and rival narrative within the film of the Iliad, of which Fritz Lang (who plays himself) is directing a film version, produced by Jeremy Prokosch (Jack Palance). As spectators we are obliged to think through the differences between the epic world of Homer and the tragic psychology of Paul's predicament, thus to think our modern condition as spectators, in and of the cinema. Godard also directs our attention to the question of the frame, contrasting Paul's narrowed look, for example, with the final shot of the wide and unpopulated expanse of the sea and sky, which offers release and redemption from the tragic love story. For Bersani and Dutoit the film plays between the two contrasting fields of desire, on the one hand, and Being, on the other. It contrasts the all too human field of psychology — in which desire is equivalent to a sadistic mastery of the other or a masochistic subjection of the self — with the field of aesthetics and the empirical neutrality of the epic, where the look is open to the full range and variation of the visual field.

But is Godard's belief in the empirical existence and accessibility of a world outside the tragedy of desire sustainable? This digression permits me to reiterate the idea of the screen as intrinsically associated with the issue of knowledge. In Proust's novel this problem is presented and explored with extraordinary acuity and depth. It is intertwined with the equally significant and pregnant issue of projection. Both terms have the virtue of referring at the same time to concrete attributes of the cinematic situation, and to mechanisms which pertain, especially in psychoanalytic literature, to aspects or operations of the psyche. Both terms, the screen to a greater extent, have been amply discussed in film theory. The screen has been, for example, a dominant motif of a powerful strand of Lacanian film theory, in the work of Joan Copjec and Kaja Silverman to name but two. But, and this is to displace the discussion temporarily onto a different terrain, this may be because both terms relate to the question of knowledge, or perhaps more specifically to the problems instantiated by the conflation of desire, knowledge, and visuality. These problems are usefully comprised in the more general issue of scepticism. They might be best articulated as a series of questions intrinsic to Proust's novel: What can I know of the world? What can I know of the Other? Does the world exist beyond my knowledge of it? How do I tell the difference between the external world and the world created by my internal processes of memory and desire? May I find myself in the world, or am I excluded from it? Is the world anything other than the image I project onto it? *Where* is knowledge? I contend that these questions are also particularly pertinent for the cinema spectator, and, more ambitiously, for individual subjects in a world in which the cinema exists. So to rethink the cinema with Proust is to explore the ways in which both fields — that of film theory and philosophy — and that of Proust's novel, may mutually illuminate each other.

But let us return now to the expression 'une étroite section lumineuse pratiquée à même l'inconnu' and to its precise context. Following an aborted visit provoked by his suspicions concerning Odette, Odette has given Swann some letters to post, of which one is addressed to his rival Forcheville. Swann reads the contents of the letter through the only part of the envelope that is not folded over ('doublée'), discovering thereby that the intimate terms she uses in her letters to him, Swann, contrast markedly with the formal tone she adopts with Forcheville. The expression Bowie uses to designate the narrow frame of Swann's jealous desire occurs via an analogy with this act of reading through the thin layer of paper, its opacity compromised:

> Il maintint immobile la carte qui dansait dans l'enveloppe plus grande qu'elle, puis, la faisant glisser avec le pouce, en amena successivement les différentes lignes sous la partie de l'enveloppe qui n'était pas doublée, la seule à travers laquelle on pouvait lire. (I, 278)

> [He took firm hold of the card that danced in the envelope, which was larger than it was, then, sliding it with his thumb, brought its different lines one after another under the part of the envelope that was not doubled, the only part through which one could read.] (I, 284–85)

Having by this means read the whole letter, Swann is in a quandary:

> Swann restait là, désolé, confus et pourtant heureux, devant cette enveloppe qu'Odette lui avait remise sans crainte, tant était absolue la confiance qu'elle avait en sa délicatesse, mais à travers le vitrage transparent de laquelle se dévoilait à lui, avec le secret d'un incident qu'il n'aurait jamais cru possible de connaître, un peu de la vie d'Odette, comme dans une étroite section lumineuse pratiquée à même l'inconnu. (I, 278)

[Swann remained there, disconsolate, embarrassed and yet happy, with this envelope which Odette had handed over to him quite fearlessly, so absolute was her confidence in his sense of delicacy, but through the transparent glazing of which was revealed to him, with the secret of an incident which he would never have believed it possible to find out, a little of Odette's life, as in a narrow illuminated section cut directly out of the unknown.] (I, 285)

I will have occasion later to comment on the image of the envelope as a window or glass partition, and to the importance of glass in Proust's visual imaginary. The key point here seems to be about knowledge, proposing the non-folded part of the envelope as allowing a privileged and improbable access to it. Reading through the 'transparent glass' of the envelope affords Swann a privileged access to a fragment of Odette's real life, like, 'comme', a narrow section cut into the unknown. However, if Swann is momentarily appeased by the knowledge that he gains from the letter, he also infers Odette's duplicity; she had pretended to Forcheville that when Swann called it was an uncle paying an inopportune visit. Her mendacity is ambivalent, and uncertain, and Swann's jealousy is only exacerbated by the partial and fragmented nature of the truth he thinks he has found.

Adam Watt has offered a persuasive reading of this scene, in the context of his sustained attention to 'le délire de la lecture' [the delirium of reading] in the *Recherche*, to the recurrent acts of reading — both the physical act and the act of interpretation — that punctuate the novel.[5] He also points to the resonance of the expression 'une étroite section' with the earlier episode in *Combray* when the narrator had observed the sexual play of Mlle Vinteuil and her friend from the darkness of the slope outside the window of their house at Montjouvain. I will call this the 'cinema of Montjouvain' and will return to the episode in Chapter 4. Watt's parallel is useful for us here in underlining the structural similarities that cut across these scenes, which both feature an illuminated frame. And this perspective also recalls the scene Bowie considers, closer in the text, in which Swann has returned to Odette's house, suspicious that she is entertaining someone and seeking to keep it from him. He positions himself outside her window, sees a glow of light from within, and hears a low murmur of voices. Certain that he now has within his grasp firm evidence of her infidelity, while sensing a curious pleasure in this assurance and in the knowledge he thinks he will gain from it, a specifically epistemological pleasure, he knocks on the window, only to discover that he is at the wrong house.

Both scenes involve a vision doubly constrained: first by the frame of the window and by the borders of the unfolded surface of the envelope, 'une section'; secondly, by the not completely transparent, semi-opaque character of a surface through or behind which things are seen or sensed, the envelope and the window.[6] The visible seems to be visible only through some kind of mediating surface, the membrane of the envelope or the blinds at the window, which allow only a suffused glow to emerge. The membrane, as mediating but also dividing surface (the word *cloison* recurs throughout the novel), will be an important factor further on in this chapter. What I want to underline at this point is the dimension of the screen, by which I understand a surface that both invites and resists the hermeneutic gaze. The screen frames, illuminates, but also excludes, and hides. What it does, I think, is to intervene between the subject and the real in order to definitively deny any sense of transparency or immediacy. The screen is not a window onto the world, but a structured and duplicitous surface; it is both geometrically and morally two-faced. The conditions of knowledge have shifted. Both the *Recherche* and the cinema inaugurate a screened world, a projected world, and thus suspend and relativize the conditions of objective knowledge.

In order to illustrate this and to explore its ramifications further, I want to turn again to the work of Bersani on Proust, which to my mind offers a particularly lucid account of the operations of epistemological desire and its negotiations with the problem of projection. In his early work *Marcel Proust: the Fictions of Life and Art* (1965), Bersani offers an insight I find entirely convincing, that there is in the *Recherche* a developmental arc which moves from a sense of hopeful belief in the truth and reality of the external world to a more resigned or sceptical position according to which, if the external world does hold truth or substance, our knowledge of it can only ever be compromised, partial, and self-interested.[7] We find only what we seek. In this light, the celebrated and triumphant notion of literature in *Le Temps retrouvé* as the 'true life', 'la vraie vie', appears at best as a compromise formation, at worst as an avoidance of the problems that this sceptical position provokes.

I will underline the elements of Bersani's argument that seem to me to speak most persuasively to the conditions of the cinema and to the position of scepticism I have just described, before addressing more frontally the kind of scepticism which I think is at stake here. Early on in his account, Bersani finds in the narrator's perspectives a 'basic anguish about the nature of the self and its relation to the external world'. This anguish, Bersani adds, is provoked by 'an extreme uncertainty about the stability of the self, a fearful fantasy of losing the self unless it can be permanently fixed in some external picture'.[8] The dynamic here is that psychic loss or emptiness is kept at bay through the fixity of an image of the world. The equation is made more tortuously complex, however, by the fact that in this image the narrator seeks, at the same time, a perceptual and experiential reality 'completely different from himself' and one which 'sends back his own image to him'.[9] To exist as a subject, and to know this, he needs an 'external picture' which affords evidence of the difference of the world but also of the persistence of the self, since it is a picture in which he can find himself. He can find himself in it since it is an image he has projected onto the world. Thus its difference is annulled and the self is dissolved in an infinite play of mirrors; the endeavour fails.

The narrator is caught in the double bind of a desire for difference and a need for sameness. This expresses an epistemological paradox — the paradox of a hopeful belief in external reality and a (fearful) scepticism concerning the consistency both of the self and of the external picture. Bersani articulates this with typical lucidity when he writes:

> One of the most interesting aspects of the book is the contradiction between the narrator's subjectivist ideas — the inexorable 'law' according to which all we can do is project images of ourselves on external reality, and what might be called the discovery of a variegated and distinct external world at the very

moment when the narrator has presumably turned his back on everything except the world of his own impressions and fantasies.[10]

It is this pattern, wherein the world intervenes unexpectedly, in Gilberte's gesture, in the 'cinema of Montjouvain' (see Chapter 4), in the appearance of the 'petite bande' at the end of the dyke, in the encounter of Charlus and Jupien in the courtyard of the Hôtel de Guermantes, in a fleeting glimpse of Robert de Saint-Loup leaving Jupien's establishment, and in the multiple experiences of involuntary memory, which fuel the narrative and prevent it from congealing into an impressionistic poetry of introspective imagined states. In the perverse logic Bersani finds here, reality impinges, in its difference, at those moments where projective reflection and reflective recognition are most assured.

The incidence of the wide and multifarious semantic range of the word *projection* has allowed me here to imply a continuity of concern between the psychic dynamics at work in Proust's novel, as drawn out by Bersani, and the cinematic experience. If I have left these inferences somewhat abstract it is because I see this continuity as virtual, potential, rather than actual, concrete. To think the cinema with Proust is to think it outside its manifest actuality. Nevertheless, Bersani offers us a more punctual point of connection with film theory in subsequent remarks about the nature of the Proustian subject.

In seeking, at first, to define the particularly vacant and indistinct nature of the Proustian narrative subject, and the way in which the narrator is thus obliged to look outside himself for a guarantee of his being, Bersani draws on an expression from one of the two drafts of *Albertine disparue*:

> Or comme le moi vit incessamment en pensant une quantité de choses, quand par hasard au lieu d'avoir devant lui ces choses, il pense tout d'un coup à soi-même, il ne trouve qu'un *appareil vide*, quelque chose qu'il ne connaît pas, auquel pour lui donner quelque réalité il ajoute le souvenir d'une figure aperçue dans la glace.
>
> [Now since the self is constantly thinking numerous things, since it is nothing more than the thoughts of those things, when by chance instead of having them as the objects of its attention, it suddenly turns its thoughts upon itself, it finds only an empty apparatus, something unfamiliar, to which, in order to give it some reality, it adds the memory of a face seen in a mirror.][11]

Bersani comments that:

> The narrator will come back often to the idea that by 'looking inside,' by attempting to define the self introspectively, we find only an 'empty apparatus.' This statement by no means expresses his whole point of view on the processes of self-awareness, but it is important to see that he emphasizes, at the beginning of his work, the way in which the self relies, for its security, on a fixed scene in the outer world.[12]

In order to illustrate this idea Bersani comments in detail on an episode in *Albertine disparue* in which the 'external picture' which gives the narrator a form of existential security has collapsed, and the world appears in the guise of a 'frightening anonymity'.[13] Learning that the baronne de Putbus and her ostensibly promiscuous maid are expected, the narrator refuses to leave Venice with his mother. After she has left in a fit of anger, the narrator finds that Venice has become alien to him; its stones do not 'take' the 'fictions' that he previously impressed upon them. The dissolution of the external picture is mirrored, internally, by the reduction of his subjectivity to nothing more than a 'throbbing heart':

> Les choses m'étaient devenues étrangères, je n'avais plus assez de calme pour sortir de mon cœur palpitant et introduire en elles quelque stabilité. La ville que j'avais devant moi avait cessé d'être Venise. Sa personnalité, son nom, me paraissaient comme des fictions mensongères que je n'avais plus le courage d'inculquer aux pierres. Les palais m'apparaissaient réduits à leurs simples parties et quantités de marbre pareilles à toutes autres, et l'eau comme une combinaison d'hydrogène et d'azote, éternelle, aveugle, antérieure et extérieure à Venise, ignorante des doges et de Turner. (IV, 231)

> [I felt [...] alienated from all things, and I was not calm enough to detach myself from my palpitating heart and impose some stability on the world around me. The city I saw before me had ceased to be Venice. Its personality and its name appeared to me as mendacious fictions that I no longer had the heart to relate to its stones. The palaces appeared reduced to their congruent parts and their portions of indifferent marble, and the waters to a combination of nitrogen and hydrogen, eternal and blind, anterior and exterior to Venice, ignorant of Turner and the Doges.] (5, 616, translation modified)

What occurs here is a failure of projection, which has the additional effect of revealing the projection as such, revealing what might appear as objective description to be conditioned and intended by the self, a 'lying fiction'. The incapacity to 'impress' an image upon the stones of Venice (surely a desublimating critique of Ruskin) is equivalent to a failure of the screen to accommodate and reflect what is projected onto it. This failure is both cause and effect of a catastrophic reduction of the self to a visceral affectivity, a degree zero of affect, nothing more than an emotional and physical pulse.

The collapse of the external picture is provoked by a failure of recognition; the narrator fails to find anything in the world that can guarantee the consistency and substance of his interiority. Bersani writes that 'The interest of the Venice passage is that it illustrates a failure of recognition and therefore — in the broadest sense — of imagination; and this failure is properly defined as a kind of ontological crisis, a sudden deprivation of self'.[14] And yet this failure of projection, and thus of the screen-effect of the external picture affords a different kind of knowledge, a different image:

> Et cependant ce lieu quelconque était étrange comme un lieu où on vient d'arriver, qui ne vous connaît pas encore, comme un lieu d'où l'on est parti et qui vous a déjà oublié. Je ne pouvais rien lui dire de moi, laisser rien de moi se poser sur lui, il me contractait à moi même, je n'étais plus qu'un cœur qui battait. (IV, 231)

> [And yet this unexceptional place was as alien as a place where you have just arrived, which does not yet know you, or a place that you have left and that has already forgotten you. There was nothing now that I could tell it about me,

nothing of mine that I could invest it with, it forced me to withdraw within myself, I was no more than a beating heart.] (5, 616)

It is as if the dysfunction of the screen, which no longer takes or fixes the image, allows external reality to seep into consciousness in its alterity, ignorant of names as of the investments the subject endeavours to introduce into it. The stones of Venice are reduced, so to speak, to their brute materiality, the water to its molecular composition. Paradoxically, however, the brute material of things and of the place is endowed with agency — they do not know the subject nor do they remember him, they reduce or contract him to himself (an echo of the opening sequence of the novel). The dynamic has been inverted; things have ceased to be (merely) the objects of a desiring investment, figures of and for a projection; they impact upon the subject in their material, indifferent presence.

Of course, from one perspective the molecular, material image of Venice is no less a picture than the Venice of the Doges and of Turner; the 'real' Venice which the failure of the screen allows to impinge is just as much a 'fiction' as the city in which the self can find consistency. Proust's fictional art lies in the oscillation between the self's projections and the intervention of the external world in the event of a failed projection. The novelist ironizes what Bersani calls the 'subjectivist' self and its almost indefatigable poetic power — always to see one thing as another — through the recurrent puncturing of the screen.

What I find interesting here, and what can lead us further in drawing out the cinematographic resonances that will I hope be felt, is, on the one hand, the physical and optical dynamics of projection and of what I referred to as the screen effect, in particular the implications of its failure. What happens when the projected image fails to take, to be imprinted, when the surface can no longer accommodate the image projected upon it? What does it mean for the subject and for knowledge if the absence or failure of the screen-effect induces an 'ontological crisis'? These questions will lead us back in due course to the very first instance of projection in the novel — the magic lantern sequence of Combray — which functions as the 'threshold of the visible world', and thus as the equivalent, in the world of Proust's *Recherche*, of Lacan's mirror stage.

The second element I want to pick up on in Bersani's discussion, however, is a second occurrence in his discussion of the notion of the self as an 'empty apparatus'. Under the subtitle 'The Self as an "*appareil vide*": A Critique of Psychological Analysis' Bersani considers the way in which Proust ironically undercuts the discourse of love through an emphasis on the dominant role of the self. The experience of love is presented by Proust, Bersani suggests, as 'a monologue masquerading as a dialogue'.[15] However, if this seems to imply that to explore the state of love and of jealousy one should examine the self, rather than the other, Bersani finds that Proust's narrator 'raises serious objections to the traditional language of introspection'.[16] For the narrator, introspection turns out to be a thoroughly useless means of enquiry, since the self is strangely devoid of content. Bersani thus finds in the Proustian account an anticipation of the Sartrean notion of consciousness as a 'transcendent activity toward objects', without content or substance:

> In fact, in one passage the narrator questions the whole process of introspection
> as a means of finding out anything about the self, and we find something close
> to the Sartrean view that consciousness is a void except insofar as it can project
> itself into objects in the outer world.[17]

Bersani then cites the expression from *Albertine disparue* with the image of the 'empty apparatus'. The notion of Proustian consciousness as a sustained, yet intermittently faulty projection onto the world should by now be familiar. What is more striking here is the supplementary idea of consciousness as an 'empty apparatus', the idea that there is nothing internal to the self which through this process finds itself externalized. This promotes the idea of consciousness as (merely) an *activity of projecting*, a kind of mechanism which gives consistency and substance to the self only in a subsequent and strangely retrospective recognition. The expression Bersani draws out from Proust suggests an equivalence between the Proustian subject and the cinematic apparatus as described by Baudry, among others, in structuralist French film theory of the 1970s. Through this analogy consciousness appears as a projecting machine which stands in the place of the I, a subjectivizing mechanism through which subjectivity is actualized only after the event. In the cinematic apparatus and in its automatism, the analogy suggests, humanity will have found a process which actualizes, reproduces, and institutionalizes the projective operations of the psyche, a process which gives a picture of the world without and despite the wilful intention of the subject.

This thought finds itself clearly articulated in the North American philosopher Stanley Cavell's philosophy of film, expressed in the central definition of film in his book *The World Viewed*: film is 'a succession of automatic world projections'.[18] One of the leitmotifs of Cavell's philosophy since the outset has been the philosophical problem of scepticism, the question of our relation to the world. Crudely, the question concerns our belief, or lack of it, in the reality of the external world; scepticism poses a threat, 'the threat that the world, and others in it, may, for all that I can know, not exist',[19] or 'the idea that we privately doubt that the world exists and ourselves and others in it'.[20] For Cavell the problem of scepticism has been an abiding preoccupation of philosophy ever since its inauguration in Descartes's doubt concerning the existence of external reality. In Hume and Kant the problem is exacerbated when they cease to find a resolution for it in the existence of God, as Descartes did. Cavell writes that 'It is in modern philosophical skepticism, in Descartes and in Hume, that our relation to things in the world came to be felt to hang by a thread of sensuous immediacy, hence to be snapped by a doubt'.[21] In Heidegger and Wittgenstein, but also in Freud and Benjamin, Cavell finds major points of reference which install the issue of our epistemological and ontological estrangement from the world as one of the dominant problems of philosophy. He writes in this vein that since Descartes, at least, 'the wish to defeat or disparage skepticism has been at philosophy's heart'.[22]

Heeding the arguments in Bersani that we discussed earlier, I find this mood of radical uncertainty about external reality, estrangement from the world, and the concurrent effort to resolve the problem, close the distance, to believe again in things and our connection to them to be central to Proust's endeavour, and to his narrator's negotiations with the world and with others. The wager, so to speak, is to pit a will to assure the existence of the world and of the self against the most severe doubts about both. It is in this sense that the *Recherche* might be considered redemptive, although the deal is by no means sealed. There is common ground between Cavell's enquiries and those of Proust's narrator as we have discussed them previously, via Bersani and Bowie. But it is in Cavell's writing on film that the parallels become more emphatic and pertinent to the effort to think Proust and cinema together, given that Cavell finds in film a solution of sorts, albeit a 'magical' one, to the suspension of the world and of our relation to it.

Cavell's major work on the cinema, *The World Viewed*, was published in 1971 following what he perceived as the failure of a seminar on cinema at Harvard in 1963, and a detour of several years during which he published a series of works focused on the philosophy of ordinary language and on issues in the philosophical aesthetics of modernity. Throughout these works the problem of scepticism was central. Cavell finds a tendency in the history and development of art and of aesthetics to move away from the representation of the world. It is 'within the threat' posed by this sceptical attitude that Cavell writes, out of a will to address, and potentially to resolve, the suspension of the reality of the external world.[23] It is in this direction that he finds in film an art which 'bears a relation to reality unprecedented in other arts'.[24] More specifically, he finds in the work of Panofsky and Bazin a 'conviction' that film does not merely represent or describe reality, but imposes it in its presence.[25] In response to this, working with the idea, yet dissatisfied with the notion that film simply *is* reality, Cavell asks questions about what relation film bears to the world and to us as spectators or viewers of film:[26] 'What Panofksy and Bazin have in mind is that the basis of the medium of movies is photographic, and that a photograph is *of* reality or nature. If to this we add that the medium is one in which the photographic image is projected and gathered on a screen, our question becomes "What happens to reality when it is projected and screened?" '[27] Cavell discerns a specific logic in the relation between painting and photography, contrary to the usual thesis whereby the latter 'defeated' the former on the terrain of realism: while, with Manet, for example 'painting [...] was *forced* to forgo likeness exactly because of its own obsession with reality, because the illusions it had learned to create did not provide the conviction in reality, the connection with reality, that it craved', photography satisfied the desire of painting for reality by removing subjectivity from the equation.[28] What photography offered was reality without a subject. Cavell puts it like this:

> It could be said further that what painting wanted, in wanting connection with reality, was a sense of *presentness* — not exactly a conviction of the world's presence to us, but of our presence to it. At some point the unhinging of our consciousness from the world interposed our subjectivity between us and our presentness to the world. Then our subjectivity became what is present to us, individuality became isolation. The route to conviction in reality was through the acknowledgment of that endless presence of self.[29]

What Cavell describes is a world in which subjectivity has become a problem, because of an estrangement that separates it from the world and redirects its focus inwardly. Subjectivity gets in the way, so to speak, of a connection to the external world. The solution is to remove the subject, and to present a reality to the subject, but from and in which the subject is excluded. The means to this end is found in the *automatism* of photography, and by extension of the medium of film:

> Photography overcame subjectivity in a way undreamed of by painting, a way that could not satisfy painting, one which does not so much defeat the act of painting as escape it altogether: by *automatism*, by removing the human agent from the task of reproduction. [...]
>
> To maintain conviction in our connection with reality, to maintain our presentness, painting accepts the recession of the world. Photography maintains the presentness of the world by accepting our absence from it. The reality in a photograph is present to me while I am not present to it, and a world I know, and see, but to which I am nevertheless not present (through no fault of my subjectivity), is a world past.[30]

The automatism of photography thus presents a solution to the problem of conviction in the existence of external reality — the epistemological and existential problem of scepticism — through the substitution of the mechanism of the camera for the look of the subject.

Cavell summarizes and extends the specificity of the medium of film with the concept of the screen:

> The world of a moving picture is screened. The screen is not a support, not like a canvas; there is nothing to support, that way. It holds a projection, as light as light. A screen is a barrier. What does the silver screen screen? It screens me from the world it holds — that is, makes me invisible. And it screens that world from me — that is, screens its existence from me. That the projected world does not exist (now) is its only difference from reality. (There is no feature, or set of features, in which it differs. Existence is not a predicate.) Because it is the field of a photograph, the screen has no frame; that is to say, no border. Its limits are not so much the edges of a given shape as they are the limitations, or capacity, of a container. The screen *is* a frame; the frame is the whole field of the screen — as a frame of film is the whole field of a photograph, like the frame of a loom or a house. In this sense, the screen-frame is a mould, or form.[31]

There are a number of conceptual moves at stake here: the screen 'holds' rather than 'supports' the image, as does the canvas; the projection is layered on it, in a mode of superimposition that does not materially impinge upon it, or does so only barely, Cavell drawing out this ontological improbability of the projected image through the felicitous trope 'as light as light'. But this projected layer is also a 'barrier', a screen which screens, in the sense of excluding; what is excluded is my visibility in this world. If the world of film is 'screened', in the sense of projection, as its viewer I am also screened (out) by it. And a further difference from the world of painting is that the screen has no frame or border; its world is unframed, and thus potentially unlimited; its only other difference from reality lies therefore in its lack of material substance. This provides the basis for an account of film as a form of magic:

> The idea of and wish for the world re-created in its own image was satisfied *at last* by cinema. Bazin calls this the myth of total cinema. [...] What is cinema's way of satisfying the myth? Automatically, we said. But what does that mean — mean mythically, as it were? It means satisfying it without *my* having to do anything, satisfying it *by* wishing. In a word, *magically*. [...] How do movies reproduce the world magically? Not by literally presenting us with the world, but by permitting us to view it unseen.[32]

While, as Cavell notes interestingly, film derives in part from the older technology of the magic lantern, the specific effect of this magic is to remove me as subject from the world, to screen me from it, while allowing me to view it. Cinema appears in this light as a fortuitous 'trick of light', which provides a kind of solution to the problem of scepticism:

> I have spoken of film as satisfying the wish for the magical reproduction of the world by enabling us to view it unseen. What we wish to see in this way is the world itself — that is to say, everything. Nothing less than that is what modern philosophy has told us (whether for Kant's reasons, or for Locke's, or Hume's) is metaphysically beyond our reach or (as Hegel, Marx or Kierkegaard or Nietzsche might rather put it) beyond our reach metaphysically.
>
> To say that we wish to view the world itself is to say that we are wishing for the condition of viewing as such. That is our way of establishing our connection with the world: through viewing it, or having views of it. Our condition has become one in which our natural mode of perception is to view, feeling unseen. We do not so much look at the world as look *out at* it, from behind the self.[33]

I see the existential and moral condition of being able to 'look out at the world, as if from behind the self' as expressing a tendency or a desire of Proust's narrator, or at least a form of solution to the problems caused by his own desiring projections on the world and the form of existential scepticism that relates to that situation. The 'as if' in Cavell's phrase is the expression of a desire; it is the magical element of the mode of being which conjurs, by means of a wish, a world from which the self is absent. This gives us a picture of the novel as determined by a 'desire for cinema', a quasi-magical desire to view a world outside the interventions of the subject and beyond the intrusions of the 'throbbing heart'. To the extent that the *Recherche* is a novel, not a film, this desire remains unsatisfied. It is in the negotiations between the projective self and the more dispassionate observer of a variegated world that Proust's fiction derives its richness and its multiplicity. The desire may also be resisted, insofar as the narrator (and the reader) gain a degree of ontological security, and perhaps of pleasure, from the self's own investments. At the outset, in the magic lantern episode of *Combray*, the projected world is something that intrudes, and provokes anxiety, but the desire for cinema, for a viewed world from which the self is excluded, nevertheless impinges in later episodes, and especially in episodes associated with homosexuality and sexual cruelty. I will endeavour in what follows to trace these motifs through close readings of the magic lantern episode and the 'cinema of Montjouvain'.

'... ces brillantes projections'

In *Death 24x a Second*, an extended meditation on stillness in the cinema, Laura Mulvey identifies the two dominant technological strands whose confluence leads to the birth of the cinema in 1895 as the camera obscura and the species of optical instruments of which the magic lantern is an example. The opening of Proust's novel, posterior in its composition to cinema's birth but anterior to it or coincident with it, one might suppose, in the fictional moment it narrates, brings both elements together, enabling us to read the novel in hindsight as an investigation into cinema's prehistory. If, as I have suggested, the opening of the novel conjures a thematics of the room and of reverie which elaborates a phenomenology which parallels but alters the model of the camera obscura and the subject supposed by it, the magic lantern is the catalyst for an exploration of the theme of light and projection which constitutes one of the most consistently powerful thematic threads of the novel.

Like the camera obscura, the magic lantern or 'lantern of fear', first recorded in the seventeenth century, has a long history which reaches back beyond its prevalence as a luxury consumer object in the mid- to late nineteenth century. Laurent Mannoni has traced the complex traffic of the device between scientific or pseudo-scientific contexts, and those closer to the realm of the 'cabinet of curiosities' and fairground or travelling entertainment.[34] The *magic* of the instrument meant that it was particularly oriented towards its marketing and dissemination as a children's toy or nursery entertainment, a development which came to the fore in the nineteenth century. The slides which were slotted into the projector were hand-painted, and on a necessarily small scale, whence a predilection for images of a relatively simplistic nature such as fairy tales or shorter narratives not requiring extensive manipulation of the machine. In the late nineteenth century magic lanterns destined for nurseries or children's bedrooms were in fairly extensive production, by firms such as Lapierre. Slides for projection in the devices would include scenes from the history of France, nursery tales or legends, uncomplicated narratives which lent themselves to the medium. An example of a series of slides, made by Lapierre, depicting the story of Geneviève de Brabant and Golo is held at the Cinémathèque française.[35] The narrative consists of a set of six slides with two panels each, showing key moments in the tale; to set them side by side or alongside one another is to create something that approximates to the *bande dessinée* or comic strip.

Historical accounts of the magic lantern, as well as some of the more biographically-oriented critical works on Proust have often identified the Lapierre slides as those viewed by the young Marcel Proust in his childhood.[36] The magic lantern and its slides, however, are textual rather than material objects. I will argue that as a textual object the magic lantern has a far more complex and indeed productive role in the novel than a straightforward historical or biographical incidence might suggest. The device and its projection instantiate a series of critical tensions — between stillness and movement (the projection is described as in motion while it is in fact still, or barely moving), around the nature of projected light and of coloured light, around narrative, and around the border or frame of the slide. The magic lantern operates, perhaps above all, as a metaphorical device; its incidence in Proust's novel thus exceeds the limits of a material history of pre-cinema, and opens questions relative to the conceptual elements which cinema brings into play, particularly around the question of projection.

The magic lantern adds to the indexical capacities of the camera obscura the operation and the poetics of projection, but also of narrative. One of the most powerful characteristics of the magic lantern is the capacity to tell a story with images, and its narrative function is to this extent also present in stained glass, in certain modes of painting, and in animated film. The magic lantern's potential for narrative and projection (understood both in terms of light and in terms of the dynamics of the psyche) will be crucial for Proust's deployment of the apparatus. It is the sequential and narrated story of Golo and Geneviève de Brabant projected onto the surfaces of his bedroom and commented (invisibly) by his great aunt which, somewhat traumatically, disengages the consciousness of the narrator from a kind of habitual continuity sunk into the environment, mediates the exterior world, and reveals it to a look and to interpretation. The magic lantern mediates the world in a specific way, however, insofar as the visual surfaces of the room, brought to life through the superimposition upon them of the evanescent and trembling colours of the magic lantern slides, are seen now through a narrative sequence in which the key motif is sexual violence: Golo's attempted seduction and abduction of Geneviève. Through this well-intentioned intrusion of the projected narrative into the interior space of his room the world is coloured by sadism; the terms of desire and of aggression are introduced into it. The magic lantern, known throughout history for its diabolical associations, is thus the symptom of a condensation of two motifs: the projection of a luminous world, and an interpretative structure determined by sexual desire and aggression.

I will argue in this light that the initial magic lantern sequence in *Combray* is a primitive or primal scene of a kind, insofar as it conditions and structures the narrator's relations to things and to people thereafter. To this extent it operates in a mode akin to Lacan's mirror stage. A key stage in the formation of the speaking subject, the mirror stage is, however, more important in terms of the formation of the visual field and of a seeing subject; insofar as Lacan construes it as affording the infant the capacity to (mis)recognize him or herself in an (ideal) image, as held together and as a kind of orthopedic scaffolding for subjectivity, the mirror stage functions, Lacan writes, as 'le seuil du monde visible' ('the threshold of the visible world').[37] This implies that the image of the world, of the things and people in it, is possible only on the basis of this scene of recognition. To think of Proust's magic lantern sequence in these terms is to propose that the visual field, in the *Recherche*, is conditioned not only by the factors of still but sequential images of projected coloured light and the instability of the projected images on the variegated surfaces of the narrator's bedroom, but also by the specific content of the story told in the slides.

If the mirror, in Lacan's schema, has a very evident theoretical status, its materiality is ambivalent; the mirror stage is not necessarily a real event. In the *Recherche*, however, the magic lantern in the narrator's bedroom is both real *and* theoretical, real and actual in the sense that what is described is a specific event in the narrator's childhood, and theoretical in the sense that the scene is endowed with a metaphorical status which will generate a number of further references in the novel, all of which are metaphorical, or virtual, rather than actual. This is to suggest that the magic lantern is the (material) basis for a *theory* of projection and of the kinds of seeing and looking associated with it. The magic lantern as theory and as metaphor has a far more powerful role in the novel than the biographical story would or could account for.

This is the first magic lantern sequence in *Combray* in its entirety:

> À Combray, tous les jours dès la fin de l'après-midi, longtemps avant le moment où il faudrait me mettre au lit et rester, sans dormir, loin de ma mère et de ma grand-mère, ma chambre à coucher redevenait le point fixe et douloureux de mes préoccupations. On avait bien inventé, pour me distraire les soirs où on me trouvait l'air trop malheureux, de me donner une lanterne magique, dont, en attendant l'heure du dîner, on coiffait ma lampe; et, à l'instar des premiers architectes et maîtres verriers de l'âge gothique, elle substituait à l'opacité des murs d'impalpables irisations, de surnaturelles apparitions multicolores, où des légendes étaient dépeintes comme dans un vitrail vacillant et momentané. Mais ma tristesse n'en était qu'accrue, parce que rien que le changement d'éclairage détruisait l'habitude que j'avais de ma chambre et grâce à quoi, sauf le supplice du coucher, elle m'était devenue supportable. Maintenant je ne la reconnaissais plus et j'y étais inquiet, comme dans une chambre d'hôtel ou de 'chalet', où je fusse arrivé pour la première fois en descendant de chemin de fer.
>
> Au pas saccadé de son cheval, Golo, plein d'un affreux dessein, sortait de la petite forêt triangulaire qui veloutait d'un vert sombre la pente d'une colline, et s'avançait en tressautant vers le château de la pauvre Geneviève de Brabant. Ce château était coupé selon une ligne courbe qui n'était autre que la limite d'un des ovales de verre ménagés dans le châssis qu'on glissait entre les coulisses de la lanterne. Ce n'était qu'un pan de château et il avait devant lui une lande où rêvait Geneviève qui portait une ceinture bleue. Le château et la lande étaient jaunes et je n'avais pas attendu de les voir pour connaître leur couleur car, avant les verres du châssis, la sonorité mordorée du nom de Brabant me l'avait montrée avec évidence. Golo s'arrêtait un instant pour écouter avec tristesse le boniment lu à haute voix par ma grand-tante et qu'il avait l'air de comprendre parfaitement, conformant son attitude, avec une docilité qui n'excluait pas une certaine majesté, aux indications du texte; puis il s'éloignait du même pas saccadé. Et rien ne pouvait arrêter sa lente chevauchée. Si on bougeait la lanterne, je distinguais le cheval de Golo qui continuait à s'avancer sur les rideaux de la fenêtre, se bombant de leurs plis, descendant dans leurs fentes. Le corps de Golo lui-même, d'une essence aussi surnaturelle que celui de sa monture, s'arrangeait de tout obstacle matériel, de tout objet gênant qu'il rencontrait en le prenant comme ossature et en se le rendant intérieur, fût-ce le bouton de la porte sur lequel s'adaptait aussitôt et surnageait invinciblement sa robe rouge ou sa figure pâle toujours aussi noble et aussi mélancolique, mais qui ne laissait paraître aucun trouble de cette transvertébration.
>
> Certes je leur trouvais du charme à ces brillantes projections qui semblaient émaner d'un passé mérovingien et promenaient autour de moi des reflets d'histoire si anciens. Mais je ne peux dire quel malaise me causait pourtant cette intrusion du mystère et de la beauté dans une chambre que j'avais fini par

remplir de mon moi au point de ne pas faire plus attention à elle qu'à lui-même. L'influence anesthésiante de l'habitude ayant cessé, je me mettais à penser, à sentir, choses si tristes. Ce bouton de la porte de ma chambre, qui différait pour moi de tous les autres boutons de porte du monde en ceci qu'il semblait ouvrir tout seul, sans que j'eusse besoin de le tourner, tant le maniement m'en était devenu inconscient, le voilà qui servait maintenant de corps astral à Golo. Et dès qu'on sonnait le dîner, j'avais hâte de courir à la salle à manger où la grosse lampe de la suspension, ignorante de Golo et de Barbe-Bleue, et qui connaissait mes parents et le bœuf à la casserole, donnait sa lumière de tous les soirs; et de tomber dans les bras de maman que les malheurs de Geneviève de Brabant me rendaient plus chère, tandis que les crimes de Golo me faisaient examiner ma propre conscience avec plus de scrupules. (I, 9–10)

[At Combray, every day beginning in the late afternoon, long before the moment when I would have to go to bed and stay there, without sleeping, far away from my mother and grandmother, my bedroom again became the fixed and painful focus of my preoccupations. They had indeed hit upon the idea, to distract me on the evenings when they found me looking too unhappy, of giving me a magic lantern, which, while awaiting the dinner hour, they would set on top of my lamp; and, after the fashion of the first architects and master glaziers of the Gothic age, it replaced the opacity of the walls with impalpable iridescences, supernatural multicoloured apparitions, where legends were depicted as in a wavering, momentary stained-glass window. But my sadness was only increased by this, because the mere change in lighting destroyed the familiarity my bedroom had acquired for me and which, except for the torment of going to bed, had made it tolerable to me. Now I no longer recognized it and I was uneasy there, a in a room in some hotel or 'chalet' to which I had come for the first time straight from the railway train.

Moving at the jerky pace of his horse, Golo, filled with a hideous design, came out of the small triangular forest that velveted the hillside with dark green and advanced jolting towards the castle of poor Geneviève de Brabant. This castle was cut off along a curved line that was in fact the edge of one of the glass ovals arranged in the frame that you slipped between the grooves of the lantern. It was only a section of castle and it had a moor in front of it where Geneviève stood dreaming, wearing a blue belt. The castle and the moor were yellow, and I had not had to wait to see them to find out their colour since, before the glasses of the frame did so, the bronze sonority of the name Brabant had shown it to me clearly. Golo stopped for a moment to listen sadly to the patter read out loud by my great aunt, which he seemed to understand perfectly, conforming his posture, with a meekness that did not exclude a certain majesty, to the directions of the text; then he moved off at the same jerky pace. And nothing could stop his slow ride. If the lantern was moved, I could make out Golo's horse continuing to advance over the window curtains, swelling out with their folds, descending into their fissures. The body of Golo himself, in its essence as supernatural as that of his mount, accommodated every material obstacle, every hindersome object that he encountered by taking it as his skeleton and absorbing it into himself, even the doorknob he immediately adapted to and floated invincibly over with his red robe or his pale face as noble and as melancholy as ever, but revealing no disturbance at this transvertebration.

Certainly I found some charm in these brilliant projections, which seemed to emanate from a Merovingian past and send out around me such ancient reflections of history. But I cannot express the uneasiness caused in me by this intrusion of mystery and beauty into a room I had at last filled with my self to the point of paying no more attention to the room than to that self. The anaesthetizing effect or habit having ceased, I would start to have thoughts, and feelings, and they are such sad things. The doorknob of my room, which differed for me from all other doorknobs in the world in that it seemed to open of its own accord, without my having to turn it, so unconscious had its handling become for me, was now serving as an astral body for Golo. And as soon as they rang for dinner, I hastened to run to the dining-room where the big hanging lamp, ignorant of Golo and Bluebeard, and well acquainted with my family and beef casserole, shed the same light as on every other evening; and to fall into the arms of Mama, whom Geneviève de Brabant's misfortune made all the dearer to me, while Golo's crimes drove me to examine my own conscience more scrupulously. (I, 13–14)

In keeping with its historical role, the magic lantern is introduced as a distraction intended to alleviate the anxiety the narrator feels due to the absence of his mother or grandmother, but, as the narrator tells us, it only serves to accentuate the anxiety through its disturbance of the familiar space of his room. Anxiety, in other words, is primordial — it is a fundamental anxiety in relation to the world, a radical insecurity of the self, which necessitates the analgesic of maternal presence; but then the absence of this presence intensifies the anxiety, for which the projection is intended as a calmative, but which only exacerbates it further, by disturbing a minimal layer of environmental security, the room. Habit has enabled the narrator to occupy his room without occupying it, so to speak, so much have its attributes become attuned to his thoughts and movements. The magic lantern's projection intervenes, as an immaterial layer placed against its variegated surfaces, in order to disengage the narrator's consciousness from this form of automatism. It has an ambivalent value; on the one hand it only intensifies the narrator's 'suffering' ('tristesse') by disturbing the already secondary analgesic of familiarity; on the other hand, it provokes him to think: 'L'influence anesthésiante de l'habitude ayant cessé, je me mettais à penser, à sentir, choses si tristes'. The syntax here, the comma in front of 'choses' and the absence of the partitive article ('des') ambivalently proposes that it is the disturbance caused by the projection which has provoked the narrator, not to think sad things, but simply to feel and to think, activities which are in themselves painful. The inference is that prior to its introduction, the narrator was so anesthetized as to be neither thinking or feeling; indeed the lack of consciousness of the doorknob — the door seems to open by itself prior to the layering of Golo's 'astral' body upon it — is a symptom of this. Why are feeling and thinking sad things, in themselves?

Perhaps because they involve the positing of an object, and the concurrent loss of continuity with that object, a loss of maternal presence. The projection thus introduces the narrator to a world of objects, of things and thoughts. It functions as the 'threshold of the visible world' insofar as it is a condition of visibility, and it will to this extent mediate the narrator's relation to the world henceforth.

But what *is* Proust's magic lantern? To ask this question of the device in Combray is, as I have suggested above, not the same as to ask it in the context of the history and chronology of optical devices. Proust's magic lantern is a composite, imaginary object; its importance is symbolic rather than material. We can nevertheless draw from the text the key conditions of its projection, and begin to reconstitute it materially within the context of the fiction. We can note that it is placed on top of the lamp ('dont [...] on coiffait ma lampe'). It is thus a relatively primitive version of the device; more advanced versions comprised their own light source. But we should perhaps understand 'relatively primitive' here in a conceptual as well as a literal sense; it is as if Proust intends to introduce his narrative and inaugurate the narrator's suffering consciousness through an explicitly regressed or regressive form of cinema, a reduction of its apparatus to the pure form of projection.[38] We will have occasion to underline further on that this is not a *moving* image. It is not strictly true, then, as Jean-François Chevrier has proposed, that the novel 'begins' with cinema, to lead back through the various stages of the photographic process, unless we are to think of cinema as defined by the particularly narrow criterion of the projection of an image, which would be to deny the specificity of the medium; the novel begins with a scene from the *infancy* of cinema.[39]

The metaphor that follows the introduction of the device is particularly elaborate: in the same way that Gothic architects and glaziers substituted the immaterial scenes of stained glass windows for the opaque walls of churches and cathedrals, the magic lantern layers the walls of the narrator's bedroom with its 'supernatural' and 'multicoloured' 'apparitions'. The metaphor is troubled, since, while the projections are 'like' the stained glass windows of old, the magic lantern's slides are also made of glass, and correspond in their manufacture and in their form to the illuminated glass window, the 'vitrail' (we can recall the use of this term to refer to the unfolded section of Odette's letter to Forcheville). The metaphor is undermined by a metonymy, producing a degree of confusion over the nature of the object and the immateriality, or not, of the image. The final part of the extended simile is also complex, but it does serve to draw us away from the domain of architecture and glass and towards that of the immaterial projected image: 'comme dans un vitrail vacillant et momentané'. The projected image is like a momentary and 'vacillating' (trembling, evanescent) stained glass window. Proust draws out the narrative, 'supernatural', transparent, and multicoloured characteristics from stained glass and supplements them here with the transience and immateriality of the projected image. The projection is presumably 'vacillating' because the variegated surface upon which it is projected does not quite hold it, as would a blank cinema screen. There is an uncertain negotiation between the surface and the image projected upon it. The 'trembling' of the projected image, 'as light as light' in Cavell's sense, suggests that the conditions of this primitive cinema are fragile, barely sustainable. As André Benhaïm has suggested, Proust's relation to the cinema is regressive; he moves back from it towards its antecedents. François Bon has also proposed that while Proust might have easily taken the step that led from the magic lantern to cinema, he in fact moves in the opposite direction. This much is clear here, in the shift from the technology of the magic lantern (and a relatively 'primitive' version of it moreover) back to the technology of stained glass.[40]

One might suppose a radical difference between the still images of stained glass windows, comic strips, and magic lanterns, and the moving images produced by the cinematograph. The movement of the former, one might say, is on the side of the spectator, whereas with cinema it is *in* the image. Materially, however, the difference is not fundamental, but one of degree. Both the first series — stained glass, comic strip, magic lantern slides — and the strip of film propose a series of framed, sequential images; movement lies in the passage *between* one frame and the next, one slide and the next.[41] Movement is construed here in terms of sequentiality, and the key difference, a difference of degree, is that of speed, the speed of projection and of reception of the sequence. The radical difference introduced by the cinema, underlined by Cavell and by Deleuze, is that the photogrammatic strip of film is a sequence of *automatic* images, 'any instants whatsoever', as opposed to the representative instant chosen and fixed by the first series of forms.[42] In the (hypothetical) regression from cinema to magic lantern, and from magic lantern to stained glass, Proust subtracts automatism from the image, and isolates the qualities of narrative sequentiality and evanescent, coloured projection.

In the eleventh paragraph of the *Recherche*, beginning 'Au pas saccadé de son cheval', the tense shifts from the imperfect to the past historic, marking a shift from the mood of habitual action and generalized pastness to the temporality of narrative acts and events. From the retrospective perception of the adult narrator remembering his childhood, the focalization shifts to that of the storyteller, in this instance the great aunt, and the narratee, in this instance the child. The reader becomes the witness to the storytelling which accompanies the projection of the slides of the magic lantern. It is the sequential character, the great aunt's narration, and the child's reception of this narration, which invests the still images of Golo and Geneviève with the movement and gestural quality required by the narrative, supported by the voice-over. Or rather, the images of the frames of the lantern are adapted into the narrative of emotions and affects narrated by the great aunt and received by the child. Thus Golo is 'seen' to stop suddenly to listen to the great aunt's 'babble' and then to move on with a haughty air. The 'pas saccadé' of Golo's horse, and his 'jerky' ('tressautant') progress are not the inherent qualities of a moving image but qualities of the narrator's affective response to the still image, a still image, moreover, whose relation to the background or screen onto which it is projected is constitutively unstable. The affective mobility of the image is thus determined by its immaterial status, by the extent to which the projection can fix and hold the relation between projected light and the surfaces of the world onto which it is projected. This surface, unlike a cinema screen, is not blank, but the site of a complex negotiation between background and foreground, the site of a superimposition.

Golo's sexual aggressivity and his forward movement are textually co-dependent. He is the grammatical subject of a series of verbs of action — 'sortait', 's'avancait', 's'arretait', 's'éloignait', 'continuait' — generated both syntactically and affectively by the 'affreux dessein' which he has contrived, which literally and textually motivates him. The sense that his advance towards the hapless Geneviève is unstoppable is, I would suggest, justified at a number of levels; certainly it is inexorable because of the narrator's affective response to it, one of expectation and fear. Golo is also unstoppable precisely because he is still; he will forever be advancing or retreating from the castle. But Golo is also unstoppable precisely because of his immateriality; here the lantern's operator, potentially the narrator himself, intervenes ('si l'on bougeait la lanterne'), to shift the projection onto a different surface, from curtains to doorknob, for example. Golo can be made to move, in other words, and can overcome any of the obstacles that the background surface proposes. Golo's 'transvertebration' is a form of magic whereby a body can overcome ('sans aucun trouble') the impedence of the real, material surface, precisely by becoming immaterial, becoming projection.[43] The immaterial will almost always win out over the material; Golo's image will *eat* the surface on which it is projected, by making it interior to himself ('en se le rendant intérieur').

Moreover, Golo's purposeful forward movement enables, or perhaps obliges, the narrator's identification with him, while Geneviève remains very much the passive victim of his nefarious design. For the narrator Golo provides the model and the embodiment, paradoxically, of a mode of desire which incorporates its objects, and incorporates them moreover by means of a projection of ideas or images upon them, which makes them interior to it. The capacity to take on the structure ('ossature') of the material object, and to interiorize it, defines, and will determine the kind of desiring projective identifications the narrator will operate on things and persons throughout the novel, even if the operation will sometimes fail as we have observed above. The incorporative nature of these projections, which practice upon objects and things what Bersani has called the 'happy' version of desire, is also suggested in this passage by the way the syllabic 'bite' of the name 'Brabant' prepares for the yellow of the castle and the moor. In an essay on Proust and Melanie Klein which we will have occasion to return to in more detail further on in this chapter, Bersani discusses what he calls the 'appetitive metonymies' of desire, or at least of a 'happy' version of desire which moves towards things and people in the world, 'happily transforming them into partial objects' in order to fragment and to consume them.[44] Golo provides an emblem for this mode of desire for the child narrator, a desire which proceeds by incorporating its objects. The 'unhappy' mode of desire, Bersani goes on to suggest, is linked to the 'constitution of persons'.[45] The narrator's troubled identification with Golo is complicated by the guilt that he feels in relation to his mother 'que les malheurs de Geneviève de Brabant me rendaient plus chère', while 'les crimes de Golo me faisaient examiner ma propre conscience avec plus de scrupules'. The anxiety associated with the existence of objects, of others, as persons, comes into being with the emergence of the conscience, of the consciousness of a guilt concerning the previous attacks upon them, and, in Kleinian terms, a need to make reparation. The doorknob, in this schema, has a role akin to the transitional object described by Winnicott which I alluded to in Chapter 1; a substitute of a kind for the familiarity of and continuity with the mother, it now serves as the 'astral body' for Golo, which has 'swallowed' it, so to speak. Projective incorporation involves the loss of the original body.

The oscillation between the doorknob as doorknob, and the doorknob as 'ossature' or 'astral body' for Golo establishes the space between projection and surface that is explored throughout the novel. In fact, there are three versions of the doorknob — the one which is strangely invisible and impalpable so much had its handling become unconscious to the narrator, the doorknob that provides the 'astral body' for Golo, and the doorknob that emerges as an object by virtue of the projection upon it, as if subtracted from the composite made by this projection. It is as if external and objective reality appears only through the subtraction, and in some instances the failure, of projection, as with the scene in Venice cited earlier. The magic lantern sequence of *Combray*, functioning as I have suggested as the 'threshold of the visible world', constitutes this world around the oscillation or *vacillement* between a projected image and a material surface, while bringing the latter to light only, it seems, through the failure or subtraction of projection.

Unknown Colours

Reference to the magic lantern beyond the initial scene of the *drame du coucher* occurs a further twelve times in the *Recherche*, more often than not as a specific recollection of the initial projection and the story of Golo and Geneviève de Brabant. This recurrence affords the magic lantern the status of a motif in the novel, of the same order as the garden gate bells of Combray, Vinteuil's compositions, or Sand's *François le Champi*. A reference back to the magic lantern scene and to this story also occurs in the concluding pages of the work, such that it also has a structural, book-ending function. The magic lantern serves moreover to intermittently anchor important scenes of the novel back to this primordial image. In its recurrences the analogical potential of the magic lantern is also developed, altering and adumbrating the conception we might have of it as a kind of cinema, and specifying further the kind of projection at stake.

At the beginning of the second part of *Combray*, as the linear narrative of the *Recherche* starts off, the narrator considers the withdrawal of the streets of the town from his memory, and his distance from it, in terms of colour:

> Et ces rues de Combray existent dans une partie de ma mémoire si reculée, peinte de couleurs si différentes de celles qui maintenant revêtent pour moi le monde, qu'en vérité elles me paraissent toutes, et l'église qui les dominait sur la Place, plus irréelles encore que les projections de la lanterne magique; et qu'à certains moments, il me semble que pouvoir encore traverser la rue Saint-Hilaire, pouvoir louer une chambre rue de l'Oiseau — à la vieille hôtellerie de l'Oiseau Flesché, des soupiraux de laquelle montait une odeur de cuisine qui s'élève encore par moments en moi aussi intermittente et aussi chaude — serait une entrée en contact avec l'Au-delà plus merveilleusement surnaturelle que de faire la connaissance de Golo et de causer avec Geneviève de Brabant. (I, 48)

> [And these streets of Combray exist in a part of my memory so withdrawn, painted in colours so different from those that now coat the world for me, that in truth all of them, and also the church that rose above them on the Square, appear to me more unreal even than the projections of the magic lantern; and that at certain moments, it seems to me that to be able to cross the rue Saint-

Hilaire again, to be able to take a room in the rue de l'Oiseau — at the old Hôtellerie de l'Oiseau Flesché, from whose basement windows rose a smell of cooking that now and then still rises in me as intermittently and as warmly — would be now to enter into contact with the Beyond in a manner more marvellously supernatural than making the acquaintance of Golo or chatting with Geneviève de Brabant.] (I, 51–52)

The narrator establishes a marked difference between the colours with which the world of the present, the perceived world, is 'dressed', and those that his memory paints onto the streets of the town, so far back in his memory. These colours are 'as unreal' as those of the magic lantern's projections, such that to cross those streets, to inhabit the town now, would be like entering into the supernatural world of Golo and Geneviève de Brabant. Distant memory, childhood memory, in other words, has a supernaturalizing effect; its colours are unreal; the distant past merges with the material of the fairy tale.

In a further recurrence in *Combray* the magic lantern is one of a series of phantasmatic and aestheticized representations of the Guermantes, who, although he knows they are 'real and actually existing persons' the narrator has not yet managed to encounter, not yet having ventured far enough 'du côté de Guermantes':

Jamais non plus nous ne pûmes pousser jusqu'au terme que j'eusse tant souhaité d'atteindre, jusqu'à Guermantes. Je savais que là résidaient des châtelains, le duc et la duchesse de Guermantes. Je savais qu'ils étaient des personnages réels et actuellement existants. Mais chaque fois que je pensais à eux, je me les représentais tantôt en tapisserie, comme était la comtesse de Guermantes, dans le *Couronnement d'Esther* de notre église, tantôt de nuances changeantes comme était Gilbert le Mauvais dans le vitrail où il passait du vert chou au bleu prune selon que j'étais encore à prendre de l'eau bénite ou que j'arrivais à nos chaises, tantôt tout à fait impalpables comme l'image de Geneviève de Brabant, ancêtre de la famille de Guermantes, que la lanterne magique promenait sur les rideaux de ma chambre ou faisait monter au plafond, — enfin toujours enveloppés du mystère des temps mérovingiens et baignant comme dans un coucher de soleil dans la lumière orangée qui émane de cette syllabe: 'antes'. (I, 169–70)

[Never, either, could we go all the way to the end-point that I would have liked so much to reach, all the way to Guermantes. I knew this was where the castellans, the Duc and Duchesse de Guermantes, lived, I knew they were real and presently existing figures, but when I thought about them, I pictured them to myself sometimes made of tapestry, like the Comtesse de Guermantes in our church's *Coronation of Esther*, sometimes in changing colours, like Gilbert the Bad in the stained-glass window where he turned from cabbage green to plum blue, depending on whether I was still in front of the holy water or was reaching our seats, sometimes completely impalpable like the image of Geneviève de Brabant, ancestor of the Guermantes family, which our magic lantern walked out over the curtains of my room or up to the ceiling — but always wrapped in the mystery of Merovingian times and bathing as though in a sunset in the orange light emanating from that syllable: 'antes'.] (I, 172)

The Guermantes are an image, a representation 'projected' from a tapestry, a stained glass window, the magic lantern's slides, and by the final syllable of their name, all of these associated with the half-historical, half-legendary 'Merovingian' times. The listing of these different forms creates associations between them, and may be seen to follow a gradation in terms of materiality — from the tapestry through stained glass, to the 'impalpable' projection, to the golden-orange colouring effect of the name. Forms of projection, the capacity of a syllable, for example, to provoke an enveloping coloration, are widened out beyond the simply optical dimension, casting the magic lantern as one among other forms of magical thinking. The link between the magic lantern and stained glass has of course already been prepared in the first scene, where the projected images were associated with the volatile, flickering image created by a shaft of light passing through the coloured glass; here the reference is to the glass itself, yet its materiality and fixity is already compromised by the shifting nuances of Gilbert the Bad's colour — from cabbage green to plum blue — that obtain when the narrator moves position. Colour seems to intervene here between the thing and the percieving subject.

In *À l'ombre des jeunes filles en fleurs*, in his picnic excursions with the 'petite bande', the narrator prefers sumptuous cakes to sandwiches, about which he has nothing to say: 'Mais les gâteaux étaient instruits, les tartes étaient bavardes' ('Whereas the cakes were privy to much, and tarts were talkative') (II, 257; 2, 481). Quite apart from their 'Gothic' construction and the memories they bring of Combray and Gilberte, the cakes remind him of certain illustrated dessert plates owned by his great aunt, with images from the Thousand and One Nights, Aladdin and his Lamp, Ali Baba, or Sinbad the Sailor. The 'vulgar' dessert plates have been lost, but, the narrator adds:

> Dans le gris et champenois Combray elles et leurs vignettes s'encastraient multicolores, comme dans la noire Eglise les vitraux aux mouvantes pierreries, comme dans le crépuscule de ma chambre les projections de la lanterne magique, comme devant la vue de la gare et du chemin de fer départemental les boutons d'or des Indes et les lilas de Perse, comme la collection de vieux Chine de ma grand-tante dans sa sombre demeure de vieille dame de province. (II, 258)

> [Their multicolured vignettes glowed among the greyness of Combray-in-Champagne, like the shimmer of the jewelled windows in the dark of its church, the illuminations from the magic lantern in the twilight of my bedroom, the buttercups from the Indies and the lilacs from Persia in the foreground of the view of the railway-station and the little local line, or the collection of old Chinese porcelain at my great aunt's, an old lady's gloomy house in a country town.] (2, 481)

Proust imposes another series of images — illustrated crockery, stained glass windows (again), the magic lantern projections, the flowers in the foreground of the view of the station, or his great aunt's porcelain collection. Irrespective of the association with more banal, clichéd forms, the magic lantern's images are proposed as a form of coloured 'insertion' into the crepuscular darkness of his room of the same order as the illustrated plates in the greyness of Combray. What Proust describes, what he provokes through the verb *s'encastrer* is akin to the 'étroite section lumineuse' discussed earlier, a form of disruptive intrusion, in this instance foregrounded as colour against a grey or dark background. It is not that Combray is grey because it is in the past, and only remembered; at this point the narrator is in Balbec; it is that Combray is, in fact, a predominantly dull, stone-grey provincial town. Grey is the colour of the present, not of the remembered past, which is written in terms of pulsing colour. Memory is in colour, the present in black and white.

In the seventh recurrence of the magic lantern motif, at the beginning of *Le Côté de Guermantes*, the narrator proposes that the image of Mme de Guermantes had begun to change, having previously been only 'le reflet d'un verre de lanterne magique et d'un vitrail d'église' ('the reflection of a magic-lantern slide and of a stained-glass window'). Significantly, this development, which coincides with his developing acquaintance with the duchesse, is described in terms of a dimunution rather than a development of colour. Having previously been lodged in the coloured glass of the magic lantern's side, the stained glass window and their mobile projections, now the Guermantes image loses colour to become endowed with the whiteness of rushing water : 'l'atmosphère où Mme de Guermantes existait en moi [...] commençait à éteindre ses couleurs, quand des rêves tout autres l'imprégnèrent de l'écumeuse humidité des torrents' ('this is how the atmosphere surrounding Mme de Guermantes [...] began to lose its colours when quite different dreams impregnated it with the bubbling water of fast-flowing streams') (II, 311; 3, 9).

Absent from the concerns of *Sodome et Gomorrhe*, in the Albertine volumes the original magic lantern scene from *Combray* seems to lose some of its purchase, and the device, or its metaphorical avatar, attains a wider projective capacity. When she is not playing the music of Vinteuil, Albertine's performances at the pianola project different images on the walls of his room in Paris:

> Ce n'était pas, du reste, que de la musique de lui que me jouait Albertine; le pianola était par moments pour nous comme une lanterne magique scientifique (historique et géographique), et sur les murs de cette chambre de Paris, pourvue d'inventions plus modernes que celle de Combray, je voyais, selon qu'Albertine jouait du Rameau ou du Borodine, s'étendre tantôt une tapisserie du xviiiᵉ siècle semée d'Amours sur un fond de roses, tantôt la steppe orientale où les sonorités s'étouffent dans l'illimité des distances et le feutrage de la neige. (III, 884)

> [In any case, it was not only his music that Albertine played for me; the pianola sometimes served us as a kind of educational (historical and geographical) magic lantern, and on the walls of that room in Paris, better equipped than the old one in Combray, I saw spread out, according as Albertine played some Rameau or some Borodin, now an eighteenth-century tapestry dotted with cherubs on a background of roses, and now the Eastern steppes where sounds are lost in the limitless distances and muffled by the snow.] (5, 353)

Loosened from the grip of the childhood memory, the magic lantern stands here for the translation of sounds, or music, into immaterial visual forms, albeit virtual ones. There is a shift from the subjective, interior space of the child's bedroom to a geographically and historically extended exterior space; the metaphorical magic lantern is in this instance a scientific technology rather than a children's toy, both of these attributes pertaining to its ambivalent origins in magical entertainment and the history of optics. The room in Paris seems to belong, moreover, to a wholly different historical era, closer to modernity and to its inventions, as distinct from the archaic past of the room in Combray. These are nevertheless transient, merely decorative images, as the narrator adds:

> Ces décorations fugitives étaient, d'ailleurs, les seules de ma chambre, car si, au moment où j'avais hérité de ma tante Léonie, je m'étais promis d'avoir des collections comme Swann, d'acheter des tableaux, des statues, tout mon argent passait à avoir des chevaux, une automobile, des toilettes pour Albertine. (III, 884)

> [And these fleeting decorations were in fact the only ones in my room, for, even though when I came into my inheritance from Aunt Léonie I had promised I would be a collector like Swann, buying pictures and statues, in fact all my money went on horses, a motor-car, dresses for Albertine.] (5, 353)

The supposedly neutral pleasures of knowledge and art cannot compete with the voracious need to keep Albertine with him through expenditure on frivolous objects in which he has no investment.

To the extent that the magic lantern scene of Combray operates as the 'threshold of the visible world', or, to put it in terms which relate to Lacan's later theorization of the visual field, as a screen which mediates the subject's relation to it, the *dispositif* of the device is also promoted as a structuring of his memory and of his mode of attention. In *Albertine disparue* the narrator proposes that the multiplicity of different versions of Albertine, which can neutralize or at least appease the pain caused by the image of her lesbianism, is akin to the 'successive forms' projected by the magic lantern:

> Ce qui vint à mon secours contre cette image de la blanchisseuse, ce fut — certes quand elle eut un peu duré — cette image elle-même parce que nous ne connaissons vraiment que ce qui est nouveau, ce qui introduit brusquement dans notre sensibilité un changement de ton qui nous frappe, ce à quoi l'habitude n'a pas encore substitué ses pâles fac-similés. Mais ce fut surtout ces nombreuses Albertines, qui était son seul mode d'existence en moi. Des moments revinrent où elle n'avait été que bonne, ou intelligente, ou sérieuse, ou même aimant plus que tout les sports. Et ce fractionnement, n'était-il pas, au fond, juste qu'il me calmât ? Car s'il n'était pas en lui-même quelque chose de réel, s'il tenait à la forme successive des heures où elle m'était apparue, forme qui restait celle de ma mémoire comme la courbure des projections de ma lanterne magique tenait à la courbure des verres colorés, ne représentait-il pas à sa manière une vérité, bien objective celle-là, à savoir que chacun de nous n'est pas un, mais contient de nombreuses personnes qui n'ont pas toutes la même valeur morale, et que, si l'Albertine vicieuse avait existé, cela n'empêchait pas qu'il y en eût eu d'autres, celle qui aimait à causer avec moi de Saint-Simon dans sa chambre; celle qui, le soir où je lui avais dit qu'il fallait nous séparer, avait dit si tristement: 'Ce pianola, cette chambre, penser que je ne reverrai jamais tout cela' et, quand elle avait vu l'émotion que mon mensonge avait fini par me communiquer, s'était écriée avec une pitié si sincère: 'Oh! non, tout plutôt que de vous faire de la peine, c'est entendu, je ne chercherai pas à vous revoir'. (IV, 110)

> [What I fell back on to help me fight against this image of the laundry-maid, was, admittedly after it had been there for some time, this image itself, because

we only really take cognizance of something which is new, something which abruptly introduces a change of tone that strikes our sensibility, something that habit has not yet replaced with its pale replicas. But it was above all this fracturing of Albertine into many parts, into many Albertines, which constituted her sole mode of existence within me. Moments recurred when she had been nothing but kind, or intelligent, or serious, or even a lover of sport above all. And was it not right that this fragmentation should soothe me? For although in itself it was quite unreal, although it depended on the successive forms of the hours when it appeared to me, forms which remained those of my memory, as the curves in the images projected by the magic lantern depended on the curves of its coloured slides, did it not in its way represent a perfectly objective truth, which is the fact that if the immoral Albertine had indeed existed, this did not preclude the existence of others, like the one who liked to chat about Saint-Simon in her room; the one who, on the evening when I had told her that we should part, had said with such sadness, 'To think that I shall never see this pianola and this room, again' and who, when she had seen what an emotional shock my own deceit had finally given me, had cried in such sincere pity, 'Oh no, anything rather than upset you, I agree, I shall not try to see you again!'.] (5, 495)

His memory of Albertine, or of the multiple versions of her, is held to or determined by the 'successive form' of the moments of his encounters with her, just as the projected images of the magic lantern are framed and contained by the material structure of the coloured glass slides themselves. Memory, Proust seems to suggest here, operates with fixed images; it has a photogrammatic structure, consisting of a series of 'views'. This is promoted as an 'objective truth' — memory is mediated by the framed and flat form of an image, like a screen.

Further on in *Albertine disparue*, in the course of the long and tortuous period of negotiation with the lost yet interiorized Albertine, the narrator comments on the way that his dreams, in which the knowledge of her real death and absence is suppressed, and which pay no attention to the passage of time, give him the somewhat spectral illusion of her real presence. Yet this presence, and his capacity to act in relation to it, to bring it further towards him, are frustrated by the fact that he is dreaming. The magic lantern intervenes again here as a structuring and delimiting *dispositif*:

Parfois, par un défaut d'éclairage intérieur lequel, vicieux, faisait manquer la pièce, mes souvenirs bien mis en scène me donnant l'illusion de la vie, je croyais vraiment avoir donné rendez-vous à Albertine, la retrouver; mais alors je me sentais incapable de marcher vers elle, de proférer les mots que je voulais lui dire, de rallumer pour la voir le flambeau qui s'était éteint — impossibilités qui étaient simplement, dans mon rêve, l'immobilité, le mutisme, la cécité du dormeur — comme brusquement on voit dans la projection manquée d'une lanterne magique une grande ombre, qui devrait être cachée, effacer la silhouette des personnages, et qui est celle de la lanterne elle-même, ou celle de l'opérateur. (IV, 119)

[Sometimes through a flaw in the internal lighting which trecherously made the room disappear, as my carefully staged memories gave me the illusion of real life, I thought that I had really arranged to meet Albertine and had really met her; but then I found myself unable to walk towards her, to utter the words which I wanted to speak, to relight my extinguished lamp in order to see her: impossibilities in my dream which were simply the immobility, the speechlessness and the blindness of the sleeper, just as we may suddenly see in a magic-lantern show a great shadow, which is that of the lantern itself, or its operator, which were meant to be hidden, blotting out the images of the characters which were meant to be projected.] (5, 504)

The analogy equates the dream images with those of the magic lantern, and the fact of dreaming — the immobility and sensory impoverishment of the dreamer — with the mechanism of the lantern itself, the physical object of the device or the shadow cast by its operator. Earlier, in *A l'ombre des jeunes filles en fleurs*, in a parenthesis on the strange logic of dreams, the narrator had established a similar equivalence between the successive nature of dream images and the *dispositif* of the magic lantern:

> Car on dit que nous voyons souvent des animaux en rêve, mais on oublie presque toujours que nous y sommes nous-même un animal privé de cette raison qui projette sur les choses une clarté de certitude; nous n'y offrons au contraire, au spectacle de la vie, qu'une vision douteuse et à chaque minute anéantie par l'oubli, la réalité précédente s'évanouissant devant celle qui lui succède comme une projection de lanterne magique devant la suivante quand on a changé le verre. (II, 177)

> [For it is said we often see animals in our dreams, fogetting that, almost always when we dream, we ourselves are animals deprived of the clarity of certainty shed on all things by our faculty of reason; instead of it, all we can turn on the spectacle of life is an infirm gaze which is abolished by oblivion at every successive moment, each reality no sooner glimpsed than vanishing in the face of the next one, as the slides projected by a magic lantern succeed one another.] (2, 400)

Running counter to the Bergsonian notion of memory as an intuitive flux, Proust promotes the apparatus of the magic lantern to the status of a veritable structuring model for the dreaming consciousness, further confirming the association of the device with archaic, primordial time and vision.

This mode of vision is close to the 'way of seeing' of the painter Elstir, which Proust famously describes as being an extra-rational return to 'la racine même de l'impression' ('the root of our impression') (II, 712; 3, 417), independent of the conceptual classification of the world in terms of words and objects. When the narrator surveys Elstir's paintings in the Hôtel de Guermantes, this proximity is supported by an anology between Elstir's mind or head and the magic lantern, and between his paintings and the projected images:

> Seulement une fois en tête à tête avec les Elstir, j'oubliai tout à fait l'heure du dîner; de nouveau comme à Balbec j'avais devant moi les fragments de ce monde aux couleurs inconnues qui n'était que la projection, la manière de voir particulière à ce grand peintre et que ne traduisaient nullement ses paroles. Les parties du mur couvertes de peintures de lui, toutes homogènes les unes aux autres, étaient comme les images lumineuses d'une lanterne magique laquelle eût été, dans le cas présent, la tête de l'artiste et dont on n'eût pu soupçonner

l'étrangeté tant qu'on n'aurait fait que connaître l'homme, c'est-à-dire tant qu'on n'eût fait que voir la lanterne coiffant la lampe, avant qu'aucun verre coloré eût encore été placé. (II, 712)

[But the moment I was left alone with the Elstirs, I completely forgot about time and dinner; once again, as in Balbec, I had before me fragments of that world of strange new colours, the projection of the great painter's particular vision, which his speech in no way conveyed. The parts of the walls that were covered by his paintings, each of them part of a homogenous whole, were like the luminous images of a magic lantern which, in this instance, was the mind of the artist, the strangeness of which one would never have suspected from simply knowing the man, in other words so long as one had seen only the lantern shielding the lamp before any coloured slide had been inserted.] (3, 417)

Beyond the broader proposition concerning Elstir's mode of vision, what is significant here is the qualification of the paintings as 'fragments de ce monde aux couleurs inconnues'. Like the magic lantern slides, the paintings are fragmented, successive views rather than a fluid, moving image, and they are of unknown colours. The projection Proust conjures here is not a moving image, but a series of fixed views, and its primary characteristic aside from this photogrammatic structure lies in colour.

In the final volume of the *Recherche, Le Temps retrouvé*, as the narrator, waiting in the ante-room of the Hôtel de Guermantes, begins to experience the series of involuntary memories which will prepare the theoretical exposition on time and memory which will lead the novel to its conclusion, the archaic, fairy-tale time of the magic lantern intervenes again, provoked in this instance by the discovery of *François le Champi,* the novel read to him by his mother in his childhood room in *Combray.* The narrator comments that while he might discuss this book or Mme de Guermantes without connecting either to his childhood at Combray, when alone, and in this moment, he can reach or be taken further back:

Mais quand j'étais seul, comme en ce moment, c'est à une profondeur plus grande que j'avais plongé. À ce moment-là l'idée que telle personne dont j'avais fait la connaissance dans le monde était la cousine de Mme de Guermantes, c'est-à-dire d'un personnage de lanterne magique, me semblait incompréhensible, et tout autant que les plus beaux livres que j'avais lus fussent — je ne dis pas même supérieurs, ce qu'ils étaient pourtant — mais égaux à cet extraordinaire *François le Champi.* C'était une impression d'enfance bien ancienne, où mes souvenirs d'enfance et de famille étaient tendrement mêlés et que je n'avais pas reconnue tout de suite. (IV, 462)

[But when I was alone, as at this moment, I was plunged down to a much greater depth. In those moments, the idea that some woman I had met in society was a cousin of Mme de Guermantes, that is, the cousin of a magic-lantern character, seemed incomprehensible, and it seemed equally incomprehensible that the finest books that I had read might be — I do not say better than, which of course they were — but even equal to the extraordinary *François le Champi.* This was an impression from long ago, in which my memories of childhood and family were affectionately mingled and which I had not immediately recognized.] (6, 192)

Significantly, this reference back to the magic lantern projection of Combray, the return of an archaic past, is contrasted with the 'absurdity' of the 'cinematographic' presentation of things. The previous paragraph had closed with the statement : 'Quelques-uns voulaient que le roman fût une sorte de défilé cinématographique des choses. Cette conception était absurde. Rien ne s'éloigne plus de ce que nous avons perçu en réalité qu'une telle vue cinématographique' ('Some even wanted the novel to be a sort of cinematographic stream of things. This was an absurd idea. Nothing was further apart from what we have really perceived than that sort of cinematographic approach') (IV, 462; 6, 191). The linear progression or procession of the cinema is contrasted with the return of the archaic time of childhood and with the procession of memory-images that it can induce. The key word here, I think, is 'défilé', literally 'procession', translated by Ian Patterson as 'stream of things'; Proust's opposition between the procession of the film-strip and the memory image of the magic lantern slide echoes Barthes's impatience and frustration with the 'voraciousness' to which the forward movement of film constrains him, in contrast with the 'pensiveness' allowed and provoked by the photograph and the photogram.[46] Bellour comments that Proust's narrator had felt something of the same impatience when he remarked of the original Combray magic lantern projection that 'rien ne pouvait arrêter sa lente chevauchée' ('nothing could arrest its slow progress') (Bellour erroneously displacing Golo's movement towards Genevieve de Brabant with the notion of the magic lantern's movement).[47] But the 'pensiveness', the latitude for slower, alternative associations, and for anamnesis, the recovery of remembered images, is given by the magic lantern, which slows or stills the progression of the cinematograph in Proust's opposition. In relation to a cinematographic *défilé*, the magic lantern occupies a place 'between-the-images', to use Bellour's expression. Like the photograph or the still *within* the film, in Bellour's seminal essay 'Le Spectateur pensif' [The Pensive Spectator], the magic lantern image 'a ainsi comme effet de décoller le spectateur de l'image [...] Elle arrache le spectateur à cette force peu précise mais prégnante: la moyenne imaginaire du cinéma' ('has the effect of uncoupling the spectator from the image [...] It pulls the spectator out of this imprecise, yet pregnant force: the ordinary imaginary of the cinema').[48]

Why and in what way does it have this effect? I have been proposing that the magic lantern, while proposing a *dispositif* which structures and determines some of the ways of seeing described in the *Recherche*, also represents an archaic, pre-history which will recurrently intervene throughout the novel as a supernaturally coloured projection. It is the image of another time. Its final occurrence in the novel will endow it with another kind of force, one which we may be able to clarify with reference to Deleuze's notion of the time-image. Observing the guests in the 'bal de têtes' of the Guermantes matinee, the narrator sees the extraordinary image of his former nemesis M. d'Argencourt, so transformed by time that he resembles a kind of puppet or doll:

> C'était trop de parler d'un acteur, et, débarrassé qu'il était de toute âme consciente, c'est comme une poupée trépidante, à la barbe postiche de laine blanche, que je le voyais agité, promené dans ce salon, comme dans un guignol

PROUST'S PROJECTIONS 95

à la fois scientifique et philosophique où il servait, comme dans une oraison funèbre ou un cours en Sorbonne, à la fois de rappel à la vanité de tout et d'exemple d'histoire naturelle. Un guignol de poupées que, pour identifier à ceux qu'on avait connus, il fallait lire sur plusieurs plans à la fois, situés derrière elles et qui leur donnaient de la profondeur et forçaient à faire un travail d'esprit quand on avait devant soi ces vieillards fantoches, car on était obligé de les regarder, en même temps qu'avec les yeux, avec la mémoire. Un guignol de poupées baignant dans les couleurs immatérielles des années, de poupées extériorisant le Temps, le Temps qui d'habitude n'est pas visible, qui pour le devenir cherche des corps et, partout où il les rencontre, s'en empare pour montrer sur eux sa lanterne magique. Aussi immatériel que jadis Golo sur le bouton de porte de ma chambre de Combray, ainsi le nouveau et si méconnaissable d'Argencourt était là comme la révélation du Temps, qu'il rendait partiellement visible. Dans les éléments nouveaux qui composaient la figure de M. d'Argencourt et son personnage, on lisait un certain chiffre d'années, on reconnaissait la figure symbolique de la vie, non telle qu'elle nous apparaît, c'est-à-dire permanente, mais réelle, atmosphère si changeante que le fier seigneur s'y peint en caricature, le soir, comme un marchand d'habits. (IV, 502–03)

[In fact to call him an actor would be an overstatement, unencumbered as he was by any kind of conscious spirit, it is more as a jigging puppet, with a beard made of white wool, that I saw him twitched about and walked up and down in the drawing-room, as if he were in a scientific and philosophical puppet-show, in which he served, as in a funeral address or a lecture at the Sorbonne, both as a reminder of the vanity of all things and as a specimen of natural history. Puppets then, but puppets which, if one were to identify them with someone one had known, needed to be read on several levels at once, levels that underlay them and gave them depth and, when faced with one of these old marionettes, forced one to make an intellectual effort, because one was obliged to look at them with the memory at the same time as with the eyes; puppets steeped in the intangible colours of the years, puppets which were an expression of Time, Time which is normally not visible, which seeks out bodies in order to become so and wherever it finds them seizes upon them for its magic lantern show. As intangible as Golo had once been on my bedroom doorknob in Combray, the new, almost unrecognizable d'Argencourt stood there as the revelation of Time, which he rendered partly visible. In the new elements which made up the face and character of M d'Argencourt one could read a certain tally of years, one could recognize the symbolic form of life not as it appears to us, that is as permanent, but in its reality, in such a shifting atmosphere that by evening the proud nobleman is depicted there in caricature, as an old clothes-merchant.] (6, 232–33)

The mode of vision or of reading which the narrator proposes one needs to adopt, in order to see more than the spectacle of ridiculous old men, and to link them to the persons he once knew, is again marked out as successive, multi-layered, 'sur plusieurs plans à la fois'. These other levels of image are positioned as if behind them, somewhat in the manner of the chronophotographic images produced by Marey and Muybridge. This temporal layering of the visual field is immaterial, although the figures do in some way embody or exteriorize time; in order to become visible time captures ('s'empare de') the body. And this mode of capture is proposed as a magic lantern's projection. In Proust's analogy, time becomes visible in the body, or in the image of the body, by means of the magic lantern, as if the successive views, the layered spectres of the body's past, were made optically visible in its rays; the magic lantern makes time visible. The immateriality of the projected image is transferred here to the immateriality of the image of time; the immaterial form of Golo on the doorknob of the Combray bedroom is analogically extended to the temporal form of M. d'Argencourt, in Proust's words to the 'symbolic figure of his life'.

In an essay on Robbe-Grillet published in 1954 Roland Barthes proposes that the author of *Les Gommes* [The Erasers] has revolutionized the literary mode of description; rather than, as in classical description, proposing a scene as a fixed and immobile spectacle, modern description (that of Robbe-Grillet) operates a 'déboîtement' [dislocation] or a spatial 'unlocking' ('déclenchement') which gives the image a kind of serial depth; Barthes writes that 'il devient profond sans cesser d'être plan' ('it assumes dimension without ceasing to be plane'). He adds: 'On reconnaît ici la révolution même que le cinéma a opérée dans le réflexes de la vision' ('We recognize here the same revolution that the cinema has worked upon our visual reflexes').[49] This cinematographic transformation of the spatial conditions of description corresponds to a parallel and consequential dislocation in terms of temporality; Barthes writes:

> Le temps classique ne rencontre jamais l'objet que pour lui étre catastrophe ou délinquesence. Robbe-Grillet donne à ses objets un tout autre type de mutabilité. C'est une mutabilité dont le processus est invisible: un objet, décrit une première fois à un moment du continu romanesque, reparaît plus tard, muni d'une différence à peine perceptible. Cette différence est d'ordre spatial, situationnel [...]. Le temps déboîte l'espace et constitue l'objet comme une suite de tranches qui se recouvrent presque complètement les unes les autres: c'est dans ce 'presque' spatial que gît la dimension temporalle de l'objet. Il s'agit donc d'un type de variation que l'on retrouve grossièrement dans le mouvement des plaques d'une lanterne magique ou des bandes de 'Comics'.

> [Classical time never encounters the object except as catastrophe or delinquescence. Robbe-Grillet gives his objects an entirely different type of mutability. It is a mutability whose process is invisible: an object, first described at a moment of novelistic continuity, reappears later on, endowed with a scarcely perceptible difference. This difference is of a spatial, situational order [...]. Time dislocates space and constitutes the object as a series of slices which almost completely overlap each other: in that spatial 'almost' lies the object's temporal dimension. This is a type of variation which we find in a cruder version in the movement of magic-lantern slides or of animated comic strips.][50]

What Barthes describes here as a temporal 'variation', which he finds in a cruder or broader form in magic lantern slides or in animated images, is a kind of serial sequentiality akin to the chronophotographic images of Marey or Muybridge; the temporal variation lies in the 'almost', the slight dislocation or *décalage* in the object's 'situation' which extends it or gives it a kind of shadow extending in space, a spectral extension or seriality which corresponds to its temporality. In *Le Temps retrouvé*, whose shadow falls over Barthes's account here, to read M. d'Argencourt, or more precisely to read him in terms of the 'symbolic form' of his life, the narrator proposes that he has to read him according to the mode of spatio-temporal dislocation Barthes describes here, as if there were several different versions of him extended 'behind him', on several levels. The difference between the 'almost' exact superimposition of one image onto the other, and the crude sequentiality of the magic lantern slides or *bande dessinée* frames is one of speed; the chronophotographic image speeds up the passage between the successive views proposed by the slides.

In associating Robbe-Grillet's radicalization of the conditions of description with the revolution in vision provoked by the cinema, Barthes remains wedded, however, to a conception of cinema which conceives it in terms of a succession of forms, a temporality defined by spatial sequentiality or situational shifts. There are elements in the description of M. d'Argencourt and the other elderly guests, moreover — the necessity to read on several different levels as if situated behind them — which also pertain to this essentially chronophotographic definition of cinema. Other elements in Proust's description — seeing with the eyes of memory, the revelation and visibility of time, the notion of time as an immaterial atmosphere, suggest a different reading, one which hinges on the proposition of the magic lantern as a projecting device, rather than on the narrative sequentiality of its slides.

The capacity of an immaterial projection to give us an image of time, which Proust accords to the magic lantern here, comes close to Deleuze's concept of the time-image. The division of Deleuze's writing on the cinema into the two volumes *L'Image-mouvement* and *L'Image-temps* expresses a major conceptual and broadly historical distinction between a cinema in which temporality is conceived on the basis of movement, and one in which time is *in* the image, irrespective of whatever movement might take place. Deleuze explains this distinction through attention to a moment in film history in which he finds a crisis of motricity, a paralysis of the human motor-schema. In post-war Italian cinema, but also earlier and more fully, in the work of Ozu, Deleuze focuses on scenes without movement, but in which time nevertheless passes. The time-image proposes a conception of cinema in which time is no longer measured and perceived in terms of movement, but simply as time passing. What the cinema of the time-image gives us, Deleuze proposes, is 'un peu de temps à l'état pur' ('a bit of time in the pure state').[51] Readers of Proust will recognize this as a quotation (unacknowledged by Deleuze) from *Le Temps retrouvé*; provoked by the series of experiences of involuntary memory in the ante-room of the Hôtel de Guermantes the narrator comments that sensation of the past given to him in the present allows the law which dictates that one can only imagine what is absent to be neutralized. This 'subterfuge' adds to the imagination (we might say, to the projection), the quality of existence, and allows the narrator to experience, in an instant, 'un peu de temps à l'état pur'. There is a continuity, then, between Deleuze's notion of the time-image, the perception in cinema of time passing, and Proust's conception of involuntary memory. Deleuze capitalizes on this further on in *L'Image-temps* when he writes:

Mais toujours l'image-temps directe nous fait accéder à cette dimension proustienne d'après laquelle les personnes et les choses occupent dans le temps une place incommensurable à celle qu'ils occupent dans l'espace. Proust parle alors en termes de cinéma, le Temps montant sur les corps sa lanterne magique et faisant coexister les plans en profondeur.

[But the direct time-image always gives us access to that Proustian dimension where people and things occupy a place in time which is incommensurable with the one they have in space. Proust indeed speaks in terms of cinema, time mounting its magic lantern on bodies and making the shots coexist in depth.][52]

The analogy between the narrator's vision of M. d'Argencourt in terms of the 'depth' of layers of time which he embodies, and the way certain films propose what Deleuze refers to as a 'temporalization' of the image anchors the conceptual continuity between Proust's novel and the cinema, or at least of the Deleuzian notion of a cinema which departs from the limits of the present. This final reference to the magic lantern in Proust's novel, and to Golo's immaterial body, refers us back to the very beginning of the work and in so doing is itself a form of 'time-image', incorporating, as if in successive layers behind it or within it, the passage of time not only of the narrative but also of our reading time. But there is also a shift in terms of agency; while the opening sequence of *Combray* staged the disengagement of the narrator's consciousness from unconsciousness and from habitual continuity, provoking the discovery of things and thoughts, through the intrusion of the magic lantern's projections on the walls of his room, here the narrator has, like Elstir, incorporated the magic lantern into his look, and endowed it with the magical capacity to see 'in time'.

Notes to Chapter 3

1. Malcolm Bowie, *Freud, Proust, Lacan: Theory as Fiction* (Cambridge: Cambridge University Press, 1997), p. 49. Bowie's quotation from Proust is I, 278 ('a narrow illuminated section cut directly out of the unknown', I, 285).
2. Ibid., p. 50.
3. Leo Bersani and Ulysse Dutoit, *Forms of Being* (London: BFI, 2004), pp. 19–73.
4. Ibid., p. 37.
5. Adam Watt, ' "Une étroite section lumineuse pratiquée à même l'inconnu": Swann et la lettre pour Forcheville', *Bulletin d'informations proustiennes*, 43:1 (2013), 133–38.
6. See Tom Baldwin's discussion of this scene in *The Picture as Spectre: Diderot, Proust, Deleuze* (Oxford: Legenda, 2001), pp. 79–80. Baldwin discusses the semantic and logical tensions around the metaphor of the window as an 'illumimated manuscript', and points to the importance of the shuttered window which makes of it a 'mottled screen of reading' which is 'translucent like a text that will not let us abandon the idea that it is connected to an image'.
7. Leo Bersani, *Marcel Proust: The Fictions of Life and Art* (Oxford: Oxford University Press, 1965), pp. 30–31.
8. Ibid., p. 6.
9. Ibid., p. 13.
10. Ibid, p. 18.
11. Translated in Bersani, *Marcel Proust*, pp. 105–06 (my emphasis).
12. Ibid., p. 21.

13. Ibid., p. 27.
14. Ibid., p. 28.
15. Ibid., p. 105.
16. Ibid., p. 106.
17. Ibid.
18. Stanley Cavell, *The World Viewed — Enlarged Edition* (Cambridge, MA, & London: Harvard University Press, 1979), p. 72.
19. Stanley Cavell, 'The Fantastic of Philosophy', in *Cavell on Film*, ed. by William Rothman (New York: SUNY Press, 2005), pp. 145–52 (p. 149).
20. Stanley Cavell, 'Two Cheers for Romance', in *Cavell on Film*, ed. by Rothman, pp. 153–66 (p. 166).
21. Stanley Cavell, 'The World as Things', in *Cavell on Film*, ed. by Rothman, pp. 241–80 (pp. 248–49).
22. Ibid.
23. Cavell, *The World Viewed*, p. 165.
24. Ibid, p. 166.
25. Cavell cites Panofsky, 'The medium of the movies is physical reality as such', and Bazin, 'The cinema is of its essence a dramaturgy of Nature' (*The World Viewed*, p. 16).
26. Spectators or viewers? It is in the substitution of the second word here for the first that Cavell's account can be further specified. The title of his book underlines that the world film gives to us is the world 'viewed', implying a whole different set of issues from those intended by the notion of spectatorship, including the idea of film as a spectacle beheld at a distance, of film as spectacular, as a diversion from our ordinary relation to things. Significantly, the translation into French of *The World Viewed* renders its title as *La Projection du monde*. In his short 'Concluding Remarks on *La Projection du monde*' (in *Cavell on Film*, ed. by Rothman, pp. 281–86) Cavell comments on this that 'I wanted the title, incorporating a translation of the German *Weltanschaung*, to capture the sense of film as imposing its own conditions of viewing, or revelation. French does not permit this incorporation, and the alternative idea of the world projected shifts the location of the conditions of film's existence. So something I liked in the original was lost. But something was gained. A danger in invoking the *Weltanschaung* for film is the suggestion that film is conditioned by a given set of circumstances and concepts, knowable in advance of the experience and history of film. "Projection", by contrast, captures the sense of the intervention of the work of humans and machines in materializing or rematerializing the world. A danger here is the suggestion that there are psychological and physical processes resulting in some well-understood set of effects which show the subjectivity of film's duplication of the world. But this danger is offset by the invocation of Heidegger's idea of "projection", which may alert us to film's capacity to reveal what we would deny' (pp. 285–86).
27. Cavell, *The World Viewed*, p. 16.
28. Ibid., p. 21.
29. Ibid., p. 22.
30. Ibid., p. 23.
31. Ibid., p. 25.
32. Ibid., pp. 39–40.
33. Ibid., p. 102.
34. Mannoni, *Le Grand art*, p. 41; *The Great Art*, p. 33.
35. Three of these six panels are reproduced on the cover of this book.
36. See Mannoni, *Le Grand Art*: 'Et puis il ne faut pas oublier [parmi les titres du catalogue Lapierre] les fameuses plaques illustrant *Geneviève de Brabant* (6 verres de 12 images, existant en plusieurs formats). Cette belle série (qui comporte encore une scène onirique) a vivement frappe l'esprit du jeune Marcel Proust, à Illiers' (p. 277) ('There was also [in the Lapierre catalogue] a famous set illustrating *Geneviève de Brabant* in six slides of twelve images, produced in several different formats. This beautiful set, which once again included a dream sequence, made a strong impression on the mind of the young Marcel Proust', *The Great Art*, p. 295). Mannoni's book includes a reproduction of an oval slide from the series, which does, despite my reservations

about the referential status of the slides, correspond to the form of the slides which feature in *Combray*.

37. Jacques Lacan, 'Le Stade du miroir', in *Écrits* (Paris: Seuil, Collection, 1966), pp. 93–100 (p. 94); 'The Mirror Stage as Formative of the Function of the I', in *Ecrits: A Selection*, trans. by Alan Sheridan (London: Tavistock, 1977), pp. 1–7 (p. 3).

38. See Benhaïm, *Panim*, pp. 149–50, for an argument about Proust's 'regressive' tendencies vis-à-vis technological 'perfection', including that of the cinema.

39. Chevrier, *Proust et la photographie*: 'Les premières images d'*À la recherche du temps perdu* sont des images de cinéma (les aventures de Golo et de Geneviève de Brabant), terrifiantes parce qu'elles ne sont pas contenues dans le cadre d'un écran ni dans l'espace spécialement adapté d'une salle de projection mais se déroulent sur les murs memes de la chambre de Marcel' [The first images of *In Search of Lost Time* are cinema images (the adventures of Golo and of Geneviève de Brabant), terrifying because they are not contained within the the frame of a screen nor in the specially adapted space of a projection room, but unfold on the very walls of Marcel's bedroom] (p. 15).

40. François Bon, *Proust est une fiction* (Paris: Seuil, 2013): 'Proust aurait pu franchir l'étape de la lanterne magique au cinématographe, mais c'est plutôt l'inverse à quoi il procède' [Proust could have moved from the stage of the magic lantern onto that of the cinematograph, but instead he moves in the opposite direction] (p. 75).

41. A further regressive model is provided by the sequential panels of Giotto's paintings; in 'Nom de lieux: le nom' the narrator proposes that the different 'compartments' of the projective images provoked by the names of Venice and Florence are 'comme certains tableaux de Giotto eux-mêmes qui montrent à deux moments différents de l'action un même personage, ici couché dans son lit, là s'apprêtant à monter à cheval' ('like certain of Giotto's paintings themselves which show us the same figure at two different moments in the action, here lying in his bed, there getting ready to mount his horse') (I, 382; I, 393).

42. See Cavell, *The World Viewed*, pp. 20–21, 101–08. Deleuze, *Cinéma 1*, pp. 13–17; *Cinema 1*, pp. 3–8.

43. Johanna Malt, in her article 'The Blob and the Magic Lantern: On Subjectivity, Faciality and Projection', *Paragraph*, 36.3 (2013), 305–23, proposes a comparative reading of the magic lantern sequence in the *Recherche* with the installation work of contemporary artist Tony Oursler. Her account focuses on conceptual issues around the ontology of projection and the 'dialectic' (p. 319) of materiality and immateriality. In the closing paragraphs of the article Malt proposes a persuasive alignment between the viewer of Oursler's projection installations and the reader of Proust's text: 'In a sense, like the screen-object of the installation, the reader is positionally aligned in the place of an absent presence (that of the author-narrator), with the novel in the mediating position of the recorder/projector — a kind of literary machine. We have the sense of being "inside" the narrator's room-consciousness, of ourselves momentarily embodying, like the doorknob which becomes the body of Golo, the virtual self projected towards us by the text. And as the structure of projection dictates, we do not become what is projected onto us, but something else, a third term or reading self, which is created in the coming together of the novel's intangible beam and the screen of our embodied being' (p. 320). Malt's notion of the text as a 'kind of machine' is evidently pertinent to my exploration here of the resonances between the spaces of Proust's novel and of the cinema, as is her proposition that 'Neither the intentional subject of phenomenology, nor the asubjective consciousness of Deleuze, the subjectivity suspended in the structure of projection brings something into being in the oscillation between the two' (p. 320).

44. Leo Bersani, 'Death and Literary Authority: Marcel Proust and Melanie Klein', in *The Culture of Redemption* (Cambridge, MA, & London: Harvard University Press, 1990), pp. 7–28 (p. 22).

45. Ibid., p. 23.

46. In a discussion of the punctum of the photographic image as a kind of supplement to it, added by the viewer, yet already there, Barthes asks: 'Est-ce qu'au cinema j'ajoute à l'image? — Je ne crois pas; je n'ai pas le temps: devant l'écran, je ne suis pas libre de fermer les yeux; sinon, les rouvrant, je ne retrouverais pas la meme image: je suis astreint à une voracité continue; une foule d'autres qualities, mais pas de pensivité; d'où l'intérêt pour moi du photogramme' (*La Chambre*

claire, pp. 89–90) ('Do I add to the images in movies? I don't think so; I don't have time: in front of the screen, I am not free to shut my eyes; otherwise, opening them again, I would not discover the same image; I am constrained to a continuous voracity; a host of other qualities, but not *pensiveness*; whence the interest, for me, of the photogram', *Camera Lucida*, p. 55).

47. Raymond Bellour, 'Quand s'écrit la photo du cinéma', in *L'Entre-images*, pp. 67–72 (p. 71); 'When the Photo of Cinema is Written', in *Between-the-Images*, pp. 82–83

48. Raymond Bellour, 'Le Spectateur pensif', in *L'Entre-images,* pp. 75–83 (p. 79); 'The Pensive Spectator', in *Between-the-Images*, p. 92.

49. Roland Barthes, 'Littérature objective', in *Essais critiques* (Paris: Seuil, 1964), pp. 29–40 (p. 34); 'Objective Literature', in *Critical Essays*, trans. by Richard Howard (Evanston, IL: Northwestern University Press, 1972), pp. 13–24, (p. 18).

50. Ibid, p. 36; p. 21.

51. Deleuze, *L'Image-temps*, p. 27; *The Time-Image*, p. 17.

52. Ibid., p. 56; p. 39.

CHAPTER 4

The Cinema of Montjouvain

On one of his frequent perambulations, on a day on which his parents have given him permission to be out as late as he wants, the narrator has walked as far as Montjouvain, where he stretches out in the shade amongst the bushes on the bank which overlooks the house of M. Vinteuil:

> Il faisait presque nuit quand je m'éveillai, je voulus me lever, mais je vis Mlle Vinteuil (autant que je pus la reconnaître, car je ne l'avais pas vue souvent à Combray, et seulement quand elle était encore une enfant, tandis qu'elle commençait d'être une jeune fille) qui probablement venait de rentrer, en face de moi, à quelques centimètres de moi, dans cette chambre où son père avait reçu le mien et dont elle avait fait son petit salon à elle. La fenêtre était entr'ouverte, la lampe était allumée, je voyais tous ses mouvements sans qu'elle me vît, mais en m'en allant j'aurais fait craquer les buissons, elle m'aurait entendu et elle aurait pu croire que je m'étais caché là pour l'épier. (I, 157)

> [It was almost night when I awoke, I wanted to stand up, but I saw Mlle Vinteuil (insofar as I actually recognized her, because I had not seen her very often in Combray, and only when she was still a child, whereas now she was growing into a young woman), who had probably just come home, opposite me, a few centimetres from me, in the room in which her father had entertained mine and which she had made into her own little drawing-room. The window was half-open, the lamp was lit, I could see her every movement without her seeing me, but if I had gone away I would have made rustling sounds among the bushes, she would have heard me and she might have thought I had hidden there to spy on her.] (I, 160)

The improbable geometry of this scene positions the narrator a few centimetres only in front of a window through which he can see Mlle Vinteuil's salon, illuminated from within. He himself is invisible, due to the fading light outside and the internal light of the room. He is able to see, but without being seen. He disavows this voyeuristic position however, in protesting that were he to leave he would alert the other parties to his presence and thus be suspected of being a voyeur.

The narrator sees the illuminated scene, framed by the window, in deep focus; he can discern the portrait of M. Vinteuil on the mantelpiece, an image which will have a significant role to play in what follows:

> Au fond du salon de Mlle Vinteuil, sur la cheminée était posé un petit portrait de son père que vivement elle alla chercher au moment où retentit le roulement

d'une voiture qui venait de la route, puis elle se jeta sur un canapé, et tira près d'elle une petite table sur laquelle elle plaça le portrait, comme M. Vinteuil autrefois avait mis à côté de lui le morceau qu'il avait le désir de jouer à mes parents. Bientôt son amie entra. (I, 158)

[At the back of Mlle Vinteuil's drawing room, on the mantelpiece, stood a small portrait of her father which she quickly went to get at the moment when the rattle of a carriage could be heard from the road outside, then she threw herself down on a couch, drew a little table close to her and set the portrait on it, just as M. Vinteuil had once placed beside him the piece that he wanted to play for my parents. Soon her friend came in.] (I, 161)

In expectation of what will ensue, suggesting that this is a recurrent ritual, Mlle Vinteuil moves the picture of her father to a more advantageous position to 'see' what is going to happen. Lying back invitingly on the *canapé*, but then feeling embarrassed by this attitude she gets up ostensibly to close the shutters at the window. In response to her friend's suggestion that she leave the shutters open, Mlle Vinteuil protests that they might be seen, to which her friend replies:

'Oui, c'est probable qu'on nous regarde à cette heure-ci, dans cette champagne fréquentée, dit ironiquement son amie. Et puis quoi ?' ajouta-t-elle (en croyant devoir accompagner d'un clignement d'yeux malicieux et tendre, ces mots qu'elle récita par bonté, comme un texte qu'elle savait être agréable à Mlle Vinteuil, d'un ton qu'elle s'efforçait de rendre cynique) 'quand même on nous verrait ce n'en est que meilleur'. (I, 159)

[' — Yes, I'm sure people are watching us at this hour, in this densely populated countryside, her friend said ironically. And what if they are? She added (thinking she had to give a mischievous, tender wink as she uttered these words, which she recited good-naturedly like a text she knew Mlle Vinteuil liked, in a tone that she tried to make cynical, 'if someone saw us, so much the better'.] (I, 162)

The irony here is double, not only through the forced and 'tender' erotic sarcasm of Mlle Vinteuil's friend, suggesting that it would be better if they were seen, but also through the fact that they are, in fact, being watched. Thus Proust includes or inscribes the look of the spectator in the scene, as a look compromised on the one hand by a perverse desire to see, and on the other by a desire to be seen, recalling Freud's instinctual pairing of voyeurism and exhibitionism.

Subsequently, in an extension of the perversion of the look to that of cruelty and suffering — thus to Freud's other instinctual pair of sadism and masochism — Mlle Vinteuil, lying underneath her friend, draws the latter's attention to the portrait of her deceased father on the mantelpiece; another look is introduced into the scene, here a look which emanates from a photograph. As if moving through the set phrases of a ritual profanation, the friend implores and conjures the disapproving look of M. Vinteuil, before then adding a further provocation in threatening, lubriciously, to spit on it.

It is at this point that the curtain falls, as it were, since Mlle Vinteuil gets up to close the shutters:

> Je n'en entendis pas davantage, car Mlle Vinteuil, d'un air las, gauche, affairé, honnête et triste, vint fermer les volets et la fenêtre, mais je savais maintenant, pour toutes les souffrances que pendant sa vie M. Vinteuil avait supportées à cause de sa fille, ce qu'après la mort il avait reçu d'elle en salaire. (I, 161)

> [I did not hear any more, because Mlle Vinteuil, with a manner that was weary, awkward, fussy, honest and sad, came and closed the shutters and the window, but now I knew that for all the suffering which M. Vinteuil had endured on his daughter's account during his lifetime, this was what he had received from her as his reward after his death.] (I, 164)

This marks the limits of the narrator's vision, but it also extends its dynamics in supposing M. Vinteuil's witnessing of the scene. Its masochistic dimensions will of course become more acutely realized upon the narrator at the end of *Sodome et Gomorrhe* when Albertine reveals to him that she is the best friend of Vinteuil's daughter's best friend, and that she knows Mlle de Vinteuil almost as well. What ensues is a form of superimposition in which the image of Montjouvain, conjured in the narrator's memory, is projected onto and conditions all other images in which he might see or imagine Albertine. On hearing Albertine's unwitting remark the narrator's visual field is transformed as if from within:

> Une image s'agitait dans mon cœur, une image tenue en réserve pendant tant d'années que, même si j'avais pu deviner, en l'emmagasinant jadis, qu'elle avait un pouvoir nocif, j'eusse cru qu'à la longue elle l'avait entièrement perdu; conservée vivante au fond de moi — comme Oreste dont les Dieux avaient empêché la mort pour qu'au jour désigné il revînt dans son pays punir le meurtre d'Agamemnon — pour mon supplice, pour mon châtiment, qui sait? d'avoir laissé mourir ma grand'mère, peut-être; surgissant tout à coup du fond de la nuit où elle semblait à jamais ensevelie et frappant comme un Vengeur, afin d'inaugurer pour moi une vie terrible, méritée et nouvelle, peut-être aussi pour faire éclater à mes yeux les funestes conséquences que les actes mauvais engendrent indéfiniment, non pas seulement pour ceux qui les ont commis, mais pour ceux qui n'ont fait, qui n'ont cru, que contempler un spectacle curieux et divertissant, comme moi, hélas! en cette fin de journée lointaine à Montjouvain, caché derrière un buisson où (comme quand j'avais complaisamment écouté le récit des amours de Swann) j'avais dangereusement laissé s'élargir en moi la voie funeste et destinée à être douloureuse du Savoir. (III, 499)

> [A picture came to life in my heart, a picture held in reserve during so many years that, even had I been able to guess, when long ago storing it away, that it had the power to do harm, I would have supposed that in the course of time it had lost it entirely; preserved alive deep inside me — like Orestes, whose death the gods had prevented so that on the day appointed he might return to his homeland to punish the murder of Agamemnon — as my torment, as my punishment perhaps, who knows, for having allowed my grandmother to die; suddenly rising up out of the depths of that darkness where it had seemed to lie forever entombed and striking like an Avenger, in order to inaugurate for me a new life, terrible and deserved, perhaps also to explode before my eyes the fateful consequences to which wicked actions give rise indefinitely, not only for those who have committed them but for those who were no more than, who

thought they were merely, onlookers at a curious and diverting spectacle, like me, alas, on the far-off day's end in Montjouvain, hidden behind a bush, where (as when I had listened complaisantly to the account of Swann's amours) I had perilously allowed to broaden out within me the fateful path of Knowledge.] (4, 507)

The new knowledge that now conditions the narrator's vision provokes a form of visual and aural hallucination, a repetition of the scene of Montjouvain, in which Albertine is almost literally cut out from the actuality of her presence and reimposed on a different background:

Derrière Albertine je ne voyais plus les montagnes bleues de la mer, mais la chambre de Montjouvain où elle elle tombait dans les bras de Mlle Vinteuil avec ce rire où elle faisait entendre comme le son inconnu de sa jouissance. (III, 502)

[Behind Albertine I no longer saw the blue mountains of the sea, but the room in Montjouvain where she was falling into the arms of Mlle Vinteuil, with that laugh in which she made you hear as it were the unknown sound of her sexual pleasure.] (4, 509)

The hallucinatory scene of Montjouvain which the narrator's masochistic and fascinated desire creates imposes itself between his eyes and the image he has before him, in a later moment back in his room. An inversion takes place whereby the imagined scene of Montjouvain takes on the qualities of the real background, onto which what he actually sees seems like a projected or painted or reflected image:

Mais derrière la plage de Balbec, la mer, le lever du soleil, que maman me montrait, je voyais, avec des mouvements de désespoir qui ne lui échappaient pas, la chambre de Montjouvain où Albertine, rose, pelotonnée comme une grosse chatte, le nez mutin, avait pris la place de l'amie de Mlle Vinteuil et disait avec des éclats de son rire voluptueux: 'Eh bien! si on nous voit, ce n'en sera que meilleur. Moi! je n'oserais pas cracher sur ce vieux singe?' C'est cette scène que je voyais derrière celle qui s'étendait dans la fenêtre et qui n'était sur l'autre qu'un voile morne, superposé comme un reflet. Elle semblait elle-même, en effet, presque irréelle, comme une vue peinte. En face de nous, à la saillie de la falaise de Parville, le petit bois où nous avions joué au furet inclinait en pente jusqu'à la mer, sous le vernis encore tout doré de l'eau, le tableau de ses feuillages, comme à l'heure où souvent, à la fin du jour, quand j'étais allé y faire une sieste avec Albertine, nous nous étions levés en voyant le soleil descendre. Dans le désordre des brouillards de la nuit qui traînaient encore en loques roses et bleues sur les eaux encombrées des débris de nacre de l'aurore, des bateaux passaient en souriant à la lumière oblique qui jaunissait leur voile et la pointe de leur beaupré comme quand ils rentrent le soir: scène imaginaire, grelottante et déserte, pure évocation du couchant, qui ne reposait pas, comme le soir, sur la suite des heures du jour que j'avais l'habitude de voir le précéder, déliée, interpolée, plus inconsistante encore que l'image horrible de Montjouvain qu'elle ne parvenait pas à annuler, à couvrir, à cacher — poétique et vaine image du souvenir et du songe. (III, 502)

[But behind the beach of Balbec, the sea, and the sunrise, to which Mama was pointing, I could see, in a fit of despair that did not escape her, the room in

Montjouvain where Albertine, pink, curled up in a ball like a big cat, with her mischievous nose, had taken the place of Mlle Vinteuil's friend and was saying, to peals of voluptuous laughter: 'Oh well, if we're seen, that'll only make things better. Me, I wouldn't dare spit on that old ape!' This was the scene I could see behind that spread out in the window, which was nothing more than a mournful veil superimposed on the other like a reflection. It seemed itself indeed almost unreal, like a painted view. Facing us, where the Parville cliffs jutted out, the leafy tableau of the little wood where we had played hunt-the-ring sloped all the way down to the sea, beneath the still golden sheen of the water, as at that hour when often, at the day's end, I had gone to have a siesta there with Albertine, we had got to our feet on seeing the sun go down. In the disorder of the night mists that still hung in blue and pink shreds over waters littered with the pearly debris of the dawn, boats were passing, smiling at the oblique light that had turned their sails and the tips of their bowsprits yellow, as when they return home in the evening: an imaginary scene, shivering and deserted, a pure evocation of the sunset, which did not rest, like the dusk, on the procession of hours of the day that I was in the habit of seeing precede it, slender, interpolated, more insubstantial even than the horrible image of Montjouvain that it had not succeeded in cancelling out, in covering, in concealing — a vain and poetic image of the memory and the dream.] (4, 521–22)

Proust plays here with the dynamics of projection; the imagined scene is of such affective acuity that it becomes the background, the screen, on which other images now appear as projections, 'mere' poetic or painterly images. What is underlined in the return to Montjouvain is the contingency of vision and the way that the visual field is not only constrained and conditioned by external factors such as the frame, the look, the field, but also by internal factors, by the hallucinatory power of projection.

Elisabeth Ladenson discusses the Montjouvain episode in some detail in *Proust's Lesbianism*, so as to indicate the paradox that lesbianism, in the novel, while much more prone to visual exhibition, remains far less knowable, and of an 'enduring opacity', compared to the closeted spectacle of male homosexuality.[1] This paradox echoes another, whereby the erotic charge of lesbian sex and sexuality is dependent on an explicit exhibitionism which both satisfies and subverts the narrator's 'disavowed voyeurism'. The Montjouvain episode in particular proposes a lesbian couple whose pleasure is enhanced by the knowledge, albeit imaginary or virtual, that they are being watched: 'the idea of being seen is an integral part of their sexual game'.[2] Their exhibitionism is double; they are watched first by M. Vinteuil in the form of his photographic portrait, and by the virtual spectator whose look they allow and invite by leaving the shutters open. The narrator's voyeurism, since he is in fact watching them, is doubly denied, first by himself — he stays there, he says, only for fear of alerting the couple to his presence by the noise he would make in moving away — and by the couple themselves; their desire to be seen subverts a fundamental condition of voyeurism, to see without being seen or without any awareness, on the part of the other, of his look. Ladenson suggests that 'This scene of voyeurism, which sets the stage for the novel's presentation of Gomorrah, thus violates the very structure of voyeurism itself, which depends on an unsuspecting object'.[3]

Ladenson's commentary is hugely insightful in its attention to the complex play of visibility in relation to sexuality and to the asymmetry of the component compulsions of exhibitionism and voyeurism. It is significant then that the dominant terms of her discussion of the Montjouvain episode derive from the theatre. The proposition of the asymmetrical overlapping of exhibitionism and voyeurism is rendered in theatrical terms: 'when the hero creates a clandestine theatre for himself, he finds the stage occupied by actors in search of an audience'. When Mlle Vinteuil closes the shutters of the open window Ladenson suggests that she and her lover are 'in charge of the curtain in their own drama'. The later episode in Jupien's brothel from *Le Temps retrouvé,* in which the narrator witnesses Charlus's flagellation through a convenient spyhole, with which Ladenson contrasts the Montjouvain episode, is 'just as much a theatricalized ritual'.[4] The theatrical terms are apt here, insofar as they capture the ritualistic attitude of the scene's participants, and resonate with Eve Sedgwick's 'epistemology of the closet', which Ladenson seeks to develop. I want to ask if they account sufficiently for the specific conditions of framing and luminosity that the Montjouvain scene seems to offer. Ladenson herself points in a later moment to the way in which 'lesbian desire is frequently described as a luminescent emanation', and this can prompt us to explore further the play of light and darkness that structures the scene.[5]

One of the conditions under which Mlle Vinteuil and her lover may be seen by the narrator, and the conditions of the exhibitionism-voyeurism dynamic is the illumination of the room, framed by the window, and the darkness of the hillside outside. The narrator can see, without being seen, because of the difference between the illuminated interior and the unlit exterior. The couple can imagine being seen, without seeing their voyeur, due to this same difference. It is as if, between the narrator as voyeur and the exhibitionistic couple the open window intervenes to make inoperable any symmetrical exchange of looks, or of desires. Without being a surface as such the window operates as a screen. It screens the viewer from its world, in Cavell's terms, and allows the narrator to view a world without being part of it. From the perspective of the couple, what the window as screen allows is the postulation of an imaginary or virtual viewer. In Lacanian terms what excites them is not the prospect of a look, but the fiction of a gaze.

I have suggested above that the luminosity of what the narrator sees tends to draw it close to the conditions of being screened, and that a screen-effect may be discerned in the exclusion of the narrator from the visible field. A further factor which seems to me to constitute the Montjouvain episode as cinematic rather than theatrical concerns the issue of the off-screen or *hors champ*, a widely discussed term in film theory, of which one of the seminal examples is André Bazin's postulation, in *Qu'est-ce que le cinema?*, of the difference between the theatre and the cinema. Bazin writes that: 'Il ne saurait exister de théâtre sans architecture [...] un espace privilegié, réellement ou virtuellement distinct de la nature' ('There can be no theatre without architecture [...] a privileged spot actually or virtually distinct from nature'). He adds that 'Parce qu'il n'est qu'un élément de l'architecture scénique le décor de théâtre est donc un lieu matériellement clos, limité, circonscrit, dont les seules "découvertes" sont ceux de notre imagination consentante' ('Because it is only part of the architecture of the stage, the decor of the theatre is thus an area materially enclosed, limited, circumscribed, the only discoveries of which are those of our collusive imagination').[6] The theatrical stage, moreover:

> Existe par son envers et son absence d'au-delà, comme la peinture par son cadre. De même que le tableau ne se confond point avec le paysage qu'il représente, qu'il n'est non plus une fenêtre dans un mur, la scène et le décor où l'action se déroule sont un microcosme esthétique inséré de force dans l'univers mais essentiellement hétérogène à la Nature qui les entoure.

> [Exists by virtue of its reverse side and its absence from anything beyond, as the painting exists by virtue of its frame. Just as the picture is not to be confounded with the scene it represents and is not a window in a wall. The stage and the decor where the action unfolds constitute an aesthetic microcosm inserted perforce into the universe but essentially distinct from the Nature which surrounds it.][7]

In contrast:

> Il en va autrement au cinéma dont le principe est de nier toute frontière à l'action. Le concept du lieu dramatique n'est pas seulement étranger, mais essentiellement contradictoire à la notion de l'écran. L'écran n'est pas un cadre comme celui du tableau, mais un *cache* qui ne laisse percevoir qu'une partie de l'événement. Quand un personnage sort du champ de la caméra, nous admettons qu'il échappe au champ visuel, mais il continue d'exister identique à lui-même en un autre point du décor, qui nous est caché. L'écran n'a pas de coulisses.

> [The basic principal of the cinema screen is a denial of any frontiers to action. The idea of a locus dramaticus is not only alien to, it is essentially a contradiction of the concept of the screen. The screen is not a frame like that of a picture but a mask which allows only a part of the action to be seen. When a character moves off screen, we accept the fact that he is out of sight, but he continues to exist in his own capacity at some other place in the décor which is hidden from us. There are no wings to the screen.][8]

Bazin thus postulates the screen as a mask (*cache*) rather than a frame (*cadre*), and constitutes the world it shows as contiguous with the world around it, with what he calls 'nature', rather than a reserved and isolated space.

The exhibitionistic and ritualistic tendencies on the part of Mlle Vinteuil and her friend, both to each other and to the two virtual voyeurs they conjure in their imagination — M. Vinteuil and the invisible spy outside — do serve to transform the room into a performance space, thus into a form of stage, and to this extent Ladenson's account draws out a crucial element of their phantasmatic relation to it, one authorized elsewhere in the novel itself. However, despite the theatricalizing desire on their part, their wish to stage or to act their desires, the world of the illuminated room is contiguous with the universe; both Mlle Vinteuil and her lover continue to exist beyond their visibility to the narrator, rather than existing only in and for the space and time of the performance. When they enter or leave the visual field, they move off-screen rather than off-stage.

The cinematic rather than theatrical character of the episode also seems to me to come to the fore if one considers the near total visibility and audibility of the couple's movements and words. Without a clear sense of the architecture of the room, despite his static position, and even beyond the fact of his apparent proximity to the open window, the narrator's look seems to be able to register everything without obstruction or any sense of distance; the volume of the room is in this sense flattened, while the look is able to roam around it and to choose its objects of focus. It is a surface with a virtual depth, a screen rather than a stage. This effect is particularly acute, I would suggest, in relation to the photographic portrait of M. Vinteuil which plays such a crucial role in the sadism of the scene. Its presence, and the narrator's (deep) focus upon it, open the scene out to the 'off-screen' dimension of M. Vinteuil's relation to his daughter, to his own disavowed exhibitionism (as noted by Ladenson), and to the subtle imbrications of art (Vinteuil's music) with sexuality and cruelty. The portrait functions as a kind of aperture within the scene through which it opens out beyond itself, an effect in which, as we have seen, Bellour, commenting the presence of photographs in films, locates a troubling or a suspension of the *défilement* (procession) of the film and of the 'ordinary imaginary of the cinema', and the provocation of a 'pensive spectator'.[9] If the Montjouvain episode, as I am suggesting here, is closer to cinema than to theatre, it is a cinema whose conditions are fragile and uncertain, occupying the space 'between-the-images' which Bellour detects as its destiny.

I will return to these concerns at the end of this chapter. I want at this point to pursue what might be called the camera-effect of the narrator's vision of the room at Montjouvain via Mieke Bal's discussion of it in *The Mottled Screen*, since it adds further purchase to a reading of it in cinematic terms, while stopping short of seeing it as a kind of film. This supports in turn the notion I have just introduced, of Proust's writing as provoking a kind of suspension or troubling of orthodox cinematographic conditions. Commenting the set-up of the Montjouvain episode, Bal writes: 'Equipped with his zoom lens, the hero suddenly sees Mlle Vinteuil "standing in front of me, and only a few centimetres away"'.[10] The 'zoom lens' is a figure Bal has employed previously in her book to convey the way in which the narrator's look seems at times to 'press against' or up against the image, which is thus construed as a surface. She develops the figure in her reading of the Montjouvain scene, in which 'the voyeur finds himself sufficiently well-placed to be able to "press himself" against the view'. This kind of launching forward of the look is effected in part by means of an identification: 'This pressing against takes place through an identification by means of which the narrator projects thoughts into Mlle Vinteuil's mind'.[11] I would add here that it is also by means of an identification with M. Vinteuil, and with the look that the narrator and the couple alike imagines to emanate from the photograph, that he is able to press himself up against the view, to enter, and to move around in it. Bal writes that: 'In order that the photograph in the photograph become a dramatic agent, the zoom lens comes to its assistance'. One of the effects of this 'pressing against' is to disturb the fixed positions of classical perspective; the position of visual and epistemological mastery assumed by the spectator in the camera obscura is troubled, as we saw in Chapter 2, by the introduction of a physiologically mobile viewer whose distance from the scene is not assured. Bal writes that 'This pressing against is necessary in order to question better the traditional epistemology in which subject and object are clearly distinguished, and, further, to explore the alternatives opened up by this questioning'.[12]

This troubles the security of Cavell's viewers and their exclusion from the world they survey, but it is a condition characteristic of Proust's subject, one from which he perhaps strives to escape, to find himself inevitably caught up in the image and implicated in it. We have already noted, through Ladenson, that his (disavowed) voyeurism finds itself to be compromised by the exhibitionistic design of Mlle Vinteuil and her friend. Bal's proposition of the visual, quasi-tactile qualities of the narrator's look also troubles the static and invisible position of the voyeur, and begins to suggest ways in which, rather than being the master of what he sees, the narrative subject may be more problematically caught in the field of the screen. Bal writes that the 'instability' that 'classical perspective is intended precisely to control' is 'made more serious because the subject projects himself outward in a heteropathic identification in order to press up against the object'.[13] The security of the voyeuristic position is not assured, and is corrupted by the forms of identification with the look of the other which desire inevitably introduces into the picture.

It is also the resurrection of the Montjouvain scene that constitutes it more thoroughly as screened rather than performed. If the scene in the room has a virtual extension, a *hors champ* dimension, the more specifically Proustian aspect to this lies in its recurrence in the narrator's memory and in its subsequent transformation of the narrator's vision. I want to approach this via a further engagement with Bersani and here specifically with his discussion of the Montjouvain episode in a key chapter of *The Culture of Redemption*, 'Death and Literary Authority: Marcel Proust and Melanie Klein'.

Like Bowie and Ladenson, and extending the direction of his earlier *Marcel Proust: The Fictions of Life and Art*, Bersani seeks to read Proust's novel against the generalized tendency to see it as essentially reparative or redemptive. These critics play off what they see as a conservative and 'amnesic' urge to attend only to the framing volumes of the *Recherche*, those that offer the most compelling argument for the redemptive triumph of art.[14] This argument is made, they propose, at the expense of the whole sequence of volumes of which Albertine is the focus, and also at the cost of the exclusion from critical visibility of the whole issue of homosexuality.

Bersani's reading of the 'resurrection' of the grandmother through the involuntary memory of her presence in the Grand Hôtel in Balbec, in *Sodome et Gomorrhe*, thus draws out a more unsettling psychology than that of the redemptive power of memory. Emphasizing the role of death, Bersani suggests that the grandmother whom the narrator finds again through this process is a figure who no longer contains the narrator's image; she is 'resurrected' as a stranger, as now 'authentically other': 'Marcel's involuntary memory returns his grandmother to him as the *outside of thought*: that is, not as someone who can be desired or appropriated or dialectically related to, but simply as someone who existed beside him, a mere other presence in the world'. This is unbearable for the narrator, of course, but it is ambivalently so, for, in a space in which 'desire [...] works to reduce the world to a reflection of the desiring subject', it offers a 'rediversification of the world'.[15] We are back with the relentless struggle between the self's desiring projections and the empirical alterity of the external world and the others in it. In a postulation that echoes the idea of the 'empty apparatus' and Cavell's notion of a world from which the subject is excluded, Bersani writes that what the narrator discovers in this instance is 'his own absence from the world', a 'radical separation of the self from the world'.[16]

Bersani then embarks on a survey of the work of Klein in order to indicate a contrast between the early notion of an unproblematic pleasure in and of the subject's desire, and the more well-known paranoid position in which the subject is gripped by the need to deal with the aggressivity both of his/her own desire and of the (fantasized) other whose attacks must be warded off. Bersani writes: 'Let us first acknowledge the outlines of a novel of *happy* desire in the *Recherche*, of a desire that exuberantly dismembers its objects'.[17] Much of the substance of the novel, in effect, consists in the untroubled recounting of 'the appetitive metonymies of desire', which fragments its objects into impressions and leads them on in a mesmerizing associative chain. However, and this is where the drama and the tragedy of the novel impinges, difficulties arise when the narrator is compelled to interrupt the metonymic logic of association, and imagine persons, in the place of impressions: 'the constitution of persons is linked to the emergence of a novel of *un*happy desire, a novel that depends we might say, on Marcel's misreading of the otherness inherent in desire'. The error in Bersani's account, is the introduction of otherness, the otherness of a person, into the sameness of the narrator's litany of 'happy' objects of desire. The very energy of his own desire is strangely inverted into a paranoiac idea of the desire of the other:

> Desire becomes identical to anxiety as soon as Marcel begins to understand the disappearance of the object not as a function of the energy of his desire but as the consequence of an evil intention on the part of the other. Thus desire's mobility is interpreted paranoiacally: the other has a secret, and that secret is itself a desire excluding Marcel.[18]

We are back on the terrain of Godard's *Le Mépris*: a paranoid psychology of persons has intervened to irretrievably transform the dynamics of desire. Rather than being led along by the procession of associations, of impressions and images, the narrator's quest now becomes one of power and mastery: 'the desexualization of desire and the invention of character are, in Proust, the preconditions for a ruthless if futile effort to absorb the other'.[19]

The emergence of the other as person or character is coextensive therefore with the perception that they are not merely objects of desire, signifiers in a metonymic chain of associations, but also subjects, with their own desires which may or may not include the narrator. The emergence of the other as a person, rather than an object, thus as a source of anxiety and jealousy, is coextensive with the perception of the other's desire. Thus, in Combray, the child narrator's anxiety concerning the knowledge that his mother is 'dans un lieu de plaisir où l'on n'est pas' ('in a place of enjoyment where you are not') (I, 30; I, 33), an anxiety that he later learns he shares with Charles Swann, the very cause of his mother's absence and thus of his suffering. If this paranoid logic is given its first substantial exposition in *Un amour de Swann*, it gains a far more powerful and intractable, impossible twist in the emergence, in later volumes, of homosexuality as *the other desire*, a desire which constitutively excludes the paranoid subject as an actual or potential object.

But Bersani's formulation is perhaps more radical than this, or proposes it to be a more disastrous, if unavoidable, kind of mistake. The mobility of the other's desire is in effect a projection of the very mobility of the self's desire, its 'appetitive metonymy'. In the paranoid constitution of a relation to Albertine as a desiring other, with other desires, at one level the narrator is 'merely' projecting the associative mobility of his own desire. The mistake is to see this as an 'evil intention' on her part. In the election of Albertine to the status of an object whose desire must be mastered, controlled, and above all *known*, the narrator constitutes his own desire as a secret. Bersani renders this as a form of internalization, drawing justification from the narrator's comment that 'once he feels convinced of Albertine's lesbianism, the only truthful way to portray her relation to him would be to "place Albertine, not at a certain distance from me, but inside me"'.[20] This internalized alterity is exacerbated by the fact that, despite all of his efforts to imagine things otherwise, the narrator is constitutively excluded from the extensive range of Albertine's potential desires:

> I spoke of Albertine's sudden displacement from outside Marcel to inside Marcel as the internalization of an impenetrable otherness. I should now refine this formula: first of all, it is her inwardness that Marcel has internalized. The Albertine now making him suffer within himself is not the body that made an excited Marcel move from her to the sea but, instead, the desiring Albertine, the girl who could give Marcel the key to her desires by letting him hear 'the strange sound of her pleasure' (*le son inconnu de sa jouissance*). This internalized interiority of otherness is, for Marcel, the experienced otherness of his own interiority.[21]

The Montjouvain episode, as Proust proposed in a letter to Paul Souday (cited by Ladenson), is in this way the cornerstone of two entire volumes of the novel — presumably *La Prisonnière* and *Albertine disparue*. It is significant then that the dynamics of paranoid jealousy and the fraught question both of the other's desire and the *other desire* of lesbianism hinge around a scene of voyeurism which offers several points of resonance with the cinema, and that the crucial event in the evolution of the narrator's relation to Albertine, thus to his own desire, is rendered as a kind of filmic superimposition.

We can now re-read the passage in question, reducing it to the formative elements of this logic of superimposition:

Une image s'agitait dans mon cœur, une image tenue en réserve [...] pour mon
supplice, pour mon châtiment, qui sait? d'avoir laissé mourir ma grand'mère,
peut-être [...] peut-être aussi pour faire éclater à mes yeux les funestes
conséquences que les actes mauvais engendrent indéfiniment, non pas seulement
pour ceux qui les ont commis, mais pour ceux qui n'ont fait, qui n'ont cru,
que contempler un spectacle curieux et divertissant, comme moi, hélas! en
cette fin de journée lointaine à Montjouvain, caché derrière un buisson où [...]
j'avais dangereusement laissé s'élargir en moi la voie funeste et destinée à être
douloureuse du Savoir. (III, 499, see above for the English translation)

The 'scene' of Montjouvain, held in reserve, has now become 'une image', and this
transformation is construed by the narrator as a form of punishment, not only for
having 'allowed' his grandmother to die, but also for the apparently innocent original
act of voyeurism, as if, unbeknownst to him, the scene he witnessed had imprinted
itself far back in his visual memory. The moral that seems to be expressed here is
that no perception may be simply 'curious and entertaining', that the disinterested
perception or contemplation of nature is never innocent, since the scenes witnessed
or stories overheard (the narrator also refers to his earlier attitude to Swann) can
return to corrupt the present. But it is the notion of 'une image tenue en réserve'
that interests me most here. Proust's writing endows the Montjouvain image with a
kind of vengeful agency, an 'evil intention'; the mastery of his voyeuristic position
on the hillside is sucked onto the side of the image itself; rather than holding it
securely within his visual grasp, he is caught in the field of the image.

The transformation of the Montjouvain scene into an image is emphasized
further as the narrator goes on to describe its effects on his perception, as he looks
out of the window of the Grand Hôtel at Balbec at the sea:

Mais derrière la plage de Balbec, la mer, le lever du soleil, que maman me
montrait, je voyais, [...] la chambre de Montjouvain où Albertine [...], avait pris
la place de l'amie de Mlle Vinteuil [...]. C'est cette scène que je voyais derrière
celle qui s'étendait dans la fenêtre et qui n'était sur l'autre qu'un voile morne,
superposé comme un reflet. Elle semblait elle-même, en effet, presque irréelle,
comme une vue peinte. [...] Dans le désordre des brouillards de la nuit qui
traînaient encore en loques roses et bleues sur les eaux encombrées des débris
de nacre de l'aurore [...] scène imaginaire, grelottante et déserte, pure évocation
du couchant, qui ne reposait pas, comme le soir, sur la suite des heures du jour
que j'avais l'habitude de voir le précéder, déliée, interpolée, plus inconsistante
encore que l'image horrible de Montjouvain qu'elle ne parvenait pas à annuler,
à couvrir, à cacher — poétique et vaine image du souvenir et du songe. (III, 502)

[But behind the beach of Balbec, the sea, and the sunrise, to which Mama was
pointing, I could see [...] the room in Montjouvain where Albertine [...] had
taken the place of Mlle Vinteuil's friend [...] This was the scene I could see
behind that spread out in the window, which was nothing more than a mournful
veil superimposed on the other like a reflection. It seemed itself indeed almost
unreal, like a painted view. [...] In the disorder of the night mists that still hung
in blue and pink shreds over waters littered with the pearly debris of the dawn,
boats were passing, smiling at the oblique light that had turned their sails and
the tips of their bowsprits yellow, as when they return home in the evening: an
imaginary scene, shivering and deserted, a pure evocation of the sunset, which

did not rest, like the dusk, on the procession of hours of the day that I was in the habit of seeing precede it, slender, interpolated, more insubstantial even than the horrible image of Montjouvain that it had not succeeded in cancelling out, in covering, in concealing — a vain and poetic image of the memory and the dream.] (4, 521–22)

The perception of the seascape, which the narrator had invested with so much projective, associative desire and which had been crucial in the metonymic chain that has led him to Albertine becomes nothing more than a thin and muted veil placed upon the more vivid scene of Montjouvain, which is described as lying 'behind' it; the view of the sea is described as superimposed upon it like a reflection, or a painted view. The vision of the dawn, despite the intensity of the poetic touches with which it is endowed, becomes an 'imaginary' or purely evocative vision, out of joint with any temporal sequence or chain of associations. There are at least two conceptual manoeuvres at work here: the relation between the unreal or virtual memory image of Montjouvain and the real and actual perception of Balbec is inverted, such that the latter becomes a mere reflection which cannot compete with the former. Perception becomes a 'vain image', and the memory image is installed as a kind of gestalt against or in relation to which all perception is now structured and affected. The virtual has become actual, so to speak. Secondly, Proust seems to imply the triumph of this logic of the image, and of its 'evil' agency over all forms of art. The image has a kind of desublimating effect on the literary description of the sea, reducing its ekphrastic touches to 'mere poetry'.

Bersani describes the Montjouvain image as having a 'spectralizing effect on reality'.[22] This captures perfectly the paradox which Proust's writing introduces: the image held in reserve (which might normally be rendered as a kind of spectral shadow of actual and real perception) transforms reality into spectre. The usual hierarchy of memory and reality is unfixed and ungrounded, such that it may not be precisely accurate to refer to the Montjouvain image as a memory. It is endowed with a perceptual reality or, at the very least, dims the intensity of real perception, turning it into merely a veil, a film. The 'spectralizing effect' transforms the phenomenal real into a projected image.

In psychoanalytic literature Bertram Lewin's notion of the 'dream screen', referenced by Baudry and discussed in Chapter 1, might seem to pertain to this particular form of hallucination. But while this may account for the attraction and effects of the cinema screen and its capacity to induce a state of 'crepuscular reverie' it does not quite capture the traumatic and potentially psychotic status of the 'spectralizing effect'; the Montjouvain image, moreover, is not a 'blank background', but a mnesic image or memory image of a sort. Despite the affinities of the crepuscular and the spectral, Lewin's dream screen appears far too benign to capture the perceptual catastrophe of Montjouvain. I would rather see the episode as translating into a visual register the logic of Freud's account of melancholia, wherein the 'shadow of the object falls upon the ego'. The 'dimming' effect on perception is akin to the impoverishment of the ego which characterizes the melancholic, for Freud. In this instance the shadow of the image has fallen on perception, so to speak.

Freud discusses a phenomenon close to this in the 1917 essay 'A Metapsychological Supplement to the Theory of Dreams', which compares the specific type of hallucination of the dream with other types such as that of the schizophrenic, and those associated with dementia praecox and with 'Meynert's amentia'. Freud writes that:

> When once a thought has followed the path to regression as far back as to the unconscious memory-traces of objects and thence to perception, we accept the perception of it as real. So hallucination brings belief in reality with it.[23]

However, finding that regression alone cannot account for the hallucination, Freud proposes that it involves an overcoming of the perceptual apparatus of the system of consciousness, and of the operations of reality-testing:

> Hallucination consists in a cathexis of the system *Cs. (Pcpt.)*, which, however, is not effected — as normally — from without, but from within, and [...] a necessary condition for the occurrence of hallucination is that regression shall be carried far enough to reach this system itself and in so doing be able to pass over reality-testing.[24]

In this light we can understand the Montjouvain sequence and its spectralizing effect as a transition in the shift from an external perception to the perception 'from within' which Freud describes here.

Is the spectralizing effect of the episode accounted for by this form of hallucination? If it is, do both phenomena find a corollary of a sort in the situation of film spectatorship? As Barthes, Metz and Baudry argue, the impression of reality of the cinematic image is heightened because the operation of reality-testing, which as Freud notes depends on motor-innervations, is diminished for the relatively immobile spectator. The spectralizing effect and the hallucinatory effect discussed by Freud might be proposed to meet, then, in the conditions of hallucination proposed by the cinema.

However, as I noted earlier, the superimposition of the image of the room at Montjouvain, with Albertine in the place of Mlle Vinteuil's friend, on the perceived image of the sea through the windows of the Grand Hotel causes the latter to appear as no more than a dim veil placed over the more vivid image of the former. The polysemy of the word *film* allows me to suggest that it is perception that has become a film, a thin layer placed *right up against* the memory image, which itself has acquired the status of the perceptual real, in a chiasmatic inversion of properties. Rather than aligning the cinema of Montjouvain with the regressive hallucination described by Freud, or as a supplement to this parallel, I would suggest that it may be more pertinently rendered as a specific trope explored both by Proust — here and at other moments in the *Recherche* — and in some of the most seminal moments within film history, within the framework of film narratives, as if the cinema were exploring its own vocation and its own limits in the indiscernibility and substitution of the real and the virtual.

The two sides of Alfred Hitchcock's *Vertigo*, those belonging, so to speak, to Madeleine on the one hand, and Judy on the other, meet in an extraordinary scene which seems to me to provide a close visual rendition of this spectralizing effect.

The sequence occurs as Scottie (James Stewart) embraces Judy (Kim Novak), in whom he thinks he has found a near exact double of Madeleine, who he believes has fallen to her death from the bell-tower of the Mission of San Juan Bautista. Scottie is attempting to mould Judy into the exact image of the dead woman, to dress and to fix her hair like Madeleine, and this visual echo prompts the sequence which the viewer is invited to see as a hallucination on Scottie's part. Judy in the image of Madeleine seems to emerge out of the already dimmed pale green light of a doorway; as the couple embrace the camera turns around them and the hotel room setting behind them is replaced, in the course of this revolution, by the stable below the bell-tower in which Scottie kissed Madeleine before her death. As it turns around further we are returned to the hotel room, just prior to Scottie's discovery of the deception: Madeleine was in fact Judy, and her death was faked to mask the death of the real Madeleine.

What I find resonant with the Montjouvain episode in this sequence from *Vertigo* is the dimming effect, visible just prior to the turn of the camera, on the already muted perceptual image of the hotel room as the camera starts to revolve, the substitution of this image by the image of the stable, which appears as if projected behind the couple, and Scottie's perplexed recognition of the hallucination that the film is visiting upon him. The ambivalent status of the hallucination, which is not fully integrated into Scottie's psychological agency, and is out of joint with the narrative viewpoint of the film, points to its liminary status at the boundaries of orthodox narrative film. The 'vertigo' of the film's title, from this perspective, refers as much to the specific pathology of its male protagonist as to the oscillation of virtual and actual that takes place at this limit. It is at limits such as these, I would venture, that cinema begins to realize its Proustian vocation.

I would like to end this chapter with a return to colour, prompted by Jean-Louis Schefer's attention to this scene of *Vertigo* and in particular by its colours. Schefer reads the scene as 'un piège guimauve' [a marshmallow trap], a succulent lure for Scottie and for the viewer alike, which, through the emphatically artificial, 'make-up' of the scene, draws them in to fascination with the *image* of the reincarnated Madeleine.[25] Schefer also refers to the pale green light as a 'poudroiement pistache' [a pistachio frosting], and to the 'alimentary' aspects of the scene, which Hitchcock has prepared for us 'comme un gateau' [like a cake].[26] Through this Schefer proposes that the film foregrounds the way in which Scottie is captured by the 'trap' of the image, in which he has re-made Judy in the image of Madeleine (Schefer exploits the term *maquillage*, make-up), and re-found Madeleine as an image, which he will subsequently find to be just that, and to have been caught in its trap from the start.

In this light we can look again at Proust's narrator's entrapment by the image of Albertine as Mlle Vinteuil's friend. He writes with full poetic force of the image of the dawn above the cliffs of Parville, cited above, which is eclipsed by that of Albertine in the room at Montjouvain. Behind the image of the dawn, 'spectralizing' it, the narrator sees: 'Albertine, rose, pelotonnée comme une grosse chatte, le nez mutin' ('Albertine, pink, curled up in a ball like a big cat, with her mischievous nose') (III, 502; 4, 521). While the original Montjouvain scene is described without colour, colour becomes particularly marked in the superimposition; the delicate Turneresque touches of Proust's ekphrastic description of the dawn are drastically reduced by the almost monstrous, bestial image of Albertine; the golden varnish of the sea, the pink and blue tendrils of the lingering night fog, the pearl-white and blue of the seascape are eclipsed by the vision of Albertine as a plump, pink cat, rolled up into a ball. I have already suggested that what occurs here is a fairly radical negation of the aestheticizing tendency, of the power of language to evoke a scene; it approaches the radical negation of Bataille's 'hatred of poetry' or of his affirmation of the 'hypermorality' of literature.[27] But what interests me particularly here is the way in which the painterly scene of the dawn is eclipsed by an image which, to use Bal's terms, seems to press outward, against the narrator's vision, and which seems almost cartoon-like in its animalistic and alimentary evocation, and in the fleshy pinkness attributed to Albertine. The subtle variations of the ekphrasis are homogenized by this pulsing intensity of the pink, an effect which we might see replicated in the capacity of film to modulate and intensify colour so as to express and provoke specific forms of affect.

One might object to this point that the history of painting already offers us an extremely rich and subtle exploration of effects of colour and the use of the play of colours and tones to propose quite specific affective responses. But the reason why I see the Montjouvain superimposition pointing us more towards cinema lies in the homogeneity of Albertine's pink, effacing the variegated tones of the dawn — pink versus blue, pink and blue, gold, yellow, and pearl. I think of this as 'cartoon-like' because of this homogeneity, the filling-in of figures by blocks of colour, the absence of shading. As a cartoon image it pertains to animation, and to the magic lantern and stained glass, in which colour is also a homogenous block. In the magic lantern projection of Combray, the forest was dark green, Geneviève wore a blue belt, the castle and the moorland were yellow, and Golo's cloak was red. This kind of colour-coding points less towards painting and more towards the 'primitive' visual form of the magic lantern, or the use of blocks of colour in stained glass. I see in it another variant of Proust's tendency towards a regression, towards the infancy of the cinema, as if to imagine its reinvention.

Notes to Chapter 4

1. Elisabeth Ladenson, *Proust's Lesbianism* (Ithaca, NY, & London: Cornell University Press, 1999), p. 63.
2. Ibid., p. 64.
3. Ibid., p. 66.
4. Ibid.
5. Ibid., p. 78.
6. André Bazin, *Qu'est-ce que le cinéma* (Paris: Editions du Cerf, 1959), p. 98; *What is Cinema?*, trans. by Hugh Gray, 2 vols (Berkeley & Los Angeles: University of California Press, 1967), I, 104.
7. Ibid., p. 100; I, 105.
8. Ibid.
9. Bellour, 'Le Spectateur pensif', p. 80; 'The Pensive Spectator', p. 82.
10. Bal, *The Mottled Screen*, p. 216.

11. Ibid., p. 217.

12. Ibid., p. 219.

13. Ibid., p. 222.

14. See, for example, Bowie, *Freud, Proust, Lacan*, p. 46; Ladenson, *Proust's Lesbianism*, pp. 58–59; Christopher Prendergast, *Mirages and Mad Beliefs: Proust the Skeptic* (Princeton, NJ, & Oxford: Princeton University Press, 2013), pp. 1–4.

15. Bersani, 'Death and Literary Authority', p. 8

16. Ibid., p. 9.

17. Ibid., p. 22.

18. Ibid., p. 23.

19. Ibid.

20. Ibid.

21. Ibid., p. 24.

22. Ibid., p. 25.

23. Sigmund Freud, 'A Metapsychological Supplement to the Theory of Dreams', in *On Metapsychology: The Theory of Psychoanalysis*, Pelican Freud Library 11 (Harmondsworth: Penguin, 1984), pp. 229–43 (p. 238).

24. Ibid., p. 240.

25. Jean-Louis Schefer, '*Vertigo*, vert tilleul', in *Images mobiles: récits, visages, flocons* (Paris: P.O.L., 1999), pp. 194–202 (p. 196): 'un piège guimauve est disposé auquel l'enquêteur se prendra, comme une mouche à la colle' [a marshmallow trap is arranged in which the detective will be caught, like a fly in fly-paper].

26. Ibid., pp. 200, 201.

27. See Georges Bataille, *La Littérature et le mal* (Paris: Gallimard, 1957); *Literature and Evil*, trans. by Alistair Hamilton (London: Penguin Books, 2012): 'La littérature est l'essentiel ou n'est rien. Le Mal — une forme aigüe du Mal dont elle est l'expression, a pour nous, je le crois, la valeur souveraine. Mais cette conception ne commande pas l'absence de morale, elle exige une "hypermorale"' (p. 9) ('Literature is either the essential or nothing. I believe that the Evil — an acute form of Evil — which it expresses, has a sovereign value for us. But this concept does not exclude morality: on the contrary, it demands a "hypermorality"', p. 4).

CHAPTER 5

Theory of Gesture

The Lost Film

Giorgio Agamben's essay 'Notes on Gesture', originally published in French in the inaugural issue of Serge Daney's new film review *Trafic*, in 1992, has provoked a powerful seam of film theory and philosophy focused around the issue of gesture.[1] The *Recherche* features as a salient reference in the essay and in its intertexts, and the figure of Proust and the logic of involuntary memory also hover spectrally over Agamben's discussion, flickering intermittently throughout Agamben's various arguments concerning gesture, which interweave arguments drawn from the work of Aby Warburg, Walter Benjamin, and Gilles Deleuze. It will be my contention in this chapter that, while it offers striking parallels and connecting points to the work of Warburg, Proust's *Recherche* is also a significant point of departure for the theoretical discourses upon which Agamben draws, and that this constellation of connections can lead us toward the virtual film which Proust's novel projects.

'Notes on Gesture' draws together a series of motifs and propositions concerning gesture in Agamben's previous writings, and in significant instances lifts sentences and paragraphs from earlier texts, indicating that the arguments concerning cinema are part of a larger constellation of concerns. For example, the principal thesis of the essay — that at the end of the nineteenth century the European bourgeoisie definitively 'lost its gestures' and 'succumbed to interiority' — repeats an argument from an earlier essay on the twentieth-century German literary critic and historian Max Kommerell, while also drawing on Agamben's close experience and sustained commentary on the work of Kommerell's contemporary Benjamin.[2] The main focus of the text on Kommerell is the gestural or 'gestic' level of criticism, which, Agamben writes, 'resolves the work's intention into a gesture (or into a constellation of gestures)'.[3] The idea of intention here gives us a purchase on one of the seams of Agamben's argument concerning gesture — it is 'closely tied to language' but is 'more originary than conceptual expression'.[4] It is 'not exhausted in communication' and to this extent it is equivalent to an 'originary' intention in speech as such, an intentionality inherent in the very act of speaking, which is not captured in conceptual communication. Gesture, however, is not a 'prelinguistic content', but 'the muteness inherent in humankind's very capacity for language'. Following Kommerell, Agamben locates gesture in relation to the 'state of speechlessness in language', or humankind's 'speechless dwelling in language'. The gesturality inherent in language is the mark of being in language or with language as such, the very fact of speaking, which as such 'has nothing to say', which is speechless. In order to explicate this sense of speechlessness inherent in language, which Kommerell had discerned in the enigma, the secret, and the mystery, Agamben has recourse to a sort of pun; the gesture is a 'gag', both in the sense of 'something put in someone's mouth to keep him from speaking', and in the sense of 'the actor's improvisation to keep him from speaking'. But the 'gag', Agamben writes, turns to 'mystery', and the confusion provoked by the enigma of this speechless dwelling turns to 'dance'.[5]

This serves to introduce Agamben's commentary on Kommerell's essay on the German Romantic writer Jean Paul, and the delineation of a 'dialectic of gesture' which moves beyond the falsity of convention and the fixity of the symbol (in Goethe) to approach the level of 'pure gesture', manifest in the 'fragments of another world in the soul of Jean Paul'.[6] For Agamben this is redolent of a 'redeemed world', and he also finds this in Benjamin's contemporaneous evocation of the 'Oklahoma Nature Theatre' in Kafka's unfinished novel *Amerika*. It is the reference to the stage which is key here — Agamben writes that if criticism is 'the reduction of works to the sphere of pure gesture', this trajectory 'opens onto a stage'. In seeking the inherent speechless core of a work, or of an era, its gestural origin, criticism points us towards a kind of speechless mime or dance, and to the 'creatures' which perform it, such as 'Harlequin, Pantaloon, Columbine', creatures 'emancipated from written texts and fully defined roles'.[7] This 'reduction', in which we might find echoes of Mallarmé's project for the Book (*Le Livre*), or Artaud's 'Theatre of Cruelty', introduces a conception of the literary work not as the communication of a content or the representation of reality, but as a form of choreography in which may be discerned the fact of being in language, the fact of inhabiting it, which is, in itself without words.

At this point Agamben writes, enigmatically:

> In the comedy that criticism substitutes for literary history, the *Recherche* or the *Commedia* ceases to be the established text that the critic must investigate and then consign, intact and inalterable, to tradition. They are instead the gestures that, in those wondrous texts, exhibit only a gigantic lack of memory, only a 'gag' destined to hide an incurable speechlessness.[8]

Proust's novel is evoked here, counter-intuitively, as 'reduced' to its gestures, to its 'gags', to those elements in it which point to an absence or lack of memory and of speech. Rather than as a literary monument to memory, a triumph of the capacity of language to capture and to represent, to communicate, the *Recherche* is stripped back to a series of 'gags', both in the sense of comic, improvised movements, pratfalls, and stumbles (the narrator's mishap with the paving stone in *Le Temps retrouvé* is evoked silently here) and in the sense of instances where memory and speech fail, where the capacity to communicate and to represent are silenced. Agamben does not expand on the brief reference to Proust here — as if to prove his point about speechlessness his work lacks any extensive analytic engagement with the *Recherche* — but it does prepare for a later proposition in both the Kommerell essay and 'Notes on

Gesture', in which Proust appears alongside silent cinema, already foreshadowed in the incidence of speechlessness and of the 'gag', as attempts to recuperate 'what humanity was soon to lose irretrievably': the sphere of gesture.

It is this third part of the essay on Kommerell which is incorporated almost word for word in the different context of the 'Notes on Gesture' essay in *Trafic*, thus in a context more specifically concerned with cinema and with a renewed orientation of film criticism. Firstly, Agamben takes from Kommerell the opening thesis of 'Notes on Gesture' (written as a numbered and italicized proposition at the head of the essay): '1. By the end of the nineteenth century, the Western bourgeoisie had definitely lost its gestures'.[9] What Agamben means by the loss of gesture here is indicated in the Kommerell essay by the following: 'The age of Jean Paul is an age in which the bourgeoisie, which in Goethe still seemed to possess its symbols, fell victim to interiority'.[10] Gesture is equivalent to symbol, to a conventionally and consensually common repertory of signs or indices in which humanity located its common inhabiting of language, which showed its common dwelling in language. The loss of gesture is a loss of commonality, of community, and it has a corollary in a 'succumbing to interiority'. Countering Kommerell's argument that this loss of common gestural language is a form of emancipation from fixed forms, ('Fully liberated spirit is a consequence of the bourgeoisie that has lost its gestures'),[11] Agamben outlines the sense in which this loss renders gesture indecipherable and foreign, and promotes gesture to the status of a 'destiny', turning humans into puppets under the sway of unknown powers and, in a more sinister manner, prey to destruction:

> But an epoch that has lost its gestures is, by the same token, obsessed with them; for men from whom all authenticity has been taken, gesture becomes destiny. And the more gestures lost their ease under the pressure of unknown powers, the more life became indecipherable. And once the simplest and most everyday gestures had become as foreign as the gesticulations of marionettes, humanity, — whose very bodily existence had already become sacred to the degree that it had made itself impenetrable — was ready for the massacre.[12]

In 'Notes on Gesture' this is rendered thus:

> An age that has lost its gestures is, for this reason, obsessed by them. For human beings who have lost every sense of naturalness, each single gesture becomes a destiny. And the more gestures lose their ease under the action of invisible powers, the more life becomes indecipherable. In this phase the bourgeoisie, which just a few decades earlier was still firmly in possession of its symbols, succumbs to interiority and gives itself up to psychology.[13]

In 'Notes on Gesture', this paragraph appears under the second, italicized proposition: '2. *In the cinema, a society that has lost its gestures tries at once to reclaim what it has lost and to record its loss*'. In the first part of the essay Agamben had marked the historical moment of the loss of gesture through reference to the recording of a 'generalized catastrophe of the gestural sphere' in the work of Jean-Marie Charcot and Gilles de la Tourette at the Salpetrière hospital towards the end of the nineteenth century, linking it to the contemporaneous experiments with human locomotion of Eadweard Muybridge and to the films which 'Marey and Lumière began to shoot exactly in those years'.[14] Agamben positions early 'film' (conflating Marey's experiments with chronophotography with Lumière and Edison's moving image projections) as both a symptom and a response to the loss of gesture. The second part begins with the slightly altered version of the argument Agamben has drawn from Kommerell (losing the Benjaminian reference to the impending 'massacre') — thus situating early cinema as a marker of the loss of gesture, but also as an attempt to recover it. Cinema becomes a symptom of a political crisis, the loss of a commonality or a consensual 'dwelling' in language, and a struggle against this loss. There is a complex dialectic at work here, which Agamben will develop in the course of the essay: cinema, and the experimental and medical procedures from which it derived (in the work of Charcot, de la Tourette and Marey) worked in the same direction as the loss of gestural 'ease' through the decomposition of bodily movement into a series of 'snapshots' and the consequential image of frenetic gesticulation in early films. However, in liberating the image of the body from the stasis of the fixed pose or the statue, cinema 'leads images back to the homeland of gesture'.[15] Further on in this chapter I will work through some of the underpinnings of this argument, in which Agamben draws on the work of Warburg and Deleuze. But Agamben's next proposition, in both the Kommerell and gesture essays, concerns me more explicitly at this stage, as it involves a positioning of silent film and of Proust's *Recherche* alongside one another as equivalent attempts to recuperate the loss of gesture.

This is the relevant paragraph in the essay on Kommerell, repeated word for word in 'Notes on Gesture':

> In modern culture, Nietzsche marks the apex of this polar tension toward the effacement of gestures and transfiguration into destiny. For the eternal return is intelligible only as a gesture (and hence solely as theatre) in which potentiality and actuality, authenticity and mannerism, contingency and necessity have become indistinguishable. *Thus spake Zarathustra* is the ballet of a humanity that has lost its gestures. And when the age became aware of its loss (too late!) it began its hasty attempts to recuperate its lost gestures *in extremis*. Isadora Duncan and Diaghilev's ballets, Proust's novel, Rilke and Pascoli's great *Jugendstil* poetry, and, finally, in the most exemplary fashion, silent film — all these trace the magic circle in which humanity tried to evoke what it was soon to lose irretrievably.[16]

While the essay on Kommerell wraps itself up in a concluding consideration of the German critic's essay on *William Meister*, 'Notes on Gesture' extends its proposition of early film as the 'most exemplary' dimension in which the recuperation of gesture is visible, through engagements with Warburg and Deleuze, and through a third proposition — that the central point of cinema is the gesture, rather than the image, and that it thus belongs essentially to the sphere of ethics and politics, rather than aesthetics.

The key argument which Agamben draws from Warburg, and which he will in turn apply to Warburg's legacy, rests on the distinction between the image and gesture. Agamben argues that the legacy of Warburg's work has been short-sightedly limited to the field of aesthetics, to a concern with the image, while its true focus is the dynamic element in art, the gesture. Warburg belongs not to the field of aesthetics and art history, but to a 'nameless science' which Agamben had promoted in a separate essay on Warburg from 1975, which thus enters the arena as a further key intertext of 'Notes on Gesture'.[17] The gesture Warburg sought is, as Agamben outlines in the latter essay, a 'crystal of historical memory', a 'decisively historical and dynamic element'. Warburg studied the tendency for the gesture to 'stiffen' into a destiny, into a fixed and immutable form, and the opposing struggle on the part of artists to 'redeem the destiny [of gesture] through a dynamic polarization'.[18]

In 'Notes on Gesture' Agamben points to Warburg's unfinished *BilderAtlas* project, also referred to as the Mnemosyne project, which featured a vast array of images from multiple and varied historical and aesthetic contexts. The point, Agamben argues, was not to collect and present an 'immoveable repertoire of images', but to propose a 'representation in virtual movement of Western humanity's gestures', as if each image were not an autonomous icon but something more akin to a film still. The Mnemosyne project is thus like one of those 'flip books', Agamben suggests, in which Walter Benjamin saw a version of the dialectical image:

> Inside each section, the single images should be considered more as film stills than as autonomous realities (at least in the same way in which Benjamin once compared the dialectical image to those little books, forerunners of cinematography, that gave the impression of movement when the pages were turned over rapidly).[19]

Underlying the distinction between image and gesture, then, is an implicit opposition between stasis and movement: the image is considered as 'autonomous reality', while the gesture is that element in an image which expresses a dynamic force, and which moves across and between (still) images. The paradigmatic shift is towards the dynamic and the dialectical, displacing the iconic stasis of classical form.

The driving force of Warburg's displacement and transgression of the boundaries of the discipline of art history is the central notion of *Nachleben* — the survival or more correctly 'afterlife', in the form of images, of memory traces, which Agamben relates to the 'engram', the preservation of energy in the form of a trace — which Warburg was to find in the work of Richard Semon. The history of art, rather than a repertory of forms, susceptible to a purely formal analysis, is the story of a struggle between the expressive force of pagan culture, embedded in the image itself, and the forms in which it might be tamed, or released. This trans-historical conception of the image positions it as a sort of symptom of the dynamic tension of historical forces; the work of art is a 'dynamogram', and 'stylistic and formal decisions at times adopted by artists appear as ethical decisions of individuals and epochs regarding the inheritance of the past'.[20] The work of art is a 'confrontation [...] with the tremendous energies stored in images'. To this extent, the work of art appears as a form of intermediary, a negotiation of sorts, benign or violent, between the forces of the present and those of the past; it is an 'interval' or *Zwischenraum*, 'between consciousness and primitive reactions', and Agamben suggests, pointing to a note by Warburg from 1929, that the nameless science be called an 'iconology of the interval'.[21] Warburg's notion of the *Pathosformeln* designates that element in the work of art by which the tension between historical forces becomes visible; it is not, as Agamben suggests it is in the work of Warburg's principal interpreter Erwin Panofsky, the expression of the innermost elements of the artist's individual personality, but a symptom of historical dynamism.[22] The liberation of the dynamic element in the work of art, which was both the aim and effect of Warburg's transgressive displacement of the boundaries of orthodox art history and aesthetics, hinges on a shift of focus away from the static image as a fixed and autonomous form towards the confrontation of conscious and unconscious forces of which the artist is only one vector. But it also hinges on a conception of the image in relation to movement, and a different conception of movement as such. This justifies Agamben's turn to Deleuze, and to the theses of *Cinéma 1: l'image-mouvement*.

Following the reference to Warburg, and significantly informed by it, Agamben writes, under the third propositional statement, '3. *The element of cinema is gesture and not image*':

> Gilles Deleuze has argued that cinema erases the fallacious psychological distinction between image as psychic reality and movement as physical reality. Cinematographic images are neither *poses éternelles* (such as the forms of the classical age) nor *coupes immobiles* of movement, but rather *coupes mobiles*.[23]

Agamben refers here in fact to the 'thèses sur le movement' proposed by Deleuze in the first chapter of *Cinéma 1*, by way of a first commentary on Bergson. Reading these two texts alongside one another is a frustrating experience of convergence and divergence; at points the Warburgian thesis of the dynamism inherent in the image seems to fall within the orbit of the 'illusions' concerning movement of which Bergson, and Deleuze following him, are critical; at other points Agamben seems to ascribe fully to the conception of the movement–image elaborated by Deleuze, and yet wants to depart from it, in 'prolonging' Deleuze's argument towards the status of the image in general, whether still or moving. In effect, Agamben proposes a partial reading of Deleuze — drawing from *Cinéma 1* the points that serve the Warburgian thesis he wishes to pursue, and the subsuming of cinema within a general argument about gesture.

Bergson, Deleuze argues, situates two 'illusions' in the conception of movement, the antique and the modern. In the antique version, movement is conceived on the basis of a transcendent and immobile Idea or Form: 'Pour l'antiquité, le mouvement renvoie à des éléments intelligibles, Formes ou Idées qui sont elles-mêmes éternelles et immobiles' ('For antiquity, movement refers to intelligible elements, Forms or Ideas which are themselves eternal and immobile'). Movement is conceived in terms of the passage from one form to another. Of course, Deleuze continues, movement can be grasped at the closest point ('au plus près') of its incarnation in the flux of matter, as potentiality.[24] Are we close here to Warburg's thesis of the dynamism inherent in the image? This much seems to be suggested by Deleuze's subsequent proposition that movement considered on this basis is expressed as a 'dialectic of forms', recalling Agamben's reference just before to Benjamin's 'image of the dialectic'. This suspicion is intensified in Deleuze's next point: 'Le mouvement ainsi conçu sera donc le passage réglé d'une forme à une autre, c'est-à-dire un ordre des *poses* ou des *instants priviligiés*, comme dans une danse' ('Movement, conceived in this way, will thus be the regulated transition from one form to another, that is, an order of poses or privileged instants, as in a dance').[25] The reference to dance might seem to comprise Agamben's displacement from image to gesture, and thus to comprise the Warburgian argument he pursues within the 'antique' illusion of movement criticized by Deleuze. Is Warburg's dynamism a passage between forms, a dialectic of forms? Or is it, rather, an approach which detects a dynamism inherent in the image itself, a force inherent in form? The distinction between these two conceptions is slippery.

The key difference between the antique and the modern illusions concerning movement lies in the difference between the recourse to a transcendent form or essence and movement conceived on the basis of an immanent analysis. The modern conception of movement abandons the postulation of the 'privileged instant' through the emergence, in the analysis of the sensible (rather than conceptual synthesis), of what Deleuze calls 'l'instant quelconque' ('any-instant-whatever').[26] This distinction, between privileged instant and 'whatever moment', paralleled in the opposition of the pose and the cut or slice (*coupe*), will prove to play a programmatic role in Deleuze's philosophy of film, since despite the critique of the 'modern' illusion of movement located in the 'immobile cut' of the instant, it is out of this illusion that the true conception of movement will emerge.

Referring to a series of 'modern' scientific methodologies — Kepler in astronomy, Galileo in physics, Descartes in geometry, Newton and Leibniz in calculus — Deleuze writes that: 'Partout la succession mécanique d'instants quelconques remplaçait l'ordre dialectique des poses' ('Everywhere the mechanical succession of instants replaced the dialectical order of poses').[27] The cinema belongs to this lineage, and it is determined, according to Deleuze, by its basis in 'whatever instant':

Les conditions déterminantes du cinéma sont les suivantes: non pas seulement la photo, mais la photo instantané (la photo de pose appartient à l'autre lignée); l'équidistance des instantanés; le report de cet equidistance sur un support qui constitue le 'film' (c'est Edison et Dickson qui perforent la pellicule); un mécanisme d'entraînement des images (les griffes de Lumière).

[The determining conditions of the cinema are the following: not merely the photo, but the snapshot (the long-exposure photo belongs to the other lineage); the equidistance of snapshots; the transfer of this equidistance on to a framework which constitutes the 'film' (it was Edison and Dickson who perforated the film in the camera); a mechanism for moving on images (Lumière's claws).][28]

It is interesting to see how Deleuze charts the technological elements which will coalesce in the cinema as it would be institutionalized in relation to the central fact of 'whatever instant', but also how he discerns within photography a dichotomy between the 'lineage' ('lignée') of the pose and that of *whatever instant*. Is this dichotomy a purely technical matter? It is true that the daguerreotype needed the subject to maintain a pose for the duration of the exposure, and that the capture of movement 'in the instant' became possible only with the development of faster lenses and instantaneous exposure times.

However, Agamben argues that the dynamism inherent in 'whatever instant' is not specific to cinema and asserts that, 'It is necessary to extend Deleuze's argument and show how it relates to the status of the image in general within modernity'.[29] This is to say that Agamben promotes Deleuze's conception of the movement-image as a displacement from the image to gesture, from the image as autonomous and static reality to gesture, following Warburg, as the element of dynamism inherent in the immobile image. This has a number of implications, not fully spelt out by Agamben. Firstly, it implies a shift away from the specificity of cinema as such as *the* technological means for the representation of movement, and towards a 'more general' concern with the dynamism inherent in the image, whether moving or still. This explains the relevance of Agamben's evocation of the Mnemosyne *BilderAtlas* as a series of film stills, and the allusion to Benjamin's note about flip books. The dynamism of the image, the movement-image, is felt as much in the still, or in a painting, as in the moving image as such. Movement, in other words, is not a quality restricted to the cinematographic apparatus. The sphere of gesture, while it is visible 'in the most exemplary fashion' in film, extends beyond it; cinema is one dimension of the gestural sphere. A second implication is that gesturality is not the sole province of cinema and is extended across other media. The extension of Deleuze's argument:

> Implies, however, that the mythical rigidity of the image has been broken and that here, properly speaking, there are no images but only gestures. Every image, in fact, is animated by an antinomic polarity: on the one hand, images are the reification and obliteration of a gesture (it is the *imago* as death mask or as symbol); on the other they preserve the *dynamis* intact (as in Muybridge's snapshots or in any sports photograph). The former corresponds to the recollection seized by voluntary memory, while the latter corresponds to the image flashing in the epiphany of involuntary memory. And while the former lives in magical isolation, the latter always refers beyond itself to a whole of which it is a part. Even the *Mona Lisa*, even *Las Meninas* could be seen not as immovable and eternal forms, but as fragments of a gesture or as stills of a lost film wherein only they would regain their true meaning. And that is so because a certain kind of *litigatio,* a paralyzing power whose spell we need to break, is continuously at work in every image; it is as if a silent invocation calling for the liberation of the image into gesture arose from the entire history of art. This is what in ancient Greece was expressed by the legends in which statues break the ties holding them, and begin to move. But this is also the intention that philosophy entrusts to the idea, which is not at all an immobile archetype as common interpretations would have it, but rather a constellation in which phenomena arrange themselves in a gesture.[30]

Before we come to the distinctive allusion to Proust in this passage, I want to note that Agamben thus supplements the appeal to Warburg with a reference to Deleuze, and specifically to the thesis on movement in Deleuze's *Cinéma 1*. This implies a wholly different conception of movement, one which does not in fact hinge on whether the image is moving or not — Warburg did not study film as such, and the comparison of Mnemosyne to a series of film stills might suggest that we are in the realm of gesture, rather than that of the moving image as such.

Despite the basis of the photograph in whatever instant, at least since the daguerreotype, the dichotomy of pose and instant might still be at work, both on the side of the subject and of the object, so to speak. This is to say that the tension between form and movement does not depend by necessity on the means of production but rather on the modalities of seeing and acting in relation to the image. And the pose brings with it a whole psychology of self-consciousness and capture which go beyond the determination of the apparatus. The possibility that, even within those media produced on the basis of whatever instant, the dichotomy of pose and whatever instant may be inherent in the modes of seeing and reading the image allows for the strategy for which Agamben argues — to draw cinema towards gesture, away from the image. Deleuze is in effect aware of the possibility of the privileged instant within film, and addresses this via Eisenstein; cinema appears to draw on 'privileged instants' in the moments of crisis and paroxysm, the 'pathetic' elements in Eisenstein's films appear as evidence of this. But this is no objection, Deleuze proposes, referring back to Marey's and Muybridge's experiments with animal locomotion and the representation of the horse's gallop by virtue of the graphic recording ('enregistrements graphiques') of the former and the equidistant snapshots ('instantanés equidistants') of the latter, which produce an organized set of images each of which is 'any-point-whatever' ('un point quelconque').[31] 'Remarkable' moments will perforce arise in the whole set of equidistant points or out of the pattern of lines and marks of the graphic method, and these might be called 'privileged instants', but they are privileged, or singular, in an entirely different sense than in the older ('ancien') modes of representation of the horse, and differ from the poses or 'generalised postures' of antique forms.[32] The privileged instants drawn from the series of whatever instants or equidistant points differ radically from the poses or postures of antique forms, and the key distinction appears to lie in in the difference between the derivation of the pose, however dynamic, from a 'transcendental synthesis' ('synthèse transcendentale') and the derivation of singular moment from the immanent analysis of movement. The privileged instant in Eisenstein, for example, is derived from movement and is immanent to it, as opposed to its movement or dynamism being a quality of a transcendent or 'average' idea of form. The privileged instant remains whatever instant among others. If there are privileged or singular moments in film it is on a wholly different basis from in media premised on a transcendent notion of form — singular moments are drawn from ('prélévés sur') the whatever.[33] The key displacement lies in the technology which allows for the production of equidistant points or the lines of the graphic method, thus an automatic recording and analytic technology from which the synthesizing consciousness is subtracted, along with the transcendent idea of form. Deleuze thus accords specificity to proto-cinematographic and to the automatism of its methods, which he designates as 'immanent'. The determining instance is equidistance and immanence.

But a further difficulty arises here, Deleuze notes, since the aims of the scientific 'revolution' which conceived movement immanently were predominantly analytic. If it was necessary to produce an image of movement through an analysis immanent to it, a synthesis based on the same principle appeared redundant, or of little interest. The scientific value of the synthetic representation of movement drawn from the analytic decomposition of movement into a series of equidistant points, that is, of a continuous representation of these points so as to recompose the movement, was null. And neither did it seem, Deleuze argues, of any artistic merit, since art seemed to maintain the privilege of transcendent poses and forms, which analytic science had repudiated. Neither Marey nor Lumière, Deleuze asserts, had much faith in the future of the cinema as invention or as an art.[34]

However, the arts were nevertheless sensitive to the change, and Deleuze points to the ways in which, at the end of the nineteenth century, dance, mime, ballet, and even painting progressively abandoned the pose in favour of 'des valeurs non posées, non-pulsées' ('values which were not posed, not measured'), relating movement to whatever instant, and becoming capable of responding to contingency, to 'les accidents du milieu' ('accidents of the environment'). 'Tout cela conspirait avec le cinéma' ('All this served the same end as the cinema'), Deleuze writes.[35] Without making explicit any causal connection Deleuze situates the birth of cinema and the new arts of movement as part of the evolution of the scientific 'revolution' which had rejected transcendental synthesis in favour of immanent analysis.

Rather than as a response to the loss of gesture, and a species of the artistic and critical tendency — in Warburg, for example, which sought to liberate movement from stasis, gesture from image — Deleuze thus situates the emergence of the cinema as a predominantly technical and scientific evolution or revolution. Agamben, on the other hand, in proposing that the central element of cinema is gesture, draws it back into a longer-term development, or even an anthropological tendency. These two quite distinct orientations, sketched in Agamben's essay, more drawn out in Deleuze, converge on an indiscernible difference between the derivation of movement as a property of form, and the notion of form as a quality of movement. In reporting or 'prolonging' Deleuze's analysis to the issue of gesture, Agamben anthropologizes Bergson's argument concerning movement and matter as such. Agamben proposes that Deleuze's delineation, via the commentary on Bergson (who Agamben does not mention) of the movement-image as a 'mobile section' ('coupe mobile') is equivalent to the dynamic potential of or in the image, the gesture in and of the image. The technical and historical specificity of the cinema, which Deleuze had argued emerges out of the analytic sciences, is collapsed back into the history of images and a conception of the image as a relation of forces, such that paintings may be seen as 'photograms', 'fragments of a lost film'. It is worth re-emphasizing this proposition in the passage cited above: 'Even the Mona Lisa, even Las Meninas could be seen not as immovable and eternal forms, but as fragments of a gesture or as stills of a lost film wherein only they would regain their true meaning'.

The 'privileged instant' or the pose is reconfigured, in this argument, as 'whatever instant'. Agamben substitutes for Deleuze's analysis a programmatic, and transgressive plea for the 'nameless science' he identifies in Warburg; on the basis of the technology which makes possible the photogram, an instant drawn out of a larger dynamism, the whole history of images can be recast as the study of force and movement rather than image and form.

A further recurrence of the Proustian motif in Agamben's essay arises in the orbit of this proposition, and is a further aspect of the passage cited above I want to address more closely. Having proposed that Deleuze's conception of the cinematographic image as a 'mobile section' should be extended to the status of the image in general in the modern era, and thus that the gestural component of the image be discerned, Agamben argues, in Warburgian mode, that the image be considered as determined by two polarities — one which reifies and thus annuls the gesture, as in the death mask or the Symbol, and the other which is dynamic, a gestural potentiality which is nevertheless preserved or conserved 'intact' in the image, however still or fixed. The Proustian resonance of the word 'conserved' seems to prepare for the subsequent comparison: 'The former [the static annihilation of gesture] corresponds to the recollection seized by voluntary memory, while the latter [the dynamic potentiality] corresponds to the image flashing in the epiphany of involuntary memory'.[36] Voluntary memory is construed here as a fixed picture, a static image of the past, which nevertheless conserves within it a dynamic force which opens memory out to becoming. Agamben refers implicitly to Deleuze's commentary on Bergson's 'third thesis on movement', that movement as a mobile section gives an image of a change in duration, a change in the whole, a whole which is not given in advance, but is open, is the Open.

This analogy, which asserts that voluntary memory is to the image as involuntary memory is to gesture, allows us to think of the instances of involuntary memory in the *Recherche* — the madeleine, bootlace, paving stone, napkin, bell, the name 'Vinteuil' — as its gestural components, those elements which open memory out beyond itself to a dynamic becoming. The *Recherche*, like silent film, would thus be an expression of the attempt to recuperate gesture in its attention to the dynamic of memory as a non-linear and multiple knot of temporal forces. This allows us also to position the 'movement-images' or gestures of film on the same terrain as the temporal disjunctions and displacements that punctuate Proust's novel, to see it as negotiating the tensions between the image as a reification of gesture and the dynamism of gesture as such, conserved intact in the image. The *Recherche* would thus offer us images as photograms of a lost film, fragments of gesture. The alignment of the Proustian theory of involuntary memory with the dynamism 'conserved' in the gesture also signals a significant importation from Proust's novel into a theory of the image and of film as such.

However, the lost film does not exist and never existed, as such, or is not possible as a pre-determined reality, since, to follow Bergson-Deleuze, this would be to give a fixed and immobile, thus false, image of time. The lost film is necessarily incomplete, open to the new. The lost film would, like Warburg's Mnemosyne project, or Benjamin's *Passagenwerk*, consist of fragments, photograms related not to a former Whole, but to an open totality, a film yet to be made.

On this issue a recent book by Janet Harbord, *Ex-Centric Cinema: Giorgio Agamben and Film Archaeology*, provides a fertile ground in relation to which to probe further the place of Proust in Agamben's philosophy of film. Harbord proposes her book as a movement towards 'an unlived history of cinema'.[37] Her method, signaled by the subtitle 'film archaeology', is drawn from Agamben, which in turn 'is more profoundly influenced in the final instance by Benjamin's thesis that the profane is not simply excluded matter but rather is that which lies dormant within the overlooked detail of the life, or cinema, that we have'.[38] Film archaeology thus looks at the traces and the margins of the cinema, the forgotten or obsolete elements of film history, in order to bring cinema as such into relief, in a form of excavation. It looks at the periphery, and reads 'for the ex-centric'.[39] Harbord's method is in keeping with Agamben's theory of gesture, where this is understood as the element of dynamic potentiality within form, which opens it up to its futural possibilities, or indeed to the virtual dimension that has not been actualized. Harbord makes explicit her aim to 'dismantle the primacy of actuality over potentiality in the realm of cinema', and thus to look for the other or negative cinema which the cinema we know and have occludes.[40] But this is not a purely historiographic or formal exercise; Harbord draws out Agamben's proposition that gesture, and thus cinema, work in the dimension of ethics, rather than aesthetics, since gesture, which is the essential focus of cinema for Agamben, is hinged into the ethical and political questions of means and ends. Harbord writes:

> Agamben positions cinema at the forefront of a transition of biopolitical relating in which human communicability (an openness to communicating with others) as gesture is caught in the act of its own disappearance. That is, the human subject's capacity to communicate is, in the earliest manifestation of cinema, found to be waning, its residue form trapped within a pathologized form of gesture including the ticks [*sic*] and spasms of a body leaking communicative disorder.[41]

In this vein, Harbord seeks to rewrite the cinema 'from within', and to focus on the 'incomplete film' described as a 'partial thing', 'a version of cinema that exists at the edges, that proffers a glimpse of an unlived cinema and yet fails to fully disclose its form'.[42] Harbord focuses on the 'film that was never completed' as an index of the potentiality of the cinema, and seeks to yoke this notion of incompletion to the Warburgian concept of *Nachleben*, or the after-life of the image. One might yet ask, however, to what extent this depends on the specific notion of the incomplete film, or the film as 'ruin', to evoke another image deployed by Harbord.[43] The notion of afterlife is not structurally dependent on incompletion, but on the lack of coincidence between experience and memory, a Benjaminian thesis, drawn as we have seen from Proust, which points to the way in which, in Harbord's words 'the image is produced at a moment in time and yet its effect lingers in memory where it continues to "live" and to take different forms'. The image, or the image construed as a gesture, is thus 'a thing that continues to live phantasmatically within us'.[44]

When, in 'Notes on Gesture', Agamben writes that Warburg's Mnemosyne project should be seen not as a vast repertory of immobile images, but as a representation 'in virtual movement' of the gestures of Western humanity, in which each image is a photogram rather than an autonomous reality, he refers, as we have seen above, to Benjamin's comparison of the dialectical image with the flip book.

This repeats a reference by Agamben, in an earlier essay on Benjamin, to 'a passage bearing the title "From a Short Speech on Proust Given on my Fortieth Birthday"' and to other fragments in which Benjamin relates the redemptive figure of the angel to the Proustian temporality of involuntary memory.[45] Agamben takes issue with Gershom Scholem's reading of the figure of the angel in Benjamin's work, a reading which he sees as casting 'a melancholic light on the entire horizon of Benjamin's reflections on the philosophy of history, in which the angel lays its properly redemptive role'. Linking the motif of the demonic, which Scholem identifies in Benjamin, to the motif of happiness, through the Greek term for happiness, *edaimonia*, Agamben proposes, against Scholem, that 'Benjamin ties the figure of the angel precisely to an idea of happiness'.[46] Citing Benjamin's unpublished fragment 'Agesilaus Santander', written in 1933, Agamben writes: 'The angel [...], "wants happiness: the conflict in which lies the ecstasy of the unique, new, as yet unlived with the bliss of the 'once more,' the having again, the lived"'.[47] Moving through an engagement with Benjamin's work on Karl Kraus, Agamben goes on to address the recurrence of the figure of the angel in the 'Theses on the Philosophy of History' of 1940. The motif of the concurrence of 'as yet unlived' with the 'lived' is given more flesh in Benjamin's second thesis, which Agamben cites, in which we may read:

> The kind of happiness that could arouse envy in us exists only in the air we have breathed, among people we could have talked to, women who could have given themselves to us. In other words, our image of happiness is indissolubly bound up with the image of redemption. [...] The past carries with it a temporal index by which it is referred to redemption.[48]

The notion of the temporal index here, and the strange conflation of different tenses and moods in 'the air we have breathed, the people we could have talked to' is interrogated by Agamben, who finds the answer in the next thesis: citing Benjamin, 'only a redeemed humanity receives the fullness of its past [...] only for a redeemed humanity has its past become citable in all its moments. Each moment it has lived becomes a citation *à l'ordre du jour* — and that day is Judgment Day'.[49]

Citation is not a return to origins, Agamben argues, it 'in no way signifies the reconstruction of something that once was'.[50] In support of this Agamben refers back to Benjamin's *Origin of German Tragic Drama*, and to the proposition there that 'Origin is an eddy in the stream of becoming, and in its current it swallows the material involved in the process of genesis. That which is original is never revealed in the naked and manifest existence of the factual: its rhythm is apparent only to a dual insight'.[51] Agamben's point is that the dialectic or 'dual insight' of restoration and incompleteness posits a future totality, a moment at which, Benjamin proposes, the phenomenon 'becomes what it was not — totality'.[52]

When Benjamin writes, in 1940, that the past contains a temporal index by means of which it is referred to redemption, the notion of a fulfilled totality or a historical consummation is echoed — that this is not a simple return to the past or a reconstruction of it is evident in the fact that the 'origin' is not revealed as such, in the 'factual', in what takes place. There is something invisible or virtual in the event and in the experience which is 'caught in the stream of becoming', and which refers forward to redemption. The figure of the angel stands at the point of this fulfilled totality, in which the temporal indices of the past are gathered up in their completeness. Agamben writes that the figure of the angel is 'the consummation of the historical totality of existence that is accomplished on the last day, such that in its figure origin and end coincide'.[53]

Agamben explains the temporal logic which is operating here as follows:

> The fact that Benjamin often writes that this redemption takes place in a 'dialectical image' does not distance us from angelology but, on the contrary, leads us to its very centre. In its essence, the dialectical image 'flashes'. It is the 'involuntary memory of redeemed humanity'. 'The past can be seized only as an image which flashes up at the instant when it can be recognized and is no longer seen again', we read in the Fifth Thesis. This is why the redemption that it accomplishes can be grasped 'always only as losing itself in the Unredeemable'. Does this mean that redemption fails and that nothing is truly saved? Not exactly. What cannot be saved is what was, the past as such. But what is saved is what never was, something new. This is the sense of the 'transfiguration' that takes place in the origin. In the 'Epistemological-Critical Preface' Benjamin states this explicitly: the phenomenon that is saved in the Idea 'becomes what it was not — totality'. In a note that bears the title 'The Dialectical Image', the method of historical knowledge is stated in this phrase 'to read what was never written'. Just as, in the end, the angel that comes to meet man is not an original image but the image that we ourselves have formed by our own actions, so in historical redemption what happens in the end is what never took place. This is what is saved.[54]

I want to draw a number of points out of this, so as to emphasize the profoundly Proustian logic at work: to read what was never written, what can be saved is what never was, what happens in the end is what never took place. The temporality of involuntary memory, which does not return to the past but provokes an experience of an 'unlived' element within it, which is 'outside time' as such, and to which Benjamin refers explicitly, parallels and underpins the notion of the dialectical image and the angel of history in Benjamin's thought.[55] The fact that the dialectical image 'flashes up' also alerts us both to the echo in 'Notes on Gesture', where Agamben writes of the 'epiphany flashing in the experience of involuntary memory', and to the intermittent flicker of the cinematographic image, of the flip book, or of Warburg's Mnemosyne, seen as a series of photograms.[56] Moreover, Agamben's insistence that redemption 'loses itself in the Unredeemable', and the earlier proposition that the original experience is 'an eddy in the stream of becoming', point us toward the equivalence of redemption and incompleteness; just as the past is not simply the past, the 'naked and manifest existence of the factual', but — to leap to a later moment in Benjamin's *oeuvre* as Agamben does — that it 'contains within it a temporal index by means of which it is referred to redemption', means that experience always carries with it an element which 'does not take place'; the virtual or potential accompanies the actual and manifest and so opens it outside any possible completion.

This constellation, wherein Benjamin situates Proust's *Recherche* as an index of the temporality of redemption and of the 'dialectical image', premised on the recovery of the 'unlived' element of experience, is given a further connection to the intermittent media of cinema and proto-cinema, and to Agamben's arguments about gesture, in Agamben's subsequent quotation and commentary of Benjamin's fortieth birthday speech, in which he said of involuntary memory:

> Its images do not come unsummoned; rather, it is a matter of images that we have never seen before remembering. This is clearest in the case of images in which we see ourselves as we do in dreams. We stand before ourselves just as we did in an originary past that we never saw. And precisely the most important images — those developed in the darkroom of the lived moment — are what we see. One could say that our deepest moment, like some cigarette packs, are given to us together with a little image, a little photo of ourselves. And the 'whole life' that is said to pass before the eyes of the person who is dying or whose life is threatened is composed of precisely those little images. They present a rapid succession, like those precursors of cinematography, the little booklets in which, as children, we could admire a boxer, a swimmer, or a tennis player.[57]

Here Benjamin proposes a radical account of involuntary memory which he will pick up again in the essay 'On Some Motifs in Baudelaire', and which I will consider in the next chapter — that the images presented to us in involuntary memory are images we have not seen before, 'unlived' elements of our experience. A parallel with Freud is also suggested through the comparison with dream images, and both of these are figured with the photographic metaphor of the 'darkroom' (*Dunkelkammer*, in the original) of the lived moment, and the flip book in which these images are seen 'in rapid succession'.

Agamben's proposition — to draw or see the image in gestural terms — and to see images as so many photograms, 'fragments of a lost film', is thus drawn out of Benjamin's philosophy of history, which itself is in part informed by Benjamin's reading of involuntary memory in the *Recherche*, a derivation which punctuates Agamben's texts recurrently. The motif of the 'fragments of a lost film' may need to be corrected; the film is not lost, time is not lost, as such, because it was not lived as such; what can be saved is what never was, what was not written. The film was never made, never seen, except insofar as it 'flashed up' in sporadic instances, and perhaps even in these flashes it remained unseen. The film is incomplete, and partial, as Harbord suggests, but not in the sense that it is unfinished, or in the sense of the ruin, the trace of a lost totality. The film is, rather, incomplete in the sense of open, a swirl in the stream of becoming; a (lost) film not yet made, to be made, impossible to make.

Proust's Gestures

These considerations might prompt us to look again at the *Recherche*, to re-imagine it, against the grain, as a flip book of a kind, to see it as a Warburgian catalogue of gestures.

Proust's narrator is in effect particularly attentive to the gestures of others, whether as an index of social interaction or of the complex and multi-layered nature of individuality. In the former case, his observation is recurrently focused on gestures of greeting and acknowledgment, and more often than not on their dysfunction; gesture is not the sign of social cohesion or commonality so much as the disjunctions caused in the social fabric by conflicting demands and allegiances. In an early instance, when the narrator and his father are walking in Combray, they encounter Legrandin, whose minimal and unfriendly acknowledgment of them is at odds with his status as a family friend:

> Comme M. Legrandin avait passé près de nous en sortant de l'église, marchant à côté d'une chatelaine du voisinage que nous ne connaissons que de vue, mon père avait fait un salut à la fois amical et réservé, sans que nous nous arrêtions; M. Legrandin avait à peine répondu, d'un air étonné, comme s'il nous reconnaissait pas, et avec cette perspective du regard particulière aux personnes qui ne veulent pas être aimables et qui, du fond subitement prolongé de leurs yeux, ont l'air de vous apercevoir comme au bout d'une route interminable et à une si grande distance qu'elles se contentent de vous adresser un signe de tête minuscule pour le proportionner à vos dimensions de marionette. (I, 118)

> [When M. Legrandin had passed near us as he was coming out of the church, walking by the side of a lady from a neighbouring château whom we knew only by sight, my father had greeted him in a way that was at once friendly and reserved, though we had not stopped; M. Legrandin had barely responded, with a surprised look, as if he did not recognize us, and with that perspective in his gaze peculiar to people who do not want to be friendly and who, from the suddenly extended depths of their eyes, seem to perceive you at the end of an interminable road and at so great a distance that they confine themselves to addressing you a miniscule nod in order to give it the proportions of your puppet-like dimensions.] (I, 120–21)

The enigma of this failure in the expected process of recognition is resolved quite quickly, but only temporarily, by a subsequent encounter with Legrandin the next evening at which he performs a more emphatic greeting and enthuses to the narrator about his poetic soul. But the riddle of Legrandin's behaviour is further compounded a little while later when his exaggerated bodily movements, when greeting a local aristocrat, alert the narrator to the possibility of a Legrandin unknown to him. As Legrandin bows excessively, with 'un renversement secondaire' ('a secondary recoil'), the narrator observes that:

> Ce redressement rapide fit refluer en une sorte d'onde fougueuse et musclée la croupe de Legrandin que je ne supposais pas si charnue; et je ne sais pourquoi cette ondulation de pure matière, ce flot tout charnel, sans expression de spiritualité et qu'un empressement plein de bassesse fouettait en tempête, éveillèrent tout d'un coup dans mon esprit la possibilité d'un Legrandin tout différent de celui que nous connaissions. (I, 123)

[This rapid straightening caused Legrandin's bottom, which I had not supposed was so fleshy, to flow back in a sort of ardent muscular wave; and I do not know why that undulation of pure matter, that quite fleshy billow, with no expression of spirituality and whipped into a storm by a fully contemptible alacrity, suddenly awakened in my mind the possibility of a Legrandin quite different from the one we knew.] (1, 126)

The enigma is exacerbated by two further encounters at which Legrandin again fails to give the expected gesture of acknowledgment to the narrator and his father, and is compounded again by his insistence, when asked by the narrator if he knows the Guermantes, that he does not, and has never sought to, an insistence contradicted by his gestural enthusiasm on being introduced to the aristocrat. The narrator concludes that Legrandin's behaviour is 'comme toute attitude ou action où se révèle le caractère profond et caché de quelqu'un' ('like any attitude or action that reveals a person's deep and hidden character') (1, 125; 1, 127–28), and that the *décalage* in his social greetings is a symptom of a snobbery related to class: he does not want the aristocratic acquaintances he so craves, despite his supposed 'independence' and profession of 'Jacobinism', to know that he frequents middle-class, bourgeois families such as that of the narrator. The narrator deduces that there are thus several layers to Legrandin, several Legrandins, 'Legrandin le causeur' [Legrandin the talker], and a 'second' Legrandin 'qu'il cachait soigneusement au fond de lui' ('whom he kept carefully concealed deep inside himself') (1 , 127; 1, 129). This second Legrandin, 'Legrandin enfant terrible, Legrandin maître chanteur' ('Legrandin the troublemaker, the blackmailer') betrays itself in 'le verbe infiniment plus prompt, composé de ce qu'on appelle "réflexes"' ('the infinitely quicker speech consisting of what are called "reflexes"') (1 , 127; 1, 130), which 'speak' before Legrandin the talker can intervene, and which the latter can only try to mitigate.

Proust thus allows his narrator to develop a theory of gesture which positions it as a social sign, but more definitively as an index of social difference, of class difference and distinction, and as an index to the multiple and conflictual layers of the personality. Gesture communicates, but as a second language, expressive of something like a corporeal unconscious, which operates below or across the level of the individual, and counter to their conscious intention. Legrandin's snobbishness, and his unremitting desire to disavow it, are deduced by the narrator through a reading of gestures which decodes their hidden meaning and resolves the enigma they propose, a reading which is moreover sanctioned and supported by the narrator's family as a whole. At this stage and in this instance gesture is an eminently readable sign, an element in the semiotic apprenticeship Deleuze discerns across the novel.

The readability of gesture, although it will be compromised further on in the novel, and specifically by the factor of sexuality, is an expression of a generalized tendency within the text to give sense to matter, and to read matter in movement as expressive. In the first extract above, although he is unaware of *how* it takes place, the narrator is nevertheless struck by the way in which the 'ondulation de pure matière' of Legrandin's backside communicates the existence of his second, hidden personality. This is symptomatic of a wider certainty in the capacity of matter to embody sense, and in the case of gesture and bodily movement, of the capacity of a moving body to communicate a sense which language and conscious intention cannot. Gesture, in other words, is another language, which operates, transversally, in spite of the self.

This postulation of another language, expressed in material movement, in reflexes, and in the differences between different levels of sense, is also present in the narrator's insight, much later in the novel, of the multiform nature of experience and its suppression by rationality and 'uniform' consciousness and memory. The fundamental elements of the theory of involuntary memory and experience developed by the narrator in the 'Adoration perpetuelle' chapter of *Le Temps retrouvé* also carries a theory of gesture:

> Je comprenais trop que ce que la sensation des dalles inégales, la raideur de la serviette, le gout de la madeleine avaient réveillé en moi n'avait aucun rapport avec ce que je cherchais à me rappeler de Venise, de Balbec, de Combray, à l'aide d'une mémoire uniforme; et je comprenais que la vie pût être jugée médiocre, bien qu'à certains moments elle parût si belle, parce que dans les premiers c'est sur toute autre chose qu'elle-même, sur des images qui ne gardent rien d'elle, qu'on la juge et qu'on la déprécie. Tout au plus notais-je accessoirement que la différence qu'il y a entre chacune des impressions réelles — différences qui expliquent qu'une peinture uniforme de la vie ne puisse être ressemblante — tenait probablement à cette cause que la moindre parole que nous avons dite à une époque de notre vie, le geste le plus insignifiant que nous avons fait était entouré, portrait sur lui le reflet de choses qui logiquement ne tenaient pas à lui, en ont été séparées par l'intelligence qui n'avait rien à faire d'elles pour les besoins du raisonnement, mais au milieu desquelles — ici reflet rose du soir sur le mur fleuri d'un restaurant champêtre, sensation du faim, désir des femmes, plaisir du luxe — là volutes bleues de la mer matinale enveloppant des phrases musicales qui en émergent partiellement comme les épaules des ondines — le geste, l'acte le plus simple reste enfermé comme dans milles vases clos dont chacun serait rempli de choses d'une couleur, d'une odeur, d'une température absolument différentes. (IV, 448–49)

[I understood only too well that what the sensation of the uneven flagstones, the stiffness of the napkin, the taste of the madeleine, had awoken in me bore no relation to what I was trying to remember about Venice, about Balbec and about Combray, with the help of a uniform memory; and I understood that life might be deemed dreary, even though at certain moments it may seem so beautiful, because for the most part it is on the basis of something quite different from it, on the basis of images which retain nothing of life itself, that we judge it and disparage it. At most I noticed incidentally that the difference between each of the real impressions — differences which explain why a uniform depiction of life cannot be a good likeness — was probably because the slightest word we have spoken at any point in our lives, the most insignificant action, was surrounded by, and was a reflection of, things which logically were not connected to it, were separated from it by the intelligence which had no need of them for its rational purposes, but in the middle of which — here, the pink reflection of the evening on the flower-covered wall of a country restaurant, a feeling of hunger, the desire for women, the pleasure of luxury —

there, the blue scrolls of the morning sea enveloping the musical phrases which partially emerge from them like the shoulders of mermaids — the gesture, the simplest action remains enclosed as if within a thousand sealed vessels each one of which would be filled with things of a completely different colour, odour and temperature.] (6, 177–78, translation modified)

The fundamental logic articulated here is an intrinsic factor of the theory of involuntary memory; the most insignificant gesture is linked through a process of association to a host of other impressions. These associations are flattened out in the 'uniform' image given by voluntary memory, informed by reason and by the intelligence. Voluntary memory thus reduces the heterogeneity of experience to a linear and unilateral plane, while a more accurate representation of the past and a more faithful recollection of it brings out its multiple and associative nature. The uniform picture or image also reduces or flattens the specific difference of each impression. A gesture, then, is not (just) a gesture, but an element in a multiform array of sensory impressions and interior affects, specific to the moment of their experiencing. In contrast to the memory of reason, involuntary memory actualizes the whole array of the experience of that instant, including elements of it which did not necessarily rise to the level of consciousness at the time. Involuntary memory actualizes the unrealized elements of past experience, through a process of association tied to the specific difference of the now.

In addition, then, to the conception of gesture as an index of deeper and hidden layers of the personality, and the notion of gesture as an element in a second, non-intentional language, gesture is embedded in a theory of temporality, which posits an unrealized or unlived portion of experience, susceptible to re-actualization, an afterlife of gesture.

But there is also in the *Recherche* a theory of gesturality and facial expression which construes it in more evolutionary, Darwinian terms. This is focused around the narrator's commentary on the facial expressions and vocal accents of the 'jeunes filles en fleurs' on the cliffs at Carquethuit. The narrator has earlier said that the real traits of the girls' faces had not yet 'showed through' ('jailli') (II, 258; 2, 482). The profile is not yet discernible. They are 'confondues' ('indistinctly suffused') in the same 'rougeur confuse de l'aurore' ('their daybreak's indiscriminate bloom') (II, 258; 2, 482). As yet they have 'rien de définitif' ('are quite undefinitive') (II, 258–59; 2, 482). But the moment comes, all too quickly, 'où le corps est figé dans une immobilité qui ne promet plus de surprises' ('when the body is static, held in an immobility which promises no further surprises') (II, 259; 2, 482).

This vision of the process of the formation of facial features expresses the idea of a certain plasticity of the flesh, which is 'worked' as if through an evolutionary process of matter itself; young girls are for the narrator 'celles chez qui la chair comme une pâte précieuse travaille encore' ('in whom the unleavened flesh, like a precious dough, has not yet risen') (II, 259; 2, 482). 'Elles ne sont qu'un flot de matière ductile petrie à tout moment par l'impression passagère qui les domine' ('They are malleable, a soft flow of substance kneaded by every passing impression that possesses them') (II, 259; 2, 482).

The metaphorical underpinning of this vision, initially set in terms of the culinary process of baking ('pâte', 'pétrir'), shifts into sculpture and statuary: 'On dirait que chacune est tour à tour une petite statuette de la gaieté, du sérieux juvenile, de la calinerie, de l'étonnement, modelée par une expression franche, complète, mais fugitive' ('Each of them looks like a brief succession of little statuettes, representing gaiety, childish solemnity, fond coquettishness, amazement, every one of them modelled by an expression which is full and frank, but fleeting') (II, 259; 2, 482). Both figures, however, express the sense of plasticity, resolved in the proposition that 'Cette plasticité donne beaucoup de variété et de charme aux gentils égards que nous montre une jeune fille' ('This plasticity lends much variety and great charm to a girl who is trying her best to be nice to us') (II, 259; 2, 482).[58]

If the features and voices of young girls are variable and plastic, those of older women have 'hardened' ('durcie'); the expressiveness even of those we love just 'de molles fluctuations' ('faint fluctuations') (II, 259; 2, 483, translation adapted). They have been 'sculpted' ('sculpté') by certain sacrifices. Adolescence precedes this 'solidification complète' ('complete stabilization') (II, 259; 2, 483), and presents a visibly mobile process of plastic modelling 'le spectacle des forms sans cesse en train de changer' ('this spectacle of ceaselessly changing forms') (II, 259; 2, 483), which evokes the sea: 'la perpétuelle recréation de la nature qu'on contemple devant la mer' ('that perpetual recreation of nature's primordial elements which we witness by the sea') (II, 259; 2, 483).

Jean-Pierre Richard, in *Proust et le monde sensible*, recognizes the sea as the sensory origin and the grounding metaphor ('la métaphore essentielle') of the young girls, 'plastique, virtuelle, mobile, changeante, renouvelée comme elles' [plastic, virtual, mobile, changing and always renewed as they are], but he postulates it as an origin or a memory which is 'oublieuse' [forgetful], in which form is continuously forgotten in a process of formation or metamorphosis.[59] Richard thus postulates a sense of consistency in the novel which lies in metamorphosis and malleability, a paradoxical consistency of formal inconsistency, and which operates in dynamic tension with tendencies towards formal stasis and fixity. Processes of trace and imprint work in tension with processes of variation, transformation, and dynamism.

The plasticity of the flesh, figured through the image of the ceaselessly changing sea, is nevertheless subject to other laws, evolutionary and moral laws which might be summarized under the general category of *atavism*. In the same scene above the cliffs of Carquethuit, the narrator hypothesizes a tendency for the plastic flesh and variable gestures and intonations of the young girls to become fixed in relation to atavistic laws determined by familial traits and habits ('le legs familial') and geographic location. But these are held 'en réserve' ('in reserve') (II, 263; 2, 486). It is as if the felicitous variability and mobility of the flesh is simply a form of parenthesis before the laws of atavism and habit, which fix gesture and intonation in 'an unchangeable mask', come into play, after an initial delay. The narrator posits a dynamic relation between gesture and physiognomy, wherein the latter is a static image of the mobile form of the former:

> Les traits de notre visage ne sont guère que des gestes devenus, par l'habitude, définitifs. La nature, comme la catastrophe de Pompéi, comme une méta-

morphose de nymphe, nous a immobilisés dans le mouvement accoutumé. De même nos intonations contiennent notre philosophie de la vie, ce que la personne se dit à tout moment sur les choses. Sans doute ces traits n'étaient pas qu'à ces jeunes filles. Ils étaient à leurs parents. L'individu baigne dans quelque chose de plus général que lui. A ce compte, les parents ne fournissent pas que ce geste habituel que sont les traits du visage et de la voix, mais aussi certaines manières de parler, certaines phrases consacrées, qui presque aussi inconscientes qu'une intonation, presque aussi profondes, indiquent, comme elle, un point de vue sur la vie. [...] Enfin, plus générale encore que n'est le legs familial était la savoureuse matière imposé par la province originelle d'où elles tiraient leur voix et à même laquelle mordaient leurs intonations. (II, 262–63)

[The features of our face are little more than expressions ingrained by habit. Nature, like the catastrophe at Pompeii or the metamorphosis of a nymph, freezes us into an accustomed cast of countenance. In the same way, the intonations of our voice express our philosophy of life, what one says to oneself at each moment about things. The facial features of these girls did not, of course, belonged just to them: they belong to their parents. As individuals, each of us lives immersed in something more general than ourselves. Parents, for that matter, do not hand on only the habitual act of a facial and vocal feature, but also turns of phrase, certain special sayings, which are almost as deeply rooted and unconscious as an inflection, and imply as much as it does a point of view on life. [...] Also, more general features than these family heirlooms were the body and redolence given to their whole speech by the far-flung regions of France from which their voices came, and which flavoured their intonations.] (2, 486–87)

The intonations and turns of phrase of an individual are the expression not of the individual but of more general laws of evolution, for which Proust gives two vectors: the family legacy ('le legs familial') and the original locale ('province'). But he also postulates a theory of gesture in terms of a dynamic of mobility, fixity, and habit or repetition. The lines ('traits') of our faces are the product of a fixative or 'definitive' arrest of a mobile gesturality, a process which the text figures as a catastrophe, or as the metamorphosis of the larval form of insects.[60]

There is also a logic of individuation implicit in this account. In their current state the bodies of the young girls, figured as a succession of statues, express a variable and multiple affective range which has not yet been individualized, in which individual and atavistic traits have not yet distinguished them from each other.[61] However, the narrator, as an 'amateur de jeunes filles' professes himself able to discern, in other words to read, already, the individuating traits of each young girl:

Dans un bois l'amateur d'oiseaux distingue aussitôt ces gazouillis particuliers à chaque oiseau, que le vulgaire confond. L'amateur de jeunes filles sait que les voix humaines sont encore bien plus variées. Chacune possède plus de notes que le plus riche instrument. Et les combinaisons selon lesquelles elle les groupe sont aussi inépuisables que l'infinie variété des personnalités. Quand je causais avec une de mes amies, je m'apercevais que le tableau original, unique de son individualité, m'étaient ingénieusement imposé aussi bien par les inflexions de sa voix que par celles de son visage et que c'étaient deux spectacles qui traduisaient, chacun dans son plan, la même réalité singulière. (II, 261–62)

[In a wood, a bird-watcher's ear will instantly pick out the chirps and warbles peculiar to different species which the uninstructed cannot tell apart. The fancier of young girls knows that human voices are even more varied. Each of them has a wider range of notes than the most versatile instrument; and the combinations it can make of them are as inexhaustible as the infinite variety of personalities. When I chatted with one of the girls, I noticed that the outline of her individuality, original and unique, was ingeniously drawn and ruthlessly imposed upon me as much by the modulations of her voice as by the shifting expressions of her face, and I was confronted by two performances, each of which rendered in its own mode the same singular reality.] (2, 485)

Even though it is not yet definitively fixed, voice and facial expression, as variants of gestural mobility, are signs of the intrinsic individuality of each girl, but this itself is the product of determining forces prior to the individual, forces 'more general' than the individual herself. The second language of gesture is paradoxically both individuating and expressive of trans-individual factors, which work against the mobile variation of singularities the narrator imagines.

If the 'jeunes filles en fleurs' thus offer the narrator the basis for a theory of gesture in which the fantasized plasticity of the flesh is countered by atavistic tendencies which will become 'catastrophically' fixed, the gestures and bodily movement of Robert de Saint-Loup are the basis for a more developed and troubled theory of gesture. The narrator's first sight of him, in the Grand Hôtel at Balbec, is couched in terms of speed and delicacy: 'Il traversa rapidement l'hôtel dans toute sa largeur, semblant poursuivre son monocle qui voltigeait devant lui comme un papillon' ('He strode right through the hotel, seeming to be in pursuit of his monocle, which fluttered in front of him like a butterfly') (II, 89; 2, 309). The equilibrium and poise of his body is emphasized further as the narrator describes him as 'équilibrant perpétuellement les mouvements de ses membres autour de son monocle fugitive et dansant qui semblaient leur centre de gravité' ('keeping his limbs in perfect equilibrium about the dancing flight of his monocle, which seemed to be their centre of gravity') (II, 89; 2, 309). But as with Legrandin, it is the gesture and posture involved in the social greeting, when he shakes the narrator's hand, that offer most purchase for the latter's propensity to posit gesture as an enigma, to be read:

Il sembla ne pas entendre qu'on lui nommait quelqu'un, aucun muscle de son visage ne bougea; ses yeux où ne brilla pas la plus faible lueur de sympathie humaine, montrèrent simplement dans l'insensibilité, dans l'inanité du regard, une exagération à défaut de laquelle rien ne les eût différenciés de miroirs sans vie. Puis fixant sur moi ces yeux durs comme s'il eût voulu se renseigner sur moi, avant de me rendre mon salut, par un brusque déclenchement qui sembla plutôt dû à un réflexe musculaire qu'un acte de volonté, mettant entre lui et moi le plus de distance possible, allongea le bras dans toute sa longueur, et me tendit la main, à distance. (II, 91)

[He gave no sign that someone's name had just been uttered in his presence; not a muscle moved in his face; and had it not been for the fact that his eyes, in which there glowed not the slightest spark of humane feeling, showed a mere exaggeration of their insensitivity and emptiness of all expression, nothing would have distinguished them from lifeless mirrors. Then, staring at me with his hard eyes, as though he wished to be informed about me before acknowledging my greeting, suddenly set in motion as though by a muscular reflex rather than by an act of will, and putting between himself and me the greatest distance possible, he thrust out his arm as far as it would go and, from a great distance, gave me his hand.] (2, 311)

The narrator resolves his initial puzzlement and disappointment through an explanation which, as with the *jeunes filles*, reads Saint-Loup's gestures as the result of a form of 'dressage' or 'moulding' specific to his family. Saint-Loup's 'distant' greetings are a result of the education of his mother, who has 'trained his body' ('plié son corps') to certain 'habitudes mondaines' specific to the Guermantes. It is thus devoid of the 'signification morale' which the narrator initially attributed to it, and is read as a 'réflexe musculaire', a defensive instinct, 'comme le geste de parer un coup' ('like the gesture of warding off a blow') (II, 91; 2, 312, translation modified), plausibly an echo of Baudelaire's description of the 'peintre de la vie moderne' in the essay devoted to Constantin Guys. Saint-Loup's corporeal movements are thus expressive of codes specific to the class status of the Guermantes, which have been so integrated as to function like reflexes. They are the expression of: 'un être plus général que lui-même, le "noble" [...] qui comme un esprit intérieur mouvait ses membres, ordonnait ses gestes et ses actions' ('a creature of wider generality than himself, the "nobleman", a being which, like some inner daemon, moved his limbs, directed his gestures and his actions') (II, 96; 2, 316). Observing Saint-Loup, 'comme un œuvre d'art' ('like a work of art'), and appreciating his movements as being regulated by 'une idée générale à laquelle elles étaient suspendues mais qu'il ne connaissait pas' ('a general idea which underlay their structure and function of which he was unaware') (II, 96; 2, 317, translation modified), the narrator feels guilty not to be attentive to the specific qualities of his friend, to sacrifice the individual specificity of Saint-Loup, to so speak, to the generality of a 'type' and the deduction of sociological laws. But this guilt only serves to underline further the extent to which gesture, in the narrator's reading of it, works as an index of forces which work across and despite the individual. Individuality is not so much something he ignores, to the benefit of his sociological speculations about more 'general' laws, as their symptom, their product; even in his desire to distance himself from his aristocratic origins, in his intellectual and political opinions, Saint-Loup remains determined, in his body, by the grace which comes from a certain disdain for other classes and the absence of self-consciousness which comes from an internalized sense of social superiority.

In another instance of a failed or enigmatic social greeting, after the narrator has stayed with him for several days at his barracks in Doncières, Saint-Loup drives past in a carriage and barely, or only remotely, acknowledges the narrator: 'sans qu'un muscle de sa physionomie bougeât, il se contenta de tenir pendant deux minutes sa main levée au bord de son képi' ('without moving a muscle of his face, his only response was to keep his hand raised for a moment to the peak of his cap') (II, 436; 3, 135). Later, back in Paris, when the narrator visits the theatre with Saint-Loup and his mistress Rachel, he proposes an explanation for this curious event, positing the same 'training' of the body for social codes:

> A côté de cette sincérité naïve de son visage dont la peau laissait voir par transparence le brusque afflux de certaines émotions, son corps avait été admirablement dressé par l'éducation à un certain nombre de dissimulations de bienséance et que, comme un parfait comédien, il pouvait dans sa vie de régiment, dans sa vie mondaine, jouer, l'un après l'autre des rôles différents. (II, 474)

> [Compared to the spontaneous sincerity of his face with that transparent skin which revealed the sudden surge of his emotions, his body had been so admirably trained to perform a number of the dissimulations demanded by etiquette, and that, like a truly skilled actor, he had the ability, in his regimental and in his society life, to play a succession of different roles.] (3, 173)

The narrator hints here, with the reference to the skill of the actor and the idea of different 'roles', at a reading of gesture as a kind of performance. This allows us to think about Robert's performance in relation to that of La Berma, described by the narrator earlier in *Le Côté de Guermantes* on the occasion of the narrator's visit to the Paris Opéra, where the actress is performing an act from Racine's *Phèdre*, his second, and more successful, encounter with the actress.

Initially the narrator observes with frustration the way in which the gestures and voices of the actors playing the supporting roles of Aricie, Ismène, and Hippolyte seem to be exterior to the role itself and to remain at the level of 'everyday life':

> Mais les membres insoumis laissaient se pavaner entre l'épaule et le coude un biceps qui ne savait rien du rôle; ils continuaient à exprimer l'insignifiance de la vie de tous les jours et à mettre en lumière, au lieu des nuances raciniennes, des connexités musculaires; et la draperie qu'ils soulevaient retombait selon une vertical où ne le disputait aux lois de la chute des corps qu'une souplesse insipide et textile. (II, 346)

> [But their unsubmissive limbs allowed a biceps which knew nothing of the part they were playing to flaunt itself between shoulder and elbow; their bodies continued to express the triviality of everyday life and to emphasize not the subtlety of Racine but the related functions of their muscles; and the hanging robes that they held up fell back into a vertical drop in which the laws governing falling bodies were challenged solely by the tame movement of textiles.] (3, 44)

In contrast to this sense of disconnection between matter and sense, between gesturality and meaning, La Berma, on this occasion, presents for the narrator a self-evident integration and interiorization of the sense of Racine's verses into bodily movement, intonation, and even into the 'fall' of the drapery of her costume. La Berma's performance is compared to that of a great musician (the narrator mentions Vinteuil) whose playing has become 'si transparent, si rempli de ce qu'il interprète que lui-même on le voit plus, et qu'il n'est plus qu'une fenêtre qui donne sur un chef d'œuvre' ('so transparent, so full of what he is interpreting, that he himself disappears and becomes simply a window opening on to a masterpiece') (II, 347; 3, 45). While the intention and dramatic 'instruction' of the minor characters is evident to the narrator, La Berma has absorbed ('résorbés') and interiorized ('intériorisé') the role 'en ses moindres cellules' ('down to its smallest cells') in a quasi-material sense, to the extent that, in the narrator's estimation, there remains no material element 'refractory' to the 'spirit' ('esprit') of the verses (II, 347–48; 3, 45). Even the movement of her veils, in an echo of the 'accessoires de mouvement' studied by Aby Warburg, appears to be animated by the sense of the play:

> Ces blancs voiles eux-mêmes, qui, exténués et fidèles, semblaient de la matière vivante et avoir été filés par la souffrance mi-païenne, mi-janséniste, autour de laquelle ils se contractaient comme un cocon fragile et frileux; tout cela, voix, attitudes, gestes, voiles, n'était, autour de ce corps d'une idée qu'est un vers [...] que des enveloppes supplémentaires qui au lieu de le cacher ne rendaient que plus splendidement l'âme qui se les était assimilées. (II, 348)

> [Those white veils themselves, exhausted and faithful, which seemed to be made of a living substance and to have been spun by the half-pagan, half-Jansenist suffering around which they clung like a frail and shrinking cocoon; all these, voice, stage presence, gestures, veils, around that embodiment of an idea represented by a line of poetry [...] were merely additional coverings which, instead of concealing revealed the greater splendour of the soul that had assimilated and spread itself through them.] (3, 46)

Proust constructs here an ideal of embodiment in which gestural language has been interiorized and worked, or absorbed, to such an extent that it becomes translucent and extends like a series of envelopes around the work. In contrast, intentional gesturality is constructed as awkward and graceless. If La Berma is the agent of this gestural performance it is at the expense of intentionality. The narrator proposes that intention as such is awkward; La Berma has internalized the role and the meaning to the extent that she absorbs it, rather than 'intending' it.

In a similar, but significantly different way, Robert's grace functions at the expense of his individual agency. In the episode of the 'soir de l'amitié' of *Le Côté de Guermantes* the narrator observes Saint-Loup move with grace along the banquettes which run along the wall of the restaurant in the Bois de Boulogne in which they are dining, vaulting over the electric wires which run to the tables. Once more the narrator feels a sense of guilt in observing and analyzing Robert's movements, especially on this evening on which he senses their mutual friendship, and especially since the pleasure he experiences in witnessing Robert's graceful acrobatics relates not to the latter's individual nature; it has its meaning ('signification') and its cause ('sa cause') on the contrary in the nature he has inherited from the 'race' of the Guermantes: 'par la naissance et par l'éducation' ('by birth and upbringing) (II, 706; 3, 411).

Robert's movements are described as a performance, the gracefulness of which derives from a competence which consists in the capacity to apply the right 'mechanism' ('mécanisme') or technique ('technique') for each situation, but more specifically in an absence of self-consciousness, a sense of social superiority and assuredness, rather than the more commonplace anxiety in relation to conventions, a disdain, therefore, which Robert has received 'par héritage en son corps' ('by inheritance in his body') (II, 707; 3, 411). The motif of corporeal plasticity recurs here, as this inheritance had 'moulded' ('plié') the manners ('façons') of his ancestors to the superiority which befits their dominant class position (II, 707; 3, 411).

Robert's gestural and corporeal competence is compared to the skill of a musician, and the meaning which it communicates is compared to the 'puissance industrieuse' ('industrious energy') which shines through a work of art, 'significatif et limpide' ('meaningful and limpid'). A further reference point for Robert's performance, and for its meaningfulness, its capacity to be read, is proposed as the narrator compares the intelligibility of Robert's movements to 'ceux de cavaliers sculptés sur une frise' ('those of horsemen on a marble frieze') (II, 707; 3, 413), drawing the comparison back to Greek statuary in the same way as with La Berma's drapery. We find here the same fusion of sense and matter as in La Berma's performance, the same integration of meaning and movement, and the same critique of conscious intention. Yet in distinction from La Berma, Robert's grace is not a purely aesthetic object; it derives from 'une certitude du goût dans l'ordre non du beau mais des manières' ('Certainty of taste (with regard not to aesthetics but to personal behaviour)') (II, 706; 3, 411). The ideal of sense integrated in matter is, with Robert, moved out of the domain of the aesthetic, which nevertheless remains its point of reference, and into the social. Robert's agility and grace constitute an ideal performance of gestural communication, in contrast to the 'opaque and dim' ('opaque et obscur') nature of the narrator's body (II, 707; 3, 412). It is, like La Berma's performance, Legrandin's grotesqueness, and the 'gazouillis' of the young girls, a model of intelligibility.

The comparison of Robert's meaningful movement with the opacity of the narrator's body suggests the extent to which the ideal intelligibility of gesture is held in tension with a more problematic opacity and unintelligibility, with a crisis of readability. The suppression of intentionality in La Berma's Phèdre and Robert's agility contrast with the troubling factors of interiority and, in the later volumes of the novel, sexuality. What is outlined with Robert and La Berma is an ideal of corporeal semiosis which compensates for a crisis of gesture elsewhere, echoing Agamben's account of the loss of gesture as a common measure, and the proposition that this loss coincides with and is provoked by a century which has 'succumbed to interiority'.

The integration of sense in material movement, and the intelligibility of gesture are compromised, in the *Recherche*, by sexuality, to the extent that, in an echo of Agamben's proposition, one might say that the crisis of gesture comes when the era 'succumbs to sexuality', sexuality functioning in the novel as a paradigmatic form of interiority. One of the first instances in the novel of an ambivalently sexual gesture which poses a challenge to intelligibility comes with the narrator's first encounter with Gilberte, on a walk 'du côté de Méséglise':

> Elle laissa ses regards filer de toute leur longueur dans ma direction, sans expression particulière, sans avoir l'air de me voir, mais avec une fixité et un sourire dissimulé, que je ne pouvais interpréter d'après les notions que l'on m'avait données sur la bonne éducation, que comme une prévue d'outrageant mépris; et sa main esquissait en même temps un geste indécent, auquel quand il était adressé en public à une personne qu'on ne connaissait pas, le petit dictionnaire de civilité que je portais en moi ne donnait qu'un seul sens, celui d'une intention insolente. (I, 139–40)

> [She allowed her glances to stream out at full length in my direction, without

any particular expression, without appearing to see me, but with a concentration
and a secret smile that I could only interpret, according to the notions of good
breeding instilled in me, as a sign of insulting contempt; and at the same time
her hand sketched an indecent gesture for which, when it was directed in public
at a person one did not know, the little dictionary of manners I carried inside
me supplied only one meaning, that of intentional insolence.] (1, 142)

Elizabeth Ladenson has observed how, in contrast to other gestures (for example
those of Legrandin, discussed earlier) the text 'does not represent the gesture itself,
thus leaving it open to readerly interpretation or misinterpetation'.[62] It is 'a gesture
which is interpreted but not actually described'.[63] Indeed, while the narrator
interprets it as unequivocal, the interpretation itself, that the gesture is 'd'une
intention insolente', leaves the content of this certainty empty. The unequivocal
yet lacunary nature of the narrator's interpretation renders the passage 'pregnant
with prolepsis', and proposes it as 'a cas-limite of Proustian interpretability'.[64]
Ladenson observes, moreover, that the incident is 'one of the most photogenic
passages of the novel' and that: 'All the elements of cinematic mise-en-scène would
seem to be present; what is described is a place, a person, and a gesture'.[65] This
propensity to visual representation seems to work at the expense, however, of the
usual proliferation of interpretative hypotheses, of reading: the gesture seems to
paralyze reading. Ladenson looks at the three visual representations of the scene
proposed in Stéphane Huet's graphic novel version of *Du Côté de chez Swann*,
Raoul Ruiz's *Le Temps retrouvé*, and a 1988 BBC documentary on Proust, in which
the scene is dramatized, and finds in them a symptomatic equivocation around
the precise sexual meaning of the gesture; while the BBC version shows Gilberte
making a circle of her thumb and forefinger and inserting the forefinger into the
circle, in a sign which, for Ladenson, 'can have no other conceivable meaning than
the metaphoric one of sexual penetration', Ruiz's film shows Gilberte making the
same shape with her left hand, but with the finger of the right hand wavering and
describing 'a sort of vacillating motion that suggests a whole panoply of alternative
metaphoric interpretations, most obviously heterosexual hesitancy or inadequacy,
lesbian sexuality or equivocal foreplay'.[66] Huet, in the more 'family-values'-
oriented version of the scene, chooses not to represent the gesture itself, but shows,
in the successive frames of the graphic novel, Gilberte's hand before or after it has
made the gesture. For Ladenson this version is the one which 'best serves Proust's
text', since it eschews direct visualization and promotes instead the processes of
interpretation and reinterpretation.[67] This absence of evidence, or the problematic
nature of evidence in Proust's text is related by Ladenson to other instances of
misinterpretation in the *Recherche*, in particular to instances of confusion between
sexual invitations and social insults, or between social and sexual invitations, thus at
the interface between the regimes of the signs of love and the social signs discerned
by Deleuze in *Proust et les signes*. In particular, Ladenson relates the scene to the
narrator's observation, immediately preceding the gesture, that he was particularly
struck by Gilberte's blue eyes, even though he later confirmed that they were
in fact black. Thus within the same sentence the reader is presented with two
incompatible perceptions. The point here, I think, is that sexuality functions as a

specifically acute example of the simultaneous existence of incompatible perceptions or interpretations, thus the relegation of the evident in favour of a conflict of interpretations, particularly around the question of penetration. The intelligibility of the evident is fundamentally problematized, and the narrator and reader are left in a mood of radical equivocation as to the meaning of the gesture, and this despite Gilberte's improbable revelation, much later in *Albertine disparue*, that she had intended the gesture as a sexual invitation, the precise sense of which remains undescribed.

However, even though Gilberte's gesture remains undescribed in the text, and thus susceptible to the 'several layers of misinterpretation' Ladenson observes it to generate, at this point the narrator is certain of what the gesture is, and, at this point of the narrative, of the meaning it carries. Metaphorically, this certainty is justified by the narrator's imaginary 'consultation' of the 'petit dictionnaire de civilité' that he carries within him. The meaning of the gesture, even though it is only 'sketched' ('esquissé'), is certified according to a supposed index of 'civil' gestural signs, a dictionary assuring their sense. Aside from the fact that, as Ladenson suggests, no 'manual of etiquette, internal or otherwise, would have featured such an entry', the narrator's curiously naïve response is to suppose, even imaginatively, that such signs can be unequivocally defined or indexed in such a way.[68] The contradiction of certainty and equivocation, definition and indeterminacy, surrounding Gilberte's gesture seem to cast doubt on the semiotic capacities of gesture as such, a symptom perhaps of the crisis of gesture which Agamben detects.

André Benhaïm, for his part, reads the narrator's encounter with Gilberte and the gesture of the latter as a kind of duel of looks, won by Gilberte, who consecrates her victory, the capturing of the narrator in her visual field, with a gesture implicitly equivalent to the digital release of a photographic shutter.[69] This can suggest a line of enquiry in which the centre of gravity of the figuration of the narrator's observation of gestures shifts from that of statuary to that of more contemporary visual technologies of photography and cinematography.[70] I hope to show in what follows that as the intelligibility of gesture and bodily movement is problematized and troubled by sexuality, it is increasingly rendered in terms which decompose movements into a succession of frames. The decline in the intelligibility of gesture goes hand in hand with the serial decomposition of movement, a move towards the style of the flip book.

The episode of the kiss with Albertine, in *Le Côté de Guermantes,* amply illustrates the way in which the troubled epistemology of desire is set in terms not of the disinterested contemplation of works of art — as with the observation of Robert de Saint-Loup's athletic grace, akin to that of a frieze from the Parthenon, or La Berma's flowing veils — but in terms of optical instruments which present a succession of images or 'planes' ('plans'). Albertine is figured here as the object of a series of visual images, of a visual variation. Sensing her to be now available to him, the narrator speculates about the three different levels or visual planes in which she has appeared to him, first as if in a theatrical tableau or projection, profiled against the background of the sea at Balbec, then, 'détaché du faisceau lumineux' ('detached from the beam of light') (II, 656; 3, 359), the real woman appears, but has none of the availability with which the first image endowed her; now, as Albertine shows herself to be available, the narrator's desire is intensified by the previous inaccessibility and by the imaginary investment and desire for something out of reach with which he has imbued her. The narrator speculates that sexual desire, which on its own proposes the cheeks to be kissed as 'sans secret, sans prestige' ('devoid of mystery and glamour'), is 'multiplied and diversified' as if by means of a series of optical instruments ('un instrument d'optique, puis un autre') (II, 657; 3, 360), adding to purely physical possession the possession of memories of desire and of the fantasy images one has dreamed of. The possession of Albertine, symbolized by the kiss, is, in the narrator's mind, the possession of an image, and of an image which he is able to manipulate technologically, so to speak:

> On a vu une femme, simple image dans le décor de la vie, comme Albertine profilée sur la mer, et puis cette image, on peut la détacher, la mettre près de soi, et voir peu à peu son volume, ses couleurs, comme si on l'avait fait passer derrière les verres d'un stéréoscope. (II, 658)

> [One sees a woman, a mere image in life's scene, like Albertine silhouetted against the sea, and then it becomes possible to detach that image, bring it close, and gradually to observe its volume, its colours, as though it had been placed behind the lens of a stereoscope.] (3, 361)

To know a woman, he says, is to be able to visually manipulate her image: 'faire varier de forme, de grandeur, de relief l'image humaine' ('to make the human image vary in shape, in size, in relief'), and moreover, Albertine is for the narrator linked to a whole series of maritime images: 'D'autre part Albertine tenait, liées autour d'elle, toutes les impressions d'une série maritime qui m'était particulièrement chère' ('There was also the fact that Albertine held in a unbroken ring around her all the impressions of a series of sea-scapes that were particularly dear to me') (II, 658; 3, 361). The image of Albertine is thus susceptible both to the technological manipulation of the zoom lens, and to serialization.

This hypertrophic faith in the epistemological and libidinal power of the image, in the narrator's capacity, in other words, to possess Albertine through the technologies of his observation, is troubled, of course, by the kiss itself. The narrator speculates that he will, in kissing Albertine, be able to add to the succession of images he already has 'ce plan nouveau' ('this new plane'), this time gained through 'la connaissance par les lèvres' ('knowledge through the lips'); his error here is to suppose that touch operates in the same way as the look, or perhaps, as he goes on to confess, that there is any such thing as knowledge through the lips. All the lips can do is to 'drift against a surface' ('vaguer à la surface') and to 'come up against the barrier of the cheek's desirable impenetrability' ('se heurter à la cloture de la joue impénétrable et désirée') (II, 659; 3, 362). And it seems that once the distance of purely visual contemplation has been reduced through the very desire that it provokes and intensifies, once, in other words, the desire to possess and to know through the eyes has crossed over or been extended into the desire to know through touch, the physical impenetrability of the other ruins the mastery and control of

the visual; as the narrator's lips approach Albertine's cheek the speed of changes
of perspective fractures her image into a succession of disparate and unintegrated
frames, which he says he would nevertheless like to pull together, before finally
being eclipsed in the moment of contact. This shift in the narrator's relation to the
image of Albertine, and in his capacity to manipulate and master the image is set in
terms relating to the perspectival illusions of photography, but also in terms of the
speed of the succession of different 'frames':

> Les dernières applications de la photographie — qui couchent aux pieds d'une
> cathédrale toutes les maisons qui nous parurent si souvent de près, presque aussi
> hautes que les tours, font successivement manœuvrer comme un régiment, par
> files, en ordre dispersé, en masses serrées, les mêmes monuments, rapprochent
> l'une contre l'autre les deux colonnes de la Piazzetta tout à l'heure si distantes,
> éloignent la proche Salute et dans un fond pâle et dégradé réussissent à faire
> tenir un horizon immense sous l'arche d'un pont, dans l'embrasure d'une
> fenêtre, entre les feuilles d'un arbre situé au premier plan et d'un ton plus
> vigoureux, donnent successivement pour cadre à une même église les arcades
> de toutes les autres — je ne vois que cela qui puisse, autant que le baiser, faire
> surgir de ce que nous croyons une chose à aspect défini, les cent autres choses
> qu'elle est tout aussi bien, puisque chacune est relative à une perspective non
> moins légitime. Bref, de même qu'à Balbec, Albertine m'avait souvent paru
> différente, maintenant — comme si, en accélérant prodigieusement la rapidité
> des changements de perspective et des changements de coloration que nous
> offre une personne dans nos diverses rencontres avec elle, j'avais voulu les
> faire tenir toutes en quelques secondes pour recréer expérimentalement le
> phénomène qui diversifie l'individualité d'un être et tirer les unes des autres,
> comme d'un étui, toutes les possibilités qu'il enferme — dans ce court trajet
> de mes lèvres vers sa joue, c'est dix Albertines que je vis; cette seule jeune fille
> étant comme une déesse à plusieurs têtes, celle que j'avais vue en dernier, si je
> tentais de m'approcher d'elle, faisait place une autre. Du moins tant que je ne
> l'avais pas touchée, cette tête, je la voyais, un léger parfum venait d'elle jusqu'à
> moi. Mais hélas ! — car pour le baiser, nos narines et nos yeux sont aussi mal
> placés que nos lèvres mal faites — tout d'un coup, mes yeux cessèrent de voir, à
> son tour mon nez s'écrasant ne perçut plus aucune odeur, et sans connaître pour
> cela davantage le goût du rose désiré, j'appris à ces détestables signes, qu'enfin
> j'étais en train d'embrasser la joue d'Albertine. (II, 660)

[Apart from the latest developments in photography — which lay down at the
foot of a cathedral all the houses that so often, from close to, seemed to us to be
as high as towers, which deploy like a regiment, in file, in organized dispersion,
in serried masses, the same monuments, bring together the two columns on the
Piazzetta that were so far apart a while back, distance the nearby Salute and, on
a pale and lifeless background, manage to contain an immense horizon beneath
the arch of a bridge, in a single window-frame, between the leaves of a tree in
the foreground that is more vigorous in tone, frame a single church successively
in the arcades of all the others — I know of nothing that is able, to the same
degree as a kiss, to conjure up from what we believed to be something with
one definite aspect, the hundred other things it may equally well be, since each
is related to a no less valid perspective. In short, just as in Balbec Albertine has
often seemed different to me, now, as if, by magically accelerating the speed of
the changes of perspective and colouring a person offers us in the course of our

various encounters, I had tried to contain them all within the space of a few seconds in order to re-create experimentally the phenomenon which diversifies a person's individuality and to draw out separately, as from a slip-case, all the possibilities it contains — now what I saw, in the brief trajectory of my lips towards her cheek, was ten Albertines; because this girl was like a many-headed goddess, the head I had seen last, when I tried to draw near, gave way to another. As long as I had not touched it, I could at last see this head, and a faint perfume came to me from it. But alas — for when we kiss our nostrils and eyes are as ill-placed as our lips are ill-made — suddenly, my eyes ceased to see, and my nose in turn, crushed against her cheek, no longer smelled anything, so, without my efforts bringing me any clearer notion of the taste of the rose I desired, I discovered, from these abominable signs, that I was finally in the process of kissing Albertine's cheek.] (3, 363)

The perspectival tricks of photography allow a kind of relativistic, visual multiplicity, to be able to see in the place of what I thought was a definitive image multiple other equally valid images. But it is the acceleration of the successive images which more tellingly leads the narrator to a crisis of visual mastery. Despite his desire to hold all the successive images of Albertine together, and to perpetuate his voyeuristic manipulation of them, at each slight movement a different Albertine, a different frame of Albertine appears, before finally cutting to black. This cinematographic figure needs to be corrected, however, since the narrator does not render the experience in terms of a moving image so much as a succession of different frames, one, then another. Albertine is subjected to what we might call a chronophotographic decomposition.

Numerous scenes in the *Recherche* suggest themselves as examples or variants of the decomposition of movement into a succession of photogrammatic instants; the successive views of the bell-towers of Martinville in *Du côté de chez Swann*, the three trees of Hudimesnil in *A l'ombre des jeunes filles en fleurs*; in both of these cases the narrator himself is moving, and the succession of images is produced by the mobility of the viewpoint. And in both cases the objects hold a secret which he is compelled to discover. This is the case in the episode of the kiss with Albertine discussed above. We might also recall the appearance of the 'petite bande' in Balbec in *A l'ombre des jeunes filles en fleurs*, where they are first described as '[faisant mouvoir] une tache singulière' '(where they made a strange mass of moving colours') (II, 146; 2, 369) and are compared to a flock of gulls, the whole composition nevertheless summarized as possessing 'une beauté fluide, collective et mobile' ('a shared, unstable and elusive beauty') (II, 148; 3, 371). From the moment of their introduction, Albertine and her friends are endowed with the emblem of mobility, and a mobility associated moreover with those animals, predominantly horses and birds, with which Muybridge and Marey had pursued their explorations in chronophotography.

However it is in the character of Robert de Saint-Loup that what I will call the Muybridge mode is most explicit.[71] Mieke Bal, in her study of visuality in Proust's writing *The Mottled Screen*, and in an earlier version of a chapter in this book, 'All in the Family: Familiarity and Estrangement according to Marcel Proust', proposes that 'Robert is a Muybridge character',[72] and that 'He is one of those figures that Etienne-Jules Marey photographed in movement, or one of Muybridge's serialized figures'.[73] Bal distinguishes Albertine from Robert; if Albertine is 'more radically other', Robert is more radically 'in movement'.[74] Just as the narrator strives to capture Albertine, ultimately by attempting to still her flight, he attempts to capture Robert's movement in a way which resonates with Muybridge and Marey's analytic decomposition of movement in a series of instantaneous photographic images in succession. Bal observes of Proust's writing here about Robert de Saint-Loup that it represents a 'drawing of movement that is reduced to a series of fixed points',[75] and that, in contrast to the way in which the multiple Albertines are presented, 'Visions of him yield not a picture album but a contact sheet of rapidly taken photos of movement'.[76] But Bal's analysis also brings out the way in which Proust's writing is not reducible to a kind of scientific experiment but is determined by desire and sexuality — Robert's desire not to be seen (to remain in the closet) and not to display this desire, and the narrator's desire for the body in movement, a desire which is epistemological and visual. With reference to Muybridge's sequence *The Wrestlers* of 1887, which shows twelve frames of two naked men closely entwined, she writes:

> Like the 19th-century photographer, Eadweard Muybridge, Proust explores through [Robert de Saint-Loup] the possibility of fixing movement. If his movement could only be fixed, allowing the desiring gaze to pin him down, the final frame of Muybridge's series could become visible.[77]

The desire to fix and to capture movement is thus an expression of desire as such, and photography, Bal proposes, is one of its most expedient visual means. The Muybridge sequence appears in this light as a compromise between the desire to capture the other in a fixed image, and the inherent sexual mobility of the other; Bal writes that in engaging with Proust visually, in this instance, 'we are dealing with something like an avant-garde photograph, which appears prior to cinema'.[78]

Bal herself identifies two scenes of particular significance: Robert's fisticuffs with the man who propositions him in after leaving the theatre with his mistress Rachel and the narrator, in *Le Côté de Guermantes*; and the narrator's momentary glimpse of Robert leaving Jupien's homosexual brothel in *Le Temps retrouvé*. This is the first episode:

> Nous quittâmes le théâtre, Saint-Loup et moi, et marchâmes d'abord un peu. Je m'étais attardé un instant à un angle de l'avenue Gabriel d'où je voyais souvent jadis arriver Gilberte. J'essayai pendant quelques secondes de me rappeler ces impressions lointaines, et j'allais rattraper Saint-Loup au pas 'gymnastique', quand je vis qu'un monsieur assez mal habillé avait l'air de lui parler d'assez près. J'en conclus que c'était un ami personnel de Robert; cependant ils semblaient se rapprocher encore l'un de l'autre; tout à coup, comme apparaît au ciel un phénomène astral, je vis des corps ovoïdes prendre avec une rapidité vertigineuse toutes les positions qui leur permettaient de composer, devant Saint-Loup, une instable constellation. Lancés comme par une fronde ils me semblèrent être au moins au nombre de sept. Ce n'étaient pourtant que les deux poings de Saint-Loup, multipliés par leur vitesse à changer de place dans cet ensemble

en apparence idéal et décoratif. Mais cette pièce d'artifice n'était qu'une roulée qu'administrait Saint-Loup, et dont le caractère agressif au lieu d'esthétique me fut d'abord révélé par l'aspect du monsieur médiocrement habillé, lequel parut perdre à la fois toute contenance, une mâchoire, et beaucoup de sang. (II, 480)

[The two of us left the theatre and walked for a while. I had lingered for a moment at the corner of the Avenue Gabriel from which I had often seen Gilberte appear in the past. I tried for a few seconds to recall those distant impressions, then as I moved on at a jog to catch up with Saint-Loup, I saw that a somewhat shabbily dressed gentleman appeared to be talking to him in a fairly confidential manner. I came to the conclusion that this was a personal friend of Robert; meanwhile, they seemed to be drawing even closer to one another; suddenly, like some astral phenomenon appearing in the sky, I saw ovoid bodies assuming with dizzying speed all the positions they needed to form an unstable constellation in front of Saint-Loup. Hurled out like missiles from a catapult, there seemed to be at least seven of them. They were merely, however, Saint-Loup's two fists, multiplied by the speed with which they were changing place in this apparently ideal and decorative pattern. But this deceptive display was merely a series of punches Saint-Loup was delivering with nothing aesthetic about it, and its aggressive nature first became obvious to me when I saw the state of the shabbily dressed gentleman, who seemed to be losing his self-possession, his jaw, and a great deal of blood.] (3, 179)

The writing of this scene moves between the narrator's perception of a single moving phenomenon, like a comet in the sky, and the perception of a series of successive positions, as if of separate bodies adopting different positions, which together make up a constellation. Proust's 'Muybridge mode' is explicit in the idea that the movement of Saint-Loup's fists is perceived as the movement of at least seven ovoid bodies around a succession of positions. The temporal sequence and speed of the movement of Robert's fists is described as a series of spatial positions, and the whole image is presented as a 'set' ('un ensemble'), with aesthetic qualities ('en apparence idéal et décoratif'). As Bal suggests, the visual form which Proust's writing comes closest to is not so much the photogrammatic sequence as the blurred motion image, in which several exposures are visible within the same frame.

The second episode runs as follows, as the narrator's curiosity is provoked by a house which appears different from the others around it as he walks through Paris at night during an air-raid:

C'était un hôtel par qui la jalousie de tous les commerçants voisins (à cause de l'argent que ses propriétaires devaient gagner) devait être excitée; et ma curiosité le fut aussi quand je vis sortir rapidement, à une quinzaine de mètres de moi, c'est-à-dire trop loin pour que dans l'obscurité profonde je pusse le reconnaître, un officier.

Quelque chose pourtant me frappa qui n'était pas sa figure que je ne voyais pas, ni son uniforme dissimulé dans une grande houppelande, mais la disproportion extraordinaire entre le nombre de points différents par où passa son corps et le petit nombre de secondes pendant lesquelles cette sortie, qui avait l'air de la sortie tentée par un assiégé, s'exécuta. De sorte que je pensai, si je ne le reconnus pas formellement — je ne dirai pas même à la tournure ni à la sveltesse, ni à l'allure, ni à la vélocité de Saint-Loup — mais à l'espèce

d'ubiquité qui lui était si spéciale. Le militaire capable d'occuper en si peu de
temps tant de positions différentes dans l'espace avait disparu, sans m'avoir
aperçu, dans une rue de traverse, et je restais à me demander si je devais ou non
entrer dans cet hôtel dont l'apparence modeste me fit fortement douter que ce
fût Saint-Loup qui en fût sorti. (IV, 389)

> [It was a hotel which (because of the money its owners must have been
> making) must have aroused the jealousy of all the neighbouring shop-keepers;
> and my curiosity was also aroused when, some fifteen metres away from me,
> that is to say too far away for me to be able, in the profound darkness, to make
> out who it was, I saw an officer hurriedly leaving it.
>
> Something about him struck me, all the same; it was not his face, which I did
> not see, nor his uniform, which was concealed under a heavy greatcoat, but the
> extraordinary disproportion between the number of different points through
> which his body passed and the small number of seconds it took for him to effect
> this exit, which looked like an attempted dash to safety on the part of somebody
> under siege. So that I was reminded, even if I did not actually recognize him —
> I will not say exactly of the frame, or the slenderness, or the gait, or the speed
> of Saint-Loup — but of the sort of ubiquity which was so peculiar to him. The
> soldier who was capable of occupying so many different positions in space in
> such a short time had disappeared down a side-street without seeing me, and
> I stood there wondering whether or not I should enter the hotel, the modest
> appearance of which made me doubt very much whether it was Saint-Loup
> who had left it.] (6, 119)

The speed of the figure barely glimpsed is again written in terms of a kind of
equation between a number of points and the time elapsed, the time of the
exposure, so to speak. This is thus Proust in Muybridge rather than Bergsonian
mode (in which movement would be duration, change); movement is analytically
decomposed into a series of spatial points. But this is also a characteristic specific to
Robert and to his psychology, which Proust consecrates with the notion of ubiquity.
In this figure Proust condenses both Robert's military and gymnastic prowess and
the desire not to be seen provoked by a closeted homosexuality. The symptom of
ubiquity, in other words, is equivalent to a Muybridge or Marey sequence in which
the visibility of the body is reduced, so rapid is its occupation of points in space in
a given lapse of time. This is also a question of efficiency: the capacity to occupy a
multiplicity of positions in a short space of time — 'd'occuper en si peu de temps
tant de positions différentes dans l'espace' — is expedient and efficient both from
the point of view of military strategy and productivity. We may recall that this was
one of the objectives of Marey's motion studies, at a time, after the crises of 1870,
when the military and industrial strength of France was in crisis.[79]

Both scenes relate to the hidden fact of Robert's homosexuality, and are but
one instance in which looking and the operations of quasi-cinematographic
visual capture on the part of an invisible narrator of scenes of the spectacle of
homosexuality are promoted to our attention throughout the novel. It is as if what
might somehow become visible in the interstices of the chronophotographic frames
of the Muybridge sequence, read via Proust, or at its end, is the encrypted spectacle
of homosexuality in its pure state. It is as if the decomposition of movement — what

I have called Proust's Muybridge mode — operates whenever there is a secret to know, a knowledge to grasp: the secret hidden in the bell-towers of Martinville or the trees of Hudimesnil, the permanence of Albertine and of her desire underneath so many versions of her, or the truth of Robert's sexuality. The decomposition of movement, while it corresponds to an aesthetic and technological tendency of the time, is realized in Proust as the constitution of a secret, something which must be read between the frames. It is always in the next frame, the next supposition, that the secret is held. Proust's Muybridge mode at the same time constitutes knowledge as something that can be fixed and captured, and removes it from our grasp. It thus serves the ends of the sustenance of desire.

Notes to Chapter 5

1. The essay was originally published in French as 'Notes sur le geste', trans. by Daniel Loayza, *Trafic*, 1 (1992), 31–36. Its publication in Italian is 'Note sul gesto', in *Mezzi senza fine* (Turin: Bollati Boringhieri, 1996), pp. 45–53. There are two versions of the essay in English translation. It appears, curiously truncated of its final paragraphs, as 'Notes on Gesture', in *Infancy and History: Essays on the Destruction of Experience,* trans. by Liz Heron (London: Verso, 1993), pp. 133–40, and, in full, as 'Notes on Gesture', in *Means Without End*, trans. by Binetti and Casarino, pp. 49–62. It is not included in the original Italian edition of *Infanzia et storia* (Turin: Einaudi, 1979). I will quote from the English version in *Means Without End*. On Agamben, film and gesture see Janet Harbord, *Ex-centric Cinema: Agamben and Film Archaeology* (London: Bloomsbury, 2016); Benjamin Noys, 'Gestural Cinema?: Giorgio Agamben on Film', *Film-Philosophy*, 8:22 (July 2004), < http://www.film-philosophy.com/vol8–2004/n22noys> [accessed 19 March 2018]; Pasi Väliaho, 'Simulation, Automata, Cinema: A Critique of Gestures', *Theory & Event*, 8:2 (2005), <http://muse.jhu.edu/article/187860> [accessed 19 March 2018]; and *Cinema and Agamben: Ethics, Biopolitics and the Moving Image*, ed. by Henrik Gustafsson and Asbjorn Gronstad (London: Bloomsbury, 2014).

2. Giorgio Agamben, 'Kommerell, or On Gesture', in *Potentialities: Collected Essays in Philosophy*, trans. by Daniel Heller-Roazen (Stanford, CA: Stanford University Press, 1999), pp. 77–85. The original Italian version is in a collection of translations of Kommerell's work edited by Agamben in 1991 (*Il poeta e l'indicible: saggi di litteratura tedesca* (Genoa: Marietti, 1991).

3. Agamben, 'Kommerell, or On Gesture', p. 77. There is an echo here of Benjamin's remarks about the 'Nature Theatre of Oklahoma' in Franz Kafka's unfinished novel *Amerika*, on which Benjamin remarks that 'One of its most significant functions [...] is to dissolve happenings into their gestic components' ('Franz Kafka', in *Illuminations*, trans. by Harry Zohn (London: Fontana, 1973), p. 116).

4. Agamben, 'Kommerell, or On Gesture', p. 77.

5. Ibid., p. 78.

6. Ibid.

7. Ibid., p. 80.

8. Ibid.

9. Agamben, 'Notes on Gesture', p. 49.

10. Agamben, 'Komerell, or On Gesture', p. 83.

11. Ibid., citing Max Kommerell, *Jean Paul* (Frankfurt: Klostermann, 1933), p. 42.

12. Agamben, 'Kommerell, or On Gesture', p. 83.

13. Agamben, 'Notes on Gesture', p. 52.

14. Ibid., p. 52.

15. Ibid., p. 55.

16. Agamben, 'Kommerell, or On Gesture', p. 83; 'Notes on Gesture', pp. 52–53;

17. Giorgio Agamben, 'Aby Warburg and the Nameless Science', in *Potentialities*, pp. 89–103.

18. Agamben, 'Notes on Gesture', p. 53.
19. Ibid.
20. Agamben, 'Aby Warburg and the Nameless Science' p. 93.
21. Ibid., p. 94.
22. As Agamben indicates in the essay on Warburg, one of the significant examples of the *Pathosformeln* and the historical dynamics at play in the latter's work focuses on the figure of the nymph.
23. Agamben, 'Notes on Gesture', p. 54.
24. Deleuze, *Cinéma 1*, p. 12; *Cinema 1*, p. 4.
25. Ibid., p. 13; p. 4.
26. Ibid.
27. Ibid.
28. Ibid., p. 14; p. 5.
29. Agamben, 'Notes on Gesture', p. 54.
30. Ibid., pp. 54–55.
31. Deleuze, *Cinéma 1*, pp. 14–15; *Cinema 1*, pp. 4–5.
32. Ibid., p. 15; p. 5.
33. Ibid., p. 15; p. 6
34. Ibid., p. 16; p. 6.
35. Ibid., p. 15; p. 7.
36. Agamben, 'Notes on Gesture', p. 54.
37. Harbord, *Ex-centric Cinema*, p. 1.
38. Ibid., p. 4.
39. Ibid., p. 5.
40. Ibid., p. 5.
41. Ibid., p. 7.
42. Ibid., pp. 7, 25, 14.
43. Ibid., p. 34.
44. Ibid., p. 46.
45. Giorgio Agamben, 'Walter Benjamin and the Demonic: Happiness and Historical Redemption', in *Potentialities*, pp. 138–59 (p. 158) (first published in Italian as 'Walter Benjamin e il demonico: felicità e redenzione storica nel pensiero del Benjamin', *aut aut*, 189–90 (1982), 39–58).
46. Ibid., p. 138.
47. Ibid., p. 144. In *Selected Writings* this passage is translated thus: 'He wants happiness — that is to say, the conflict in which the rapture of the unique, the new, the unborn, is combined with that bliss of experiencing something once more, of possessing once again, of having lived' (Walter Benjamin, 'Agesilaus Santander (Second Version)', in *Selected Writings*, ed. by Michael W. Jennings, Howard Eiland and Gary Smith, trans. by Rodney Livingstone, 4 vols (Cambridge, MA, & London: Harvard University Press, 1999), II, 715).
48. Agamben, 'Walter Benjamin and the Demonic', p. 151. The quotation from Benjamin can be found in 'On the Concept of History', in *Selected Writings*, ed. by Jennings, Eiland, and Smith, IV, 389, or 'Theses on the Philosophy of History', in *Illuminations*, p. 245.
49. Agamben, 'Walter Benjamin and the Demonic', p. 151. See also Benjamin, 'On the Concept of History', p. 390; 'Theses on the Philosophy of History', p. 246.
50. Agamben, 'Walter Benjamin and the Demonic', p 152.
51. Ibid., p. 156, citing Walter Benjamin, *The Origin of German Tragic Drama*, trans. by John Osborne (London: Verso, 1998), p. 45.
52. Agamben, 'Walter Benjamin and the Demonic', p. 157.
53. Ibid.
54. Ibid.
55. Agamben refers to the 'Epistemological-Critical Preface', otherwise known as the 'Paralipomena to "On the Concept of History"' which can be found in *Selected Writings*, ed. by Jennings, Eiland, and Smith, IV, 403: 'In drawing itself together in the moment — in the dialectical image — the past becomes part of humanity's involuntary memory'.

56. Agamben, 'Notes on Gesture', p. 54.
57. Agamben, 'Walter Benjamin and the Demonic', p. 158.
58. The work of contemporary French philosopher Catherine Malabou on plasticity is particularly important here. See in particular *Ontologie de l'accident: essai sur la plasticité destructrice* (Paris: Editions Léo Scheer, 2009); *Ontology of the Accident: An Essay on Destructive Plasticity*, trans. by Carolyn Shread (Cambridge: Polity Press, 2012).
59. Jean-Pierre Richard, *Proust et le monde sensible* (Paris: Seuil, 1974), p. 137.
60. Proust's reference to the 'metamorphosis of the nymph' is susceptible to opening up a seam of associations, due to its very ambivalence. Given Proust's predilection for entymological imagery, it seems likely as I have suggested that he is referring here to the way in which the plastically fluid form of the larvae transforms into the short-lived final entity of the insect. However, the continuity of this transformation with the Greek myth of the nymph, for example in Ovid's *Metamorphoses*, and the currency of this transformation in art history, also move us towards a concern of Warburg with the nymph as a specific vector of pagan dynamism in Renaissance art, and of Georges Didi-Huberman, in whose work an entymological poetics (generating such works and titles as *Phasmes, Phalènes*, and *La Survivance des lucioles*) is combined with a search for the modern and postmodern avatars of Warburg's *ninfa*, for example in *Ninfa moderna: essai sur le drapé tombé* (Paris: Gallimard, 2002), *Ninfa fluida: essai sur le drapé-désir* (Paris: Gallimard, 2015), and *Ninfa profunda: essai sur le drapé-tourmenté* (Paris: Gallimard, 2017).
61. Proust's account of the mobility of expression across the 'jeunes filles en fleurs' resonates here with Gilles Deleuze's notion of singularity, as articulated for example in his testamentary essay 'Immanence: une vie', in *Deux régimes de fous: textes et entretiens 1975–1995* (Paris: Minuit, 2003), pp. 359–63; 'Immanence: A Life', in *Two Regimes of Madness: Texts and Interviews 1975–1995*, trans. by Ames Hodges and Mike Taormina (New York: Semiotexte, 2006), pp. 384–89: 'Les singularités ou les événements constitutifs d'*une* vie coexistent avec les accidents de *la* vie correspondante, mais ne se groupent ni ne se divisent de la meme façon. Ils communiquent entre eux de toute autre façon que les individus. Il apparaît meme qu'une vie singulière peut de se passer de toute individualité ou de tout autre concomitant qui l'individualise. Par exemple les tous petits enfants se ressemblent tous et n'ont guère d'individualité, mais ils ont des singularités — un sourire, un geste, un grimace — événements qui n'ont pas de caractère subjectifs' (p. 362) ('The singularities or the events which constitute *a* life coexist with the accidents of the life that corresponds to it, but they are not arranged or distributed in the same way. They relate to one another in a completely different way than individuals do. It even seems that a singular life can do without any individuality at all, even without any of the concomitants that individualize it. For example, infants all resemble one another and have hardly any individuality; but they do have singularities — a smile, a gesture, a grimace — such events are not subjective traits', p. 387).
62. Elizabeth Ladenson, 'Gilberte's Indecent Gesture', in *Proust in Perspective: Visions and Revisions*, ed. by Armine Kotin Mortimer and Katherine Kolb (Urbana and Chicago: University of Illinois Press, 2002), pp. 147–56 (p. 147).
63. Ibid., p. 148.
64. Ibid., pp. 148, 151.
65. Ibid., p. 148.
66. Ibid., pp. 150, 152.
67. Ibid., p. 153.
68. In a suggestive parallel, Didi-Huberman points to Warburg's interest in the Italian scholar Andrea del Jurio's study of the persistence of antique gestures in popular Neapolitan culture, *La mimica degli antiche invesigata nel gestire napoletano* (1832), and includes plates from de Jurio's study, which corresponds to something like Proust's 'petit manuel de civilité'. See Georges Didi-Huberman, *L'Image survivante: histoire de l'art et temps des fantômes selon Aby Warburg* (Paris: Minuit, 2002), pp. 215, 216; *The Surviving Image: Phantoms of Time and Time of Phantoms: Aby Warburg's History of Art*, trans. by Harvey Mendelsohn (University Park, PA: Penn State University Press, 2016).
69. See Benhaïm, *Panim*, p. 90.

70. Tristan Garcia, in *L'Image* (Paris: L'Atlande, 2007), has read the episode of Gilberte's indecent gesture against the prevailing tendency to emphasize its photographic or cinematographic potential. Gilberte's gesture is an example of an 'image-sujet' which is an event and a process rather than an object, and as such is irreducible to any specific 'image-objet' (pp. 129–33).

71. I have not focused in this chapter on the gestural multiplicity of the figure of Charlus, which I would suggest is more explicit in terms of voice and vocality rather than chronophotographic decomposition.

72. Mieke Bal, 'All in the Family: Familiarity and Estrangement According to Marcel Proust', in *The Familial Gaze*, ed. by Marianne Hirsch (Hanover, NH, & London: University Press of New England, 1999), 223–47 (p. 232).

73. Bal, *The Mottled Screen*, p. 226.

74. Bal, 'All in the Family', p. 233.

75. Ibid., p. 231.

76. Ibid., p. 232.

77. Ibid.

78. Bal, *The Mottled Screen*, p. 213.

79. See Marta Braun, *Picturing Time: The Work of Etienne-Jules Marey (1830–1904)* (Chicago, IL: University of Chicago Press, 1992). Braun places Marey's work, and his collaboration with Georges Demeny, in the context of a social and medical concern with fatigue and 'degeneracy' and an effort to counter this through the study and application of human movement and productivity (see pp. 65–70, 320–48). See also Anson Rabinbach, *The Human Motor: Energy, Fatigue and the Origins of Modernity* (Berkeley & Los Angeles: University of California Press, 1990), pp. 84–119. Rabinbach links Proust to Marey in a common exploration of 'physiological time' (p. 93).

CHAPTER 6

Screen Memories/
Screen Histories

Freud's essay 'Screen Memories' ('Über Deckerinnerung', 1899), and his subsequent return to the question in *The Psychopathology of Everyday Life* (1901) consider the paradox of the vivid childhood memory of an indifferent or insignificant event, and the forgetting of life events which one might expect to have retained a strong hold on the memory due to their importance.[1] The paradox is explained, Freud proposes, by the proposition that the ostensibly insignificant event or scene which is recalled is a substitute for a more significant life event, to which it is linked through a process of displacement. The indifferent memory relates to the significant occurrence through an 'associative relation'.[2] Freud's article names these kinds of memory 'Deckerinnerung', where the prefix *Deck-* signifies *to cover*. Freud's English translators render *Deckerinnerung* as 'screen memory', drawing on the verb *to screen* in the sense of *to screen off or out*, and on the sense of the noun *screen* as something which covers or hides. The French translations offer *souvenir-écran* or *souvenir de couverture*.[3] The sense of *screen* indicating the cinematographic screen, the surface onto which an image is projected, is not intended in Freud's concept, except indirectly, insofar as the projection surface is conceived as something that screens off or displaces something else, as it is in the mobilization of the concept in the work of Stanley Cavell (on which see Chapter 3). The term *screen memory* and, to a greater extent perhaps, the French *souvenir-écran* (since the noun *écran* lacks the verb form which English offers with *to screen (off)*) thus mistranslate *Deckerinnerung* if they are taken to refer to the projection surface, rather than the function of covering.

It would be perverse, then, to ignore this potential translation error and think through the implications of *screen memory* or *souvenir-écran* as if they bore a special significance for film by virtue of the misleading ambivalence of the word *screen*. This is nonetheless the path we will take, since the error will prove instructive in pointing to what in fact turns out to be a specific kind of connection between the anachronistic memory effects Freud considers, and the experience of the cinema.[4] Both of these find a place in Proust's *Recherche*. We may find some justification in this perverse path insofar as Freud thinks of screen memories as operating in a particularly a–chronological manner, akin to the variations of temporality that we find at work in the *Recherche*. The screen memory can relate to 'the content that is screened off by it' in a manner which is 'retrospective' or 'retrogressive' — where a memory of an early event displaces a later occurrence — or through a 'displacement forward', more commonly found, in which an impression of 'recent date' is associated via displacement with an earlier experience, or contiguously, where the two mental experiences are contemporary.[5] We will return to these temporal variations further on. Of equal importance, however, is Freud's contention that the memories of early childhood, those which clinical experience has told him are particularly prone to present themselves as screen memories, have an explicitly *visual* character. They are 'plastically visual' in a way that memories of later life may not be. Even the childhood memories of Charcot's 'auditifs', those individuals more susceptible to remembering aurally, present themselves visually, in a way which is 'comparable to representations on the stage', and also bears comparison to the 'childhood memories that a nation preserves in its store of legends and myths'. This is surprising, Freud suggests, especially given the idea that children are less exclusively attentive to external impressions, being more focused on themselves. The 'plastically visual' form of childhood memories is thus a sign of their extensive revision by 'a variety of later psychical forces'.[6] This moves towards a conception of the screen memory (the memory that covers another) as a specifically constructed visual form, an image which has a peculiarly visual plasticity, a 'scene' (whence Freud's comparison with theatrical representation), but one with an exclusively visual character, a scene that is screened, in the sense of projected.

Bringing the two senses of *screen* together — covering or displacing something more significant or traumatic, and projected, constructed in a specifically visual form — offers a powerful way of thinking the relation between memory and the screen image. Proust's *Recherche* exploits this conceptual matrix, while departing, in its own way, from the stricter terms of Freud's interpretative schema. The *drame du coucher*, for example, is recalled as only a 'pan lumineux', an illuminated scene limited to the bedroom, staircase, and dining room of the house in Combray, as if framed by the limits of the affectively-charged architecture of the goodnight kiss and Swann's inopportune visit. The *madeleine* offers a particularly expansive example of a screen memory, in the sense that the whole of Combray and the ensuing narrative unfolds from the revitalization of the past sensation; while the sensation itself is gustative, the taste of the madeleine-tea, the memory it resuscitates is marked as visual: 'Certes, ce qui palpite au fond de moi, de doit être l'image, le souvenir visuel, qui, lié à cette saveur, tente de la suivre jusqu'à moi' ('Undoubtedly what is fluttering this way deep inside me must be the image, the visual memory which is attached to this taste and is trying to follow it to me') (1, 45; 1, 48–49). Like the kaleidoscopic rooms of the novel's opening sequences, the memory is sensed initially as an 'insaisissable tourbillon de couleurs remuées' ('the elusive eddying of stirred-up colours') (1, 46; 1, 49), a visual form which eventually coagulates into the image of Combray, adding itself 'comme un décor de théâtre' ('like a stage-set') (1, 47; 1, 50) to the delimited patch ('pan') of the bedroom and staircase. While this memory is provoked by taste, as if to access the memory itself the narrator had to be triggered by a repeated and contiguous sensation he conceives as a more 'faithful' ('fidèle') (1, 46; 1, 49) container of the past, once remembered the memory functions like a screen memory in the sense that the ostensibly indifferent event of having tea with his great aunt carries the 'édifice immense du souvenir' ('the immense edifice of memory') (I, 46; 1, 50), the larger span of events, habits, and ideas that will constitute the novel.

The *covering* element of the memory is not marked here, however; the recovery of the memory of Combray is largely a happy process. This screen memory effect recurs with a more devastating and traumatic effect at two significant junctures of the novel, both marked out and linked by Proust through the inter-title 'Les Intermittences du cœur'. The first instance occurs in Balbec, when the narrator bends down to tie his bootlaces and recalls the same gesture on the part of his now deceased grandmother on the occasion of his first visit, as well as the image of solicitude in her face. The memory of the gesture itself is associated with the more painful one of his grandmother's care, the recognition of her definitive absence, and of his own previous indifference to her death. This first instance of the 'intermittences du cœur' is followed later in *Sodome et Gomorrhe* with the equally painful memory of Montjouvain, discussed in Chapter 4. Here the screen memory effect is enmeshed with the dynamics of jealousy, as Albertine's ostensibly innocent and insignificant mention of her friendship with Mlle Vinteuil and her friend triggers the narrator's memory of the scene he had witnessed as a child, traumatic in itself perhaps but even more so since it is now cathected with and overlaid by his suspicions about Albertine's sexuality, and his projection of her into the Montjouvain scene. The screen memory here threatens to transgress the strict parameters of Freud's account, since each memory seems to hide or cover another, in a potentially endless series of screens; the words 'l'amie de Mlle Vinteuil' recall the scene of Montjouvain, which screens, both in the sense of *covering* and in the sense of *projecting*, Albertine's sexuality, the imagined scene in which she takes the place of the friend, which may itself displace the 'danse contre seins' with Albertine and Andrée pressed up against one another, lubriciously so according to Cottard's crude insinuation, which may in turn displace the primitive, yet also imagined, scene of his mother's presence in 'un lieu de plaisir' ('a place of enjoyment') where he is not, back in Combray (III, 191; 4, 197; and 1, 30; 1, 33).[7] In both of the 'intermittences du cœur', something like a screen memory occurs, although Proust's rendering of it both troubles and extends Freud's more precise account. Rather than the childhood memory of a specifically visual scene which recalls a more significant event, Proust's memories are triggered by a word, a gesture or a sensation, which nevertheless brings to light a past which has somehow remained inaccessible in the present, which has been forgotten through habit, and which now colours the present in a different light, more often than not a painful one. Proust's screen memories are not necessarily therapeutic, then, but they do also function as narrative devices, puncturing the linear progress of the novel and provoking a resetting or a recalibration of the narrator's perspectives, and those of the reader. They are also fictional devices, in the sense that they allow the positioning and the relativization of differential narrative perspectives, giving the image of a series of screens positioned one behind the other, with slight displacements. They offer opportunities to the reader to reframe the narrative as a whole, through the temporal and psychic disjunctions they introduce.

The account of screen memory as a resurrection of a forgotten experience brought about through a contingent association is complicated, however, by the proposition that the original experience has been repressed due to elements within it which are unacceptable to consciousness. The original memory, the one *covered* by the screen memory, has in other words not been experienced or registered as such. Proust offers a slightly different version of this Freudian logic; the experience that is recovered through involuntary memory has not only been lost or covered over due to the deadening and flattening force of habit and everyday recurrence, but also because the self which the experience relates was not accessible or actual at the time. Proust conceives of a multiplicity of virtual selves co-existing alongside the present and conscious self; involuntary memories are thus not so much memories in the strict sense as ambivalently recovered experiences of a virtual experience. There is also a temptation to go further in this dislocation of memory from the conscious subject; insofar as it is not simply a moment of the past recalled by the subject in the present, but another present now co-existing alongside the actual present, the memory does not belong to a subject, but seems to reside in the sensations and objects with which the subject has interacted: the taste of madeleine-tea, a name, a napkin, the title of a book. Proust's subject or subjects are enmeshed in a network of objects and sensations which themselves seem to contain or at least to conserve the memories which are visited upon him. It is the memory conserved within the madeleine-tea, the paving stone, the name François le Champi, which is unleashed through the narrator's encounters with them, provoking a reliving of a past he never experienced, in the strict sense.

There is of course a reading of Proust's *Recherche* which construes it as a narrative oriented towards and an argument in favour of the triumphant capacity of memory to recapture and redeem the forgotten past. According to this argument, the narrator would be saved from the desolation of loss and the conviction of his lack of literary talent by the series of 'moments bienheureux' which occur in the waiting room of the Hôtel de Guermantes, which establish analogical relations with the past and lead to the project to write on the basis of a theory of 'incorporated time', and to write the novel which we have just read. This is an argument which takes the theory constructed in the second half of *Le Temps retrouvé* at face value and thus reads the novel as a kind of self-fulfilling prophecy, the realization of the project it announces. Despite the doubt thrown on voluntary memory within its pages the *Recherche* would thus be wholly affirmative, in the end, about the capacity of memory to recover the past.

There are serious objections to this reading of the novel, however.[8] First, the triumphant, redemptive reading assumes the thematic and compositional unity of the novel; it assumes that its extensive and uneven span is unproblematically synthesized in the project it turns out to have been. Critics of the triumphalist reading have seen it as the repression of a large element of the text at the expense of another, and a denegation of its heterogeneity. Another serious objection is raised by the narrator himself and it relates to the sense, rare in the novel, of time running out: his age and impending death will prevent the completion of the novel whose project he sets out; the *Recherche* is not the realization of the project, but only its preface. Closer to my concerns here, however, are objections to the triumphalist account of memory raised within the operations of memory in the novel itself. In opposition to the instances of a recapturing of past experience in the operation of involuntary memory (in the madeleine, the paving stones, *François le Champi*) are those instances where nothing is recaptured save the subject's absence from the experience at stake; here the memory points to an absence of knowledge, of affect, of presence. This argument is presented primarily in the two scenes Proust foregrounds and links through the independent title of 'Les Intermittences du cœur'. The memory of Montjouvain provoked by Albertine's mention of the name Vinteuil brings to light a subject who did not know what he was looking at, who did not at that point have the sexual knowledge necessary to interpret the scene, and who, moreover, was not present at the scene he retrospectively imagines, since it is a fantasy, rather than a memory: what he remembers is Albertine falling into the arms of Mlle Vinteuil.[9] This lack of presence at the original scene and the Freudian operation of *Nachträglichkeit*, or *afterwardness*, allow the scene to be filled with the paranoid fantasy of the other's desire. In the previous episode of 'intermittence' what is brought to light is the narrator's affective absence from the event of his grandmother's death. Something did not take place when it ought to have; knowledge, in the first instance, emotion, in the second.[10]

This *not-having-taken-place* of that which is remembered has provided a strong impetus to readings of Proust which place greater emphasis on the Freudian operations of *Nachträglichkeit* and on the dislocation between memory and consciousness. In a contentious essay titled 'Les Juifs', in the book *Heidegger et 'les juifs'* [Heidegger and the 'Jews'], in which he uses the expression in inverted commas to designate a 'non-lieu', a not-having-taken-place, of which the Jews, in particular, have suffered the real consequences, Jean-François Lyotard proposes a radical conception of the Forgotten and its rememoration: 'Non pas se rappeler pour ce qu'il a été et ce qu'il est, car il n'a été et n'est rien, mais se rappeler comme ce qui ne cesse de s'oublier' ('The Forgotten is not to be remembered for what it has been and what it is, because it has not been anything and is nothing, but must be remembered as something that never ceases to be forgotten').[11] Lyotard goes on to link this not-having-taken-place to a lineage in French literature:

> Reste vrai, pourtant, que les 'Français', s'ils y sont plus sensibles que d'autres, c'est que depuis longtemps, par Rimbaud, Mallarmé, Flaubert, Proust, Bataille, Artaud, Beckett, — par ce qu'ils appellent 'écriture' — , attestent que la littérature (pour ne parler que d'elle) n'a jamais eu pour objet véritable que de révéler, représenter en mots, ce qui manque à toute représentation, ce qui s'y oublie. Cette 'présence', quelque nom qu'elle porte chez l'un ou l'autre, qui persiste non pas tant aux confins, mais au cœur des représentations. Cet innommable dans le secret des noms. Un oublié, qui ne résulte pas de l'oubli d'une réalité, rien n'ayant jamais été mémorisé, et que l'on ne peut rappeler que comme oublié 'avant' la mémoire et l'oubli, et en le répétant.

[It remains true, however, that if the 'French' are more susceptible to it than others, it is because they have for a long time, with Rimbaud, Mallarmé, Flaubert, Proust, Bataille, Artaud, Beckett, and what they call 'writing', testified to the fact that the real objective of literature (to speak only of that for now) has always been to reveal, represent in words, what every representation misses, what is forgotten there: this 'presence', whatever name is given by one author or another, which persists not so much at the limits but rather at the heart of representation; this unnamable in the secret of names, a forgotten that is not the result of the forgetting of a reality — nothing having been stored in memory — and which one can only remember as forgotten 'before' memory and forgetting, and by repeating it.][12]

Lyotard thus posits a forgetfulness before memorization, an absence at the heart of representation, to which he links the name of Proust, among others.[13] Concerned with the 'politics of forgetting', Lyotard proposes that the notion of the past that is at stake here is:

Un 'passé' qui n'est pas passé, qui ne hante pas le présent, au sens où il lui fait défaut, lui manquerait, se signaleraient présentement même comme un spectre, une absence, qui ne l'habite pas non plus au titre d'une belle et bonne réalité, qui ne fait pas l'objet à mémoire comme quelque chose qui serait oublié et doit être rappelé (aux fins de 'bonne fin', de bonne connaissance). Qui n'est donc même pas là comme blanc, absence, *terra incognita*, mais qui est là pourtant.

[A past that is not past, that does not haunt the present, in the sense that its absence is felt, would signal itself even in the present as a spectre, an absence, which does not inhabit it in the name of full reality, which is not an object of memory like something that might have been forgotten and must be remembered (with a view to a 'good end', to correct knowledge). It is not even there as a 'blank space', as absence, as *terra incognita*, but it is there nevertheless.][14]

In support of this argument, which he also relates to Freud's hypothesis of an unconscious without 'formations représentatives' ('representational formations'), Lyotard points to Deleuze's *Proust et les signes*, in which, Lyotard avers, Deleuze detects:

Cette sorte de passé qui nous préoccupe, qui est en deçà de l'oublié, beaucoup plus près de l'actuel que tout passé, en même temps qu'incapable d'être sollicité par la mémoire volontaire et consciente. Et dont il dit, de ce passé, qu'il n'est pas passé, mais toujours là.

[This sort of past that interests us here, a past located this side of the forgotten, much closer to the present moment than any past, at the same time that it is incapable of being solicited by voluntary and conscious memory — a past Deleuze says that is not past but always there.][15]

For Lyotard, then, the 'Freudian (and Proustian) hypothesis' means that there is no dialectical 'overcoming' of the immemorial past: 'La recherche du temps perdu commence à la fin. Et rien n'est à la fin surmonté, de l'aveu final de Marcel (*Recherche*)' ('The remembrance of things past begins at the end. And nothing is overcome at the end, by Marcel's final admission (Proust)'). If writing involves the laying bare of the time that 'does not take place', it nevertheless does not triumphantly integrate it into a representation: 'Chaque écriture, digne de ce nom, engage le combat avec l'Ange, et au mieux s'en tire en boitant' ('Every writing worthy of its name wrestles with the Angel and, at best, comes out limping').[16]

An earlier reference by Lyotard allows us to connect the Angel he alludes to here with the 'Angel of History' of Benjamin's ninth thesis in 'On the Concept of History', that angel which is being blown into the future by the wind of progress, but faces back towards the past, observing the catastrophes of the past and the debris piling up at its feet:

> Where we see a chain of events, he sees one single catastrophe which keeps piling wreckage upon wreckage and hurls it at his feet. The angel would like to stay, awaken the dead, and make whole what has been smashed. But a storm is blowing from Paradise; it has got caught in his wings with such violence that the angel can no longer close them. This storm irresistibly propels him into the future to which his back is turned, while the pile of debris before him grows skyward.[17]

What is broken cannot be made whole; the shards of past experience cannot be retrospectively integrated into a coherent whole; Lyotard shares with Benjamin, and indeed draws from him, among others, this conception of a non-dialectical relation to past experience, and this is something Benjamin also finds in Proust. In the essay 'On Some Motifs in Baudelaire', written around the same time as the theses on history, Benjamin considers the relation between consciousness and memory, and the Freudian proposition of their incompatibility:

> The basic formula of this hypothesis is that 'becoming conscious and leaving behind a memory trace are processes incompatible with each other within one and the same system'. Rather, memory fragments are 'often most powerful and more enduring when the incident which left them behind was one that never entered consciousness'. Put in Proustian terms, this means that only what has not happened to the subject as an experience, can become a component of *mémoire involontaire*. According to Freud, the attribution of 'permanent traces as the basis of memory' to processes of stimulation is reserved for 'other systems', which must be thought of as different from consciousness.[18]

This account of the 'non-lieu' of the original experience obliges us to alter our conception of the screen memory; the 'plastically visual' 'scene' recalled by memory is in these instances a displacement of an experience which 'did not take place', or which took place in 'another system'.

This Proustian logic is articulated in exemplary fashion in Chris Marker's 1962 work *La Jetée*, which hovers uncertainly between photography and cinema, opening and allowing multiple exchanges between the media. Marker incorporates the logic of the screen-memory into the simple narrative proposition of the film: a man is haunted (or 'marked') by an image from childhood, an image he initially recalls as being that of a woman's face on the observation jetty at Orly airport. The protagonist returns to or travels into the past, to find the woman, only to find that the image that has haunted him, which now expands into a sequence, was that of his own death.[19]

This reduced version of the narrative obscures the science-fictional premises on which it is based and which, through the motif of time-travel, allow for the impossible, 'scandalous' proposition (in Barthes's sense): the memory of one's own death. However, it has the virtue of bringing to light the way in which the structure of the film depends on the capacity of the image to enter into sequence (or association) with other images. It is as if the tragedy of the protagonist's death is provoked by his own hermeneutic quest to find the larger sequence from which his screen memory, a fragmentary or still image, has been as if extracted, or the chain of associations which draw it back to the traumatic event (a logic also played out in Michael Haneke's *Caché*). The proposition — that the image itself has a memory, which it imposes or visits upon the subject, like a kind of curse — is a corollary, and a reversal, of the underlying proposition of the film, that the past can be recovered through the production and projection of images. The science-fictional elements of the film, which place the protagonist as a guinea pig of a scientific experiment to move in time, so as eventually to win hope for the future, *from* the future, are only thinly separable from a metaphysical proposition that the past can be recovered through images, a proposition which is also an affirmation of the capacities of film-form itself, more devastatingly realized in *Nuit et brouillard*, the film about the concentration camps by Alain Resnais and Jean Cayrol, on which Marker collaborated, made a few years before. However, as *Nuit et brouillard* makes evident, images, as traces or scars of the past, have a degree of independence from the conscious intentions of the subject, from their agency, which gives them a potentially lethal power. The same logic which underpins the joyful recovery of the past through the image also underpins its disastrous potential; the image has two sides, one which faces towards the life that it records, and the other which faces towards the past that it is, the death that it marks, the haunting it instigates, a duality expressed in Barthes's well-known proposition about the 'noeme' of the photograph: 'ça a été' ('that has been').[20] In *La Jetée* Marker articulates these two sides and powers of the image, to bring to life and to mark death, across the structure of the narrative, and also in and around the materiality of film form. The bringing to life of the woman whom the narrator has sought out reaches its apex in the momentary and all too brief switch of the procession of still frames into the speed required for the illusion of continuous movement; the moving image, in the orthodox sense, appears redemptive and vital in drawing the woman out from the stillness of the frames in which she has been captured up to that point. The image of the protagonist's death, on the other hand, which captures his body in the parabola of its fall, his arm stretched up to the sky, emphasizes the frozen instantaneity of the photograph, and further affirms its photographic nature in its reference to Robert Capa's famous photograph of Federico Garcia Borrel at the exact moment of his death.[21]

In 'The Remembered Film', a chapter of his book of the same name, Victor Burgin considers his own fascination with a double set of film sequences featuring a woman in a landscape. The sequences — from Tsai Ming-Lang's film *Vive l'amour* and from Powell and Pressburger's *A Canterbury Tale* — have become detached from their wider narratives, and as fragments, are now related analogously to each other, each echoing the other. Continuing his discussion via a reference to Barthes's account of his response to the James van der See Harlem family photograph in *La Chambre claire*, Burgin points to the Freudian proposition that 'emotions, affects may become detached from the "representations", such as memory-traces or fantasy images, to which they were first attached', and 'experienced in isolation from the representation with which [they were] originally associated'. The affect may, moreover, be 'displaced' onto other representations. By 'retracing the path taken by the affect', Burgin continues, we may be led back to 'its origin in a repressed or suppressed idea'.[22] This retracing is a form of work, and can take the form of a 'silent and unselfconscious process'.[23] Burgin relates this process or 'work' to a point made by Barthes in his commentary on the Harlem family photograph. The photo, Barthes suggests, 'worked within him', and this process led him from the group portrait to the *punctum* of the ankle-strap on the shoes of one of the women, to the same woman's necklace, to the memory of an aunt who had spent her life caring for her mother.[24] This unconscious work, which Burgin relates to Freud's 'dream-work', does not necessarily have a definitive end-point, a final origin; the series of displacements may reach down into the inaccessible region which Freud calls the 'navel' of the dream.[25] But what interests Burgin particularly in the way in which the clusters or chains of images along which the affect is displaced are formed from a fluid set which includes both memory images and images from the 'everyday environment' or 'envelope', the potentially infinite multiplicity of images we encounter in our everyday lives.[26] Our experience, and the affectively charged 'scenes' we encounter in fantasy, dream or recollection, draw, Burgin posits, on this 'everyday environment of images' or 'image envelope'. The chain of associations which constitutes the 'work' of the image is made up of a contingent mixture of 'residues' from one's everyday encounters and experience and mnesic traces of more distant experiences. Our recollections and fantasies thus draw on what Burgin identifies, via a reference to Winnicott, as 'the location of cultural experience'.[27] Compromising Barthes's will to singularize the 'work' of the photograph, to claim it as an irreducible facet of his own 'unique being', the crucial point that Burgin works towards here is this: our experience of photographic images and of film is a significant element of this 'cultural experience'; our fantasies and affective responses are woven from the material of our unconscious and from the 'residues' of our cinematic experiences, among others, in such a way that the specifically cinematographic sense of *screen* in screen memories can be actively emphasized; our screen memories are woven in part out of our memories of the screen.

Burgin adds to this consideration, however, the important corollary that just as the link between an affect and a representation can be loosened, allowing for the displacement of that affect onto other content, or other forms, so film sequences can be dislodged from their original narratives, enter into associations with other sequences or other images, and thus enter into the unconscious 'work' of the image. Burgin proposes this argument via an engagement with Barthes's key essay 'Le Troisième Sens' [The Third Meaning], and the distinction made by Barthes between the 'obvious' ('obvie') sense of the image and the 'obtuse' ('obtus') sense;

while the first — akin to the *studium* in Barthes's later book *La Chambre claire* — includes the general cultural meaning or connotation of the image, the second, close to Barthes's later notion of the *punctum,* is more singular, less bound to a general cultural meaning. Burgin describes the way in which, for him, certain film sequences, whose bond to their original narratives has been loosened, enter into the zone of what Barthes calls the obtuse, 'a fleeting association of discrete elements': 'the fragments go adrift and enter into new combinations, more or less transitory, in the eddies of memory: memories of other films, and memories of real events'.[28]

In the introduction to *The Remembered Film* Burgin considers the way in which the narrative order of a film may be disrupted by self-consciously resistant practices (such as those adopted by André Breton and Jacques Vaché in their random *dérive* around Nantes movie houses) or the more contemporary, and less subversive, practices in the 'demotic space' opened up between cinema viewing and video technologies.[29] He refers again to Barthes, in this instance to the account, in *Roland Barthes par Roland Barthes*, of the 'stereophony' of a bar in a Tangiers souk, where, half asleep, Barthes considers the plurality of languages within his earshot, comparing it to the 'interior speech' that speaks within him. The significant point Barthes makes is that in both cases the discourse is 'outside the sentence'; the texture of this material is formed of 'small syntagms, ends of formulae', lacking the closure and hierarchy of propositional syntax.[30] What I want to draw out of Burgin's subsequent discussion is the proposition of the 'sequence–image' as the filmic equivalent of the fragmentary 'small syntagm' identified by Barthes. Burgin's 'sequence–image' is a minimal 'configuration' of elements which nevertheless occurs in a specific order; sequences withdrawn from larger narratives, yet retaining sequentiality. As the medium in which movement is presented as an image the cinema seems predisposed to offer such 'sequence–images' to the psyche as a privileged material with which to construct memory or fantasy images. In proposing to the viewer a stock of such fragmentary fragments or gestures of movement the cinema offers itself as a kind of vocabulary, a lexical stock of screen-memories. As proposed above, and by way of 'sequence–images' withdrawn from the representational space of their original narratives, now free to enter into association with other sequences or with other unconscious content, cinema forms part of the 'image envelope' available for the construction of memories, offering a different sense of the expression *screen memories.*

The Freudian resonances of Proust's logic of involuntary memory, along with Burgin's argument concerning the way our fantasies and memories draw on a repertory of 'sequence–images' in our memories of cinema can serve to re-emphasize the productive ambivalence of *screen memories.* Our screen memories can incorporate memories of screens. If we add to this the consideration in Freud's essay that childhood memories have a marked propensity towards the 'plastically visual' we might conclude that the last century provides, in the cinema, a rich and privileged resource of visual scenes and sequences, on to which our affects may be displaced or to which they may be attached. Our memories are made of films, woven with the thread of our early lives and our experiences of film. Deleuze remarks critically that the only contribution psychoanalysis has made to the philosophy of film is the notion of the 'primal scene'. He is critical of the tendency to draw film back to this Oedipal origin, to anchor it in an 'original crime'. It is feasible, however, to turn Deleuze's criticism around, and to suggest that cinema offers the psyche the material for its primal scenes, whether real or imaginary, and that in certain instances the primal scene, if not an experience of the cinema as such, is, as I argued in Chapter 1, cinematic in its construction and its phenomenology.

Deleuze's criticism of the tendency to construe cinematic experience in relation to an original crime is directed, in part, at the work of Jean-Louis Schefer, whose 1981 work *L'Homme ordinaire du cinéma* [The Ordinary Man of Cinema] was otherwise a significant influence on Deleuze's two volumes on cinema.[31] For Schefer, film has a privileged relation to childhood and to memory for several reasons; his thinking of film departs radically from film theories concerned with the representation of the real (Bazin) or the illusion of reality (Metz), and from apparatus theories concerned with the spectator as subject and their capture in the frame of ideology (Baudry). For Schefer, the spectator is primarily a body, and the reality of film is the affective experience it produces in the spectator. Film allows us the experience of movement emancipated from the substance of a body and thus from the physics determined by that substance; the 'dancing grains' of a projected film, and the improbable bodies that move on the screen, are relieved, for example, from the determination of gravity; these are bodies without a centre of gravity.[32] For Schefer cinema conjures in the spectator an 'inceptive' and formless being ('être inchoative'), constrained to the beginnings of gestures and movements lived in the body, and not subject to normalization (thus the value of Schefer for Deleuze). Neither a represented world, nor an illusory world fitted to the subject's imagination, film for Schefer is the birth of a world, a realm of inchoate affect which has not yet found a language, which seeks it in the spectator. Film thus has a privileged relation to childhood because of the resemblance of the affective economy of the two situations, where the charge of affect of the image, of experience, exceeds the limits of the language — the names and concepts — the subject has at his or her disposal. The cinema returns us to a pre-subjective situation in which the affects we experience fall outside the normal and normativizing zone of representation.

But childhood is also significant in Schefer's work beyond this theoretical analogy, and it is in this instance that cinema and history come into relation with each other in a manner which brings into relief the absence of the cinema in the represented reality of Proust's *Recherche*, like a negative space. Schefer belongs to a generation for whom the experience of cinema in childhood is formative, and, since this generation (that of Schefer, Deleuze, Claude Ollier, Serge Daney, but also, with a degree of chronological license, of Chris Marker and Jean-Luc Godard) had its childhood during the years of 1939–45, the defeat of France, the Occupation, the camps, the experience of cinema and the memory of cinema are bound up with this history, affectively bound to it, and knotted around it in different ways. This does not necessarily mean that this history finds its place in post-war cinema, as a representation; cinema and history are bound up with each other in such a way that the war, the Occupation, or the holocaust appear as a blank space, a space brought into relief by its absence. In Schefer's work in particular we find an argument which posits the cinema as a form of screen memory, a memory that screens off and excludes the memory of the defeat and the Occupation of France.[33] In Godard's work we find an argument which posits the history of the cinema as determined by a constitutive exclusion of the history of the Occupation, of collaboration, and of the camps. If history is mediated now via film-history, memory mediated via memories of films, the lacunae of film history point to telling instances of forgetfulness, if not of repression. The importance of Proust here is in the example the *Recherche* provides of alternative operations of memory; just as the narrator's conscious memory of events is constrained by the intermittence of the multiple selves of which he is composed, the deadening force of habit, and the inevitable entropy of forgetting, but recurrently dislocated and fractured, opened up by the non-linear instances of involuntary memory, film history can be opened up by the uncanny return of the past within it. This version of memory, and the account of history it supports, finds echoes in the observations by Lyotard I cited earlier, and more profoundly in the philosophy of history developed in the later work of Benjamin, in which we can find the trace of his intense engagement with Proust, and in which we might also discern elements of a Proustian theory of cinema and of history.

Tom Conley, in an illuminating article on the work of Schefer, draws on the motif of the screen memory in order to configure a conflation of its different senses, a folding of the semantics of covering into those of projection, and thus the history of cinema. For Conley, Schefer's work on film offers 'a model of an uncommon and vitally affective relation with cinema'.[34] Conley draws out of Schefer's work, in conjunction with Michel de Certeau's theorizations of practices of the everyday, the proposition that the cinema is 'practiced' by its viewers, that it forms part of a personal narrative, and that it is thus a constituent element of our memories, a 'lieu de mémoire', in which personal history merges with cultural history:

> The spatial story that ordinary persons afford themselves in gaining spatial consciousness leads to silent or inner narratives of the self: points of reference become sites in an arrangement or disposition that the user assembles with the ambient world and with the resurgent memory of cinema, bearing on the given places, which causes them to be experienced as they are and across the filter of movies.[35]

The experience of films may in certain instances be brought to bear upon the experience of the present; experience in everyday life is mediated via the memories of films:

> The cinematic practice of everyday life in Schefer's vision would not necessarily be the bailiwick of an entitled cinephile: it could be mantled wherever an art of the everyday uses cinematic memory-flashes to intensify the experience of walking, running, talking, reading and thinking.[36]

Conley goes on to suggest, if only in order to dismiss the proposition subsequently, that cinema offers us a rich material for the reliving of our own 'primal scenes', that the screen offers us screen memories, sequences through which we 'remember' the traumas of childhood.[37] But this overly straightforward operation — we remember *through* film — is overturned by a more radical proposition on Conley's part, again drawing on Schefer's work, and akin to Lyotard's postulations on forgetfulness which we discussed earlier, which posits that the screen memories compensate for and substitute for an 'absence of figuration'. Conley writes:

> But no, we cannot gain access by merely comparing our memories to those by which cinema would turn us into its own children. Film occults the scene of an 'inner history' exactly where it invites us to retrieve it. It thus accrues critical force by setting the primal scene into an area where figuration is absent.[38]

The 'inner history' to which film would give us access is itself phantasmatic, a story that does not take place, that has not taken place. Conley cites an important proposition by Schefer from *L'Homme ordinaire du cinéma* in which film comes to fill the empty, negative place left by an inner history without substance or duration:

> J'ai tenté d'expliquer comment le cinéma était en nous, à la manière d'une chambre ultime où tourneraient à la fois l'espoir et le fantôme d'une *histoire intérieure*: parce que cette histoire ne se déroule pas et ne peut, pourtant, si peu qu'elle ait lieu, que rester invisible, sans figure, sans personage mais surtout sans durée. Nous acclimatons tous ces films, par leurs rémanences d'images, à cette absence de durée et à cette absence de scène où serait possible l'histoire intérieure.
>
> [I have been trying to explain how the cinema exists within us as a kind of ultimate chamber where the hope and the ghost of an *interior history* circulate. Because this history does not unfold, and even if it occurs, can only remain invisible, without a face, without characters, and most of all, without duration. Through the persistence of their images, we acclimatize all films we see to this absence of duration and of a scene where that interior history might be possible.][39]

For Schefer, 'inner history' is without form or figure, a site or space of non-figuration, a site to which he gives the form or shape of a room or a chamber. The primal scene is in other words not simply recovered by memory or via the primal scenes with which cinema provides us, since in itself this primal scene lacks figuration; it is *informe*, negative and formless, without duration. Schefer writes that we 'acclimatize' films through the fragments of images that they leave behind in us, as traces, to this interior absence, to this formless non-figure, which is to say that we fit them to this inner life.

In Schefer's account, therefore, the primal scene, the inner history of childhood is not accessible via memory, nor is it figured straightforwardly or given figurative form by a sequence drawn from our experience of cinema. It is conjured as a formless and invisible 'chamber' in us wherever something in the film provokes that sense of absence or formlessness, wherever the negative space of our 'inner history' is brought into relief. Cinema provides us with triggers for a memory without content, the memory of an unlived life.

But Schefer also postulates, as Conley and others have shown, a specific form of relation between the early experience of cinema and the experience of history; he confesses to a sense that the films watched as a child were enjoyed at the expense of, thus as a kind of cover, a screen, for the destruction taking place elsewhere, outside the cinema. Film is a form of compensation and sublimation for the experience of the war, just as its violence screens us from the violence outside. In keeping, however, with his critique of an account of spectatorship centred on the subject, Schefer reverses this dynamic, referring to 'the films that have watched our childhood', as if the very absence of figuration, of history, from the represented space of cinema brought it to bear, as a negative image, for the spectator.

This proposition is cited and echoed in a justly revered late essay on French film history and theory by the former *Cahiers du cinéma* critic Serge Daney, 'Le Travelling de *Kapo*' [The Tracking Shot in *Kapo*]. Following a recollection of his first viewing of Resnais's *Nuit et brouillard*, Daney notes the chronological superimposition of his own biography on that of a certain portion of cinema history, precisely that which corresponds to the post-war, post-holocaust period: 'Né en 1944, deux jours avant le débarquement allié, j'avais l'âge de découvrir en meme temps *mon* cinéma et *mon* histoire' ('Born in 1944, two days before D-Day, I was old enough to discover *my* cinema and *my* history at the same time').[40] A portion of Daney's biography and of his memory is lived through a history of cinema; that memory is mediated through the experience and memory of the cinema. Like Schefer he notes, however, that there is a dislocation between the experience and the knowledge of the child and the films that he watched as a child. It is as if the cinema has a delayed effect, an effect after the event, *nachträglich*; Daney plays here on the inversion of the subject and object around the verb *regarder*, and cites Schefer to this effect:

> Que sait un enfant! Et cet enfant Serge D. qui voulait tout savoir sauf ce qui le regardait en propre? Sur quel fond d'absence *au* monde la présence aux images *du* monde sera-t-elle plus tard requise? Je connais peu d'expressions plus belles que celle de Jean-Louis Schefer quand, dans *L'Homme ordinaire du cinema*, il parle des '*films qui ont regardé notre enfance*'. Car une chose est d'apprendre à regarder les films 'en professionnel' — pour vérifier d'ailleurs que ce sont eux qui nous regardent de moins en moins — et un autre est de vivre avec ceux qui nous ont regardés grandir et qui nous ont vus, otages précoces de notre biographie à venir, déjà empêtrés dans les rets de notre histoire.

> [What does a child know? Especially this child, Serge D., who wanted to know everything except that which concerned him? What absence *from the world* will later require the presence of images *of the world*? I know of few expressions more beautiful than Jean-Louis Schefer's in *L'Homme ordinaire du cinéma* when he speaks of 'the films that have watched our childhood.' It's one thing to learn to watch movies 'professionally' — only to verify that movies watch us less and less — but it is another to live with those movies that watched us grow up and saw us — prematurely hostage to our coming biographies — already entangled in the snare of our history.][41]

Daney postulates that certain films, those films that 'concern' us ('qui nous regardent') 'hold us hostage' in a temporal sense. The films that concerned us, that watched us and our situation in childhood, have the capacity to return, on the basis of our originary absence from the experience. Daney mobilizes a number of theoretical motifs here around the temporal dislocation at stake, which I would characterize, heeding Benjamin's mobilization of the two arguments, as Freudian — the mutual exclusivity of consciousness and leaving a memory trace — and Proustian, in the sense that that experience can be conserved or stocked ('enmagasiné') in a living state ('conservée vivante au fond de moi'), despite, and even because of, a lack of consciousness of it at the time of its first occurrence.[42] The distinctive point made by Daney is that this anachronism operates precisely in the conjuncture of history and of the history and experience of cinema.

Daney offers two examples of films which 'awoke' the dormant memory in him of an absent experience, a *not-having-taken-place*, both by Alain Resnais: *Nuit et brouillard* and *Hiroshima mon amour*, both of which are concerned with the catastrophes of the Second World War and with the absence of the event itself from the field of representation. Daney writes: 'Les corps de *Nuit et brouillard* et, deux ans plus tard, ceux des premiers plans d'*Hiroshima mon amour* sont de ces "choses" qui m'ont regardé plus que je ne les ai vues' ('The corpses in *Nuit et brouillard* and then two years later those in the opening shots of *Hiroshima mon amour* are among those "things" that watched me more than I saw them').[43] Playing on the oft-repeated refrain 'Tu n'as rien vu à Hiroshima' [You saw nothing in Hiroshima] Daney considers thus that in some sense he has not *seen* the images of the bodies shown in these films, but they have looked at him, or 'concerned him'. To explain this dislocation, which he also extends to certain images and sequences in the work of Hitchcock (for example the shower scene in *Psycho*), Daney images the perceptual apparatus as operating a kind of screening effect, a screening which is also a *screening out*:

> A l'effroi vécu en commun succède alors le calme d'une solitude résignée: le cerveau fonctionne comme un appareil de projection *bis* qui laisserait filer l'image, laissant le film et le monde continuer sans lui. Je n'imagine pas d'amour du cinéma qui ne s'arcboute sur le présent volé de ce 'continuez sans moi' là.

> [From the collectively experienced fear follows a calm of resigned solitude: the brain functions as a second projector allowing the image to continue flowing, letting the film and the world continue without it. I can't imagine a love for cinema that does not rest firmly on the stolen present of this 'continue on without me'.][44]

The traumatic image, in an echo of Barthes's critique of the 'voracity' of the moving image, which disables any 'pensiveness' in response to the image, is allowed to slip away (*se filer*); it is a 'lost present', the absence of which is a condition for the continuation of the film, and of living as such. There is thus an historical image which is not experienced as such, and yet which 'looks at us', which concerns us fundamentally; Daney weaves together a lacunary conception of subjectivity and of history, a historical subjectivity characterized by a *not-having-taken-place*.

The screen-memory motif is introduced to conceptualize this experience:

> Cet état, qui ne l'a vécu? Ces souvenirs-écrans, qui ne les a connus? Des images non-identifiées s'inscrivent sur la rétine, des événements inconnu ont fatalement lieu, des mots proférés deviennent le chiffre secret d'un impossible savoir sur soi.

> [Who hasn't experienced this state or known these screen memories?

> Unidentified images are engraved in the retina; unknown events inevitably happen and spoken words become the secret code of an impossible self-knowledge.][45]

Daney introduces the notion of retinal persistence here in order to ground a metaphorical construction in which the images at stake, which consciousness has barely registered, while the film continues, become the index of an 'impossible knowledge', perhaps not only of oneself in the strict sense but rather of one's place in relation to history. They are the index of the unlived element of experience by which it is referred to involuntary memory. Such images also form, in Daney's account, the primal scene of the 'amateur of the cinema':

> Ces moments de 'pas vu pas pris' sont la scène primitive de l'amateur de cinéma, celle *où il n'était pas alors qu'il ne s'agissait que de lui*. Au sens où Paulhan parle de la littérature comme d'une expérience du monde 'quand nous ne sommes pas là' et Lacan de 'ce qui manque à sa place'.

> [Just as Paulhan speaks about literature as an experience of the world 'when we are not there' and Lacan speaks about 'that which is missing from its place,' these moments 'neither seen nor taken' are the primitive scene of the lover of cinema, the scene *in which he wasn't present and yet it was entirely about him*.][46]

On the basis of this conception of cinematic experience, but also of historical knowledge, compromised or conditioned by 'what lacks in its place', Daney proposes the work of the cinephile, his own work, as one of looking again, a work not so much of memory (as the recollection of a past event) but of living again: 'Histoire de faire son retard, de "se refaire" et de se faire' ('A question of making up for lost time, to "remake" oneself, and to make oneself').[47] The autobiographical tenor of these remarks, underlined by Daney's account of his 'second birth' on deciding to devote his life to cinema, does not for all that attenuate its historical importance; it is in this sense that Daney's biographical experience of the two films by Resnais binds the lacunary subject to the specific history of the twentieth century. The 'revolutionary' importance of Resnais lay in the choice or the chance, Daney suggests, of subject matter in *Nuit et brouillard* and *Hiroshima mon amour*: 'rien moins que l'espèce humaine telle qu'elle était sortie des camps nazi et du trauma atomique' ('nothing less than the human species coming out of the Nazi camps and the atomic trauma, disfigured and ruined').[48]

The power of Resnais's films, as Daney recognizes, is not, however, so much in what they show as in what they show to be absent or unseen. It is the mantra of *Hiroshima mon amour*, 'Tu n'as rien vu à Hiroshima', or the colour sequences of *Nuit et brouillard* of the abandoned spaces of Auschwitz in 1958, which bring into relief, as if in a virtual negative, what is not seen there; Resnais proposes an 'anti-spectacular' cinema in which a voice addresses us and tells us (the viewer) that they have seen nothing at Hiroshima, or in which the horror of the camp can only be conjured as the spectre of what there is to be seen, or in the archival photographs which interrupt the colour sequences, a cinema of 'non-images'.[49] Daney thus professes his dismay with the retrospective aestheticization of history and his preference for films which recognize the paralysis of narrative and historical continuity at stake.

He puts this significantly in terms of an 'arrest' in the progression of history: 'Ces films-là avaient au moins l'honnêteté de prendre acte d'une même impossibilité de raconter, d'un même cran d'arrêt dans le déroulé de l'Histoire, quand le récit se fige ou s'emballe à vide' ('At least these films had the honesty to acknowledge the impossibility of telling a story, the stopping point in the course of history, when storytelling freezes or runs idle').[50]

The critical trope of the 'arrêt sur l'image' thus becomes a significant centre of gravity for a conception of cinema which incorporates an awareness of the incomplete, lacunary nature of its relation to history, a correlate of what has not taken place at the level of conscious reflective experience. Daney writes:

> Soit c'est le spectateur qui soudain 'manque à sa place', et s'arrête alors que le film, lui, continue. Soit c'est le film qui, au lieu de 'continuer', se replie sur lui-même et sur une 'image' provisoirement définitive qui permette au sujet-spectateur de continuer à croire au cinéma et au sujet-citoyen à vivre sa vie. Arrêt sur le spectateur, arrêt sur l'image: le cinéma est entré dans son âge adulte. La sphère du visible a cessé d'être tout entière disponible: il y a des absences et des trous.

> [Either it's the spectator who is suddenly 'missing from his place' and is stilled while the film continues, or it's the film which, instead of 'continuing', folds back onto itself and onto a temporarily definitive 'image' that allows the spectator to continue believing in cinema and the subject-citizen to live his life. Spectator-stilled, image-stilled: cinema entered adulthood. The sphere of the visible had ceased to be wholly available: there were gaps and holes.][51]

Published only shortly before Daney's premature death, 'Le Travelling de *Kapo*' is a melancholic, if not tragic, meditation on the decline of this critical and aesthetic sensibility to historical incompletion, since he will mark the decline in the efficacy of the 'arrêt sur l'image' as the event of the concentration camps recedes in generational memory, and with the developing capacity of electronic media to cover over the lack and seal the breach through the animation of other images. Writing in the early 1990s, Daney sees the current era as one in which the image has passed over to the side of promotion, advertising, and power, and seems, in the latter sections of 'Le Travelling de *Kapo*' to abandon his faith in the capacity of cinema and its 'modern' vocation to arrest the image, in the face of the relentless power of contemporary media to re-animate the image, to pull it into the sphere of promotion and advertising, and, on the other hand, to fictionalize the historical event.[52]

The melancholic mood of Daney's meditation on the interweaving of history and the cinema and the decline of a consciousness of history in the culture of the image bears many points of comparison with the later work of Jean-Luc Godard, and indeed Daney is among the few privileged interlocutors of the Swiss director, particularly in a key chapter of Godard's six-part video project *Histoire(s) du cinéma*, completed in 1999. Godard's project addresses history as mediated by the history of cinema, and indeed Godard proposes that the history of the twentieth century *is* to all intents and purposes the history of cinema. For Kaja Silverman, writing on Godard's *Histoire(s)* under the Benjaminian title 'The Dream of the Nineteenth

Century', his project assumes a radical reversal of the usual understanding of the relation between the real and its representation, a reversal whereby 'actuality can only become "itself" by means of a representational intervention'.[53] According to the Benjaminian logic inherent to Godard's approach, the cinema has the capacity to 'realize' or 'actualize', in an image, what remained only dreamt or virtual in the past; the cinema is thus 'a nineteenth-century matter that was resolved in the twentieth century'.[54] Rather than being solely a reflection or representation of history, cinema is 'the primary place where history happens'.[55] This actualization takes place through a process of montage, wherein, for Silverman, who cites Benjamin from the *Passagenwerk*, moments of time are 'blasted' out of the continuum of the past, thus making manifest the 'resemblances linking temporally divergent moments to each other'.[56]

The strong resonances between Godard's practice of montage and the theory of involuntary memory as it occurs in Proust's *Recherche* should be much in evidence here. Indeed the substantial affinities between Proust's novel and Godard's project have been a recurrent feature of critical work on the *Histoire(s) du cinéma*, and have provoked a number of specific studies, most explicitly Miriam Heywood's book *Modernist Visions*, and an article and a chapter by Alessia Ricciardi. Both Heywood and Ricciardi point to the ways in which the cinematic technique of montage, a conceptual and methodological paradigm for the *Histoire(s)*, is also an explicit formal principle of the *Recherche*. Ricciardi suggests that Godard's *Histoire(s)* is 'the most Proustian of films' and that, in contrast to the other less successful film 'versions' of Proust's novel by Schlöndorff, Akerman, and Ruiz, and the failed projects of Joseph Losey and Luchino Visconti, Godard's video project is an ' "involuntary" adaptation' of *A la recherche du temps perdu*.[57] Both Heywood and Ricciardi pay substantive attention to the explicit allusions to Proust's novel in Godard's *Histoire(s)*.

Rather than add to these already substantial accounts of the Proustian inflections of Godard's video project, and the analysis of the citations of Proust that it includes, I want to follow in the wake of the recognition by Silverman and Ricciardi that Godard's 'adaptation' of Proust is mediated via Benjamin's theory of history and of the dialectical image, which themselves bear the influence of Benjamin's reading of Proust, and the long-term meditation on the *Recherche* ever since his immersive encounter with Proust through the translation of *A l'ombre des jeunes filles en fleurs* and *Le Côté de Guermantes*. I will argue, however, that Benjamin's relation to Proust is not uncritical; it is troubled by a tension between the stupefying immersion in the aesthetic, in the image, more likely to induce a state of political torpor, and the consequent necessity of a convulsive shock, provoked by a dialectical image, recognized in a moment of critical danger, which would provoke an 'awakening' from the dream and a lucid consciousness of the political present. What is at stake here is the use-value of Proust for history, for cinema history, and for a historical consciousness attuned to the traumas of the past.

The problematic has been posed with particular acuity in the polemic which arose between Godard and Claude Lanzmann, whose nine-hour film *Shoah* bears a number of points of conceptual contrast with the *Histoire(s) du cinéma*, and between Georges Didi-Huberman, in his commentaries on the image of the camps, and writers aligned with Lanzmann who objected to the valorization of the image and of montage as a praxis of memory and of history. In an essay on four photographs taken by members of the *Sonderkommando* in Auschwitz in 1944 of the process of incineration of the victims of the camps, Didi-Huberman proposes the methodological value of the evidence of the image and of the practice of analytic montage, in relation to the historically traumatic event, arguing against the proposition that such events, and the experience of them, are unimaginable or unrepresentable.[58] Didi-Huberman thus affirms the potential of a work of image-montage for a consciousness of history, drawing, both implicitly and explicitly, on Benjamin's theory of the dialectical image and his philosophy of history; the essay is recurrently punctuated by quotations from Benjamin's 'Theses on the Philosophy of History' and from 'Convolute N', the methodological foundation of the *Passagenwerk*.[59] The image, Didi-Huberman argues, is not 'all', yet 'in spite of everything' ('malgré tout') it can offer evidence, and provide a mode of 'survivance', a trace of sorts, of the victims whose presence it was the intention of the final solution to erase, 'without remainder'. Accordingly Didi-Huberman prefaces his essay with a quotation from Godard's *Histoire(s) du cinéma*:

> Même rayé à mort
> un simple rectangle
> de trente-cinq
> millimètres
> sauve l'honneur
> de tout le réel.
>
> [Even scratched to death
> a simple rectangle
> of thirty-five
> millimetres
> saves the honour
> of all the real.][60]

Shortly after its publication a vituperative critique of Didi-Huberman's initial essay was launched in the journal *Les Temps modernes*, of which Lanzmann was the general editor, in essays by Gérard Wajcmann and Elisabeth Pagnoux.[61] Their rejoinder to Didi-Huberman, crudely summarized, is that the real, the real of the camps in this instance, was not likely to be 'saved' by an image, and that Didi-Huberman's essay promoted the domain of aesthetics at the expense of a politically and ethically resolute consciousness of the event of the holocaust, and the testimony of those 'survivors' who remain. For Libby Saxton, in an illuminating essay on the debate, Lanzmann and his colleagues objected to the 'obscenity' of such 'sense-making projects', to the 'logic of proof' that seemed to be implied in Didi-Huberman's attention to the four photograms 'arrachés de l'enfer' ('torn from hell'), to the suspicion of voyeuristic complicity that the attention to the images raised in them, and to the arguably Christological logic of redemption with which both Didi-Huberman's arguments and Godard's *Histoire(s)* seemed to be imbued, pointing to the Pauline thesis, explicit in the *Histoire(s)* and recurrent throughout Godard's later work, that 'L'image viendra au temps de la résurrection' [The image will come at the time of the resurrection].[62]

Against Didi-Huberman's affirmation of the practice of image-montage, which finds a powerful exemplar in Godard's *Histoire(s)*, Lanzmann and his colleagues propose the value of anamnesis, the process and the experience of remembering; Lanzmann's *Shoah* is held as the example of a sustained focus on the event of the holocaust through the filming of surviving participants, uniquely in the present, remembering and to some extent reliving their experience in their spoken testimony and in the physiognomy and gestures which accompany these testimonies. *Shoah* features no archival footage, in contrast to Resnais's *Nuit et brouillard*, although like the latter it also shows the place, the site of the camp, in the present, and in doing so provokes its interviewees to revisit the events that took place there in their memories and in their words.

My point here is not to propose a further opinion on the 'imaginability' of the camps as such, which has been extended in Didi-Huberman's work, but to point to the problematic status of Proust, and of the reference to Proust, in these discussions. Saxton, for example, construes Godard's project in explicitly Proustian terms: 'Godard's histories coincide teleologically (a coincidence reinforced through explicit allusion) with a Proustian narrative of mnemonic recuperation', and 'such a narrative makes a redemptive claim, since time is regained'.[63] In *Images malgré tout*, addressing the way in which the images of the camps, rather than inviting the viewer into voyeuristic complicity, oblige an ethically charged encounter with alterity, Didi-Huberman, referring to the narrator's account of the photograph of his grandmother, writes that 'Nul mieux que Proust, peut-être, n'a parlé de cette necessaire *approche désappropriante*' ('No-one, perhaps, has spoken better than Proust of this necessary *disappropriating approach*').[64] Proust is thus postulated as an authority or a guarantee of sorts for the encounter with the photograph as form of othering. Ricciardi, in her 'Cinema Regained', aligns Proust with Godard on the side of an ostensibly redemptive vision of the capacity of the memory image to 'save the honour of the real', although she will propose a different argument in her book *The Ends of Mourning*.[65] But Proust is also enlisted in support of Lanzmann's ostensibly quite different project. Writing on Lanzmann's *Shoah* in an essay titled 'Le Lieu malgré tout', Didi-Huberman brings together, in a move characteristic of his theoretical style, a constellation of references in which Proust somewhat alarmingly appears as a paradigm for Lanzmann's approach to the camps.[66] Following a reference to Daney's 'Le Travelling de *Kapo*', indicating the absence of manipulation in Lanzmann's method, Didi-Huberman points to the way in which *Shoah* responds to the critical demand posed by Benjamin's theory of the dialectical image: 'c'est à dire qu'elle [l'œuvre d'art] produise une collision du Maintenant et de l'Autrefois' [this is to say that it [the work of art] produces a collision of the Now and the Before].[67] Didi-Huberman then cites Convolute N of Benjamin's *Passagenwerk*, proposing in this light that Shoah seeks to situate itself at the 'perilous critical moment', that it is constituted of such 'genuinely historical' images, which offer themselves to 'intelligibility'.[68] On the back of this Didi-Huberman then refers to an essay on

Lanzmann's *Shoah* by the historian and critic of revisionism Pierre Vidal-Naquet, in which the latter compares Lanzmann's film to Proust's *Recherche*, in terms of its 'mise en mouvement de la mémoire' [putting memory into movement], and to a further reference by Vidal Naquet to Proust, in which he refers to Lanzmann as doing 'en somme pour l'histoire ce que Proust avait fait pour le roman' [doing for history what Proust had done for the novel].[69]

Across these differing and conflicting constituencies and arguments, Proust's *Recherche* is enlisted variously and ambivalently for a redemptive theory of the image, the practice of montage, and an anamnestic recovery of the past, through language.[70] In both instances — the production and montage of the image, and the linguistic testimony — Proust stands for a 'mise en mouvement de la mémoire', a mobilization of memory. This ambivalence draws from an ambivalence in Proust's novel itself, between remembering and forgetting, and from a partial appropriation of the theory of involuntary memory for a theory of history.

The contemporary anthropologist Michael Taussig, in his book *What Colour is the Sacred?*, weaves an extended enquiry into the bodily unconscious into and around recurrent references to Proust.[71] In a crucial chapter of his work Taussig draws out the Proustian dimensions of Walter Benjamin's later philosophy of history. Taussig evokes a 'climatological' attention in the operation of involuntary memory, wherein what is retrieved is the 'sensuous clustering' of the recovered memory, which the intellect and habit have annulled.[72] Involuntary memory pulls at the 'proto-imageric realness that precedes actual images in the workings of memory', a sense which Taussig relates to Benjamin's expression 'the weight of the catch' in the essay 'The Image of Proust'.[73] This characteristically enigmatic expression comes towards the end of Benjamin's essay of 1929, as part of a discussion of the relation of Proust's 'psychogenic asthma' to his work. Proust's 'paratactic sequences' ('the endless succession of "soit que…" '), Benjamin writes, are a symptom of a certain weakness and the absence of 'the slightest penchant for construction' (Benjamin citing Jacques Rivière), a sign that the writer 'fell back on the bosom of nature — not to drink from it, but to dream to its heartbeat'.[74] This 'inexperience' (Rivière) expresses a renunciation of the intellect in relation to the 'crushing weight of memories', which the writer nevertheless manages momentarily to shake off. Benjamin evokes an image of Proust suffocating under the weight of the relentless stream of memories and images his writing has conjured: 'This asthma became part of his art — if indeed his art did not create it'.[75] The 'weight of the catch' has to be interpreted in the context of this evocation:

> Anyone who wishes to surrender knowingly to the innermost overtones in this work must place himself in a special stratum — the bottommost — of this involuntary memory, one in which the materials of memory no longer appear singly, as images, but tell us about a whole, amorphously and formlessly, indefinitely and weightily, in the same way the weight of his net tells a fisherman about his catch. Smell — this is the sense of weight of someone who casts his net into the sea of the *temps perdu*. And his sentences are the entire muscular activity of the intelligible body; they contain the whole enormous effort to raise this catch.[76]

In Benjamin's reading, Proust's body suffocates under the weight of this catch, while making this suffocation a part of the work itself. Benjamin's text is characteristically ambivalent, yet it is difficult not to discern a critical attitude towards Proust's submission to nature, to his 'weakness', to an indulgence in the sensory world of memory and a propensity to be crushed by it. Taussig, however, goes on to link Benjamin's 'weight of the catch' to his philosophy of history, pointing to the theoretical matrix of the Arcades Project, Convolute N, in which Benjamin incorporates allusions to the logic of involuntary memory into an epistemology of the dialectical image. Taussig cites Benjamin's proposition that 'In order for a part of the past to be touched by the present actuality there must be no continuity between them'.[77] He continues:

> This also parallels Proust's definition of reality as bound not merely to memory but to a montage of memories as *slices in time* laid on top of one another — a *now* overlaid by a *back then*: 'what we call reality is a certain connection between the immediate sensations and memories which envelop us simultaneously' [...]. With Benjamin this is the montage of memories that flashes up at a moment of danger, meaning especially in political crisis. 'The true picture of the past flits by', begins one of Benjamin's famous theses on the philosophy of history, 'The past can be seized only as an image which flashes up at the instant when it can be recognized and is never seen again.' This has Proust's fingerprints all over. The image Benjamin has in mind is that of the *mémoire involontaire*, grafted onto a Marxist vision of world history and revolution. It is an image that can affect, if not alter, the deepest layers of one's being where habit reigns, such that bodily dispositions are transferred to another register altogether — from homogenous empty time to 'time filled by the presence of the now' blasted out of the continuum of history. This unexpected, abrupt and tearing change of pace is of a piece with *awakening* — as when in 'File N' Benjamin comments: 'Thus, in Proust, the importance of staking an entire life on life's supremely dialectical point of rupture: awakening. Proust begins with an evocation of the space of waking up... The realization of dream elements in the course of waking up is the canon of dialectics. It is paradigmatic for the thinker and binding for the historian'.[78]

While Taussig's recognition of the 'grafting' of Proustian involuntary memory onto a 'Marxist vision of world history and revolution' is valuable, I hesitate around the suggestion of a transformation in terms of 'bodily disposition', precisely in the light of Benjamin's critique, in 'The Image of Proust', of Proust's suffocation. The dialectical image, while informed by the logic of involuntary memory, inflects the notion of the image differently, and orients it away from the cloying weight of Proustian sensory indulgence, towards the lucidity of an 'awakening', rather than the undecideable kaleidoscope of reverie.

However, to stay with Benjamin's attention to Proust for a moment, it is clear that the fact that one of his significant engagements with Proust bears the title 'The Image of Proust' ('Zum Bilde Proust') hints at the way in which for Benjamin the *Recherche* may 'resolve itself' into a visual form, an image; 'Zum Bilde Proust' might suggest not just the image of the author, but Proust's image, Proust's conception of the image. This image arises, according to Benjamin, from a crisis in the relation between literature and life, at the extreme point of their paradoxical distance from and proximity to one another:

> The outstanding literary achievement of our time is assigned a place at the heart of the impossible, at the center and also at the point of indifference — of all dangers, and it marks the great realization of a 'lifework' as the last for a long time. The image of Proust is the highest physiognomic expression which the irresistibly growing discrepancy between literature and life was able to assume. This is the lesson which justifies the attempt to evoke this image.[79]

The image as a 'physiognomic expression' echoes the notion of *gesture* which Benjamin will develop in his essay on Kafka of 1934. This suggests the extent to which 'the image' is not necessarily to be understood in a purely optical sense, but in a sense which has a profoundly ethical and historical dimension, insofar as it entails a specific dynamic between the present and the past, and insofar as it engages the individual life in a collective life, and, beyond this, in a primal or natural history ('Urgeschichte').

Benjamin underlines the extent to which the *Recherche* is not so much a work of the remembering of lived experience as of forgetting. It is not a remembering in the sense that it is the recall of experience, but the 'weaving' of memory, the 'Penelope work of recollection' which Benjamin suggests we might equally call 'the Penelope work of forgetting', where forgetting stands for the extraction of 'lived life' from the diurnal task of 'purposeful activity' which in turn 'unravels' the web woven at night, in the dream-world. Benjamin thus positions Proust's activity at the threshold between the dream-world and likens this work of weaving, this production of a texture, to dream, in a way which echoes Freud's conception of the dream work: 'When we awake each morning, we hold in our hands, usually weakly and loosely, but a few fringes of the tapestry of lived life, as loomed for us by forgetting'. Proust, for Benjamin, devotes his life to this work of weaving, by night, 'in his darkened room', the 'intricate arabesques' of memory.[80]

This memory, we should underline, is not memory in the strict sense, and appears more akin to a texture of images related to another in an open-ended manner. The work of forgetting is a production of images, drawn out of the dream-world, images related to another according to laws of similitude familiar to children and to their play:

> The similarity of one thing to another which we are used to, which occupies us in a wakeful state, reflects only vaguely the deeper resemblance of the dream-world in which everything that happens appears not in identical but in similar guise, opaquely similar to one another.[81]

Benjamin thus conjures an image of Proust which is inflected by Surrealism, as a writer obsessively attentive to the imagistic contiguities he was able to draw out of the dream-world, due to a fragile position at the threshold of night and day, in a state of reverie: '[Proust] lay on his bed racked with homesickness, homesick for the world distorted in the state of resemblance, a world in which the true surrealist face of existence beaks through'.[82] This world, Benjamin writes, 'bears a fragile, precious reality: the image'. The Proustian memory image, in the sense given to it by Benjamin here, is not a finite event in a progressive narrative, the recollection of a single event, but the key to an infinite texture in which history becomes an open-ended process: 'For an experienced event is finite — at any rate, confined to one sphere of experience; a remembered event is infinite, because it is only a key to everything that happened before and after it'.[83] The Proustian image, drawn from the dream world, relinquished from 'purposeful activity', and opening out into a play of similitude, is also given an intermittent, ephemeral, 'fleeting' quality which Benjamin suggests by way of an emphasis on the 'vegetative' environment in which Proust's characters exist:

> Proust's most accurate, most convincing insights fasten on their objects as insects fasten on leaves, blossoms, branches, betraying nothing of their existence until a leap, a beating of wings, a vault, show the startled observer that some incalculable individual life has imperceptibly crept into an alien world. The true reader of Proust is constantly jarred by small shocks.[84]

While this description resonates with Deleuze's vision of Proust's narrator as a spider, sensitive to 'la moindre vibration qui se propage à son corps en onde intensive, et qui la fait bondir à l'endroit nécessaire' ('the slightest vibration at the edge of her web, which propagates itself in her body as an intensive wave and sends her leaping to the necessary place'), it does so also with Benjamin's attention to the 'innervations' of the cinematic image, provoked in the spectator, and likely to innervate the collective.[85] In a plastic sense it speaks more to the flickering quality of early cinema than to the continuous progression of conventional narrative film, and more to the singular flash of the isolated image than to the durational time-image in which Deleuze sees the destiny of cinema. The Proustian image as a 'beating of wings', a 'small shock', is almost imperceptible, and temporally fleeting, in both the literal and metaphorical sense.[86]

The instantaneous, flashing or flickering quality of the Proustian image is rendered by Benjamin as a kind of intensive concentration of time; it is released in a 'dewy fresh' 'instant' provoking a 'painful shock of rejuvenation' which counters the weight of ageing: 'Proust has brought off the tremendous feat of letting the whole world age by a lifetime in an instant. But this very concentration in which things that normally just fade and slumber consume themselves in a flash is called rejuvenation'.[87] The motifs of concentration and of the flash here begin to outline the dialectical image which Benjamin will theorize in his last writings, but they can also serve to remind us of the resonance of the motif of crystallization which Warburg, and later Deleuze and Agamben, will configure with the notion of gesture as the 'crystal of historical memory', and of the 'crystal image' embodying the smallest possible circuit between the actual and the virtual, the point of their greatest proximity. But to the extent that Benjamin's writing enacts and performs a materialist critique, a method in which the physiological and plastic form of things is never far from view, the concentration and the intermittent, 'flashing' form of the image should also alert us to the materiality of the cinematic image, to the pulse of projection and the isolated fragment of the photogrammatic frame.

Proustian images are not *just* images, nonetheless. In the closing paragraphs of

'The Image of Proust', which we considered earlier with Taussig, Benjamin evokes the possibility of a 'physiology of style' for which the author's asthma would be a privileged factor, highlighting the importance of the heightened sensibility to the sense of smell. Benjamin writes:

> To be sure, most memories that we search for come to us as visual images. Even the free-floating forms of the *mémoire involontaire* are still in large part isolated, though enigmatically present, visual images. For this very reason, anyone who wishes to surrender knowingly to the innermost overtones in this work must place himself in a special stratum — the bottommost — of this involuntary memory, one in which the materials of memory no longer appear singly, as images, but tell us about a whole, amorphously and formlessly, indefinitely and weightily, in the same way as the weight of his net tells a fisherman about his catch.[88]

The image of involuntary memory, visual or olfactory, however singular and isolated, reaches down into the deeper recesses of the dream-world, evoking its weight. The 'physiological' conception construes the image as more than an optical perception, as the index or allegory of a submerged whole; it evokes the *gestus* in which Benjamin saw the opaque heart of Kafka's works. This opacity, and 'weight of the catch', under which Benjamin imagines Proust suffocates, constitutes in some senses a failure of response to modern experience. Howard Caygill has read a similar implicit critique of Proust across Benjamin's work. He describes how the original genesis of the Paris Arcades Project coincided with the plan for a collection of critical essays informed by the aim to create a 'form capable of doing justice to modern experience', and by the 'formal principle of citability, closely allied with "montage" or "allegory"'.[89] Caygill looks closely at Benjamin's essays on the work of the nineteenth-century Swiss-German writer Gottfried Keller and the Austrian Adalbert Stifter. While the landscapes evoked in the work of Stifter create a purely visual evocation of space, from which language is alienated, in Keller language becomes the space for a 'play of mutual recognition' between the visual and the aural. In this context landscape and spectator/viewer meet each other in a 'community of recognition'. Benjamin's concept of 'aura', developed later and surfacing in 'The Work of Art' and 'The Storyteller', in which the landscape looks back at the viewer, signals the decay of this community. Caygill writes that:

> The complex experience of the mutual recognition of nature and humanity was arrested in modernity and distributed across the plane of subject and object. Benjamin's subsequent critical essays examine the formal principles of modernist works in terms of the mourning of a distorted recognition, whether in memory or in 'aura' — the unreturnable gaze of the object. His finest essay on the substitution of memory for a community of recognition is 'The Image of Proust' from 1929. The infinite movement of recognition discerned in Keller becomes in Proust the 'convoluted time' of memory. Benjamin locates the formal principle of this convolution as the folding into each other of narration and narrated, but this is a movement in which description melts into lyric intensity. The infinite is present in this experience, but less in the movement of recognition than in the weaving and unweaving of memory: 'For an experienced event is finite — at any rate, confined to one sphere

of experience, a remembered event is infinite, because it is only a key to everything that happened before and after it' (1929c, 204). But this memory is already a mourning, since for Benjamin the completeness of time is remembered *d'outre tombeau*: the movement of recognition in Keller, experienced as sensual joy, becomes the weight of an impossible recollection experienced as fear of suffocation, or as the extinction of courage and hope before death as absolute explored in the critiques of Hölderlin and Goethe becomes in the Proust essay a 'Poetic' of modern experience governed by the mood of suffocation.[90]

By locating the essay on Proust in the context of Benjamin's work on Keller, Caygill situates it as a recognition of the already compromised (or 'distorted') nature of modern experience: Proust's response is evoked as an absorption or suffocation in the 'lyric intensity' of infinite recollection. In the place of the 'community of recognition' Benjamin sees in Proust a kind of stupefied intoxication in the images of memory, severed from the moment, from the now, and from the community. The *Recherche* is situated on the side of a 'subjective' 'mourning of recognition'.[91]

Beatrice Hansen has pointed to a similar sense of frustration with the limits of the Proustian image, on Benjamin's part, and the risk it represents:

> It is clear that in its earliest phase, *The Arcades Project* had much in common with Proust's *Remembrance of Things Past*, or his theory of reconstructive involuntary memory (*madeleine*) which Proust likened to a Japanese game; for the object of the past 'sprang into being' in his cup of tea much like the unfolding pieces or paper which the Japanese, for their amusement, set afloat in a porcelain bowl of water. Tellingly, Benjamin increasingly became aware of the fact that the Proustian text might become a drug, a narcotic, whose overindulgence might become fatal, as he confided to Adorno. When applied to *The Arcades Project*, the Proustian paradigm presented the threat that the vast expanse of historical space might become reduced to the porcelain-filled salon of a bourgeois subject, in which ornamental archaic images adorned the parlour of modernity. Reflecting this awareness, Benjamin would now complement his early reflections on surrealist dream-work by calling for a dialectical moment of awakening, a rude shock-like awakening that snatched the sleeper out of his enveloping visions.[92]

The risk is that the images conjured by the subject attuned to the Baudelairean *correspondances* of the world might be reduced to the contemplation, in interior space, of one's own room, that the *flâneur* might retreat inside to their bedroom and turn their back on the shock experience of modernity.

This suggests that Benjamin's sustained attention to Proust, gained in part through his translation, with Hessel, of *A l'ombre des jeunes filles en fleurs*, produces an ambivalent and critical attitude which on the one hand recognizes the value of the separation of the image from 'purposeful activity' and the correspondences of memory, while on the other hand recognizing the risk of stupefaction and political torpor represented by a subjective indulgence in such images, the risk of suffocation. Benjamin's later philosophy of history and theory of the 'dialectical' image must then extract the theory of involuntary memory from the 'synthetic' manufacturing of experience and the inertia of Proustian reverie, and re-direct it towards the moment of 'awakening'.[93]

Benjamin's notations in Convolute N are punctuated by the occurrence of the single word 'Awakening', as if indexing the propositions on the dialectical image and the method of the Arcades Project described here to the opening of Proust's novel. Benjamin makes the link explicitly, framing it in terms of dialectics:

> Is awakening perhaps the synthesis of dream consciousness (as thesis) and waking consciousness (as antithesis)? Then the moment of awakening would be identical with the 'now of recognizability' in which things put on their true — surrealist — face. Thus in Proust, the importance of staking an entire life on a supremely dialectical point of rupture: awakening. Proust begins with an evocation of the space of someone waking up.[94]

This affords Benjamin the opportunity to cast his *Passagenwerk* within the perspective opened up by Proust's attention to the threshold between sleep and wakefulness:

> Just as Proust begins the story of his life with an awakening, so must every presentation of history begin with an awakening; in fact, it should treat of nothing else. This one, accordingly, deals with awakening from the nineteenth century.[95]

The motif or paradigm of 'awakening' is also indexed to Benjamin's account of the epiphanic 'flash' of the image, which arrests history conceived as progress or progression, and wherein, in an echo of Proust's rendering of involuntary memory, the past and the present come together to form a 'constellation':

> It's not that what is past casts its light on what is present, or what is present its light on what is past; rather, image is that wherein what has been comes together in a flash with the now to form a constellation. In other words, image is dialectics at a standstill. For while the relation of the present to the past is a purely temporal, continuous one, the relation of what-has-been to the now is dialectical; is not progression but image, suddenly emergent. — Only dialectical images are genuine images (that is, not archaic); and the place where one encounters them is language. ★Awakening★.[96]

The purpose of the dialectical image, thus conceived, is 'to carry over the principle of montage into history' and 'to discover in the analysis of the small individual moment the crystal of the total event'.[97] Benjamin's method, in the *Passagenwerk*, is thus premised on a citational practice, on a montage of citations, in which each citation is figured as a monad or an 'image', extracted from its original context and set into a new constellation.[98] The *Passagenwerk* montage is thus made of images, not stories.[99]

The logic of involuntary memory is explicitly invoked by Benjamin in his account of the dialectical image as an interruption of the telos of history conceived as progress. This sustained attention to the image is evident in Benjamin's long-standing interest in the visual technologies of photography and cinema, and in particular in their instantaneity, exhibited in Benjamin's account of the 'innervations' provoked in cinematic spectatorship by the innervated movement of such figures as Chaplin, for example, alongside an attention to the method of montage, to the shocks induced by the juxtaposition of images in Dada photomontage (the work of John Heartfield, for example) and in Surrealism, less as a theory and more as a generalized method of image juxtaposition.[100] On these terms the (surrealist) image produced through the technique of montage disrupts the ideological narrative and the myth of progress through a form of short circuit between the archaic past and the present, or, in different terms, between the dream-world and the historical present, between the world of childhood and the work of politics. In the contingency and experimentation of play, in the lightning flash gestures of gambling, Benjamin foregrounds the capacity of the instantaneous image to provoke an epiphany with historical potential.

So while the essay of 1929, 'The Image of Proust', and the multiple engagements with the figure of Proust as author and with the *Recherche* foreground the image of Proust as a 'metaphysical' writer, articulating a profound vision of memory, subjectivity, and the relation of art to life, in his last writings it is the Proustian formula of involuntary memory which forms and shapes Benjamin's conception of his own fragmentary and iconographic method (both in the philosophy of history and in the Arcades Project), both of which are intended as a form of extension and parallel to the Marxist philosophy of history. Benjamin mobilizes this aspect of Proust's novel — involuntary memory as the convulsive spark of the connection of the past with the present — towards an 'awakening' from the dream of history.

Notes to Chapter 6

1. Sigmund Freud, 'Screen Memories', in *The Uncanny*, trans. by David McLintock (London: Penguin, 2003), pp. 1–22 (originally published as 'Uber Deckerinnerung', in *Gesammelte Werke*, 17 vols (Frankfurt: Fischer Verlag, 1953–68), I, 531–54); 'Childhood Memories and Screen Memories', in *The Psychopathology of Everyday Life*, trans. by Alan Tyson, Pelican Freud Library 5 (Harmondsworth: Penguin, 1975), pp. 83–93.
2. Freud, 'Childhood Memories and Screen Memories', p. 83.
3. See Laplanche and Pontalis, *Vocabulaire de la psychanalyse*, pp. 450–52.
4. Guy Rosaloto adopts a similar approach in 'Souvenirs-écran', *Psychanalyse et cinéma*, special issue of *Communications*, 23 (1975), 79–87.
5. Freud, 'Childhood Memories and Screen Memories', p. 84.
6. Ibid., p. 88.
7. In 'La "danse contre seins"' Antoine Compagnon proposes that this scene functions as a kind of 'primal scene' for the Albertine sequence of the Recherche: 'Il s'agit d'une sorte de scène primitive annonçant l'inflexion de la Recherche du côté de Gomorrhe', in *Marcel Proust: écrire sans fin*, ed. by Rainer Warning and Jean Milly (Paris: CNRS Éditions, 1996), pp. 79–97 (p. 79).
8. See Bowie, *Freud, Proust, Lacan*, p. 47.
9. Jean Laplanche's notion of the 'enigmatic signifier' can be a useful concept to frame this idea. See Jean Laplanche, *Problématiques V* (Paris: PUF, 1998).
10. This sense of an event or an experience 'not taking place when it ought to have' gains a perhaps unexpected purchase in a crucial article by the British psychoanalyst Donald Winnicott, 'Fear of Breakdown' (in *Psycho-Analytic Explorations* (London: Karnac, 1989), pp. 87–95), in which Winnicott writes of the 'breakdown that has already taken place', that 'The patient needs to "remember" this but it is not possible to remember something that has not yet happened, and this thing of the past has not happened yet because the patient was not there for it to happen to' (p. 92).
11. Jean-François Lyotard, *Heidegger et 'les juifs'* (Paris: Galilée, 1988), p. 14; *Heidegger and 'the Jews'*, trans. by Andreas Michel and Mark Roberts (Minneapolis: University of Minnesota press, 1990), p. 3.

12. Ibid., pp. 16–17; p. 5.

13. For a critique of this argument, cf. Jacques Rancière, *La Mésentente: politique et philosophie* (Paris: Galilée, 1995); *Dis-agreement: Politics and Philosophy*, trans. by Julie Rose (Minneapolis & London: University of Minnesota Press, 1999).

14. Lyotard, *Heidegger et 'les juifs'*, pp. 27; *Heidegger and 'the Jews'*, p. 11.

15. Ibid., p. 29; p. 12.

16. Ibid., p. 64; p. 34.

17. Benjamin, 'Theses on the Philosophy of History', p. 249.

18. Walter Benjamin, 'On Some Motifs in Baudelaire', in *Illuminations*, trans. by Harry Zohn (London: Fontana, 1973), pp. 152–96 (p. 157). Benjamin is citing Freud's 'Beyond the Pleasure Principle', in *On Metapsychology: The Theory of Psychoanalysis*, Pelican Freud Library 11 (Harmondsworth: Penguin, 1984), 269–339 (p. 296).

19. Janet Harbord, in *Chris Marker: La Jetée* (London: Afterall Books, 2009), points to Marker's proposition that *La Jetée* was a 'remake' of Hitchcock's *Vertigo*, and to Mark Fisher's hypothesis that Hitchcock named the object of its protagonist Scottie's desire 'Madelaine' after Proust's memory catalyst (see Mark Fisher, 'Six re-Views of Chris Marker: The Art of Memory', *Mute* (December 2002), <http://www.metamute.org/editorial/articles/six-re-views-chris-marker-art-memory> [accessed 1 June 2017]). Both Harbord and Fisher point to Marker's CD-Rom *Immemory*, where Marker interweaves references to Proust and Hitchcock around the question 'What is a madeleine?'.

20. Barthes, *La Chambre claire*, p. 120; *Camera lucida*, p. 77.

21. For a discussion of this dimension of *La Jetée*, see Patrick ffrench, 'The Memory of the Image in Chris Marker's *La Jetée*', *French Studies*, 59:1 (January 2005), 31–37.

22. Burgin, *The Remembered Film*, p. 61.

23. Ibid., p. 62.

24. Ibid., p. 60. Barthes: 'cette photo a travaillé en moi' (*La Chambre claire* , p. 87; *Camera Lucida*, p. 53).

25. Sigmund Freud, *The Interpretation of Dreams*, trans. by James Strachey, Pelican Freud Library 4 (Harmondsworth: Penguin, 1976), p. 671.

26. Burgin, *The Remembered Film*, pp. 65, 66.

27. Ibid., p. 65.

28. Ibid., pp. 67, 68.

29. Ibid., p. 8.

30. Ibid., p. 14. Burgin is citing from *Roland Barthes par Roland Barthes* (Paris: Seuil, 1975), pp. 144–45; *Roland Barthes by Roland Barthes*, trans. by Richard Howard (London: Macmillan , 1977), pp. 140–41.

31. See ffrench, 'Memories of the Unlived Body'.

32. Jean-Louis Schefer, *L'Homme ordinaire du cinéma* (Paris: Cahiers du cinéma, 1981), p. 105; *The Ordinary Man of Cinema*, trans. by Max Cavitch, Paul Grant, and Noura Wedell (Pasadena, CA: Semiotexte, 2016), p. 121.

33. See Schefer, *L'Homme ordinaire du cinéma*, pp. 79–82; *The Ordinary Man of Cinema*, pp. 95–98.

34. Tom Conley, 'Jean-Louis Schefer: Screen Memories from *L'Homme ordinaire du cinéma*', *The New Review of Film and Television Studies*, 8:1 (2010), 12–21 (p. 13).

35. Ibid., p. 15.

36. Ibid.

37. One example Conley considers is Marc Augé's memoir *Casablanca* (Paris: Seuil, 2007), in which the author engages with the memory of the war through his own fascination with Michael Curtiz's 1942 film, which he sees as a 'déclencheur de souvenirs' [trigger of memories] (p. 27). Personal and political history are thus remembered 'through' the film.

38. Conley, 'Jean-Louis Schefer', p. 16.

39. Schefer, *L'Homme ordinaire du cinéma*, p. 12; *The Ordinary Man of Cinema*, p. 17.

40. Daney, 'Le Travelling de *Kapo*' p. 20; 'The Tracking Shot in *Kapo*', p. 20. There is an echo here of Schefer's proposition that 'une partie de notre vie passe par des souvenirs de films, parfois les plus indifférents aux contenus de cette vie' ('a part of our life passes into our recollections of

films, including films that might seem completely unrelated to our lives' actual circumstances') (*L'Homme ordinaire du cinéma*, p. 7; *The Ordinary Man of Cinema*, p.11). Daney's essay originally appeared in *Trafic*, 4 (Autumn 1992). It is perhaps the most salient example of a seam in writing on the cinema in France in the relatively recent past which interweaves biographical and historical concerns, specifically around the experience of the war, the Occupation and, in some instances, the holocaust. The figure of the screen memory operates, implicitly or explicitly, across a number of these texts. An early example appears in Sartre's autobiography *Les Mots*, in which he recalls visits to the cinema with his mother in his early childhood, and the first real encounter with a human community which he found there, an experience he says he recaptured only upon his internment in a prisoner of war camp in the first years of the war. For a comparative analysis of this episode alongside Barthes's 'En sortant du cinéma', see Patrick ffrench, 'Catastrophe, Adherence, Proximity: Sartre (with Barthes) in the Cinema', *Sartre Studies International*, 19:1 (2013), 35–54. The screen memory motif may also be found more emphatically in Claude Ollier, *Souvenirs-écran* (Paris: Cahiers du cinéma/Gallimard, 1981), and Hubert Damisch, *La Dénivelée: à l'épreuve de la photographie* (Paris: Seuil, 2001). Ollier writes that the childhood experience of cinema was his first experience of fiction and that it thus programmed his subsequent work as a writer: 'Le cinéma fut ainsi donnée d'avance' [The cinema was there already] (p. 10). Damisch explores, in the chapters 'Au risqué de la vue' and 'Trouer l'écran' of *La Dénivelée*, the multiple associations between the 'primal scene' of a visit to the cinema, in this instance Victor Tourjanki's silent *Michael Strogoff* (1926), the psychoanalytic thematics of the scopic drive and the violence associated with it, and the figure of the screen. See also Hubert Damisch, *Ciné-fil* (Paris: Seuil, 2008), which considers across a number of essays the fraught relation between cinematographic representation and the concentrationary regime.

41. Daney, 'Le Travelling de *Kapo*', p. 20; 'The Tracking Shot in *Kapo*', p. 20.
42. See my discussion of Benjamin's 'On Some Motifs in Baudelaire' above. The expressions cited here are from the second 'instalment' of the 'Intermittences du cœur' in *Sodome et Gomorrhe*, the Montjouvain episode (III, 499; 4, 507).
43. Daney, 'Le Travelling de *Kapo*', p. 20; 'The Tracking Shot in *Kapo*', p. 20.
44. Ibid., p. 21; p. 21.
45. Ibid.
46. Ibid. Daney alludes here to Jean Paulhan's *Les Fleurs de Tarbes* and to the Lacanian concept of foreclosure, which Daney defines as 'le retour hallucinatoire dans le réel de ce sur quoi il n'a pas été possible de porter un "jugement de réalité"' ('the hallucinatory return in the real of that which it has not been possible to carry out a "judgement of existence") ('Le Travelling de *Kapo*', p. 25; 'The Tracking Shot in *Kapo*', p. 24, translation modified).
47. Ibid. (translation modified).
48. Ibid., p. 22; p. 22.
49. Ibid., p. 23, p. 25.
50. Ibid., p. 25; p. 24.
51. Ibid., p. 26; p. 25.
52. Gilles Deleuze, in 'Lettre à Serge Daney: optimism, pessimisme et voyage' (in *Pourparlers* (Paris: Minuit, 1990), pp. 97–112; *Negotiations*, trans. by Martin Joughin (New York: Columbia University Press, 1995), pp. 68–79), engages with Daney's 'critical pessimism' ('pessimisme critique'). See also Garin Dowd, 'Pedagogies of the Image between Daney and Deleuze', *New Review of Film and Television Studies*, 8:1 (2010), 41–56.
53. Kaja Silverman, 'The Dream of the Nineteenth Century', *Camera Obscura*, 51, 17:3 (2002), 1–29 (p. 2).
54. Ibid., Silverman citing Godard in conversation with Daney, from Chapter 2A of the *Histoire(s) du cinéma*.
55. Ibid.
56. Ibid., p. 3, Silverman citing Benjamin from the 'Theses on the Philosophy of History'.
57. Ricciardi, 'Cinema Regained', pp. 645, 644.
58. Georges Didi-Huberman, 'Images malgré tout', in *Images malgré tout* (Paris: Minuit, 2003), pp. 11–65; *Images in Spite of All: Four Photographs from Auschwitz*, trans. by Shane B. Lillis (Chicago,

IL: University of Chicago Press, 2008), pp. 1–48. The essay was first published in the catalogue *Mémoire des camps: photographies des camps de concentration et d'extermination nazis (1933–1999)* (Paris: Marval, 2002), pp. 219–41, and constitutes the first part of the book. In the second part Didi-Huberman responds to the criticisms by Wajcmann and Pagnoux, referenced below.

59. Didi-Huberman, *Images malgré tout*, pp. 46, 65; *Images in Spite of All*, pp. 31, 47.

60. Ibid., p. 9; p. 2.

61. Gérard Wajcman, 'De la croyance photographique', *Les Temps modernes*, 56:613 (2001), 47–83; Elisabeth Pagnoux, 'Reporter photographe à Auschwitz', *Les Temps modernes*, 56:613 (2001), 84–108.

62. Libby Saxton, 'Anamnesis and Bearing Witness: Godard/Lanzmann', in *Forever Godard*, ed. by Michael Temple, James S. Williams, and Michael Witt (London: Black Dog, 2004), pp. 364–79 (pp. 366, 368). See also Monica dall'Asta, 'The (Im)possible History', in *Forever Godard*, ed. by Temple, Williams, and Witt, pp. 350–63, for an account of Benjamin's presence in and influence on Godard's later work, including the *Histoire(s) du cinéma*.

63. Saxton, 'Anamnesis and Bearing Witness', p. 367.

64. Didi-Huberman, *Images malgré tout*, p. 113; *Images in Spite of All*, p. 88.

65. Ricciardi, 'Cinema Regained', p. 345. In the chapter of *The Ends of Mourning* suggestively titled 'Cool Memories', Ricciardi compares Proust's rendering of involuntary memory and Jean Baudrillard's 'postmodern souvenirs' (p. 73), proposing that Proust's novel progressively disavows the pain of mourning, dissolving 'historicist angst' into 'ahistorical ecstasy' (p. 72), displacing the experience of shock through a 'simulacrum of experience' (p. 85).

66. Georges Didi-Huberman, 'Le Lieu malgré tout' in *Phasmes: essais sur l'apparition* (Paris: Minuit, 1998), pp. 228–42 (originally in *Vingtième siècle — Revue d'histoire*, 46 (1995), 36–44.

67. Ibid., pp. 240–41.

68. Ibid., p. 463. Didi-Huberman cites Benjamin from *The Arcades Project*, p. 463.

69. Didi-Huberman cites Pierre Vidal-Naquet, 'L'Épreuve de l'historien: réflexions d'un géneraliste', in *Au sujet de Shoah: le film de Claude Lanzmann* (Paris: Belin, 1990), pp. 198–208, and *Les Juifs, la mémoire et le present II* (Paris: La Découverte, 1991), p. 221.

70. In his subsequent work Didi-Huberman has moved beyond a focus on the capacity of the image and of the imagination and towards a stress on the 'readability' ('lisibilité') of the image, although the operation of reading was arguably already active in his exploration of the 'image-montage' in *Images malgré tout*. The recurrent reference to Benjamin persists, particularly perhaps in the second volume of Didi-Huberman's currently six-volume series *L'Œil de l'histoire*, titled *Remontages du temps subi* (Paris: Minuit, 2010). The Proustian echo of its title is confirmed in the first epigraph for the book, cited from *Le Temps retrouvé*, in which the narrator proposes that the creative intelligence 'donne une sorte de survie à des sentiments qui n'existaient plus' ('gives a sort of afterlife to feelings which are no longer in existence') (IV, 484; 6, 214). Didi-Huberman returns to the quotation in the final chapter of the book, on the artist Christian Boltanski, while the previous parts of the book focus on Sam Fuller and Harun Farocki.

71. Michael Taussig, *What Colour is the Sacred?* (Chicago, IL: University of Chicago Press, 2009). Taussig draws his title from an enigmatic question in Michel Leiris's 'Le Sacré dans la vie quotidienne', a 1938 lecture for the Collège de Sociologie.

72. Ibid., pp. 195, 190.

73. Ibid., p. 197. The quotation from Benjamin is from 'The Image of Proust', in *Illuminations*, pp. 197–210 (p. 210).

74. Benjamin, 'The Image of Proust', p. 208.

75. Ibid., p. 209.

76. Ibid., pp. 209–10.

77. Taussig, *What Colour is the Sacred?*, p. 198, citing *The Arcades Project*, p. 470.

78. Ibid., p. 247, citing *The Arcades Project*, p. 464.

79. Benjamin, 'The Image of Proust', p. 197.

80. Ibid., p. 198.

81. Ibid., p. 200.

82. Ibid.

83. Ibid., p. 198.
84. Ibid., p. 204
85. Gilles Deleuze, *Proust et les signes* (Paris: PUF, 2003), p. 218; *Proust and Signs: The Complete Text*, trans. by Richard Howard (Minneapolis: University of Minnesota Press, 2000), p. 182.
86. See Ricciardi, 'Cinema Regained', p. 649.
87. Benjamin, 'The Image of Proust', pp. 206, 207.
88. Ibid., pp. 209–10.
89. Howard Caygill, *Walter Benjamin: The Colour of Experience* (London: Routledge, 1998), p. 64.
90. Ibid., p. 66.
91. Ibid., p. 67.
92. Beatrice Hanssen, 'Introduction: Physiognomy of a Flâneur: Walter Benjamin's Peregrinations through Paris in Search of a New Imaginary' in *Walter Benjamin and The Arcades Project*, ed. by Beatrice Hanssen (London & New York: Continuum, 2006), pp. 1–11.
93. For further reading on the difficult presence of Proust in Benjamin's philosophy of history, see: Max Pensky, '*Geheimmittel*: Advertising and Dialectical Images in Benjamin's *Arcades Project*', in *Walter Benjamin and The Arcades Project*, ed. by Hanssen, pp. 113–31, and 'Tactics of Remembrance: Proust, Surrealism and the Origin of the *Passagenwerk*', in *Walter Benjamin and the Demands of History*, ed. by Michael P. Steinberg (Ithaca, NY: Cornell University Press, 1996), pp. 164–89; Elissa Marder, 'Walter Benjamin's Dream of "Happiness"', in *Walter Benjamin and The Arcades Project*, ed. by Hanssen, pp. 184–200; Stathis Gourgouris, 'The Dream-Reality of the Ruin', in *Walter Benjamin and The Arcades Project*, ed. by Hanssen, pp. 201–24; Michael Löwy, *Fire Alarm: Reading Walter Benjamin's 'On the Concept of History'* (London: Verso, 2016); Walter Benjamin, *Baudelaire*, ed. by Giorgio Agamben, Barbara Chitussi, and Clemens-Carl Härle (Paris: La Fabrique, 2013).
94. Benjamin, *The Arcades Project*, pp. 463–64. Convolute N: p. 456.
95. Ibid., p. 464.
96. Ibid., p. 462.
97. Ibid., pp. 462, 461.
98. Ibid., p. 476.
99. Ibid. In a similar vein, Godard's *Histoires(s) du cinéma* extracts images and sequences from their original narratives, and through the practice of citation repeats them as fragments. This resonates with one of Godard's global arguments in the *Histoire(s)*, to the effect that the image-making capacity of cinema was historically and ideologically recuperated by the triumphal realization of cinema as a narrative art. Jacques Rancière has proposed a critical reading of this strategy in 'Godard, Hitchcock and the Cinematogaphic Image', in *Forever Godard*, ed. by Temple, Williams, and Witt, pp. 214–31. Rancière suggests that Godard's 'dream of iconic virginity' (p. 231) obscures a more subtle opposition between the 'dialectical and symbolist' modes of linkage or connection of images, and that Godard's project ultimately shows a predilection for the symbolist mode, wherein the 'mystery' of the image displaces a dialectical attentiveness to history (p. 231). See also Rancière, *La Fable cinématographique*, pp. 217–37.
100. See, among other texts, Benjamin's 'Surrealism', in *Selected Writings*, ed. by Jennings, Eiland, and Smith, II, 207–21; 'The Author as Producer' in *Selected Writings*, ed. by Jennings, Eiland, and Smith, II, 768–82; and 'The Work of Art in the Age of its Technological Reproducibility', in *Selected Writings*, ed. by Jennings, Eiland, and Smith, III, 101–33. See also Patrick ffrench, 'Convulsive Form: Benjamin, Bataille and the Innervated Body', in *What Forms Can Do: Essays in Honour of Michael Sheringham*, ed. by Shirley Jordan and Patrick Crowley (Liverpool: Liverpool University Press, forthcoming).

CONCLUSION

In 'The Image of Proust' Benjamin writes of 'Proust's blind, senseless, frenzied quest for happiness', and, further on in the same essay, that: 'it is the Elegaic idea of Happiness [...] which for Proust transforms existence into a preserve of memory'.[1] For John McCole, Benjamin construes the happiness which Proust sought as essentially the 'restoration of a lost state', a return to childhood, or, as Benjamin puts it elsewhere in 'The Image of Proust', a 'slumping back' onto the 'bosom of nature'.[2] In this view the temporality Proust seeks, and which his novel promotes, is ahistorical, 'time in its pure state'. Against this timeless, ahistorical rendering of the operation of involuntary memory, Benjamin proposes the essentially disruptive shock of the 'now'; his re-writing of the process of involuntary memory privileges the interruptive instance of the dialectical image, which connects past to present, or more exactly actualizes the un-experienced and unrealized past in the present, in a moment of intelligibility. The 'now' of intelligibility is an awakening from the dream-sleep induced by the phantasmagoria, and it is in this sense that Benjamin's quotation from Michelet, 'Chaque époque rêve la suivante' ('Each epoch dreams the one that follows'), gains its historical sense; it is a question of awakening from the 'dream of the nineteenth century'. The awakening Benjamin sought appears antithetical to the timeless happiness he discerns as the ultimate object of Proust's search, and from the 'synthetic manufacture' of experience he discerns in the *Recherche*.

Yet in the essay on Proust Benjamin had proposed two sides to happiness:

> There is a dual will to happiness, a dialectics of happiness: a hymnic and an elegiac form. The one is the unheard of, the unprecedented, the height of bliss; the other, the eternal repetition, the eternal restoration of the original, the first happiness.[3]

In an essay I cited earlier, Agamben devotes considerable attention to this dynamic.[4] He cites an unpublished fragment by Benjamin, 'Agesilaus Santander', written in 1933, in which Benjamin had written of the angel: 'He wants happiness — that is to say, the conflict in which the rapture of the unique, the new, the yet unborn is combined with that bliss of experiencing something once more, of possessing once again, of having lived'.[5] The 'hymnic' and the 'elegiac' form of happiness are combined here. If Proust 'slumps back onto the bosom of nature' in a restoration of an anterior order, albeit one which was never experienced as such, Benjamin seeks a happiness in which the rapture of the unique and unlived instant is combined with the convulsive memory of the past. This contradiction is resolved in the proposition of those images of the past that are, as Benjamin puts it in the 'Short Speech on Proust Given on my Fortieth Birthday', 'developed in the darkroom of the lived moment'.[6] For Agamben such images are of a past that 'has never happened'.[7]

The problematics of happiness and awakening, and of the relation between the two, surface in Jean-Luc Godard's ludic rewriting of the incipit of the *Recherche* in a sequence of Chapter 2B of *Histoire(s) du cinéma*, 'Fatale beauté'.[8] The sequence is characteristically multi-layered, involving a complex interaction of image, text, voice, and music: following the appearance on the screen of the words LE TEMPS PERDU, then LE TEMPS RETROUVÉ we hear Godard's voice intone the name 'Albertine', followed by the word 'disparue', and then the expression 'Longtemps je me suis couché de bonne heure', twice. On the screen a series of images of young girls follows — fragments of paintings (Seurat's *Une baignade à Asnières*, Renoir's *La Baigneuse blonde*, Courbet's *La Plage de Saint Aubin*), as we then hear Godard's voice speak these words:

> Longtemps je me suis couché de bonne heure. Longtemps je me suis couché de bonne heure. Je dis ça, et tout à coup c'est Albertine qui disparaît, et c'est le temps qui est retrouvé, et c'est parce que c'est le romancier qui parle. Mais si c'était l'homme de cinéma, s'il fallait dire sans rien dire. *Les Enfants du capitaine Grant, Parti de Liverpool*, par exemple. Je me suis réveillé de malheur. Il faut le cinéma, et pour les mots qui restent dans la gorge, et pour désensevelir la vérité.[9]

> [For a long time I used to go to bed early. For a long time I used to go to bed early. I say that, and suddenly Albertine disappears, and time is regained, and it is because it is the novelist who speaks. But if it was the man of cinema, if one had to speak without saying anything. *The Children Of Captain Grant, Embarked from Liverpool*, for example. I awoke unhappy. Cinema is needed, for the words that stick in the throat, and to uncover the truth.]

On the soundtrack we hear the first movement of Hindemith's *Sonate en fa majeur pour alto et piano*, op. 11, no. 4, giving way to the noise of Godard's electric typewriter. Godard's rewriting of 'Je me suis couché de bonne heure' should be read in the context of his critique, throughout this chapter, of the narrative motif of the sacrifice of a woman (whence the chapter title 'Fatale beauté'). The allusion to the 'jeunes filles' and their maritime origin, and the invocation of the name 'Albertine' are interwoven with the proposition that the redemptive triumph over loss and forgetfulness announced with the title 'Le Temps retrouvé', and the happiness encrypted in 'de bonne heure' at the start of the novel, is won at the cost of Albertine's disappearance; Albertine must disappear, be sacrificed, and then forgotten, in order for time to be regained and the novel to be generated from this anamnesis. Against this Godard postulates that the cinema, once separated from its narrative dimensions, has the capacity to 'speak without speaking', to attend to that which is not said, or to that which cannot bear being voiced. 'Je me suis couché de bonne heure' thus becomes 'Je me suis reveillé de malheur'. Godard's trademark typographic displacements deliberately misread 'de bonne heure' as a profession of happiness, rather than as indicating the time of the evening; he thus counters the happy sleep of the *Recherche*, which the *Recherche* may allow, with the unhappy awakening which his own *Histoire(s) du cinéma* are intended to provoke, an awakening to history, to that element in history which has been foreclosed from the stories told by cinema. A critical attention to the image, a resistance to narrative and to the gendered hierarchy implicit within it, propose an awakening which is both unhappy and untimely (if we read Godard's 'de malheur' against Proust's 'de bonne heure'). This thesis is re-affirmed in a further distortion of Proust's text in 'Fatale beauté', immediately following the first, in which the phoneme *trou* in the title *Le Temps retrouvé* is highlighted, bringing to light the disappearance — that of Albertine, and the absence of experience on which the operation of involuntary memory depends. Godard's dislocation of the expression also resonates with Benjamin's critique of Proust's 'synthetic' manufacturing of experience, with the foregrounding of 'Le Temps rêvé' resulting from the 'subtraction' of the phoneme *trou* (*Le Temps retrouvé*). The *Recherche* produces a 'dreamed' time, a dream-time, from which it is urgent to awake, with a renewed attention to what is absent from this time, to what it has foreclosed. For Ricciardi Godard escapes the 'solipsistic framework of the Proustian enterprise' through the importation of a Benjaminian consciousness of history. At the same time Godard seems to realize Agamben's postulation, via Benjamin, that the time recovered in involuntary memory is a time that did not take place, or which has not taken place in the dimension of consciousness or representation.[10]

The argument articulated across Godard's inter-medial practice supports the idea of a critical cinema, a cinema resonant with Daney's vision of it as having the potential to bring to light that which is screened out, what is foreclosed. It is underpinned by Benjamin's call for an attentiveness to the irruption of fragments of unrealized past experience in the present, which is itself informed by Benjamin's extraction of Proustian involuntary memory from the texture of Proust's narrative. The kind of happiness with which this argument is aligned, and towards which it is oriented, is the 'hymnic', the rapture of the new.

A different argument, and a different account of happiness, of awakening, and of the place of cinema is suggested by Roland Barthes's essay 'En sortant du cinéma'. There Barthes writes that it is on *leaving* the cinema that he feels he has awakened from a hypnotic trance, a form of sleep construed as a relaxation of social morality, a space of irresponsibility; he experiences his body as something 'mou comme un chat endormi' ('limp as a sleeping cat'). But Barthes senses this hypnotic state as having a curative function, as having 'le plus vieux des pouvoirs: le guérissement' ('the most venerable of powers: healing'). As a musical parallel he refers to the castrato Farinelli's voice as having 'put to sleep' ('endormit') the morbid melancholy of King Phillip V of Spain. For Barthes, beyond any potential critical function of the image as such, it is the situation of the cinema, the reverie it can induce, which allows a space and time of political and moral irresponsibility, the happiness of an absence of demand and a cure for melancholy. Farinelli's song offers just such a cure for melancholy, just as, perhaps, the cinema offers the occasion for a moral vacancy, a vacation. Indeed in considering the conditions under which one enters the cinema Barthes postulates 'disponibilité', and 'vacance' as plausible affective states.[11] We have seen how, despite, and to some extent because of, his close engagement with the *Recherche*, Benjamin is led to an ambivalent resistance to the weight of its images, to the potentially stupefying happiness it can induce, synthetically. Would Proust's *Recherche*, like the cinema, thus offer the occasion for a curative sleep, a suppression of melancholy?

The experiences of reading Proust and of cinematic spectatorship might be seen to move between these two affective modes: an 'unhappy' or melancholic critical sensitivity to the irruption of the past in the present, to the 'return' of that which has not taken place; and the happiness of the relaxation of social demand, the 'crepuscular state' evoked by Agamben to account for 'what Proust had in mind'.

Notes to the Conclusion

1. Benjamin, 'The Image of Proust', p. 200.
2. John McCole, *Walter Benjamin and the Antimonies of Tradition* (Ithaca, NY, & London: Cornell University Press, 1993), p. 261; Benjamin, 'The Image of Proust', p. 208.
3. Benjamin, 'The Image of Proust', p. 200.
4. Agamben, 'Walter Benjamin and the Demonic'.
5. Benjamin, 'Agesilaus Santander', p. 715. Cited by Agamben in 'Walter Benjamin and the Demonic', p. 144.
6. Cited by Agamben in 'Walter Benjamin and the Demonic', p. 158.
7. Agamben, 'Walter Benjamin and the Demonic', p. 159.
8. See Ricciardi, *The Ends of Mourning*, p. 196, and Heywood, *Modernist Visions*, p. 33, for discussions of this sequence.
9. Jean-Luc Godard, 'Fatale beauté', Chapter 2B of *Histoire(s) du cinéma*. For a detailed breakdown of the sequence, see Céline Scémama's analysis: <http://cri-image.univ-paris1.fr/celine/2b.html> [accessed 29 October 2017].
10. Ricciardi, *The Ends of Mourning*, p. 197.
11. Barthes, 'En sortant du cinéma', p. 383; 'Leaving the Movie Theater', p. 345 (translation modified).

BIBLIOGRAPHY

Primary Works

PROUST, MARCEL, *A la recherche du temps perdu*, 4 vols (Paris: Gallimard, Pléaide, 1987–89)
——*In Search of Lost Time*, ed. by Christopher Prendergast, trans. by Lydia Davis and others, 6 vols (London: Penguin, 2002)

Secondary Works

ABEL, RICHARD, *French Film Theory and Criticism: A History/Anthology, 1907–1939*, 2 vols (Princeton, NJ: Princeton University Press 1988)
AGAMBEN, GIORGIO, 'Aby Warburg and the Nameless Science', in *Potentialities: Collected Essays in Philosophy*, trans. by Daniel Heller-Roazen (Stanford, CA: Stanford University Press, 1999), pp. 89–103
——*Infanzia et storia* (Turin: Einaudi, 1979)
——'Infancy and History: An Essay on the Destruction of Experience', in *Infancy and History* (London: Verso, 1993), pp. 11–64
——'Kommerell, or On Gesture', in *Potentialities: Collected Essays in Philosophy*, trans. by Daniel Heller-Roazen (Stanford, CA: Stanford University Press, 1999), pp. 77–85
——'Notes sur le geste', trans. by Daniel Loayza, *Trafic*, 1 (1992), 31–36
——'Notes on Gesture', in *Infancy and History: Essays on the Destruction of Experience,* trans. by Liz Heron (London: Verso, 1993), pp. 133–40
——'Note sul gesto', in *Mezzi senza fine* (Turin: Bollati Boringhieri, 1996), pp. 45–53
——'Notes on Gesture', in *Means Without End: Notes on Politics*, trans. by Vincenzo Binetti and Cesare Casarino (Minneapolis: University of Minnesota Press, 2000), pp. 49–62
——'Walter Benjamin e il demonico: felicità e redenzione storica nel pensiero del Benjamin', *aut aut*, 189–90 (1982), 39–58
——'Walter Benjamin and the Demonic: Happiness and Historical Redemption', in *Potentialities: Collected Essays in Philosophy*, trans. by Daniel Heller-Roazen (Stanford, CA: Stanford University Press, 1999), pp. 138–59
AUBOUY, VÉRONIQUE, *Proust lu*, <http://www.aubouy.fr/proust-lu/images-lecteur.html> [accessed 24 March 2017]
AUGÉ, MARC, *Casablanca* (Paris: Seuil, 2007)
BACHELARD, GASTON, *La Poétique de l'espace* (Paris: PUF, 1964)
——*The Poetics of Space*, trans. by Maria Jolas (Boston: Beacon Press, 1969)
BAL, MIEKE, 'All in the Family: Familiarity and Estrangement According to Marcel Proust', in *The Familial Gaze*, ed. by Marianne Hirsch (Hanover, NH, & London: University Press of New England, 1999), pp. 223–47
——*The Mottled Screen: Reading Proust Visually*, trans. by Anna-Louise Milne (Stanford, CA: Stanford University Press, 1997)
BALDWIN, TOM, *The Picture as Spectre: Diderot, Proust, Deleuze* (Oxford: Legenda, 2001)
BALSOM, ERICA, *Exhibiting Cinema in Contemporary Art* (Amsterdam: Amsterdam University Press, 2013)

BARTHES, ROLAND, *La Chambre claire* (Paris: Gallimard, Seuil, Cahiers du cinéma, 1980)
—— *Camera Lucida*, trans. by Richard Howard (London: Vintage, 1982)
—— 'En sortant du cinéma', in *Le Bruissement de la langue* (Paris: Seuil, 1984), pp. 383–87
—— 'Leaving the Movie Theater', in *The Rustle of Language*, trans. by Richard Howard (New York: Hill & Wang, 1986), pp. 345–49
—— 'Littérature objective', in *Essais critiques* (Paris: Seuil, 1964), pp. 29–40
—— 'Objective Literature', in *Critical Essays*, trans. by Richard Howard (Evanston, IL: Northwestern University Press, 1972), pp. 13–24
—— 'La Mort de l'auteur', in *Le Bruissement de la langue* (Paris: Seuil, 1984) pp. 63–69
—— 'The Death of the Author', in *The Rustle of Language*, trans. by Richard Howard (New York: Hill & Wang, 1986), pp. 49–55
—— 'Longtemps je me suis couché de bonne heure', in *Le Bruissement de la langue* (Paris: Seuil, 1984), pp. 313–25
—— 'Longtemps je me suis couché de bonne heure', in *The Rustle of Language*, trans. by Richard Howard (Berkeley: University of California Press, 1989), pp. 277–90
—— *Le Neutre: cours au Collège de France 1977–78* (Paris: Seuil/IMEC, 2002)
—— *The Neutral: Lecture Course at the Collège de France (1977–1978)*, trans. by Rosalind E. Krauss and Denis Hollier (New York: Columbia University Press, 2005)
—— *Roland Barthes par Roland Barthes* (Paris: Seuil, 1975)
—— *Roland Barthes by Roland Barthes*, trans. by Richard Howard (London: Macmillan, 1977)
—— 'Le Troisième sens', in *L'Obvie et l'obtus* (Paris: Seuil, 1982), pp. 43–61
—— 'The Third Meaning', in *Image, Music, Text*, trans. by Stephen Heath (London: Fontana, 1977), pp. 52–68
BATAILLE, GEORGES, *La Littérature et le mal* (Paris: Gallimard, 1957)
—— *Literature and Evil*, trans. by Alistair Hamilton (London: Penguin Books, 2012)
BAUDELAIRE, CHARLES, *Le Spleen de Paris: petits poèmes en prose*, in *Œuvres complètes*, 2 vols (Paris: Gallimard, Plèaide, 1975–76), I, 273–374
—— *Paris Spleen: Little Poems in Prose*, trans. by Keith Waldrop (Middletown, CT: Wesleyan University Press, 2009)
—— 'La Morale du joujou', in *Œuvres complètes*, 2 vols (Paris: Gallimard, 'Pléaide', 1975–76), I, 581–87
—— 'Réflexions sur quelques-uns de mes contemporains: Victor Hugo', in *Œuvres complètes*, 2 vols (Paris: Gallimard, 'Pléaide', 1975–76), II, 129–41
BAUDRY, JEAN-LOUIS, 'Le Dispositif: approches métapsychologiques de l'impression de réalité', *Psychanalyse et cinéma*, special issue of *Communications*, 23 (1975), 65–72
—— 'The Apparatus', trans. by Jean Andrews and Bertrand Augst, *Camera Obscura*, 1:11 (1976), 104–26
BAZIN, ANDRÉ, *Qu'est-ce que le cinéma* (Paris: Editions du Cerf, 1959)
—— *What is Cinema?*, trans. by Hugh Gray, 2 vols (Berkeley & Los Angeles: University of California Press, 1967)
BELLOUR, RAYMOND, *Le Corps au cinéma: hypnoses, émotions, animalités* (Paris: POL, 2009)
—— *L'Entre-images: photo, cinéma, vidéo* (Paris: La Différence, 1990)
—— *Between-the-Images*, trans. by Allan Hardyck (Zurich and Dijon: JRP/Ringier & Les Presses du réel, 2012)
—— *L'Entre-images 2: mots-images* (Paris: POL, 1999)
BENHAÏM, ANDRÉ, *Panim: visages de Proust* (Villeneuve d'Ascq: Presses universitaires du Septentrion, 2006)
BELLOUR, RAYMOND, THIERRY KUNTZEL, and CHRISTIAN METZ (eds.), *Psychanalyse et cinéma*, special issue of *Communications*, 23 (1975)

BENJAMIN, WALTER, 'Agesilaus Santander (Second Version)', in *Selected Writings*, ed. by Michael W. Jennings, Howard Eiland and Gary Smith, trans. by Rodney Livingstone, 4 vols (Cambridge, MA, & London: Harvard University Press, 1999), II, 715

—— *The Arcades Project*, trans. by Howard Eiland and Kevin McLaughlin (Cambridge, MA, & London: Harvard University Press, 1999)

—— 'The Author as Producer', in *Selected Writings*, ed. by Michael W. Jennings, Howard Eiland and Gary Smith, trans. by Edmund Jephcott, 4 vols (Cambridge, MA, & London: Harvard University Press, 1999), II, 768–82

—— *Baudelaire*, ed. by Giorgio Agamben, Barbara Chitussi, and Clemens-Carl Härle (Paris: La Fabrique, 2013)

—— 'Epistemological-Critical Preface, or Paralipomena to "On the Concept of History"', in *Selected Writings*, ed. by Michael W. Jennings and Howard Eiland, trans. by Edmund Jephcott and Howard Eiland, 4 vols (Cambridge, MA, & London: Harvard University Press, 2003), IV, 401–11

—— 'Franz Kafka', in *Illuminations*, trans. by Harry Zohn (London: Fontana, 1973), pp. 108–35

—— 'The Image of Proust', in *Illuminations*, trans. by Harry Zohn (London: Fontana, 1973), pp. 197–210

—— 'On Some Motifs in Baudelaire', in *Illuminations*, trans. by Harry Zohn (London: Fontana, 1973), pp. 152–96

—— 'On the Concept of History', in *Selected Writings*, ed. by Michael W. Jennings, Howard Eiland and Gary Smith, trans. by Harry Zohn, 4 vols (Cambridge, MA, & London: Harvard University Press, 2003), IV, 389–400

—— *The Origin of German Tragic Drama*, trans. by John Osborne (London: Verso, 1998)

—— 'Surrealism', in *Selected Writings*, ed. by Michael W. Jennings, Howard Eiland and Gary Smith, trans. by Edmund Jephcott, 4 vols (Cambridge, MA, & London: Harvard University Press, 1999), II, 207–21

—— 'Theses on the Philosophy of History', in *Illuminations*, trans. by Harry Zohn (London: Fontana, 1973), pp. 245–55

—— 'The Work of Art in the Age of its Technological Reproducibility', in *Selected Writings*, ed. by Howard Eiland and Michael W. Jennings, trans. by Edmund Jephcott and Harry Zohn, 4 vols (Cambridge, MA, & London: Harvard University Press, 2002), III, 101–33

BERSANI, LEO, *Marcel Proust: The Fictions of Life and Art* (Oxford: Oxford University Press, 1965)

—— 'Death and Literary Authority', in *The Culture of Redemption* (Cambridge, MA, & London: Harvard University Press, 1990), pp. 7–28

BERSANI, LEO, and ULYSSE DUTOIT, *Forms of Being* (London: BFI, 2004)

BION, WILFRED, *Attention and Interpretation* (London: Tavistock, 1970)

—— *Learning from Experience* (Oxford: Aronson, 1962)

BON, FRANÇOIS, *Proust est une fiction* (Paris: Seuil, 2013)

BOWIE, MALCOLM, *Freud, Proust, Lacan: Theory as Fiction* (Cambridge: Cambridge University Press, 1997)

BRASSAI, *Marcel Proust sous l'emprise de la photographie* (Paris: Gallimard, 1997)

—— *Proust in the Power of Photography*, trans. by Richard Howard (Chicago, IL: Chicago University Press, 2001)

BRAUN, MARTA, *Picturing Time: The Work of Etienne-Jules Marey (1830–1904)* (Chicago, IL: University of Chicago Press, 1992)

BURGIN, VICTOR, *The Remembered Film* (London: Reaktion, 2004)

BUTLER, JUDITH, *The Psychic Life of Power: Essays in Subjection* (Stanford, CA: Stanford University Press, 1997)

CARRIER-LAFLEUR, Thomas, *L'Œil cinématographique de Proust* (Paris: Classiques Garnier, 2016)

CARROY, JACQUELINE, and NATHALIE RICHARD (eds.), *Alfred Maury: érudit et rêveur* (Rennes: Presses universitaires de Rennes, 2007)

CAVELL, STANLEY, 'Concluding Remarks on *La Projection du monde*', in *Cavell on Film*, ed. by William Rothman (New York: SUNY Press, 2005), pp. 281–86

—— 'The Fantastic of Philosophy', in *Cavell on Film*, ed. by William Rothman (New York: SUNY Press, 2005), pp. 145–52

—— 'Two Cheers for Romance', in *Cavell on Film*, ed. by William Rothman (New York: SUNY Press, 2005), pp. 153–66

—— 'The World as Things', in *Cavell on Film*, ed. by William Rothman (New York: SUNY Press, 2005), pp. 241–80

—— *The World Viewed — Enlarged Edition* (Cambridge, MA, & London: Harvard University Press, 1979)

CAYGILL, HOWARD, *Walter Benjamin: The Colour of Experience* (London: Routledge, 1998)

CHEVRIER, JEAN-FRANÇOIS, *Proust et la photographie: la résurrection de Venise* (Paris: L'Arachnéen, 2009)

CHION, MICHEL, *La Voix au cinéma* (Paris: Cahiers du cinéma/Éditions de l'étoile, 1982)

—— *The Voice in Cinema*, trans. by Claudia Gorbman (New York: Columbia University Press, 1999)

CLÉDER, JEAN, and JEAN-PIERRE MONTIER (eds.), *Proust et les images: peinture, photographie, cinéma, vidéo* (Rennes: Presses universitaires de Rennes, 2003)

COLOMBANI, FLORENCE, *Proust-Visconti: histoire d'une affinité elective* (Paris: Philippe Rey, 2006)

COMPAGNON, ANTOINE, 'La "danse contre seins"', in *Marcel Proust: écrire sans fin*, ed. by Rainer Warning and Jean Milly (Paris: CNRS Éditions, 1996), pp. 79–97

CONLEY, TOM, 'Jean-Louis Schefer: Screen Memories from *L'Homme ordinaire du cinéma*', *The New Review of Film and Television Studies*, 8:1 (2010), 12–21

COOPER, SARAH, *The Soul of Film Theory* (London: Palgrave, 2013)

CRARY, JONATHAN, *Suspensions of Perception: Attention, Spectacle and Modern Culture* (Cambridge, MA: MIT Press, 1999)

—— *Techniques of the Observer: On Vision and Modernity in the Nineteenth Century* (Cambridge, MA: MIT Press, 1990)

CULLEY, PETER, 'Two Works by Stan Douglas', *Vanguard*, 16:4 (October 1987), <http://ccca.concordia.ca/c/writing/c/culley/cul002t.html> [accessed 24 March 2017]

DALL'ASTA, MONICA, 'The (Im)possible History', in *Forever Godard*, ed. by Michael Temple, James S. Williams, and Michael Witt (London: Black Dog, 2004), pp. 350–63

DAMISCH, HUBERT, *La Dénivelée: à l'épreuve de la photographie* (Paris: Seuil, 2001)

—— *Ciné-fil* (Paris: Seuil, 2008)

DANEY, SERGE, 'Le Travelling de *Kapo*', in *Persévérance: entretien avec Serge Toubiana* (Paris: POL, 1994), pp. 13–39

—— 'The Tracking Shot in *Kapo*', in *Postcards from the Cinema*, trans. by Paul Grant (London: Bloomsbury, 2007), pp. 17–38

DANIUS, SARA, *The Senses of Modernism: Technology, Perception and Aesthetics* (New York: Cornell University Press, 2002)

DE MAN, PAUL, *Allegories of Reading: Figural Language in Rousseau, Nietzsche, Rilke and Proust* (Newhaven, CT: Yale University Press, 1979)

DELEUZE, GILLES, *Cinéma 1: l'image-mouvement* (Paris: Minuit, 1983)

—— *Cinema 1: The Movement-Image*, trans. by Hugh Tomlinson and Barbara Habberjam (London: Athlone, 1986)

—— *Cinéma 2: l'image-temps* (Paris: Minuit, 1985)

—— *Cinema 2: The Time-Image*, trans. by Hugh Tomlinson and Robert Galeta (London: Athlone, 1989)

—— 'Immanence: une vie', in *Deux régimes de fous: textes et entretiens 1975–1995* (Paris: Minuit, 2003), pp. 359–63

—— 'Immanence: A Life', in *Two Regimes of Madness: Texts and Interviews 1975–1995*, trans. by Ames Hodges and Mike Taormina (New York: Semiotexte, 2006), pp. 384–89

—— 'Lettre à Serge Daney: optimisme, pessimisme et voyage', in *Pourparlers* (Paris: Minuit, 1990), pp. 97–112

—— 'Letter to Serge Daney: Optimism, Pessimism and Travel', in *Negotiations*, trans. by Martin Joughin (New York: Columbia University Press, 1995), pp. 68–79

—— *Le Pli: Leibniz et le baroque* (Paris: Minuit, 1988)

—— *The Fold: Leibniz and the Baroque*, trans. by Tom Conley (London: Athlone, 1993)

—— *Proust et les signes* (Paris: PUF, 2003)

—— *Proust and Signs: The Complete Text*, trans. by Richard Howard (Minneapolis: University of Minnesota Press, 2000)

DIDI-HUBERMAN, GEORGES, 'Images malgré tout', in *Mémoire des camps: photographies des camps de concentration et d'extermination nazis (1933–1999)* (Paris: Marval, 2002), pp. 219–41

—— 'Images malgré tout', in *Images malgré tout* (Paris: Minuit, 2003), pp. 11–65

—— *Images in Spite of All: Four Photographs from Auschwitz*, trans. by Shane B. Lillis (Chicago, IL: University of Chicago Press, 2008), pp. 1–48

—— *L'Image survivante: histoire de l'art et temps des fantômes selon Aby Warburg* (Paris: Minuit, 2002)

—— *The Surviving Image: Phantoms of Time and Time of Phantoms: Aby Warburg's History of Art*, trans. by Harvey Mendelsohn (University Park, PA: Penn State University Press, 2016)

—— 'Le Lieu malgré tout', in *Phasmes: essais sur l'apparition* (Paris: Minuit, 1998), pp. 228–42

—— *Ninfa fluida: essai sur le drape-désir* (Paris: Gallimard, 2015)

—— *Ninfa moderna: essai sur le drape tombé* (Paris: Gallimard, 2002)

—— *Ninfa profunda: essai sur le drape-tourmenté* (Paris: Gallimard, 2017)

—— *Remontages du temps subi* (Paris: Minuit, 2010)

DOWD, GARIN, 'Pedagogies of the Image between Daney and Deleuze', *New Review of Film and Television Studies*, 8:1 (2010), 41–56

FFRENCH, PATRICK, 'Barthes and the Voice: The Acousmatic and Beyond', *L'Esprit créateur*, 55:4 (2015), 56–69

—— 'Catastrophe, Adherence, Proximity: Sartre (with Barthes) in the Cinema', *Sartre Studies International*, 19:1 (2013), 35–54

—— 'Convulsive Form: Benjamin, Bataille and the Innervated Body', in *What Forms Can Do: Essays in Honour of Michael Sheringham*, ed. by Shirley Jordan and Patrick Crowley (Liverpool: Liverpool University Press, forthcoming)

—— 'The Immanent Ethnography of Chris Marker, Reader of Proust', *Film Studies*, 6 (Summer 2005), 87–96

—— 'Memories of the Unlived Body: Jean-Louis Schefer, Georges Bataille, Gilles Deleuze', *Film-Philosophy*, 21:2 (2017), 161–87

—— 'The Memory of the Image in Chris Marker's *La Jetée*', *French Studies*, 59:1 (January 2005), 31–37

—— 'Proust, Deleuze and the Spiritual Automaton', in *Beckett's Proust/Deleuze's Proust*, ed. by Mary Bryden and Margaret Topping (London: Palgrave, 2009), pp. 104–16

—— *Roland Barthes and Film: Myth, Photography and Leaving the Cinema* (London: I. B. Tauris, forthcoming)

—— ' "Time in the pure state": Deleuze, Proust and the Image of Time', in *Time and the Image*, ed. by Carolyn Bailey Gill (Manchester: Manchester University Press, 2000), pp. 161–71

FISHER, MARK, 'Six re-Views of Chris Marker: The Art of Memory', *Mute* (December 2002), <http://www.metamute.org/editorial/articles/six-re-views-chris-marker-art-memory> [accessed 1 June 2017]

FRAMPTON, DANIEL, *Filmosophy* (New York & Chichester: Wallflower, 2006)

FREUD, SIGMUND, 'Beyond the Pleasure Principle', in *On Metapsychology: The Theory of Psychoanalysis*, Pelican Freud Library 11 (Harmondsworth: Penguin, 1984), pp. 269–339

—— 'Childhood Memories and Screen Memories', in *The Psychopathology of Everyday Life*, trans. by Alan Tyson, Pelican Freud Library 5 (Harmondsworth: Penguin, 1975), pp. 83–93

—— *The Interpretation of Dreams*, trans. by James Strachey, Pelican Freud Library 4 (Harmondsworth: Penguin, 1976)

—— 'A Metapsychological Supplement to the Theory of Dreams', in *On Metapsychology: The Theory of Psychoanalysis*, Pelican Freud Library 11 (Harmondsworth: Penguin, 1984), pp. 229–43

—— 'Uber Deckerinnerung', in *Gesammelte Werke*, 17 vols (Frankfurt: Fischer Verlag, 1953), I, 531–54

—— 'Screen Memories', in *The Uncanny*, trans. by David McLintock (London: Penguin, 2003), pp. 1–22

FREUD, SIGMUND, and JOSEF BREUER, *Studies in Hysteria*, trans. by Nicola Luckhurst (London: Penguin, 2004)

GARCIA, CARLA AMBRÓSIO, *Bion in Film Theory and Analysis* (London: Routledge, 2017)

GARCIA, TRISTAN, *L'Image* (Paris: L'Atlande, 2007)

GORDON, RAE BETH, *Why the French love Jerry Lewis: from Cabaret to Early Cinema* (Stanford, CA: Stanford University Press, 2001)

GORKY, MAXIM, 'In the Kingdom of Shadows', in Jay Leyda, *Kino: A History of Russian and Soviet Film* (London: Allen, 1960), pp. 407–09

GOULBOURNE. RUSSELL, 'Introduction', in Jean-Jacques Rousseau, *Reveries of the Solitary Walker* (Oxford: Oxford University Press, 2011), pp. ix–xxviii

GOURGOURIS, STATHIS, 'The Dream-Reality of the Ruin', in *Walter Benjamin and The Arcades Project*, ed. by Beatrice Hanssen (London & New York: Continuum, 2006), pp. 201–24

GREEN, ANDRÉ, *La Folie privée* (Paris: Gallimard, 1990)

GUSTAFSSON, HENRIK, and ASBJORN GRONSTAD (eds.), *Cinema and Agamben: Ethics, Biopolitics and the Moving Image* (London: Bloomsbury, 2014)

HANSSEN, BEATRICE, 'Introduction: Physiognomy of a Flâneur: Walter Benjamin's Peregrinations through Paris in Search of a New Imaginary', in *Walter Benjamin and The Arcades Project*, ed. by Beatrice Hanssen (London & New York: Continuum, 2006), pp. 1–11

HARBORD, JANET, *Chris Marker: La Jetée* (London: Afterall Books, 2009)

—— *Ex-centric Cinema: Agamben and Film Archaeology* (London: Bloomsbury, 2016)

HAUSTEIN, KATJA, *Regarding Lost Time: Photography, Identity and Affect in Proust, Benjamin and Barthes* (Oxford: Legenda, 2012)

HENRY, ANNE, *Marcel Proust: théories pour une esthétique* (Paris: Klinksieck, 1983)

—— *La Tentation de Marcel Proust* (Paris: PUF, 2000)

HEYWOOD, MIRIAM, *Modernist Visions: Marcel Proust's A la recherche du temps perdu and Jean-Luc Godard's Histoire(s) du cinéma* (Bern: Peter Lang, 2012)

KOFMAN, SARAH, *Camera obscura: de l'idéologie* (Paris: Galilée, 1973)

KOMMERELL, MAX, *Jean Paul* (Frankfurt: Klostermann, 1933)

—— *Il poeta e l'indicibile: saggi di litteratura tedesca* (Genoa: Marietti, 1991)

KRAVANJA, PETER, *Proust à l'écran* (Paris: Editions internationales, 2003)

—— *Visconti — lecteur de Proust* (Paris: Portaparole, 2005)

LACAN, JACQUES, 'Le Stade du miroir', in *Écrits* (Paris: Seuil, Collection, 1966), pp. 93–100

—— 'The Mirror Stage as Formative of the Function of the I', in *Ecrits: A Selection*, trans. by Alan Sheridan (London: Tavistock, 1977), pp. 1–7

—— *Le Séminaire Livre XVI: d'un autre à l'autre* (Paris: Seuil, 2006)

LADENSON, ELISABETH, 'Gilberte's Indecent Gesture', in *Proust in Perspective: Visions and Revisions*, ed. by Armine Kotin Mortimer and Katherine Kolb (Urbana and Chicago: University of Illinois Press, 2002), pp. 147–56

—— *Proust's Lesbianism* (Ithaca, NY, & London: Cornell University Press, 1999)

LAPLANCHE, JEAN, *Problématiques V* (Paris: PUF, 1998)

LAPLANCHE, JEAN, and JEAN-BERTRAND PONTALIS, *Vocabulaire de la psychanalyse* (Paris: PUF, 1967)

LEWIN, BERNARD, 'Inferences from the Dream Screen', *The International Journal of Psycho-Analysis*, 29 (1 January 1948), 224–31

—— 'Sleep, the Mouth and the Dream Screen', *The Psychoanalytic Quarterly*, 15 (1946), 419–34

—— 'Le Sommeil, la bouche et le rêve', *L'Espace du rêve*, special issue of *Nouvelle revue de psychanalyse*, 5 (1972), 211–24

LÖWY, MICHAEL, *Fire Alarm: Reading Walter Benjamin's 'On the Concept of History'* (London: Verso, 2016)

LYOTARD, Jean-François, *Heidegger et 'les juifs'* (Paris: Galilée, 1988)

—— *Heidegger and 'the Jews'*, trans. by Andreas Michel and Mark Roberts (Minneapolis: University of Minnesota Press, 1990)

MALABOU, CATHERINE, *Ontologie de l'accident: essai sur la plasticité destructrice* (Paris: Léo Scheer, 2009)

—— *Ontology of the Accident: An Essay on Destructive Plasticity*, trans. by Carolyn Shread (Cambridge: Polity Press, 2012)

MALT, JO, 'The Blob and the Magic Lantern: On Subjectivity, Faciality and Projection', *Paragraph*, 36:3 (2013), 305–23

MANNONI, LAURENT, *Le Grand Art de la lumière et de l'ombre: archéologie du cinéma* (Paris: Nathan, 1999)

—— *The Great Art of Light and Shadow: Archaeology of the Cinema*, trans. by Richard Crangle (Exeter: University of Exeter Press, 2000)

MARDER, ELISSA, 'Walter Benjamin's Dream of "Happiness"', in *Walter Benjamin and The Arcades Project*, ed. by Beatrice Hanssen (London & New York: Continuum, 2006), pp. 184–200

MAURY, ALFRED, *Le Sommeil et les rêves* (Paris: Didier, 1865)

MAXWELL, DONALD R., *The Abacus and the Rainbow: Bergson, Proust and the Digital-Analogic Opposition* (New York: Peter Lang, 1999)

McCOLE, JOHN, *Walter Benjamin and the Antinomies of Tradition* (Ithaca, NY, & London: Cornell University Press, 1993)

MERLEAU-PONTY, MAURICE, *Phénoménologie de la perception* (Paris: Gallimard, 1945)

—— *Le Visible et l'invisible* (Paris: Gallimard, 1964)

—— *The Visible and the Invisible*, trans. by Alphonso Lingis (Evanston, IL: Northwestern University Press, 1968)

METZ, CHRISTIAN, 'Le Film de fiction et son spectateur', *Psychanalyse et cinéma*, special issue of *Communications*, 23 (1975), 108–35

—— 'The Fiction Film and the Spectator', in *The Imaginary Signifier*, trans. by Alfred Guzzetti (modified by Ben Brewster and Celia Britton) (Bloomington: Indiana University Press, 1982), pp. 99–147

MORRISSEY, ROBERT J., *La Rêverie jusqu'à Rousseau: recherches sur un topos littéraire* (Lexington, KY: French Forum, 1984)

MULVEY, LAURA, *Death 24x a Second* (London: Reaktion, 2006)

NERVAL, GÉRARD DE, *Œuvres complètes*, 3 vols (Paris: Gallimard, Pléaide, 1984–93)

NOYS, BENJAMIN, 'Gestural Cinema?: Giorgio Agamben on Film', *Film-Philosophy*, 8:22 (July 2004), <http://www.film-philosophy.com/vol8–2004/n22noys> [accessed 19 March 2018]

OLLIER, CLAUDE, *Souvenirs-écran* (Paris: Cahiers du cinéma/Gallimard, 1981)

PAGNOUX, ELISABETH, 'Reporter photographe à Auschwitz', *Les Temps modernes*, 56:613 (2001), 84–108

PENSKY, MAX, '*Geheimmittel*: Advertising and Dialectical Images in Benjamin's *Arcades Project*', in *Walter Benjamin and The Arcades Project*, ed. by Beatrice Hanssen (London & New York: Continuum, 2006), pp. 113–31

—— 'Tactics of Remembrance: Proust, Surrealism and the Origin of the *Passagenwerk*', in *Walter Benjamin and the Demands of History*, ed. by Michael P. Steinberg (Ithaca, NY: Cornell University Press, 1996), pp. 164–89

PEREC, GEORGES, *Un homme qui dort* (Paris: Denoël, 1967)

PHILLIPS, ADAM, *On Kissing, Tickling and Being Bored* (London: Faber & Faber, 1993)

PLEYNET, MARCELIN, and JEAN THIBAUDEAU, 'Economique-formelle-idéologique', *Cinéthique*, 3 (1969), 7–14

POE, EDGAR ALLAN, 'Marginalia', in *The Collected Writings of Edgar Allan Poe*, 5 vols (New York: Gordian Press, 1981–97)

PRENDERGAST, CHRISTOPHER, *Mirages and Mad Beliefs: Proust the Skeptic* (Princeton, NJ, & Oxford: Princeton University Press, 2013)

—— *The Order of Mimesis: Balzac, Stendhal, Nerval and Flaubert* (Cambridge: Cambridge University Press, 1986)

PROUST, MARCEL, *Contre Saint-Beuve, précédé de Pastiches et mélanges, suivi de Essais et articles* (Paris: Gallimard, Pléaide, 1971)

—— *By Way of Sainte-Beuve*, trans. by Sylvia Townsend Warner (London: Chatto & Windus, 1958)

QUESNOY, PIERRE, *Littérature et cinéma* (Paris: Le Rouge et le noir, 1928)

RABINBACH, ANSON, *The Human Motor: Energy, Fatigue and the Origins of Modernity* (Berkeley & Los Angeles: University of California Press, 1990)

RANCIÈRE, JACQUES, *La Mésentente: politique et philosophie* (Paris: Galilée, 1995)

—— *Dis-agreement: Politics and Philosophy*, trans. by Julie Rose (Minneapolis & London: University of Minnesota Press, 1999)

—— *La Fable cinématographique* (Paris: Seuil, 2001)

—— *Film Fables*, trans. by Emiliano Battista (Oxford & New York: Berg, 2006)

—— 'Godard, Hitchcock and the Cinematogaphic Image', in *Forever Godard*, ed. by Michael Temple, James S. Williams, and Michael Witt (London: Black Dog, 2004), pp. 214–31

RAYMOND, MARCEL, *Romantisme et rêverie* (Alençon: José Corti, 1978)

REYNER, IGOR, *Listening in Proust* (unpublished PhD thesis, King's College London, 2017)

RICCIARDI, ALESSIA, 'Cinema Regained: Godard Between Proust and Benjamin', *Modernism/modernity*, 8:4 (November 2001), 643–61

—— *The Ends of Mourning: Psychoanalysis, Literature, Film* (Stanford, CA: Stanford University Press, 2003)

RICHARD, JEAN-PIERRE, *Proust et le monde sensible* (Paris: Seuil, 1974)

ROMAINS, JULES, 'L'Art de la foule commence', in *Le Cinéma: naissance d'un art 1895–1920*, ed. by Daniel Banda and José Moure (Paris: Flammarion, 2008), pp. 287–88

ROSALOTO, GUY, 'Souvenirs-écran', *Psychanalyse et cinéma*, special issue of *Communications*, 23 (1975), 79–87

SACKS, OLIVER, 'On the Threshold of Sleep', in *Hallucinations* (New York: Random House, 2012), pp. 198–217

SAID, EDWARD, *On Late Style: Music and Literature Against the Grain* (London: Bloomsbury, 2006)

SAXTON, LIBBY, 'Anamnesis and Bearing Witness: Godard/Lanzmann', in *Forever Godard*, ed. by Michael Temple, James S. Williams, and Michael Witt (London: Black Dog, 2004), pp. 364–79

SCHEFER, JEAN-LOUIS, *L'Homme ordinaire du cinéma* (Paris: Cahiers du cinéma, 1981)

—— *The Ordinary Man of Cinema*, trans. by Max Cavitch, Paul Grant, and Noura Wedell (Pasadena, CA: Semiotexte, 2016)

—— 'Vertigo, vert tilleul', in *Images mobiles: récits, visages, flocons* (Paris: P.O.L, 1999), pp. 194–202

SCHMID, MARION, and MARTINE BEUGNET, *Proust at the Movies* (London & New York: Routledge, 2004)

SILVERMAN, KAJA, 'The Dream of the Nineteenth Century', *Camera Obscura*, 51, 17:3 (2002), 1–29

—— *The Threshold of the Visible World* (New York & London: Routledge, 1996)

TADIÉ, YVES-JEAN, *Le Lac inconnu: entre Proust et Freud* (Paris: Gallimard, 2012)

TAUSSIG, MICHAEL, *What Colour is the Sacred?* (Chicago, IL: University of Chicago Press, 2009)

VÄLIAHO, PASI, 'Simulation, Automata, Cinema: A Critique of Gestures', *Theory & Event*, 8:2 (2005), <https://muse.jhu.edu/article/187860> [accessed 19 March 2018]

VIDAL-NAQUET, PIERRE, 'L'Épreuve de l'historien: réflexions d'un géneraliste', in *Au sujet de Shoah: le film de Claude Lanzmann* (Paris: Belin, 1990), pp. 198–208

—— *Les Juifs, la mémoire et le present II* (Paris: La Découverte, 1991)

WAJCMAN, GÉRARD, 'De la croyance photographique', *Les Temps modernes*, 56:613 (2001), 47–83

WATT, ADAM, *Reading in Proust's A la recherche: 'le délire de la lecture'* (Oxford: Oxford University Press, 2009)

—— '"Une étroite section lumineuse pratiquée à même l'inconnu": Swann et la lettre pour Forcheville', *Bulletin d'informations proustiennes*, 43:1 (2013), 133–38

WATT, CALUM, *Blanchot and the Moving Image* (Oxford: Legenda, 2017)

WATTS, PHILIP, *Roland Barthes's Cinema* (Oxford: Oxford University Press, 2016)

WINNICOTT, DONALD WOODS, *Human Nature* (London: Free Association Books, 1988)

—— 'Fear of Breakdown', in *Psycho-Analytic Explorations* (London: Karnac, 1989), pp. 87–95

—— *Playing and Reality* (London: Routledge, 2005)

YHCAM, 'Un réalisme invraisemblable', in *Le Cinéma: naissance d'un art 1895–1920*, ed. by Daniel Banda and José Moure (Paris: Flammarion, 2008), pp. 237–39

INDEX

Abel, Richard 47 n. 77
absorption 12, 25–26, 37, 42, 81, 111, 142–43, 182
Adorno, Theodor 182
Agamben, Giorgio 3, 22–23, 26, 34, 36, 40, 43 n. 5,
    119–33, 144, 146, 153 n. 1 & 3, 154 n. 22, 180,
    189–92
Akerman, Chantal 1, 57, 59–60, 174
Althusser, Louis 41
apparatus 1–4, 5 n. 2, 25, 33–38, 42, 46 n. 62, 50,
    52–53, 56, 59, 61, 63, 63 n. 5, 64 n. 10, 71, 73–74,
    79, 83, 92, 111, 115, 126–27, 167, 171
arrêt sur l'image 173
Artaud, Antonin 33, 120, 161–62
asthma 177, 181
atavism 138
attention 3, 8, 10, 12, 22–26, 29, 31, 52, 54, 59, 71,
    81–82, 90–91, 152, 177
Aubouy, Véronique 61, 65
Augé, Marc 185 n. 37
Aumont, Charles 42
automatism 24, 34, 74, 76–77, 82, 84, 127
awakening 4, 10, 13–14, 17, 31, 54, 63, 174, 178,
    182–84, 189–91

Bachelard, Gaston 30–31, 46 n. 64
Bal, Mieke 2, 6 n. 4, 109–10, 140–51, 117 n. 10,
    156 n. 72
Baldwin, Thomas 98 n. 6
Balsom, Erica 62–63, 65 n. 35
Bardot, Brigitte 67
Barthes, Roland 3–5, 9–12, 19, 23, 32, 34, 36–42,
    53 n. 7, 48 n. 106, 49 n. 109, 57, 63, 65 n. 32, 94,
    96–97, 100 n. 46, 115, 164–66, 171, 185 n. 24 &
    30, 186 n. 40, 191
Bataille, Georges 117, 118 n. 27, 161–62
Baudelaire, Charles 18, 26–28, 45 n. 18, 46 n. 59, 55,
    133, 141, 163
Baudrillard, Jean 187 n. 65
Baudry, Jean-Louis 3, 32, 34–38, 41–42, 46 n. 62,
    48 n. 90 & 91, 64 n. 10, 74, 114–15, 167
Bazin, André 19, 33, 75, 77, 99 n. 25, 107–08, 167
Beckett, Samuel 58, 161–62
Bellour, Raymond 2, 34, 48 n. 104, 57–61, 63,
    65 n. 21 & 31 & 32, 94, 109
Benhaïm, André 6 n. 6, 83, 100 n. 38, 146, 155 n. 69
Benjamin, Walter 3, 4, 22, 74, 119–20, 122–24, 126,

129–33, 153 n. 3, 154 n. 47 & 48, 163, 168, 171,
    173–84, 185 n. 18, 186 n. 42 & 56, 187 n. 62 & 68
    & 70 & 73, 188 n. 93, 189–92
Bergson, Henri 18–19, 22, 32, 43 n. 6, 45 n. 23 & 24,
    46 n. 55, 92, 124, 128–29, 152
Bernheim, Hippolyte 33, 39
Bersani, Leo 3, 67, 70–75, 85, 110–12, 114
Bertrand, Aloysius 47 n. 77
Bion, Wilfred 30–31, 44 n. 13, 47 n. 71 & 72
Blanchot, Maurice 41, 49 n. 112
Boltanski, Christian 187 n. 70
Bon, François 83, 100 n. 40
Borrel, Federico Garcia 164
Bowie, Malcolm 66–69, 75, 98 n. 1, 110, 118 n. 14,
    184 n. 8
Brassaï 6 n. 3
Braun, Marta 156 n. 79
Brecht, Bertolt 41
Breton, André 166
Breuer, Joseph 39–40, 49 n. 109
Buñuel, Luis 32
Burgin, Victor 42, 49 n. 116, 164–66, 185 n. 22
Butler, Judith 24, 45 n. 33

camera obscura 3, 24, 37, 42, 50–56, 59–61, 64 n. 10 &
    16 & 18, 78–79, 110
camps, the 164, 167–68, 172–73, 175–76, 187 n. 58
Canudo, Ricciotto 32–33
Capa, Robert 164
Castex and Surer (literature textbook) 49 n. 106
Cavell, Stanley 3, 74–77, 83–84, 99 n. 25 & 26, 107,
    110–11, 157
Caygill, Howard 181–82, 188 n. 89
Cayrol, Jean 164
Cendrars, Blaise 47 n. 77
Chaplin, Charlie 183
Charcot, Jean-Marie 32–33, 39, 121–22, 158
Chévrier, Jean-François 2, 6 n. 3, 7, 65 n. 21, 83,
    100 n. 39
childhood 8–9, 12–13, 26, 30–31, 58, 78, 80, 84, 87,
    89, 93–94, 157–59, 163, 166–67, 168, 169–70, 184,
    186 n. 40, 189
Chion, Michel 7 n. 26
choreography 120
chronophotography 2, 32, 44 n. 17, 45 n. 20 & 23,
    95–97, 122, 149, 152, 156 n. 71

Cocteau, Jean 32
colour 29, 53, 78–79, 81, 83–89, 91, 93–95, 116–17, 137, 147–49, 158, 177
comic strip 78, 84, 96
Communications 3, 32–34, 36–38
Compagnon, Antoine 184 n. 7
Companeez, Nina 1
Conley, Tom 168–69, 185 n. 34 & 37 & 38
Cooper, Sarah 32, 48 n. 78
Copjec, Joan 68
Courbet, Gustave 190
Crary, Jonathan 3, 6 n. 8, 23–25, 29, 32, 34, 37, 44 n. 17, 45 n. 27 & 34, 50–52, 63 n. 2 & 5, 64 n. 10 & 16
Creede, Gerald 62
crepuscular state 22–23, 26, 28–29, 36, 40, 43 n. 5, 192, 49 n. 109
Culley, Peter 62
Curtiz, Michael 185 n. 37

daguerreotype 125, 127
Dalí, Salvador 32
Damisch, Hubert 186 n. 40
dance 120, 125, 128
Daney, Serge 3, 119, 167, 170–73, 176, 185 n. 40, 186 n. 46 & 52 & 54, 191
Danius, Sara 18, 45 n. 23
Darwin, Charles 137
Da Vinci, Leonardo 126, 128
Davis, Lydia 43 n. 4
daydream 25, 34–36
de Certeau, Michel 168
de Fontanelle, Bernand le Bovier 26
de Man, Paul 65 n. 19
Delasalle, Jean-François 27
Deleuze, Gilles 2, 4–5, 18–19, 33, 43 n. 6, 44 n. 14, 45 n. 23, 58, 64 n. 18, 84, 94, 97–98, 100 n. 43, 119, 122, 124–29, 135, 145, 155 n. 61, 162, 166–67, 180, 186 n. 52
Delluc, Louis 32
Descartes, René 10, 12, 24, 53, 64 n. 16, 74, 125
Diaghilev, Sergei 122
Dickson, William 17, 125
Didi-Huberman, Georges 155 n. 60 & 68, 175–76, 186 n. 58, 187 n. 70
dispositif 1, 2, 5 n. 2, 24, 34, 36–38, 50, 53, 62–63, 90–94
Douglas, Stan 62–63
drapery 142, 144
dream 4, 12–13, 22, 25, 37, 28–37, 39–40, 46 n. 55, 48 n. 91, 58, 89, 91–92, 99 n. 36, 106, 114–15, 133, 165, 173–74, 177–84, 189
Dulac, Germaine 31–33
Duncan, Isadora 122
Durkheim, Émile 33
Dutoit, Ulysse 67

Edison, Thomas 17–18, 44 n. 17, 62–63, 122, 125
Eisenstein, Sergei 127
engram 123
Epstein, Jean 32–33, 47 n. 77
exhibitionism 103, 106–07, 109
exteriority 14

Farinelli 48 n. 106, 191
Farocki, Harun 187 n. 70
Fisher, Mark 185 n. 19
Flaubert, Gustave 161–62
flicker 42, 88, 119, 132, 180
flip book 123, 126, 131–34, 146
fold 10, 64 n. 18, 81
forgetting 14, 24, 130, 138, 157, 159–62, 168–69, 177, 179
Foucault, Michel 24, 45 n. 33, 51
frame 10, 59, 66–69, 76–79, 81, 84, 86, 91, 97, 100 n. 39, 102, 106–08, 125, 145–46, 148–53, 158, 164, 180
Frampton, Daniel 31–33, 47 n. 77
Freud, Sigmund 3, 12–13, 25, 29, 32–36, 39, 40, 46 n. 55, 49 n. 109, 74, 103, 114–15, 133, 157–63, 165–66, 171, 179, 185 n. 18
Fuller, Sam 187 n. 70

Galileo, Galilei 125
Galton, Francis 46 n. 55
Garcia, Carla Ambrosio 44 n. 13
Garcia, Tristan 156 n. 70
gaze 38, 41, 58, 60–61, 69, 107, 150, 181
Geneviève de Brabant (magic lantern slides) 78
gesture 3, 61, 71, 119–46, 153 n. 1, 155 n. 61 & 68, 156 n. 70, 159, 166–67, 176, 179–80, 184
Giotto 100 n. 41
Godard, Jean-Luc 2, 3, 6 n. 22, 67, 111, 167–68, 173–76, 186 n. 54, 188 n. 99, 190–91
Goethe, Johann Wolfgang von 120–22, 182
Gordon, Rae Beth 32
Gorky, Maxim 31, 42
Goudal, Jean 32
Goulbourne, Russell 26
grace 141, 143–44, 146
graphic method 14–15, 127
Green, André 29, 47 n. 71
Guys, Constantin 141

hallucination 13, 27, 36–37, 42, 46 n. 55, 105–06, 114–16, 186 n. 46
Haneke, Michael 164
happiness 131, 154 n. 47, 189–92
Harbord, Janet 130, 133, 153 n. 1, 185 n. 19
Heartfield, John 183
Hegel, Georg Wilhelm Friedrich 77
Heidegger, Martin 74, 99 n. 26
Henry, Anne 46 n. 55

Hessel, Franz 182
Heywood, Miriam 3, 6 n. 22, 174
Hill, Gary 57–58
Hindemith, Paul 190
Hitchcock, Alfred 59, 115–16, 171, 185 n. 19,
    188 n. 99
Hölderlin, Friedrich 182
Holocaust, the 167, 170, 175–76, 186 n. 40
Homer 67
homosexuality 77, 106, 110, 112, 152
Houssaye, Arsène 27–28
Howard, Richard 42
Huet, Stéphane 145
Hugo, Victor 26–27, 47 n. 77
Hume, David 74, 77
Husserl, Edmund 43 n. 6
hypnagogic state 19, 27–28, 46 n. 55, 53
hypnoid state 49 n. 109
hypnosis 23, 25–26, 32–40, 48 n. 104, 49 n. 109
hysteria 32–33, 39, 49 n. 109

immateriality 20, 82–85, 89, 95–98, 100 n. 43
individuation 139
infancy 12, 22, 39–40, 83, 117
intelligibility 4, 144, 146, 176, 189
interiority 54, 60, 72, 112, 119, 121, 144
intermittence 8, 10, 42, 43 n. 5, 52, 60, 62, 74, 86–87,
    119, 132–33, 159, 161, 168, 180, 186 n. 42
interval 57, 123–34
intimacy 26, 30, 58, 68
involuntary memory 2–4, 22, 31, 47 n. 77, 63, 71, 97,
    110–11, 119, 126, 129, 131–33, 136–37, 154 n. 55,
    160–61, 166, 168, 172, 174, 177–78, 181–84,
    187 n. 65, 189, 191

jealousy 67, 69, 73, 112, 159
Jean Paul 120, 121
Jurio, Andrea del 155 n. 68

Kafka, Franz 120, 153 n. 3, 179, 181
kaleidoscope 10, 15, 43 n. 4, 178
Kant, Immanuel 10, 23, 24, 32, 34, 43 n. 5, 74, 77
Keller, Gottfried 181, 182
Kepler, Johannes 125
Kierkegaard, Søren 77
kinetoscope 1, 17–19, 44 n. 17, 62
Klein, Melanie 39, 85, 111
knowledge 6 n. 8, 8, 12–13, 22, 24, 29, 43 n. 5, 50–53,
    61, 64 n. 16, 66–70, 72–73, 90–91, 105–06, 112,
    132, 147, 153, 161–62, 170–72
Kofman, Sarah 64 n. 16
Kommerell, Max 119–22, 153 n. 2
Kraus, Karl 131
Kristeva, Julia 34
Kuntzel, Thierry 34, 58–60, 65 n. 31

Lacan, Jacques 34, 39, 41, 43 n. 11, 44 n. 16, 100 n. 37,
    68, 107, 172, 186 n. 46
Ladenson, Elisabeth 106–10, 112, 145–46
Lang, Fritz 58, 67
Lanzmann, Claude 174–77
Lapierre 78, 99 n. 36
Laplanche, Jean 49 n. 109, 67, 184 n. 9
Larcher, David 65 n. 21
Lautrèamont, Comte de 47 n. 77
Leibniz, Gottfried 64 n. 18, 125
Leiris, Michel 187 n. 71
lesbianism 90, 106–07, 112, 145
Lewin, Bertram D. 36–37, 48 n. 91, 114
lieu de mémoire 168
light 9, 16–17, 21, 41–42, 50, 52, 54–56, 58–59, 60, 69,
    76–79, 81–84, 87–88, 91, 102, 106–07, 113, 116,
    147, 159, 183 *see also* luminosity
listening 4, 7 n. 25, 23, 52, 53
Locke, John 77
Losey, Joseph 1, 5 n. 1, 174
love 67, 73, 138, 145
Lumière, Auguste and Louis 2, 18, 31, 62, 122, 125, 128
luminosity 42, 66, 107
Lyotard, Jean-François 161–63, 168–69

magic 42, 53, 75–78, 85, 88–89, 98, 122, 126, 148
magic lantern 1, 3, 39, 53, 73, 77–98, 100 n. 40 & 43,
    117
Malabou, Catherine 155 n. 58
Mallarmé, Stéphane 120, 161–62
Malt, Johanna 100 n. 43
Manet, Edouard 75
Mannoni, Laurent 44 n. 17 & 18, 45 n. 20, 78,
    99 n. 36
Marey, Étienne-Jules 2, 18, 44 n. 17, 45 n. 19 &
    20, 45 n. 23, 95–96, 122, 127–28, 149–50, 152,
    156 n. 79
Marker, Chris 3, 56, 59, 65 n. 31 & 39, 163–64, 167,
    185 n. 19
Marx, Karl 40, 77, 178, 184
masochism 67, 103–05
materiality 41, 42, 56, 73, 76, 78–81, 83–86, 88, 91,
    99 n. 26, 100 n. 43, 108, 136, 143, 144, 164–66,
    180
Maury, Alfred 45 n. 55
McCole, John 189
melancholia 3, 48 n. 106, 81, 114, 131, 173, 191–92
Méliès, Georges 33
membrane 69
memory trace 115, 123, 163, 165, 171
memory 2–4, 8–9, 12–19, 26, 28, 30–31, 36, 47 n. 77,
    55, 60, 65 n. 39, 68, 71, 86–95, 97, 104, 106, 110,
    113–15, 120, 123, 126, 129–30, 136–38, 157–82,
    184, 185 n. 19 & 37, 189 *see also* involuntary
    memory, memory trace, screen-memory
Merleau-Ponty, Maurice 12, 43 n. 9, 44 n. 15

Mesmer, Franz 39
Metz, Christian 3, 5 n. 2, 32–36, 38, 115, 167
Meynert, Theodor 115
Michelet, Jules 189
Miller, Gérard 48 n. 103
Ming-Lang, Tsai 164
mirror stage 39, 44 n. 16, 57, 73, 79, 90
montage 19, 47 n. 77, 60, 65 n. 31, 174–78, 181,
    183–84, 187 n. 70
Montaigne, Michel de 25–26
Moravia, Alberto 67
Morrissey, Robert J. 45 n. 44
Mulvey, Laura 50, 78
music 1, 5, 6 n. 22, 29, 48 n. 106, 55, 89, 109, 142,
    144, 190–91
Muybridge, Eadweard 2, 18, 45 n. 20, 95–96, 122,
    126–27, 149, 150–53

Najab, Khalid 39
narrative 6 n. 25, 8–9, 23, 26, 32, 36, 46 n. 55, 60,
    61, 67, 71, 78–79, 83–84, 86, 97–98, 110, 115–16,
    146, 158–60, 163–66, 168, 172, 176, 180, 184,
    188 n. 99, 190–91
Nerval, Gérard de 25–26, 28, 46 n. 66, 47
Newton, Isaac 125
Nietzsche, Friedrich 77, 122
Novak, Kim 116
nymph 139, 154 n. 22, 155 n. 60

Occupation, the 167–68, 186 n. 40
off-screen (hors-champ) 107–10
Ollier, Claude 167, 186 n. 40
ontology 10, 19, 30, 33, 50, 53, 55–56, 72–77, 100 n. 43
optics 24, 38 42, 44 n. 17, 50–52, 67, 73, 78, 83, 88–89,
    96, 146, 147, 179, 181
Ornicar? (review) 39
Oursler, Tony 160 n. 43
Ovid 155 n. 60
Ozu, Yasujirō 2, 97

Pagnoux, Elisabeth 175, 187 n. 58
painting 1, 75–76, 79, 92, 93, 100 n. 41, 108, 117, 126,
    128, 190
Palance, Jack 67
Panofsky, Erwin 75, 99 n. 25, 124
paranoia 111–12, 161
Pascoli, Giovanni 122
Patterson, Ian 94
Paulhan, Jean 172, 186 n. 46
Perec, Georges 43 n. 13
performance 25, 31–32, 61–62, 89, 108–10, 120, 134,
    140, 142–44
perversion 40–42, 71, 103
phenakistoscope 18, 44 n. 18
photogram 10, 18–19, 45 n. 23, 59, 84, 91, 93–94,
    100 n. 46, 128–29, 131–33, 149, 151, 175, 180

physiognomy 67, 138, 176
Piccoli, Michel 67
Pichois, Claude 27
Pinter, Harold 1
plasticity 28, 137–38, 140, 143, 155 n. 58 & 60, 158, 180
Plateau, Joseph 18
Plato 36
Pleynet, Marcelin 41, 64 n. 10
Poe, Edgar Allan 27–28, 46 n. 53 & 55
Pontalis, Jean-Baptiste 48 n. 91, 49 n. 109
postmodernity 187 n. 65
Powell, Michael 164
Prendergast, Christopher 46 n. 60
Pressburger, Emeric 164
primal scene 39, 57, 79, 159, 167–69, 172, 184 n. 7,
    186 n. 40
projection 1, 3, 31, 36, 41–42, 45 n. 23, 53, 57, 62,
    66–98, 99 n. 26, 100 n. 39 & 43, 106, 111–12, 117,
    122, 146, 157, 159, 164, 168, 171, 180
proprioception 17, 21–22, 31, 44 n. 15 & 16, 52, 61
Proust, Adrien 45 n. 19
Proust, Marcel:
    A la recherche du temps perdu:
        volumes:
            Du côté de chez Swann 8–22, 28, 52–56, 61–62,
                66–69, 71, 78–87, 94, 98 n. 6, 100 n. 41
                & 43, 102–04, 108–09, 112, 117, 134–35,
                144–46, 149, 156 n. 70, 158–59
            À l'ombre des jeunes filles en fleurs 71, 88, 92,
                137–42, 149, 153, 155 n. 60 & 61, 182
            Le Côté de Guermantes 89, 92–93, 141–44,
                146–51, 153, 174
            Sodome et Gomorrhe 89, 104–07, 110–17, 159,
                161, 186 n. 42
            La Prisonnière 54, 59, 61, 89–90, 110, 112
            Albertine disparue (La Fugitive) 71–74, 86,
                90–92, 110, 112, 146
            Le Temps retrouvé 13, 53, 64 n. 16, 70–71,
                93- 98, 107, 120, 136–37, 150–53, 160–61,
                187 n. 70
        chapters:
            'L'Adoration perpetuelle' 136
            Un amour de Swann 66, 112
            'Combray' 53, 69, 77, 79–80, 86, 89, 93, 98,
                100 n. 36
            le drame du coucher 86, 158
            les intermittences du cœur 43 n. 5, 159, 161, 186 n. 42
            'Ouverture' 61
        characters:
            Albertine 54, 61, 89, 90–91, 104–06, 112–17,
                146–50, 153, 159, 161, 184 n. 7, 190–91
            l'amie de Mlle Vinteuil 69, 103–08, 110, 113,
                155–56, 159
            Andrée 159
            d'Argencourt, M. 94–98
            Charlus 13, 64 n. 16, 71, 107, 156 n. 71

Cottard 159
Elstir 92–93, 98
father 134–35
Forcheville 69, 83
Geneviève de Brabant 78–82, 84–87, 94,
　160 n. 39, 117
Gilberte 71, 88, 144–46, 150–51, 156 n. 70
Golo 79–82, 84–87, 94–96, 98, 100 n. 39 &
　43, 117
grandmother 7 n. 26, 81–82, 104, 110–11, 113,
　159, 161, 176
great-aunt 79, 81, 84, 88, 159
great-uncle 12–13
Guermantes, Duc de 87, 89, 94, 135, 141, 143
Guermantes, Duchesse de 87, 89, 91, 93–94,
　135, 141, 143
'jeunes filles en fleurs' or 'petite bande' 71, 88,
　137, 139, 140–41, 149, 155 n. 61, 190
Jupien 13, 64 n. 16, 71, 107, 150
La Berma 142–44, 146
Legrandin 134–35, 140, 144–45
mother 9, 54, 72, 81–82, 85, 93, 112, 159
Odette 66, 68–69, 83
Putbus, baronne de 71
Rachel 141, 150
Saint-Loup, Robert de 2, 71, 140, 142–44,
　146, 149, 150–53
Swann, Charles 43 n. 9, 66–69, 90, 104–05,
　112–13, 158
tante Léonie 90
Vinteuil, M. 43 n. p, 86, 89, 102–04, 106,
　108–09, 129, 142, 161
Vinteuil, Mlle 13, 69, 102–10, 113, 115–16,
　159, 161
places:
　Balbec 89, 92–93, 105, 110, 113–14, 136, 140,
　　146, 148–49, 159
　Bois de Boulogne 143
　Carquethuit 137–38
　Combray 8, 16, 61, 73, 80–82, 86–90, 93–96,
　　102, 112, 117, 134, 136, 158–59
　Doncières 141
　Hôtel de Guermantes 71, 92–93, 97, 160
　Hudimesnil 149, 153
　Méséglise 144
　Martinville 149, 153
　Montjouvain 69, 102, 104–07, 109–17, 159,
　　161
　Parville 105–06, 116
　Venice 72–73, 86, 100 n. 41, 136
objects:
　doorknob 81–82, 85–86, 95–96, 100 n. 43
　'pan lumineux' 158
　madeleine 129, 136, 158, 160–61, 182, 185 n. 19
Contre Sainte-Beuve 28
Esquisses 10–11

psychoanalysis 3, 12, 13, 25, 29–32, 26, 37–39, 44 n. 13
　& 16, 48 n. 103, 67–68, 114–15, 166, 184 n. 10,
　186 n. 40

Quesnoy, Pierre 31–32, 47 n. 77
Queysanne, Bernard 43 n. 13

Rabinbach, Anson 156 n. 79
Racine, Jean 142
Ramain, Paul 32
Ramuz, Charles-Ferdinand 47 n. 77
Rancière, Jacques 2, 185 n. 13, 188 n. 99
Raymond, Marcel 25–26
reading 4–5, 6 n. 16, 55–56, 60–63, 65 n. 19, 65 n. 39,
　68–69, 95, 98, 98 n. 6, 100 n. 43, 127, 135, 141–
　42, 145, 168, 187 n. 70, 192
readability 4–5, 135, 144, 187 n. 70
reality-testing 115
recognition 71–72, 74, 79, 116, 134, 159, 181–82
redemption 3, 14, 22, 67, 75, 110, 120, 123, 131–33,
　160, 164, 175–77, 190
Renoir, Auguste 190
reparation 85, 110
Resnais, Alain 164, 170–72, 176
retreat 48 n. 106, 60, 182
reverie 3, 5 n. 2, 19–20, 22–32, 34–36, 38–40, 45 n. 44,
　46 n. 59, 47 n. 71, 49 n. 109, 53, 78, 114, 178–79,
　182, 191
Reyner, Igor 7 n. 25, 64 n. 17
Ricciardi, Alessia 3, 174, 176, 187 n. 65, 191, 192 n. 8
Richard, Jean-Pierre 138
Rilke, Rainer Maria 122
Rimbaud, Arthur 47 n. 77, 161–62
Rivière, Jacques 177
Robbe-Grillet, Alain 96–97
Romains, Jules 31
room 3, 8–23, 25, 28, 30–31, 34, 37–38, 41, 44 n. 14,
　49 n. 59, 49 n. 106, 50, 52–62, 78–83, 87–91, 93,
　95–96, 98, 100 n. 39 & 43, 102–03, 105, 107–10,
　113, 115–16, 158, 169, 179, 182, 190
Rosaloto, Guy 184 n. 4
Rousseau, Jean-Jacques 25–29
Ruiz, Raoul 1, 145, 174
Ruskin, John 72

Sacks, Oliver 46 n. 55
sadism 13, 67, 79, 103, 109
Said, Edward 5 n. 1
Saint-Denis, Hervey de 46 n. 55
Salpetrière (hospital) 32–33, 39, 121
Sand, George 86, 93, 160–61
Sartre, Jean-Paul 34, 40, 73–74, 186 n. 40
Saxton, Libby 175–76
scepticism 68, 70, 74–77
Schefer, Jean-Louis 33, 116, 118 n. 25, 167–70,
　185 n. 40

Schilder, Paul 44 n. 16
Schlondorff, Volker 1, 174
Scholem, Gershom 131
Schopenhauer, Arthur 24, 46 n. 55
Schumann, Robert 29
screen 1, 3–5, 5 n. 2, 9, 33–34, 36–38, 41–42, 50, 53,
    56, 58–59, 63, 66–77, 83–84, 90, 91, 98 n. 6,
    100 n. 39 & 43, 101 n. 46, 106–10, 114, 157–71,
    186 n. 40, 190–91
screen memory 3, 157–71, 186 n. 40
Scudéry, Mme de 26
Sedgwick, Eve 107
Semon, Richard 123
sequentiality 31, 84, 96–97, 114, 151, 164–66, 168–69,
    177, 188
seriality 96–97, 146–47, 150
Seurat, Georges 190
sexuality 12, 39, 106–07, 109, 135, 144–46, 150, 153,
    159
silent film 3, 59, 61, 121–22, 129
Silverman, Kaja 44 n. 16, 68, 173–74, 186 n. 54 & 56
Situationists 23
sleep 4, 8–30, 35–36, 38–40, 46 n. 55, 48 nn. 91 & 106,
    58, 60–61, 81, 92, 166, 182–83, 189–92
Snow, Michael 57, 60
somnambulism 33
Souday, Paul 117
sound 4–5, 6 n. 22, 8, 41, 52–53, 55, 60, 62, 89, 102,
    105, 112, 190
spectrality 31, 50, 53–54, 56, 91, 96, 114–16, 162, 172
speed 15–17, 45 n. 23, 47 n. 77, 84, 97, 140, 148,
    151–52, 164
stained glass 79, 81, 83–84, 87–89, 117
Stanford, Leland 18
stereoscope 1, 51, 147
Stewart, James 116
Stifter, Adalbert 181
suggestion 32–34
superimposition 47 n. 77, 60, 76, 79, 84, 97, 104, 112,
    115, 117
surface 36, 52, 66, 69–70, 73, 79, 82–86, 107, 109, 147,
    157
Surrealism 32, 47 n. 77, 48 n. 80, 179, 182–84

Tadié, Yves-Jean 39, 48 n. 105
Tarde, Gabriel 33, 46 n. 55
Taussig, Michael 177–78, 181, 187 n. 71
technology 18, 25, 33, 50, 62–63, 63 n. 5, 65 n. 39, 77,
    83, 89, 127, 129

Tel Quel 32, 36, 48 n. 40, 64 n. 10
theatre 37, 58, 107–09, 120, 122, 158
Thibaudeau, Jean 64 n. 10
threshold 4, 8–10, 12–13, 16–19, 22, 27–30, 39–40,
    43 n. 11, 53, 57, 73, 79, 82, 86, 96, 179, 183
'time in the pure state' 2, 13, 97
Tourette, Gilles de la 121–22
Tourjanki, Victor 186 n. 40
toys 18, 78, 89
Trafic 65 n. 22, 119, 121, 153 n. 1, 186 n. 40
transparency 55, 68–69, 83, 142
trauma 3, 12, 22, 79, 114, 158–59, 164, 168, 171–72,
    174–75
Truffaut, François 58
Turner, Joseph Mallord William 72–73, 117

unconscious, the 11, 23, 25, 29, 31–34, 36, 39, 82, 86,
    98, 115, 124, 135, 162, 165–66, 177

Vaché, Jacques 166
vacillation 9, 10, 43 n. 5, 46 n. 60, 83, 86, 145
van der See, James 165
variation 31, 96, 117, 138, 140, 146, 157–58
Velásquez, Diego 126, 128
vertigo 53, 116
Vidal-Naquet, Pierre 177, 187 n. 69
video 2, 57–61, 65 n. 21, 166, 173–74
Viola, Bill 57–60
Visconti, Luchino 1, 5 n. 1, 174
voice 5, 6 n. 22, 7 n. 26, 48 n. 106, 61–63, 84, 138–40,
    142–43, 156 n. 71, 172, 190–91
voice-off 5
voyeurism 5, 13, 66, 102, 103, 106–10, 112–13, 149,
    175–76
Vuillermoz, Emile 32, 33

Wajcmann, Gérard 175, 187 n. 58
Wallon, Henri 44 n. 16
Warburg, Aby 119, 122–26, 128–29, 130, 132, 134, 143,
    154 n. 22, 155 n. 60 & 68, 180
Watt, Adam 69
Winnicott, Donald 30, 31, 39, 47 n. 71, 85, 184 n. 10
Wittgenstein, Ludwig 74

Ycham 31

zoom 60, 109, 147

Milton Keynes UK
Ingram Content Group UK Ltd.
UKHW050624170924
1691UKWH00033B/251